The Seven Deadly Sins: Society and Evil

BY STANFORD M. LYMAN

The Asian in the West

The Black American in Sociological Thought:
A Failure of Perspective

Chinese Americans

The Asian in North America

A Sociology of the Absurd (co-author)

The Revolt of the Students (co-author)

The Drama of Social Reality (co-author)

Structure, Consciousness, and History (co-editor)

STANFORD M. LYMAN

New School for Social Research

The Seven Deadly Sins: Society and Evil

ST. MARTIN'S PRESS, INC.
NEW YORK

Library of Congress Catalog Card Number: 77-89994
For information, write St. Martin's Press, Inc.,
175 Fifth Avenue, New York, N.Y. 10010

cover design: Melissa Tardiff

cloth ISBN: 0-312-71324-X
paper ISBN: 0-312-71325-8

Acknowledgment
Excerpts reprinted from *The Three Sisters* by Anton Chekhov,
trans. Tyrone Guthrie and Leonard Kipnis. Copyright © 1965
Avon Book Division, The Hearst Corporation. Reprinted by
permission of Avon Books.

PREFACE

This study of sin and evil grew out of my personal experiences as much as my academic concerns. I am of course not alone in being a witness to much evil in the past forty years. Indeed, it is a peculiarly complacent soul who has not marveled at and shrunk from the horrors of war, racism, poverty, and moral defection in the twentieth century. In my own case, however, the evils raised a gnawing question: how is man's inhumanity to man a part of humanity itself?

In 1942, as a nine year old, I watched as innocent Japanese Americans— ultimately 120,000 humans of all ages: men, women, children, aliens and citizens, grandparents and infants, fathers and mothers, sons and daughters—were unjustly taken out of their homes, away from their livelihoods, off their farms, and incarcerated in prison camps especially set aside for them in the wastelands of America. A few years later I became a habitué of San Francisco's Chinatown. There, hidden behind the tinseled glitter of that gilded ghetto I saw the poverty, squalor, and disease that racism had fostered. My parents owned a grocery store in the black and—until the summer of 1942—Japanese ghetto of the city. Racial prejudice and victimization were daily features of the lives of the people there. What emerged from these experiences was my life-long interest in the study of race relations, that is, of racism, race discrimination, and race prejudice especially as they have affected the lives and life chances of Chinese, Japanese, and Black Americans.

Evil, however, has many faces. Naturally, I have not seen them all. However, some of recent years are especially remarkable. In the 1960s the march toward civil rights and the elimination of poverty were interrupted by yet another war—this time in Vietnam. A student revolt broke out in America and in many parts of the world. Professors and students became embroiled in the agony of political revolution and social reform and the ecstasy of innovative communalism and personal salvation. Teaching in California and Nevada in those years, I became more and more impressed by the existential features of the situation. Together with Marvin B. Scott I formulated an idea that seemed to sum up the scene in theoretical terms. Scott and I called it a sociology of the absurd, and we meant by that to refer to the condition wherein the social world makes no essential sense but nevertheless is made sensible by the actions and beliefs of the peoples who participate in it. Applying this idea to the revolt of the students, we sought to uncover both the instrumental and expressive elements in an uprising that included both programs of societal reorganization and prophecies of individual redemption. Although the war in Vietnam came to an end at long last, neither the fragile society nor the fractured self were redeemed.

Evils continue. The anger, greed, envy, and pride that encourage racial divisions at home and ever more destructive wars abroad have given impetus to a malaise; sloth and *acedia*, lust and gluttony characterize an aimless sensibility that haunts America in the 1970s and makes predictions about its future difficult. It seems that we are witnesses at a great convulsion and a watershed. The world that we thought we knew and understood in the 1950s—when some sociologists hailed the end of ideology and the beginning of a well-ordered society that required only occasional tinkering to keep it smooth and efficient—is no more. The world that is to come is not yet visible. In the interim we muddle through, shaping the scenarios of our existence like actors in a guerilla theater—acting without a script, criticizing in the absence of a theory of criticism, directing without a final act in mind. And the dramas we create are comedies, tragedies, and farces. Absurdity gives voice to the spontaneous outpouring of unplanned plays of existence. The existential claim that normal men do not know that everything is possible is overthrown as normality itself is undermined. And evil is let loose at the very moment that the capacity to criticize it is subverted.

It is my conviction that we lack a rhetoric of criticism for social evils. For nearly a century radicals have fallen back on the materialist critique of society— tracing the past in historical materialism and employing the endless twists of the dialectic to comprehend and oppose the present. What is required is an ideational critique of society, a rhetoric that grasps the structures of consciousness, the phenomenology of history, and the dramaturgy of contemporary scenes. Such a new rhetoric would regard culture, thought, and ideas as such, and it also would see the precise relationship between values and acts. More to the point it would take evil as a topic in its own right, seeking to uncover its historical backgrounds, describe its social forms and architectonics, and examine its supports and strengths.

The present work is my suggestion of a beginning for that project. It is a prolegomena to the study of evil, written as an examination of the seven deadly sins. Central to these sins is their alienating quality. The inhumanity of humanity is located in the sins' capacity to separate man and woman from their kind, and ultimately from themselves. Sin has been neglected by sociology. Evil, here represented as the structures of alienating sins, has wreaked havoc on society for too long without this notice. Sin and evil are ever with us, but they need not be so mysterious.

This study could never have been written without the advice, help, and criticism of colleagues and students. In printing my thanks for their aid I can only acknowledge a debt that cannot be repaid.

Marvin B. Scott, my collaborator on three earlier books, has been guide, counsel, and critic on this project from its inception. It was he who first suggested the idea, and he is the virtual co-author of the chapters on sloth, anger, envy, gluttony, and greed. Professor Scott provided me with outlines, opportunities for discussion, and expert criticism throughout the first year of manuscript preparation. It is only because of his other personal commitments and his high sense of professional responsibility that he refused to let his name appear on the title page.

My research on the seven deadly sins led me to seek a print of their unforgettable representation in Fritz Lang's film, *Metropolis*. After several weeks of futile search, it was suggested that I request the assistance of Herman G. Weinberg, whose writings on cinema constitute a major contribution to modern culture. A week after I wrote my letter Mr. Weinberg appeared in my office. Not only did he provide me with the print from *Metropolis*, but also he obtained and showed me many other prints depicting aspects of the seven deadly sins in European and American films. Moreover, Mr. Weinberg took an interest in the entire project, and his reconstruction of von Stroheim's *Greed* proved to be an important resource in research on that topic. For his gracious attention and generous services I shall always be grateful.

Herbert Hill, until recently national labor director of the National Association for the Advancement of Colored People, has been a constant intellectual and moral support. I am especially grateful for his suggestions about the importance of Herman Melville's novel, *The Confidence Man*, for this project.

Peter Rose and Edward Sagarin have each given me the benefit of their sociological expertise by independently reading the entire manuscript and providing painstaking and meticulous criticisms of every chapter. I have not always followed their advice, and, indeed, I have vigorously disagreed with one or both over a few matters of interpretation, but I am extremely grateful for their aid, criticism, and confidence in the project.

Arthur J. Vidich, my colleague at the New School for Social Research, has been an ever-faithful friend, resource, and critic. He guided me to a sociological understanding of the particular form of *acedia* that overcame the Oceanic peoples in the nineteenth century and critically evaluated my analysis of the social economics of greed. Two of his sons, Paul and Joseph, each a promising writer in his own right, agreed to listen to my readings of certain chapters aloud and gave me the benefit of their substantive and stylistic criticism.

A portion of the chapter on greed was presented at a conference sponsored by the Humanistic Transdisciplinary Association at the University of Chicago. I am especially grateful for the invitation and the advice given by John Raphael Staude and Randall Collins.

A fine place to do research and much time for reflection was provided when a sabbatical leave from the New School for Social Research permitted me to become Senior Member in residence at Linacre College, Oxford, during the Michaelmas Term, 1975. I am very grateful to my sponsor and host, Rom Harre, for his many kindnesses, to Bryan Wilson of All Souls College for an entertaining and enlivening evening of sociological discussion, to the students of Oxford for their cordiality and intelligence, and to the brilliant and sparkling wit of H.R. Trevor-Roper, whose lectures on Macaulay, Gibbon, and Burckhardt were one of the delights of my stay at Oxford. My thoughts and research on the seven deadly sins were also enhanced during my visit to England by opportunities to lecture at Cambridge through the kind invitation of Anthony Giddens; at Warwick under the sponsorship of John Rex; and before the sociology faculties of Bedford, Chelsea, and Goldsmith Colleges of the University of London because of the efforts put forth in my behalf by John MacDonald. Through the good offices of the United States Information Service I have also benefited from the chance to lecture on aspects of my research before academic and journalistic audiences in Singapore, Taiwan, Hong Kong, and Japan.

Research assistance on this project has been provided through the work/ study program at the New School for Social Research. I am especially grateful for the bibliographic searches conducted by some expert "hunters and gatherers" among my students, including Ying-jen Chang, James Cleland, Cecil Greek, Gary Johnson, Gary Kriss, and Steven Seidman.

Over the years my general outlook has been much influenced by certain sociologists who have been friends and colleagues. The late Donald W. Ball is outstanding among these. His tragic and untimely death removes from the scene one of the finest sociologists and one of my dearest friends. He is already sorely missed. The works of and my friendships with Jack Douglas, Sherri Cavan, John Irwin, John Lofland, Lyn Lofland, and Peter Manning have been invaluable. Certain former students, who have now become active and productive members of the profession, have been helpful as critics, advisers, and supporters of my research. These include David Altheide, Richard Brown, Charles R. "Chuck" Freeman, John Johnson, Tetsuden Kashima, and Dennis Lum.

Without the all-purpose help of Daria Cverna this manuscript as well as several others could never have been completed. Keeping my copies and letters on the subject in order, typing parts of the manuscript, warding off all manner of importunities, and cheering me up when the doldrums set in, Ms. Cverna has been a mainstay of the project.

The final draft of the manuscript was typed by Shirley Baker, who showed unusual skills and a remarkable knowledge of the various type faces appropriate to each part of the manuscript. Ms. Baker's skills and her cordiality are very much appreciated.

The editors and staff of St. Martin's Press have been most helpful and cooperative. I am especially grateful to Tom Broadbent, Glenn Cowley, Bert Lummus, and Sheila Friedling for their advice and support, and to Arthur Strimling, who first introduced me to the people at St. Martin's.

For all sins of commission and omission I alone am responsible.

STANFORD M. LYMAN
New York City, December, 1977

CONTENTS

PREFACE   vii

Sin and Sociology   1

ONE
Sloth   5

TWO
Lust   53

THREE
Anger   110

FOUR
Pride   135

FIVE
Envy   184

SIX
Gluttony   212

SEVEN
Greed   232

Society and Evil   269

NOTES   277
INDEX   317

The Seven Deadly Sins: Society and Evil

Sin and Sociology

The problem of the meaning of history is always the problem of the meaning of life itself, since man is an historic creature involved, and yet not involved, in the flux of nature and time, but always involved in a false solution of his predicament.

*Reinhold Niebuhr**

The struggle continues. Civilization becomes more complex.

*Kenneth Scott Latourette***

This book is a study in the sociology of evil. As such it devotes itself to an area of investigation too often eschewed by modern sociology. Evil is a term that is rarely found in a modern sociology text. The "science of society" seems to go about its task without the gnawing encumbrance of ethics. That subject is abandoned to a branch of moral philosophy where it also languishes, unstudied, unread. Evil seems to be too great, too impersonal, and too absurd to be a serious topic for sociological concern. Its very omnipresence, grossness, and grotesqueries defy and transcend the sociological imagination.

The failure of a sociological perspective on evil to develop arises from several causes. Originally sociology, as Auguste Comte perceived it, was to be a moral science suited to the scientific, rational, and technological breakthroughs that were occurring everywhere in the Occident. Sociology was associated with the social construction not only of present-day realities but also of utopias—communities of the future, which, under the guidance of melioristic social managers, would banish poverty, hunger, crime, inequities, and tyranny. The politics of the present would be overcome and bypassed. Revolution in the literal sense of the word would overturn the social order. New orders of an only-dreamed-of bliss would be established. Edenic man would be realized in man-made paradises, shorn perhaps of their natural beauty, but pleasant and trouble-free nonetheless. Sociologists were optimistic then and believed that a new morality might develop and spread over the face of the world as rapidly and easily as Western civilization seemed to be overtaking remote regions once settled only by "savages," "barbarians," and "pagans."

The advent of Darwinistic thought added new dimensions to this sociological dream. Although it is both unfair and incorrect to saddle "Social Darwinism" with too much intellectual and ethical originality, the popularity of its doctrines and, more significantly, the rhetoric of its explanatory theories did much to relegate the issues of social and personal evil to the "prescientific" historical dustbin. A civilization that advanced by "tooth and claw" toward the realization of a higher plane of existence might be justified by the end toward which it was inexorably directed. Moreover, the more liberal-minded and optimistic Social Darwinists perceived a role for active and moral man in advancing civilization. Once man understood the nature and direction of history, he might harness his own energies in its behalf, hacking away at the obstacles to social progress and hastening the inevitable end. Those passive spectators of the social scene, who believed that both natural and social science had moved man away from the center of active intervention in societal and civilizational change, nevertheless believed that change was going on. Indeed, social change was all too easily made synonymous with social progress, and an irresistible, irreversible movement toward the Good Society seemed to be accelerating.

There can be little doubt that sociological optimism was a major casualty of World War I. The promising development of society and civilization was revealed as a grand illusion that had captivated and blinded sociologists. A more complex understanding of societal processes would have to precede any attempt at utopia building, or even prediction of the shape of things to come. Positivism replaced utopianism and Darwinism in sociological thought; and it emphasized research using a "scientific" methodology imitative of the natural sciences. The idea of a social science seemed to require ethical neutrality, sociometric scaling, and a recognition of a universe of diverse means and ends.

The development of an unsanguine sociology paralleled the multiplication and intensification of societal evils. Totalitarian tyrannies arose in places that only recently had been centers of artistic, cultural, and intellectual freedom. The vast reaches of Russia, China, Africa, and Asia were convulsed in revolutions and blood. From 1933 to 1945 the Nazi regime prosecuted a new war against the Jews with such fierceness that for the first time in modern history that ancient people were threatened with extinction.[1] Evils of race pride and race prejudice ran rampant over much of the earth, corroding the moral bases of advanced as well as backward societies. The United States of America—that supposedly most progressive bastion of freedom and equality—was so shorn of its pretensions that Gunnar Myrdal, a Swedish Social Democrat, could, in the midst of the war to end the Nazi and Fascist tyrannies, describe an as yet unresolved "American Dilemma" of racism and unfreedom at its very heart. Technological advances in the craft of killing transformed whole cities and entire populations into cinders with a single bomb. And the violation of human rights of privacy, security, creed, and belief proceeded well into the postwar era.

As world war gave way to cold war, the methods of the opposing parties merged more and more. Science, technology, and supposedly neutral social science were pressed into service—sometimes unwittingly, sometimes out of patriotism, sometimes for money—for purposes that were rarely debated in a public or ethical forum. Man and nature became victims of a seemingly ineradicable destructive force. The bloodless entelechy that sociological system building produced in the postwar era seemed both to shrink before and yet to encompass all these forms of antisocial systems. Utopias (or rather, dystopias) were already present, sociologists seemed to say, and they might house any individual, group, or outlook proceeding toward any kind of goal.

To the extent that sociological thought embraces the study of evil today, it does so under the embarrassing, neutered morality of "deviance." Adopting for the most part an uncritical stance toward the normative structure of any given society, the sociologist of deviance can only locate those violations of the norms that evoke sanctions of one kind or another. Presuming to have no relevant standards of morality by which he might independently judge the situation, the positive sociologist of deviance takes his cue from whatever the forces of law and restriction define as evil. Hence, the concerns of the vocal and powerful elements of a society become the resources for a sociological investigation of evil. Alternatively, the sociologist becomes the self-appointed advocate of an allegedly oppressed group, or of history itself, and seeks to define and locate evil in just those official elements that move against and demoralize his chosen people or trajectory of history. Sociologists are asked to take sides in a kind of intellectual contest of moral and social superiority; in the outcome of that game, there will emerge good and evil.

The concept of sin is a rara avis in sociology.[2] Indeed, it is a rare word these days altogether if we except the thundering warnings of religion.[3] It is not that there are no transgressions for which we might atone or repent, but rather that the atomization of society, the alienation characteristic of social relationships, the collectivization of guilt and pride make the designation of sinners all too difficult. There has been a division of labor in sin as well as in virtue, and each person can now point an accusatory finger toward others or toward a faceless massive monolith—the corporate structure of modern society. It is precisely in this recognition of division, corporatism, and neutrality that sin has reached its greatest heights.[4] For modern sin is peculiarly non-human in its use of things and exploitative in its use of men. Just as man reaches new understandings of human nature and social order, those very understandings lead him to see evil as outside his control. It is the Frankensteinian vision that haunts the world today. Man has created great corporate automatons, empowered them with money, endowed them with strength and potency, and freed them from personal, social, or moral responsibility. Once imagined to be his neutral servants, who would keep him from the temptations of pride, avarice, envy, and gluttony, coerce him away from sloth, reduce and cabin his lust, and chasten his anger, these corporate men *manqué* have become his masters, driving him on, determined to achieve in their soulless domination a hitherto unimagined kind of tyranny. They have appropriated and neutralized sin, liberating men from their obligations to one another at the precise moment when these same men become slaves to their own immortal and untiring creations.

The chapters of this book report on the soul-destroying journey of each of the seven deadly sins. In each case we have a beginning in slowly recognized evil, a meandering course of changing definitions, a sublimation of the sin, and a dramaturgic rendering of its ambiguous legacy. The list of seven great transgressions allows us to return sociology to the *topic* of evil in its own right, to discern how the several forms of sin, arising in different epochs and eras, wrest evil from its lair, exploit and employ it, purify and deny it, create good from it, and suffer the manifold damnations it brings.

This book offers no way out, no elimination of evil, or promise of good. Rather it tries to see evil in its many masks and personae; to look at it closely, delineate some of its processes, determine some of its forms, and dramatize its existence. Evil appears in tragedy and comedy, in pathos and farce. Its sociology ought to display it in terms of a great theater of human activities, a drama of social reality that is part of a sociology of the absurd.

ONE

Sloth

The world has become a world 'given over to death,' and this is the more terrible because there exists in the world a basic despair that seems impossible to remedy.

*Jacques Choron**

Tomorrow I am going to work again. I work to buy the admission-price into society, the ticket to the great theater of life, the great game. But now I am lonely . . .

*The Journal of Andrew Bihaly***

ON THE MEANING OF SLOTH

Perhaps the most difficult sin to define, and, indeed, to credit as a sin, is sloth. The term, in fact, refers to a peculiar jumble of notions, dating from antiquity and including mental, spiritual, pathological, and physical states. *Sloth* is but one medieval translation of the Latin term *acedia* (Middle English, *accidie*) and means "without care." Spiritually, *acedia* first referred to an affliction attending religious persons, especially monks, wherein they became indifferent to their duties and obligations to God. Mentally, *acedia* has a number of distinctive components of which the most important is affectlessness, a lack of any feeling about self or other, a mind-state that gives rise to boredom, rancor, apathy, and a passive inert or sluggish mentation. Physically, *acedia* is fundamentally associated with a cessation of motion and an indifference to work; it finds expression in laziness, idleness, and indolence. The scope and range of sloth is, thence, very great. It can grip both the body and soul of its victim, paralyzing both action and thought. Although its status as a cardinal sin has been called into question, its dangers to individuals, groups, and history itself have been frequently noted.

The spiritual dangers of *acedia* were well recognized in the early Christian and medieval eras. Vagrius (d. c. 400 A.D.), a putative "father" of the interpretation of the seven cardinal sins and a desert dweller himself, believed that *tristitia* ("melancholy") and *acedia* held particular terrors for hermits and gave these sins a special place in the temptations of the desert fathers.[1] Gregory the Great merged *acedia* with *tristitia*, utilizing the latter term to describe the sin, probably out of adherence to the earlier Egyptian monastics' belief that one should serve God with joy rather than sadness,[2] and certainly in consideration of the religious defections of monks who succumbed to "slothfulness in fulfilling the commands, and a wandering of the mind on unlawful objects."[3] In the isolated environment of the hermit desert-priest and, later, the cloistered enclosure of the monastery, the greatest fears of sinfulness grew up around the temptations threatening chastity and the tedium of the slow-paced life. While the fleshly demands were very difficult to subdue, a deeper danger lay in "spiritual dryness" (or *taedium cordis*, as Cassian, who had included *acedia* and *tristitia* as separate sins, referred to it).[4] According to the Carolingian theologian Alcuin—who wished to retain Gregory's synthesis of *acedia* and *tristitia* but returned to the former term because he saw a positive side to Christian sadness—*acedia* arose out of irascibility, the second of the three divisions of the soul, and, of course, the one to which not only monks but men in general might frequently be subject. The evils attendant upon the irascible element of the soul lent wider scope to the play of *acedia*. In the later Middle Ages it comes to refer to a particular kind of ubiquitous sloth—laziness in performing one's duties to God, and more especially failing to attend church, or, even more sinfully, choosing to attend a tournament or fair on Sunday instead of church. As the special bane of all mystics and meditators, *acedia* refused to be cloistered in monastic seclusion. Rather, it spread to plague the spirit of all those who might begin to dwell on the infinite sadness of the cosmos or lament over the sorrows of the world.[5]

Emotionally and cognitively, the evil of *acedia* finds expression in a lack of any feeling for the world, for the people in it, or for the self. *Acedia* takes form as an alienation of the sentient self first from the world and then from itself. Although the most profound versions of this condition are found in a withdrawal from all forms of participation in or care for others or oneself, a lesser but more noisome element was also noted by the theologians.[6] From *tristitia*, asserted Gregory the Great, "there arise malice, rancour, cowardice, [and] despair. . . ."[7] Chaucer, too, dealt with this attribute of *acedia*, counting the characteristics of the sin to include despair, somnolence, idleness, tardiness, negligence, indolence, and *wrawnesse*, the last translated variously as "anger" or better as "peevishness."[8] For Chaucer, man's sin consists of languishing and holding back, refusing to undertake works of goodness because, he tells himself, the circumstances surrounding the establishment of good are too grievous and too difficult to suffer. *Acedia* in Chaucer's view is thus the enemy of every source and motive for work. It opposes the work of the innocent Adam, whereby he praised and adored God; the labor of the sinful man, to which he is compelled in expiation of his sins; and the arduousness of the seeker after grace, who performs works of penitence. Sloth not only subverts the livelihood of the body, taking no care for its day-to-day provisions, but also slows down the mind, halting its attention to matters of great importance. Sloth hinders man in his righteous undertakings and thus becomes a terrible source of man's undoing.

Acedia is associated not only with the conditions of the spirit and the states of the mind but also the inactions of the body. The medieval literature associates it with motionlessness, depicting it as the *feet* of the devil that halt man in his tracks. In the illustrations of the sins for Spenser's *Faerie Queen* (1590), idleness is the guide animal to the three pairs of sins that follow and is presented as the "the nourse of sin," dressed as a somnolent monk, constantly wracked by fever.[9] In *The Pricke of Conscience*, a fourteenth-century work associated with the "school of Richard Rolle," the connection of sloth to motion is again made in the diseases promised to the slothful in Purgatory: "potagre" and gout in the limbs.[10] Sleepiness and remaining in bed through the morning hours are typical descriptions of this form of sloth.[11]

SLOTH AND SIN:
THE AMBIGUITIES OF ACEDIA

In Guillaume de Deguileville's *Pélerinage de la vie humaine*, an early-fourteenth-century work,[12] sloth is represented as an old hag carrying an axe. She attacks and binds the pilgrim hero of this moral tale and tells him that she is a principal servant of her master, the chief butcher of hell. Her duty is to ensnare and lead all pilgrims to destruction. She goes to bed with young people and makes them fall asleep; she also induces sleep in the sailor so that his ship is sunk; and she carries the cords of her attendant subsins to bind her victims and render them helpless. Once in Hell, her captives, the slaves of sloth, are punished by having their legs and feet broken. Sloth is depicted as one of the worst of sins; indeed, it is hinted in this tale that sloth is the *primary* sin. That *acedia* might be the first of all of the sins is argued in an anonymous fifteenth-century religious encyclopedia, *Jacob's Hell*,[13] wherein the devil, spying an idle man, leads him into committing all the other sins. The adage "idle hands are the devil's workshop" here finds its force: for it is among the idle that Satan goes to work, inducing boredom, enervation of the will, and trouble making.[14] Indeed, in testimony to the significance of sloth as a truly evil sin, note that it is sometimes personified as the chamberlain in the devil's castle; that it is at one point numbered after pride, envy, and anger, despoiling sins, as the one that knocks man down; that it is at another point compared to the barrenness of the sea in that it produces neither fruit nor grass; that it is named as one sin that, unrepented, will certainly doom man to hell; and that together with pride it is the sin that can be forestalled by concentrating on the Crucifixion and its meaning.[15]

A further testimony to the significance of sloth as a sin may be derived from Jewish Kabbalistic mysticism, especially that of the Sabbateans, and one of that sect's greatest scholars, Nathan of Gaza.[16] Although terms like sloth, *acedia*, and related phrases are not to be found in Nathan's theology, his doctrine of creation suggests a similar kind of evil. According to Nathan, the act of creation did not exhaust the "lights" or powers of *En-Sof*—"the Hidden God, the Divine Thought by whose words the world was created"—but instead exhibited only half of them. The other half was "the light that did not contain thought." While the first and creative light was active, the second was self-absorbed and passive. Because of its constitutionally inactive state, this second light resisted all creative movements of innovation, growth, and change emanating from its twin. The drama of this struggle between the ultimate forms of creation and their actualization is played out on earth, although the precise nature of the conflict and its eschatology is obscure and fraught with contradictions. Suffice it to say, nevertheless, that, as Gershom Scholem puts it: "This resistance [to change] turned the light without thought into the ultimate source of evil in the work of creation."[17] Based on the premise that the principles of good (creative light) and evil (thought-less inert light) coexist in the mind of the Supreme Deity, and are set in dialectical motion by Him on earth, it would seem to follow that human inertia would be *a*, if not *the*, one-sided capitulation to the forces of thought-less light, that is, the forces of darkness.

Acedia: *The Passive Aspect*

From the Christian and kabbalistic analyses of sloth, we are in a position to grasp its peculiar qualities of sinfulness. In fact, *acedia* contains both passive and active elements. The passive aspects are perhaps more visible, although their evil nature is not quite so easy to discern. *Acedia* constitutes a withdrawal of one's self, one's thoughts, one's talents, and one's endeavors from society, or from service to God. The meditative or contemplative life is especially subject to the accusation or the affliction of *acedia*. For example, the hermit priests, desert fathers, and cloistered monks and nuns who withdrew from worldly pursuits because of their oath of obligation to God had constantly to concentrate on God, and have their actions indicate this concentrated devotion. However, two modes of *acedia* challenged and threatened their oaths and duties. First, the life of prayer, contemplation, and study might result in melancholia or despair and be followed by a descent into lethargy, lifelessness of the spirit, and paralysis of the will. Such a sinking had to be resisted, fought against, and prayed over—*acedia*, in effect, could retire from service those especially charged to serve God. Second, precisely because they had forsworn worldly incentives and aspirations, ascetics ran the risk of succumbing to somnolence or sloth. No external pressure existed to prod them into motion; neither was there the incentive of a substantive reward for their efforts. Absent the push of force or the pull of hope, and man is free to choose whether to activate his will in righteous thought or in useful activity. Refusal to choose at all is an unwarranted indulgence of the self, a willful renunciation of the human obligation to be or to become, and a denial of the fundamental gifts of sentience and sapience that distinguish man from the beasts. That is a sin.

The problem of passivity inherent in the idea of *acedia* provokes further inquiry into the nature of its sinfulness. From a theological point of view man has a duty to do more than resist evil; he must also undertake to do good. Sloth falls along the invisible line that separates the sins of commission from those of omission. The indolent man may eschew those sins of flesh and action that require effort, but still by his inaction he permits evil to flourish or fails to contribute to the good. The sin of sloth consists, in this sense, then, not in committing an overt blasphemy against God but in failing to act for the good by allowing the mind to drift aimlessly or by succumbing to a paralysis of the will. For this notion of the sin of sloth to be credible, the world must be conceived dramatically, as a place where the advance of good or evil depends on man's attitudes and actions. By man's silence in the face of all that is going on, all that might be done, he sins. Where inevitability, either as fatalistic doom or eschatological promise, operates despite man's thoughts or actions, the inactivity of sloth and the attitudes of *acedia* seem venial.

It is precisely in the development of deterministic or fatalistic theories and doctrines that sloth is made at least potentially less evil than it might be in a more humanistic world. When the promise of messianic religion or the forces of historical destiny are regarded as set and immutable and where the pace of development is also governed by divine or superhuman controls, man's day-to-day activities seem irrelevant to any future, dissociated from every past. Passivity, sloth, sluggishness, and melancholy are here not only a possibility but a reasonable course of inaction. Only when an element of humane voluntarism and control is granted to human beings, or when duty and obligation to God or history are required in the face of destiny, can the sinful nature of sloth be secured. Hence, in the Calvinistic doctrines of faith and duty and in the teleological evolutionist's requirement of human catalytic and synergistic action, we find a moral prohibition and a social proscription against withdrawal and lassitude. It follows, therefore, that the sinfulness of sloth is dependent upon the perception of the endowed nature of man. Belief in man's freedom and control makes of sloth a sin; the dehumanization of man threatens to neutralize its evil or even elevate it to a virtue.

Acedia threatens whenever man is conceived as participating in a great chain of being, a long lineage of ancestors and successors, a linear and secular history, or a waiting for the end. In each of these instances man suffers the inconveniences of *time*. What to do while the chain of being is still becoming, in relation to the ever-long epochs and seemingly infinite eras of man's unfolding story, turns out to be one of the most awesome of all mankind's searching questions. No answer as given by theologians, philosophers, scholars, sociologists, or psychologists can discount the potentiality for lethargy, lassitude, boredom, apathy, and restive reactions to these states. The generally offered defenses against sinking into mourning for an active contemporary world or melancholy over the ennui of temporal existence are fortitude and faith. Chaucer's parson, for example, urges that "Against this horrible sin of Sloth, and the branches of the same, there is a virtue that is called *Fortitudo* or Strength; that is, a devotion through which a man despises harmful things."[18]

However, there is another cultural or societal alternative. Mircea Eliade has described (indeed, perhaps created) another kind of man, "archaic man," who by definition has the capacity to relieve himself of the burden of history, ancestry, destiny, and inevitability—he can abolish history at will and begin life anew.[19] But, while this reconstruction of life and history will separate man from the enervating dilemmas of secular time, it will not absolve him from the sinful aspects of his sloth. Instead, it will impose another obligation of effort upon him. He must actively undertake the rituals and tasks associated both with the exorcism of the past and the beginning of a new existence. He may not withdraw or shrink from this task no matter how much it frightens him. To do so would be to succumb to fatalism and the deadening fate that history, ancestry, or evolution has in store.

Tristitia: *The Roots of Melancholy and Ennui*

Passive *acedia* has yet other evils attendant upon it, evils that connect it to almost all the other deadly sins. Both theologians and psychologists have addressed themselves to the particularly troublesome component of (or, for some, the separate sin closely related to) *acedia* called *tristitia:* melancholy and ennui. It may at first seem strange that Gregory the Great included "rancour" as one of the consequences of *tristitia*, but in fact his perception on the matter anticipates the psychoanalytic discoveries of Freud, Karl Abraham, and Sandor Rado.

The psychoanalytic tradition has identified the common elements in grief and melancholy and distinguished the more pathological elements in the latter.[20] Central to this focus is the discovery of cloaked anger and unconscious hostility at the base of the melancholic attitude. Both mourning and melancholia have their origins in the loss of a loved object. Freud outlined the steps of the process leading to abnormal melancholic attitude.[21] Once the loved object has been lost, the person withdraws libido—sexual interest and energy—from that object. After such withdrawal, however, the ego becomes enraged with the loved one for leaving it; the anger, in turn, causes part of the ego to regress to an oral-sadistic level. But, at the same time, unable to accept the loss of its loved one, the ego remains ambivalent, splits and one part regresses to the oral-receptive state, internalizing or "introjecting" the lost love object and subsequently identifying with it. To Freud's and Abraham's penetrating analyses Rado added one focusing on the symptoms of hurt, rebellion, and arrogance that melancholics often display and explained these in terms of a fundamental narcissistic wound experienced in childhood.[22]

The melancholic state so assiduously studied by the psychoanalysts bears a striking resemblance to the *tristitia* that was the bane of hermits, monks, and contemplative men of earlier epochs. Indeed, the process whereby withdrawal from the workaday world led to melancholy and rancor can be duplicated in the lives of these isolates and outsiders.[23] In ascetic service to God or to knowledge, these people suffered the misfortune of losing affection for the object of their intense if private search. In the case of Christian monastics a loss of faith attended some of those who retired to concentrate on the love of God; philosophers and scholars suffer a world-weariness, a "sickness unto death"[24] with mundane affairs, a sense that life has left them and that, alone and rejected, they are gone stale and flat.

Acedia is not confined to the Occident. The psychoanalyst Franz Alexander has noted the comparability of melancholia to the second stage of the Buddhist progress toward nirvana.[25] In that stage the monk's experience of the lost love object is perceived by him as his loss of the world-as-object, and it becomes in turn sadistically depreciated, turned against the ego, and then reclaimed by introjection, and protected by narcissism. Alexander saw the Buddhist pursuit of nirvana as, in effect, the asocial construction of an artificial catatonia and the subsequent attribution of value to it. In true Occidental tradition, the psychoanalyst condemns the Oriental doctrine as wrong because it encourages absolute withdrawal from involvement with the world rather than dynamic adjustment to it. Moreover, according to Alexander, precisely because Buddha experienced a personal melancholia and yet taught its derivative doctrine to disciples, he contradicted his own basic principles. Noting that Buddha had considered but rejected the option of keeping his new knowledge to himself, Alexander asserts that he deserved his fate—death, rather than eternal life: "He completely withdrew from the world, yet one thread he left unsevered—his spiritual connection with his disciples. Here it is that he receives his mortal blow. He denied the world, and the denied world revenged itself upon him in the form of the unconscious parricidal wishes of his followers."[26] The wages of Buddha's sin of *acedia* are death.

Tristitia becomes a mortal sin in the eyes of many because it may set in motion all the other sins. As a reaction to loss melancholy generates *anger* at the once loved object for departing; *envy* of any that might possess it; *greed* in the desire to own and control the thing loved; *lust* in the introjection and symbolic sexual defloration of it; *pride* in the narcissism of its ego involvements; and *gluttony* in its engorgement of the whole of the once-loved other.[27] Modern psychoanalysis is no less harsh on melancholia than the medieval theologians, pointing to its pathological and abnormal status, its containment of so many unhealthy emotions, its negative effect on interpersonal relations, and its peculiar role in causing troubles for all concerned. The melancholic, by his withdrawal and peevishness, has a powerful and unpleasant effect on the world. His sin is in his infliction of the effects of his sadness on the world.

That *acedia* finds form in mourning and melancholia and ultimately paralyzes the will to act is perhaps nowhere better illustrated than in Hamlet.

Hamlet has suffered a grievous loss in the death of his beloved father. Moreover, the deadly assault on his father is exacerbated by his terrible suspicion that his uncle and new step-father is the murderer. Hamlet suffers both injury and insult; indeed, the full scope of his suffering can be understood as a deep and incurable narcissistic wound. While others go through a normal period of mourning for the dead king, Hamlet sinks into melancholy. His symptoms have attracted the interest of psychoanalysts as well as Shakespearean scholars because they are such a fine presentation of the pathological syndrome: dejection, loss of appetite, insomnia, irrational behavior, delirious seizures, and uncontrolled rage.[28] More to the point of our own study, however, is Hamlet's almost complete reversion to that affliction of contemplative men who have lost a love-object—melancholia. It is Hamlet who discourses with the ghost of his father, who finds himself unable to place his complete trust in this apparition of his dearly departed sire, but who reluctantly takes over the task assigned to him by it. And it is this same Hamlet who, having done all this and also plotted craftily against his enemies, still cannot carry off his awesome duty; he invents unsatisfactory rationalizations to account for his moral paralysis and his physical incapability.

Hamlet's sin is certainly that of *acedia*, here taking form as holding back at the opportune moment, refusing to accept God's "charity," the will of God and the plea of the ghost that Hamlet revenge the murder that placed his uncle in the bed of his mother and on the throne of his father. Melancholia not infrequently leads to violence and aggression, as the diseased sinner acts to alleviate the boredom that has ensued since his separation from the world. For Hamlet, however, it leads to withdrawal, self-doubt, and uncertainty. Hamlet has lost faith in his world and in himself.

It is very early in the play that Claudius, the recently crowned King of Denmark, observes most presciently the precise nature and deviance of Hamlet's melancholic conduct, calling it a course

> Of impious stubbornness; 'tis unmanly grief;
> It shows a will most incorrect to heaven,
> A heart unfortified, a mind impatient,
> An understanding simple and unschool'd:
> For what we know must be and is as common
> As any the most vulgar thing to sense,
> Why should we in our peevish opposition
> Take it to heart? Fie! 'tis a fault to heaven,
> A fault against the dead, a fault to nature,
> To reason most absurd . . .
> *Hamlet*, I:2

Hamlet's melancholia is here correctly referred to as "a fault . . . to reason most absurd. . . ." It is indeed meaningless with respect to reason, a product of wounded pride and thwarted self-love, a fool's attempt to flout *Fortuna* followed by a refusal to take action against it. On the one hand we have the much aroused *virtu* of the outraged Hamlet; on the other hand we have an inertness when the time to strike is at hand.[29] Hamlet's *acedia*, a mixture of boredom, despondency, and despair, is projected on the world:

> How weary, stale, flat and unprofitable
> Seem to me all the uses of this world.
> Fie on't! O fie! 'tis an unweeded garden
> That grows to seed; things rank and gross in nature
> Possess it merely. . . .

A world so worthless is also unworthy of corrective action.

The melancholic attitude is inordinately egoistic in rejecting efforts appropriate to ameliorating an unjust world. However, bowed down by his unredeeming sadness, the miserable sufferer from *acedia* considers suicide, removing himself from this world altogether, surely a most sinful act. Hamlet, however, trembles before this ultimate choice. His weakness in the face of terrible but seemingly necessary choices—acquiescence, revenge, suicide—is presented as a wavering of direction, a vacillation induced by mental anguish, ultimately a paralysis of the will to act decisively. His unfulfilled plots and mad craft, shared only with Horatio, have isolated him, perhaps intentionally, at the cost of great enhancement of his melancholy. Laertes, a less complicated and certainly less contemplative man than Hamlet, takes his revenge for Hamlet's part in the death of his sister, Ophelia, and in the confusion that ensues all die except the faithful Horatio. Ultimately, Hamlet's indecisiveness leads to the undoing of his kingdom: the once-rotten state of Denmark is left leaderless, its elite wiped out in a "grand guignol" of vengeance and inadvertence. No one profits from this except the nonparticipating soldier Fortinbras, who acquires the crown by default. *Acedia* has unfolded a tale of absurdity.

Acedia: *Boredom and the Activation of Sloth*

Acedia is associated with a restlessness of spirit, a nagging anxiety that coexists fitfully with the despair of the world and a despondency of the soul that characterizes melancholy. It is not so surprising, then, that this complex attitude should do more than just paralyze its victims; it may also activate efforts aimed at release from its torments. The kinetic component of the sin of *acedia* consists precisely in those terrible and terrifying acts that are generated to relieve or remove the gnawing corrosiveness of the spirit. To put the matter bluntly: Boredom begets aggression, and aggression releases the victim of *acedia* from its prison house of torments.

That boredom and melancholia might lead to aggression and troublemaking seems first to have been appreciated in the Homeric stories. As the Greek poet saw it, the condition of soul-rendering ennui was first produced as an unintended by-product of the leisurely life of the gods, and only later began to afflict man. Separated from the world and living on Olympus, the gods were exempted from need, necessity, or care.[30] It is the absence of this last element, care, that was to be so painful. Literally meaning "uncaring," *acedia* had been inadvertently institutionalized in the leisure world of the Greek deities. Free to do as they wished, they at first frolicked amongst themselves, dining on the best of foods, drinking the finest of wines, and enjoying pleasure as they pleased. The gods had their heavenly pursuits, but these were hardly of the character of the "calling" that would centuries later evoke the Puritan to labor so diligently.[31]

Indeed the pursuits of the Homeric gods correspond to just those much-feared activities that Christian theologians supposed would come from sloth; Zeus was an insatiable philanderer, Apollo, the archer, often gave himself up to minstrelsy, and Ares encouraged battles and wars. Only one amongst them, Hephaestus, the god of the forge, deviated from the life of leisure to which the Olympians had dedicated themselves. And this virtuous worker was physically defective; burly and with a hairy chest, he was also lame and could not participate in sports and games nor was he, despite his marriage to Aphrodite, attractive to women. In contrast to the honor accorded to those engaged in the noble pursuit of pleasure and fancy, Hephaestus is frequently ridiculed by Zeus and the others, and is regarded as a figure of fun. His special treatment is stark testimony to the Olympian ethos that favored the sweet life over the sweated existence. And, as Albert G. Keller has noticed, these gods lived in a land from which oppressive gloom had been all but banished. They do become upset over infringements on their rights by mortals. Mortals did not require the mediation of a priest to deal with these playful gods; indeed, as Keller observed: "The divinities might act like spoiled children, but [they] were easily cajoled."[32]

However, if the early period of Olympus' history is remarkable for its sun-drenched, fun-filled, hedonistic, and promiscuous leisure life and for its vigorous, active, resourceful, and cunning group of gods, the later years—those in which the story of the *Iliad* and the *Odyssey* occur—are marked by a definite disillusion, a condition of *dis-ease*. Except for Hephaestus, who is sustained by the private joy of his work, the once happy gods have become moody and irritable. They are all too frequently bitter, jaded, jealous, sullen, unsmiling, and in a fearful temper. They are often at odds with one another and argue and quarrel over fancied slights and slight injuries. The particular dis-ease that the Olympians were suffering from is a variant of *acedia*—boredom.[33] Precisely because they had no needs, no desires that could not be instantly gratified, they also came to have no hope. Hopes and longings are founded on *un*realized desires, on wants for which effort and energy must be expended and luck implored. Lacking any hope, because there was no need for it, the gods became sunk in restlessness. Without an opposition to challenge them, their gnawing boredom gave rise to the artificial social reconstruction of one another as obstacles to their desires, to gratuitous conflicts, to conspiracies, intrigues, and deceit. As Gregory the Great was later to observe, *tristitia* gives rise to malice.[34] However, the world of the Greek gods was too small and too concentrated to contain the meddlesome malice that had been sown by its slothful life of leisure. Like a stone thrown into a placid pond, this malice spread out, and its emanations began to touch the lives of others not subject to the torments of *acedia*.

It is in this movement outward that we see another evil consequence of the troublesome search for release from an all-consuming boredom—its capacity to overtake and engulf the lives of those who come in contact with its victims. Lenin referred to imperialism as the highest stage of capitalism. But there is an "imperialism" of the malicious spirit that is the highest stage of boredom. Homer and other Greek poets have described it in the intervention of the gods in the affairs of mortals. Bored with their own lives, the gods begin to take an interest in the lives of less privileged beings with whom they can have sport, cause trouble, and in general identify. Mortals and their problems offer the chance for a zestful and exciting direction of the gods' energies.

A further hint of the medicinal value of incentive-oriented labor for relieving the dis-ease of sloth is to be found in the debate between Poseidon and Apollo. They argue over which side the gods should favor in the Trojan War. Poseidon denounces Apollo for his unqualified support of the Trojans, pointing out that on orders of Zeus the gods had been hired out to Laomedon, king of Troy, as contract laborers rebuilding the wall around the city, only to be cheated out of their pay at the end of the year and driven away with threats.[35] In terms of our own argument, Poseidon is angry at Apollo's treachery because he is siding with those who introduced effort-bent hope into the lives of the gods and then cheated them out of this blessing. Without promising work and rewarding incentive, the bored gods can only continue to meddle, stir up trouble, and make themselves merry with the miseries of ordinary men.

The moral message of the Homeric tale is this: A leisure life rooted in indolence might give man temporary pleasure but it will never guarantee him permanent happiness. The delights of gourmandizing and unbridled sensuality grow stale. Life soon becomes boring, miserable, and anxious. Everything that makes life worth living has been removed from the scene of sloth: challenge, stress, endeavor, initiative, and the joys that come from using one's own talents to counteract obdurate forces. Humans or gods sentenced to an eternity of sloth will eventually struggle to break out of its stranglehold on their unspent energies. In that liberation struggle there will be released an awesome aggression whose objects and limits cannot be predicted.

In the evolution of Homeric thought about boredom and its effects, the condition of slothful god is exchanged for the status of leisurely aristocrat. The human representative of this exchange is Odysseus.[36] Odysseus is certainly a man who does not need to work in order to live. He can afford to be away from home for a decade of siege at Troy and another decade of wanderings. Moreover, although he is strong and supple, he disdains common labor. It is true that he can plow, till, and herd as well as wrestle and shoot, but he is not *compelled* to work. He is, after all, a king and neither a freeborn laborer nor a slave. He is also not a merchant,[37] a point revealed when Odysseus takes umbrage at Euryalus' description of him as "some skipper of a merchant crew, who spends his life on a hulking tramp, worrying about his outward freight, or keeping a sharp eye on the cargo when he comes home with the profits he has snatched."[38] As the king of Ithaca he leads a leisurely life, spending most of his days at sport.[39] Yet Odysseus took the time to erect his own nuptial bedroom and with his own hands constructed and decorated a bed with gold, silver, and ivory yet still attached to the olive tree growing on the site, surely an indulgence even for a wealthy man steeped in luxury. On the eve of the Trojan War Odysseus' career presents the picture of a prosperous, contented, minor monarch, who might have disappeared from history had not Paris set world-historical events in motion by his abduction of Helen.[40]

However, the torments of *acedia* do not come to plague Odysseus until his ten-year travail on the sea keeps him from returning to his beloved wife. His situation is one that could literally sink him into more than mourning and melancholia, and certainly one of the longest periods of boredom recorded on lonely and barren water. Indeed, one minor Greek poet, Herakleitos (first century A.D.), interprets Odysseus' wanderings and adventures as a moral struggle against eight sins, although the Greek list does not correspond entirely to the later Christian enumerations of the seven deadly sins. To Herakleitos the Lotus-eaters represent the temptation of gluttony; the Cyclops, the menace of savage anger; Circe, the allurement of exotic perversions; Charybdis, unwarranted extravagance; Scylla, unalloyed and ubiquitous shamelessness; the Cattle of the Sun, the pangs of aching hunger; the Sirens, inordinate curiosity about the past; and the Land of Shades, the forbidden search for secret lore.[41]

What is significant about this list, however, is that it does *not* include *acedia*. One might say that the entire odyssey is a struggle against succumbing to this unnamed sin, and that Odysseus achieves his release from it in his imprudent and impractical bon mot hurled at the blinded giant Polyphemus. When first asked his name by the Cyclops, Odysseus replies, "My name is Nobody. That is what I am called by my mother and father and by all my friends."[42] Absent from home for so long and suffering the outrages of ever more cruel fortune punctuated by long enervating periods of drifting on an unknown sea, Odysseus has become not only estranged from family and friends but also indifferent to himself. He has become a nobody. But, after seizing the moment to put out the eye of Polyphemus and effect the escape of his friends and himself, Odysseus is restored to a distinctive personal status. He is a somebody once more. From his ship he hurls back to the howling giant his restored identity and proud patrimony: "Cyclops, if anyone ever asks you how you came by your unsightly blindness, tell him your eye was put out by Odysseus, Sacker of Cities, the son of Laertes, who lives in Ithaca."[43] And with this active mastery of Cyclops, Odysseus is released from ennui. As Andrew L. Bowman concludes, "For whatever else it may or may not have done, it managed to assuage—for more than ten years—the boredom that a man of war must inevitably experience in an age of peace."[44]

Modern Versions of Acedia

The examples of Hamlet, the Greek gods, and Odysseus illustrate the troublesome potentialities of *acedia* for individuals, groups, and whole societies. Boredom is experienced as a special and most tortuous form of frustration. The world provides no zest, interest, sparkle, or challenge to energize the expenditure of human effort. Response seems a futile gesture, since that to which it would be directed is uninviting, uninteresting, and obdurate. Torpor of both body and mind, the characteristic condition of boredom, is itself an uncomfortable and disquieting experience. Seemingly at ease, the bored person cannot relax; he is fatigued but not tired, exhausted but unable to sleep, restive but denied any rest. Energy seeks outlets. Where exciting and inviting challenges are present, the person can leap into exhilarating action; where flatness and staleness seem to be everywhere, some will seek to create, to stir up the conditions to which they can respond with cheerful sprightliness or daring endeavor.

It is in the variety of individual and collective outbursts that boredom produces the many faces of its peculiar evil. Boredom finds its quintessential feeling in the anguishing sense that one is "full of emptiness," possessed by a longing that knows no object, and indeed converted from being to nothingness. Modern civilization seems peculiarly prone to boredom. Individuals experience it as an unpleasant feeling of despairing separation from everything and everyone, accompanied by a sense of deadness within and a loss of *élan vital*.

Simmel captured a portion of the mood of boredom and *acedia* in his powerful portrait of the modern metropolis and its mordant mental life. Although he did not employ the terms *acedia*, boredom, or sloth, Simmel observed that urban life was characterized by what he called a blasé attitude, defined as an "incapacity . . . to react to new sensations with the appropriate energy."[45] With the blasé attitude as his basic approach to daily life, the city dweller perceives the several material objects and life processes around him, but the "meaning and differing values of things, and thereby the things themselves, are experienced as insubstantial." Interestingly, Simmel links the possible origin of this attitude to the "boundless pursuit of pleasure" that "agitates the nerves to their strongest reactivity for such a long time that they finally cease to react at all," and to the money economy, whose capital is the metropolis, and whose characteristic consequence is the leveling of all things and the reduction of all measures of value to a single common denominator. It is in the city, with its market economy and money exchange, that the blasé attitude is concentrated so that "the nervous system of the individual" is stimulated "to its highest achievement" until "it attains its peak." But such concentrated intensity eventually produces an enervation of the responsive nerves as a defense against excessive stimulation. And with this cessation of responsiveness comes *acedia*. "The self-preservation of certain personalities is bought at the price of devaluating the whole objective world," concluded Simmel, "a devaluation which in the end unavoidably drags one's own personality down into a feeling of the same worthlessness."

It remained for Simmel's American disciple, Robert E. Park, to see and describe the forms of activation of the distract spirit in the modern city. Taking his cue, undoubtedly, from Simmel's depressing observation that "the individual has become a mere cog in an enormous organization of things and powers which tear from his hands all progress, spirituality, and value in order to transform them from their subjective form into the form of a purely objective life," Park pointed to the collective outbursts of magic, madness, and missions in the mental life of the metropolis.[46] Leisure, Park observed, had become a "restless search for excitement," and manifested itself in a "wish to escape reality." From the boring routines and enervating practices of everyday life, individuals and groups set forth on romantic quests, which from Park's point of view found their "most outrageous expression in the dance halls and jazz parlors,"[47] but were also to be seen in the lure of exotic places, political revolutions, social reform movements, millennarian religions, missionary enterprises, crime waves, an efflorescence of juvenile delinquency, and the many popular fads[48] that swept over urban populations. "We are everywhere hunting the bluebird of romance, and we are hunting it with automobiles and flying machines," Park asserted. "But," he added, "this physical mobility is but the reflection of a corresponding mental instability." Although he gave no name to this instability it is clear that Park had in mind the age-old dis-ease of *acedia*. And, giving emphasis to his argument, Park added that it is through the misuses of leisure in thrill-seeking that real progress is retarded: "This restlessness and search for adventure is, for the most part, barren and illusory, because it is uncreative," Park pointed out: "We are seeking to escape from a dull world instead of turning back upon it to transform it." The sin of sloth, here perceived as an energized leisure animated by the desire to escape from ennui, leads to "the great wastes in American life."[49]

The dangers posed by boredom and melancholy to social order have not gone entirely unnoticed. In a recent paper on the subject heavily influenced by a psychoanalytic model, Franz Goetzl charges boredom with being "the root of discontent and aggression." Likening the victim of boredom to a man caught in a jawlike vise, Goetzl describes one jaw as the inhibition against reaching out and securing from nature, the world, or other humans the assistance required to avert the agony of one's melancholic isolation, and the other jaw as the inhibition against acknowledging and utilizing the passionately longed-for objects even when they are available and offer their services. Eager to escape from his fetters, yet unable to effect his escape through practical means and the employment of his own resources, the individual regresses to a childlike stage in which he succeeds "in maintaining his self-esteem through passive-receptive mastery over the external world."[50]

However, as Goetzl points out, "Caught in that vise, he feels bored: empty, alienated, lonely, and worthless; he may appear apathetic, yet he is tense and demanding help from without." The tension cries out for resolution as, in effect, the soul cries out for pastoral rest. However, the jaws of boredom permit no easy release. Instead, as Goetzl observes, "The vise . . . has caused a shift of the struggle for maintaining self-esteem from a level of mature tranquillity to one of primitive impulsiveness." And, just as Herakleitos saw in Odysseus' lonely sea journey a morality play on the struggle against sin, so Goetzl, in the language of the scholarly clinician, describes the moods and behavior of the bored personality as expressions of and conducive to the commission of sins:

> Prominent among these disorders of mood and behavior, which may be present in variable intensity and combination, are the following: a morbid exaggeration of variations in mood not unlike that seen in overt manic-depressive disease; restlessness and inability to concentrate; greed for things and persons combined with a conspicuous predilection for change and novelty; tendency toward immature identification with possessions; impulse neuroses, addictions and perversions; proneness to promiscuous conduct; conversion reactions; hypochondriasis; states of depression, unmasked or masked, neurotic or psychotic, dependent upon the depth of narcissistic regression; and above all, an all-pervasive aggressiveness with a striking readiness to respond to frustration with violence, a proclivity to destroy, to ruminate and even to commit murder and suicide.

The train of evil that follows from boredom and melancholy is formidable indeed, and it is not only theologians and psychoanalysts who have observed it. Kenneth Burke has symbolized the longing for a pastoral tranquillity that cannot be found in modern frenetic yet boring civilization by contrasting the peace of mind available to somnolent white oxen in a zoo with the restive rage and sneering suspicion that attends a caged lion.[51] The oxen seem to be content despite the fact that they lead a sluggish existence. "They were chewing in deliberate contentment," he writes, and appeared to be calm, harmless and sleepy as they lolled about in their enclosure. The visitor to the zoo, subject to the pangs of an ubiquitous but gnawing boredom, envies the oxen: "To them the supreme gift of God was to sleep and know that one is sleeping." Modern man cannot accept this gift of God, Burke seems to say. And, in his anguish he wishes he could be transformed into oxen: "He yearned to see things with their dull, slow-blinking eyes, to retire into their blissful sloth of semi-sensation."[52] Denied the "blissful sloth" of oxen, man is permitted only the anxious boredom of *acedia.* Adam Smith had pointed out earlier that the lofty and tranquillizing disinterest of Stoic philosophy had been denied to modern men, its "perfect apathy" having no play in "the great business and occupation of our lives."[53] Burke goes even further. While commenting on Nietzsche's problem of coming to terms with the inconsistency of human purpose, he observes that "whereas the organism has developed an equipment for attaining the benign sluggishness of satiety, the very equipment for bringing about such a world Nirvana is in itself the essence of turbulence and struggle."[54] The paradoxical contradiction of a leisure that does not pacify finds its expression in violence and war. Assuring his readers that he does not wish to glorify the element of combat underlying all action, Burke points out that it is only "in moments of great stress, as in extreme personal anguish or under the present disorders of our economic system, that the purely combative emphasis must come to the fore." Nevertheless, the thrust of his comments vitiates the solace offered by this qualification, for if "pure" combat is expressed only in moments of great stress, a less than pure but no less destructive aggressiveness arises from the general condition of *acedia* that dominates the current age. That struggle against boredom, that vain attempt to escape into the peace of the white oxen, produces the fanaticism, tenacity, pugnacity, and aggression that characterize contemporary existence.

SLOTH: SIN OR DISEASE?

In light of the dangers and evils attendant upon sloth, it may seem puzzling that it has had an inconsistent history as a sin. In fact, the history of attitudes toward sloth indicates that it has enjoyed a cyclical career in the Occident—considered a disease among the ancients, elevated to a sin by the early medieval theologians, reassigned to disease status (or to being a general tendency in man) in the later medieval period, and then rediscovered as the deadliest sin tempting those who subscribed to the Protestant ethic. In the medieval period, *acedia* was sheared off from sloth proper, resulting in a two-pronged division of the evil. On the one hand there was melancholy, lassitude, and malice; on the other there was laziness, indolence, and idleness. In the modern period the two have been reunited; a deadly synthesis of sloth and *acedia* has become the bane of a burgeoning leisure era. But in truth the issues connected with *acedia* transcend the scope of pathology, and the problems of sloth are not confined to the arenas of pleasure. The sinfulness of sloth has not been lost in the fusion of the term occasioned by the modern era; indeed the sinful qualities loom as large as ever.

Among the ancients Hippocrates resisted succumbing to a popular supernatural theory of mental states and formulated a humoral theory that among other things accounted for the dark, doleful, sad, and solitary expression of certain persons by referring these symptoms to *melancholia*, that is, black bile, a substance that when generated in excess from the liver produced the sorrowful countenance associated with *acedia*.[55] Opposed to the prevalent theories of demonic possession, the humoral theory was spread among medical circles of the Greek physician Galen, and continued in some measure through the medieval period and into modern times.[56] Humoral and other theories of the organic origin of melancholy are significant because they relieve the sufferer in part or in whole of personal and voluntary responsibility for his untoward and antisocial conduct. However, the sinful aspects of even a humorally induced melancholy were not entirely eliminated by the medical approach. In Robert Burton's *Anatomy of Melancholy*, an *omnium gatherum* on the subject, melancholy, although still considered bilious in origin, opens people to becoming the prey of the devil, who "spying his opportunity of such humours, drives them many times to despair, fury, rage, etc., mingling himself among these humours," and who might sign up the melancholic by "diabolic temptations and illusions" to commit other sinful acts.[57] To Burton want of faith, incredulity, weakness, or distrust in God might become the devil's workshop for melancholy.

Perhaps the most significant change in the moral status of sloth occurred during the waning of the Middle Ages.[58] For the second time in its history the Western world was swept by an epidemic of melancholy. In the earlier epidemic, during the first century of the Christian era, boredom assumed such great proportions that its victims were given a special name, *ardeliones*, and considered a troublesome nation within a nation, interrupting the affairs of other people, indifferent to their own welfare, annoying to the social order, and a cause for general alarm.[59] In the second instance, the rise of general *acedia*, although having a variety, indeed, a jumble of disparate consequences, is notable for the growth of the argument that separates *accidie* from laziness pure and simple.[60] Monks were again reminded of their special susceptibility to the *daemon meridianus* ("the demon at noontide"), a satanic holdover from the period of the desert fathers, who, once he gained a grip on the cloistered penitent, would deprive him of hope, blow him down with sadness, sink him to the depths of despair, and turn him away from his prayerful obligations to God.[61] Laziness in secular matters, on the other hand, sheared off from *acedia*, began to lose some of its sinful qualities; indeed, in some instances, it was seen as merely a tendency, and in other cases a useful preventative against the excesses of greed.[62] As the nobility of the feudal period fought against a burgeoning bourgeoisie by emphasizing the evils of avarice, the counterattack leveled its sights on the immoral nature of sloth. However, a secularized indolence, while perhaps a disturbance to material progress and an inhibition to diligence, could not arouse a moral fervor until it regained the status of true sin.

The restoration of sinfulness to sloth is the great accomplishment of the Protestant era and its ethic. As Max Weber has so carefully pointed out, the thrust of post-Calvinistic admonitions, especially the exhortations and homilies of the seventeenth-century English churchman Richard Baxter, is to raise sloth not merely to its former status as one of the seven deadly sins, but indeed as the principal moral lapse on the list. Once ordinary work is elevated to the status of the layman's glorification of God, resistance to one's calling—by idleness, indolence, or relaxed acceptance of the fruits of one's accomplishments—becomes blasphemy. "Waste of time," Weber writes, "is thus the first and in principle the deadliest of sins."[63] Sloth, the Puritan divines argued, permits individuals to relax their vigilance with respect to election or damnation, encouraging a false sense of security in the enjoyment of their material possessions; it also stimulates the pleasureful employment of wealth in frivolous but dangerous temptations of the flesh; and, most important, it introduces a host of distractions from the dutiful pursuit of a righteous life. Precisely because the span of human life was so short, individuals were morally bound to use every moment in actions that would promote their election. "Loss of time through sociability, idle talk, luxury, even more sleep than is necessary for health, six to at most eight hours, is worthy of absolute moral condemnation."

Whereas Thomas Aquinas had argued that labor was necessary only for the maintenance of the individual and the community, the fundamental change introduced by the Protestant ethic is the transvaluation of it into the moral duty of every man. Thus, Baxter insisted that Paul's command, "He who will not work will not eat," is a universal injunction against sloth and applies to everyone regardless of wealth or station. Since God's Providence provides a calling for every man, no one is permitted to shrink from the assumption of his duty to labor for the greater glory of God. Moreover, the contemplative life and the acceptance of irregular and transitory work are condemned. "A man without a calling ... lacks the systematic, methodical character which is ... demanded by wordly asceticism." Thus did Protestant ethical casuistry rescue sloth from its degradation as a mere mundane condition; it was restored to its pristine place as a deadly sin.

The most recent chapter in the wavering career of sloth includes the secularization and pathological reconstruction of *acedia* and the routinization of sloth. *Acedia*—like asceticism—has been carried out of monastic cells and into everyday life.[64] Aldous Huxley has described a portion of the historical and cultural process whereby *acedia* moved "from the position of being a deadly sin, deserving of damnation, to the position first of a disease, and finally of an essentially lyrical emotion, fruitful in the inspiration of much of the most characteristic modern literature."[65] But *acedia* has since progressed beyond its status as the peculiar possession of poets and novelists. Stripped of its romantic shibboleth, it survives as a major element in the corrosive social psychology of current civilization, contributing to revolt, rebellion, crime, and delinquency and causing concern and consternation wherever it emerges.

And what of sloth? It too has suffered a certain diminution in its moral status without losing its gnawing capacity to enervate. Still, it retains its power to produce guilt in its practitioners. Deprecated by the apostles of the self-made man in America,[66] it exists as both a lure and a horror to the diligent and prudent working man. Seeking on the one hand to attain a state of existence wherein he can afford to enjoy the fruits of his accumulated labor, he also fears to undertake the realization of this dream lest his upward mobility be threatened by a surcease of his efforts, or his moral standing in the community be cast into doubt through the taint of egoism or unwarranted gratification.[67] And in the perhaps inevitable conflict of generations that ensues, his children rebel by cultivating the arts of sloth and indolence, only to discover that they have not escaped from the *daemon meridianus*, their season in the sun subverted by a growing sense of *acedia*.

THE DRAMATIZATION OF SLOTH

"Dramatic" is one of the key words of the vocabulary of culture and society in the present era.[68] Its relationship to sloth is complex and paradoxical. One interpretation of the dramatic emphasizes the common-sense meaning attached to theatrical, and suggests emotive exaggeration, heightened expression, and arresting display.[69] On the other hand, a sociological approach to dramatism calls attention to life as theater and seeks to uncover the performance aspects of everyday affairs.[70] Sloth appears to conjoin and yet to confound these two meanings, since in the first instance it seems least likely to excite the interest or evoke the attention of those who would observe the more exciting dramas in the theater of everyday life, and in the second, it would appear to be too pervasive and yet too intertwined with other matters to deserve theatrical notice in its own right. Yet, there is a drama in the routine, and a sociology rooted in theatricality would do well to attend just those dramatic stages of seemingly undramatic conduct that the ordinary theatergoer would be sure to avoid.[71] In the ennui and enervation of sloth there is a strategic research site for the further development of a sociologically informed dramatism.

As with all other conventional practices—and for sloth to be a sin it must find a locus in convention—sloth has its theatrical settings, its time for performance, and its dramatic manner. Moreover, these spatial, temporal, and rhetorical patterns change across the span of history and among the various cultures. To the desert fathers, sloth appeared as a fearsome devil, the *daemon meridianus*, who stalked the souls of monks during that part of the day when the sun shone so bright and hot that the mind would begin to wander, and when enervating tedium would begin to gnaw its way into the pious heart.[72] The boring tedium of the intense desert sun at midday initiated the drama of the long dark night of the soul. To the aristocrats of the antebellum South, on the other hand, sloth took form as the rightful luxury that certain men deserved as a measure of their station in life. It found dramatic expression in the gracious living, hedonistic excesses, cultivated gentility, and flaunted idleness of southern white gentlemen; it displayed a dramatically heightened contrast when viewed against the backdrop of the backbreaking labor and moral degradation of the black slaves toiling in the fields.[73] For our own times, we shall illustrate some dramatic elements of sloth that occur in contemporary theaters of work, education, and leisure. In each case we shall find the sin playing its part as a corrupter of good morals, even though it often comes in disguises, bringing what appears to be a blessing instead of a curse.

Work: From Asceticism to Acedia

The drama of workaday reality takes place quintessentially in large, densely populated theaters of operations called factories, plants, or offices. On the stages of these theaters people perform work in accordance with pre-established time schedules, rather rigid rituals of movement and motion, and a studied, impersonal, and attentive manner that concentrates on the task at hand. At least that is the scenario imagined by management, by industrial engineers, and by all those efficiency experts and students of time and motion who do not know the difference between the *pre-text*, that is, the imagined scenario, of modern labor and the *text*, or the performed reality, of modern work.[74] In fact the actors performing in the workplace enact a very different drama from that imagined by the corporate playwrights who write its formal and idealized scenario. Sociology has only just begun to comprehend the actual text and texture of workaday reality,[75] but even in these rude beginnings there is a glimpse of the central part played by sloth and the multiform subversions of work that it can encourage. To be sure, it is rare to see sloth create havoc with the work situation; more likely it acts as an interruption and an interference—a character who has stepped onto the stage during an act in which he was not to appear.

Although the role of sloth has rarely been recognized even as a supporting player in the workplace, its character is expressed in deactivated or energized boredom, foolish pranks, and hostile aggression. Max Weber made the mordant observation that "the Puritan wanted to work in a calling; we are forced to do so." And he went on to point out that the modern economic order "is now bound to the technical and economic conditions of machine production which today determine the lives of all the individuals who are born into this mechanism, not only those directly concerned with economic acquisition, with irresistible force. Perhaps it will so determine them until the last ton of fossilized coal is burnt."[76] Sentenced to an eternity of mechanized petrification, the working man is ever threatened by the fatal mood of boredom which sets in as a consequence of the monotony of his drudgery. To be sure, "elite" theorists of industrial life have pointed to the fact that boredom among worker "aborigines"—as Clark Kerr ironically refers to them—is less likely where mechanization has made daydreaming possible or when concentrated attention to the task is required.[77] But daydreaming, fantasy, and other mental trips from the stationary stage on which the undramatic performance of labor must go on are but the most passive expressions of the *acedia* that gnaws at productive actors in contemporary industrial civilization.

Literally, monotony means "one tone," and it is the sense that one's work is all of the same tone—flat, devoid of interesting rhythmic changes, colorless—that evokes a sense of boredom in relation to it. The evidence indicates that the sense of monotony varies greatly in the several kinds of work settings and differs among men and women.[78] However, there are some data to suggest that those who do not report themselves to be bored by their work have very little hope in general for an interesting existence. Descendants of and bound in service to the Frankenstein firm created by the Puritans to carry off their sins, they are even more zombielike than their progenitor. Their undramatic lives herald the routinization of *acedia*.

Playfulness and pranks are part of the *text* of daily work, but never part of the *pre-text* that establishes the scenario and setting, defines the roles and costumes, and writes the lines and silences that are expected of the performing worker. Indeed, official notice of the serious import of horseplay has so rarely been given that it could become a cause for revolt. In the 1960s a counter-culture revolutionary, Abbie Hoffman, advocated and attempted to carry off an insurrection based on the playful disruption of ordinary workaday occasions, a "revolution for the hell of it."[79] More serious was the rising of French students and workers in 1968, animated in part by an ideology that denounced the teachings and practices of a "human relations" oriented industrial sociology, imported to the class-rooms of the Sorbonne from the Western Electric Company researchers in the United States.[80] That research, significant as it has been, constitutes an incomplete account of the nature and extent of boredom in the work situation.[81] The empirical materials reveal that the jokes, games, and horseplay that a team of investigators discovered to be modifying and sometimes controlling productivity in a bank wiring room were largely the consequences of boredom and a kind of deadening ennui. "Monot-ony," Sir Geoffrey Vickers points out, "is as great a stress to one man as responsibility is to another."[82] The stress of their monotonous wiring task led the employees to make bitter jokes about the "slavery" of their output requirements, to get into angry squabbles over insignificant matters such as the opening of a window, and to devise a cruel game, called "binging," in which one worker was permitted to strike another as hard as possible for the slightest of social infractions or in order to keep the output of each worker at an even level.[83] Something of the mindless aggression generated by the boredom of their situation is revealed by this exchange between a sociological observer and "W9," a worker in the bank wiring room:

W9 suddenly binged W7.
Obs. (to W9): "Why did you do that?"
W9: "He swore. We got an agreement so that the one who swears gets binged. W8 was in it for five minutes but he got binged a couple of times and then quit."
Obs: "Why don't you want W7 to swear?"
W9: It's just a bad habit. There's no sense to it, and it doesn't sound good. I've been getting the habit lately and sometimes swear when I don't want to. I never used to swear until I got next to W8, there, and now I find myself doing it all the time."[84]

It is not laziness that lies submerged as the subtext of the modern drama of daily work, but *acedia*. Searching for the motivation of the laborer who jokes, swears, fights with and then helps his fellow worker, the student of the seven deadly sins would no doubt uncover that ancient evil known to the desert fathers and the medieval theologians. And just as some succumb to *acedia* by sinking into melancholy, while others become restive, anxious, and aggressive, so some workers retreat into the private worlds of their own reveries, while others strike out in black comedy or even blacker anger. The theater of industrial drama conceals a subtextual tragicomedy of grotesque *acedia*.

The School: Yawns and the Tapping of Feet

An educational drama is played out in the theater of learning created by the public schools in America. Designed originally to ensure that the polyglot population of immigrants would be molded into a single nation,[85] the educational curriculum was reduced to a low common denominator and the art of teaching to a standardized method. Characterized by lesson plans, grouping of students according to age and measured intelligence, and tracking of pupils along a streamed trajectory, the schools order life chances to a considerable extent.[86] One result is that for considerable numbers of students classroom education becomes a dull, boring, and enervating experience. Both *acedia* and sloth proper set in, with the usual results—daydreaming, restlessness, playful distractions, aggression, and absenteeism. The dull drama of the schools becomes a years-long rehearsal for the even duller drama of the workplace.

The dramatic expression of schoolchildren's boredom takes on forms in part associated with the physiology of the human organism but also contingent upon the setting and props associated with classroom activities. Most frequently noticed as an expression of boredom and underspent energies are yawning and foot tapping.[87] Both of these acts, typically regarded as signs of bored fatigue or anxious escape, arise in the first instance because of physiological circulatory processes. When running, walking, or even standing there is sufficient muscular work going on to keep the blood circulating to the heart. However, sitting—the usual posture dictated by the classroom setting, and one approved by pedagogical leaders for its effectiveness in keeping order and communicating the authority of the teacher—tends to permit the pooling of the blood in the lower legs and the feet. Sedentary persons not infrequently claim that their feet "go to sleep." One escape from this body-induced and setting-encouraged form of sloth is limb exercise. Smaller children, not yet socialized in the ways of polite attention, often fidget and squirm when ordered to sit quietly in a chair for any length of time. Restricted by the rules of classroom deportment, the role of pupil, and the relationships enjoined by educational scenario and school setting, the bored student rebels reflexively in the manner permitted by these restraints—he taps his foot. Yawning arises from a similar situation. Sitting restricts pulmonary respiration and slows down the exhalation of surplus carbon dioxide. In an extreme case, a sedentary person suffers from *stagnant asphyxia*. However, the body rescues the individual from such extremities by reflexively ordering the yawn. Unstifled and frequent, these yawns are all too often interpreted as an affront to the teacher, an expressive assault on the lesson in progress, or a form of passive aggression against the educational situation. In reacting harshly to the yawning student, the teacher may initiate a drama of humiliation and degradation that not only exaggerates the dangers present but also fails to perceive how the body reflex has rescued the individual from physiologically induced ennui.

However, there is another function of boredom in the schools.[88] "Education" derives from a Latin word meaning "to lead out" or "to draw out." In effect, education produces a drama of social and personal metamorphosis that is quite frightening to some young unformed minds because of the drastic changes that might occur. On a collective level whole groups have actively resisted public education because of the threat it poses to cherished values and traditional beliefs. However, the individual who lacks the protective support available to members of such educational resistance groups as the Amish, Mennonites, Hutterians, or Doukhobors[89] is left to his own devices. In his apprehensions over the new and unfamiliar and whatever other dangers he believes education holds in store for him, the pupil might artfully assume the *role* of one who is bored, putting on a show of apathy, lack of interest, or carelessness as a protective armor. Boredom strikes here in the form of a seductive devil, who in effect possesses the pupil and invites him to become slothful and indifferent to his own educational welfare. By succumbing to the siren song of sloth, slouching in his seat, shifting his gaze, and steeping himself in reverie, the lazy student avoids the pain and challenge that learning has to offer. However, his retreat into boredom is not without dangers of its own. And these include more than the ignorance that goes unchecked. Isolated and alone, the bored pupil might fall prey to melancholy. The drama of school life tells many sad stories.

Like war and work settings, schools also are scenes of structured competition and unstructured aggression. A certain recognition of the dangers of boredom and also of children's limited capacity for concentration on a single subject for very long has led public schools to pace education like a theatrical play, dividing the school day into several separate periods, scenes punctuated by intermissions in which the pupil is free to exercise his unspent energies and relieve his boredom through fun, games, and horseplay. The gymnastics, contests, and sports provided by the schools are in effect short-lived playlets offering a brief eudaemonic release from boredom. Apparently, however, they are not exhilarating enough to still the nagging voice of *acedia*; for the restive boredom of the students strikes out beyond the permissible forms of excitement and occasionally erupts in schoolyard violence and classroom disruption. The intermissions between classes give inadvertent license to troublemaking. But the mischief committed by young people often constitutes not only a declaration of a moral holiday but also the dramatic construction of an escape from boredom and fatalism.[90] In one case, reported by Willard

Waller, a minister's son recalled years later how a particularly vulgar set of pranks he and his friends played on some adults buoyed him up in the face of his otherwise constricted existence: "That was one time I thoroughly escaped my role for a few hours and enjoyed what seemed to be entire freedom. The escape and the ecstasy of it still glow in my memory. Of course it all seems crude now, but then it was the living out for me of a great dream of escape to freedom."[91] Thus have *acedia* and sloth sometimes acted as the puppet master, directing the subtext of the learning experience. And it is sloth or its consequences that frequently interrupts and sometimes subverts altogether both the text and the pre-text of the educational drama.

Leisure: Blessing or Curse? A Morality Play

Leisure, like hell, holds out much dread and little hope for all who enter its realm. To be sure it beckons as a utopia in the minds of all those who consider the toil of this world to be a nightmare from which man should ultimately awaken. But at the same time it threatens man with agonies of unguided but ultimate choice, the emptiness of contentless time, and the ennui that sloth encourages. Every discussion of modern leisure is in fact a terrifying morality play, opening upon a scene of apparently boundless pleasure and revealing it to be a prison allowing no exit, devoid of true happiness.

The moral ambivalence surrounding the scenario of leisure is nicely illustrated by the debate over it in the family of Karl Marx. Marx himself never imagined the disappearance of labor altogether. Rather he foresaw the social transformation of labor into communal production, wherein the quality of work determined its value; he hoped for the abolition of the monetary quantification of labor and of calculated exchange value; and he prophesied an increase in leisure time, affording individuals untold opportunities for humanistic enhancement.[92] Marx scoffed at the idea that the abolition of private property would bring about the cessation of work and the engulfment of the world in universal laziness. "Communism deprives no man of the power to appropriate the products of society; all that it does is to deprive him of the power to subjugate the labor of others by means of such appropriation."[93] And, in a passage in the *Grundrisse*, he speaks of the work appropriate to cultural production: "Really free labour, the composing of music for example, is at the same time damned serious and demands the greatest effort."[94] Marx's utopian vision embraced not a slothful world of idleness, but a productive worthwhile life in which not labor but its divisions, not work but its roles, had been absolished:

In communist society, . . . where nobody has an exclusive area of activity and each can train himself in any branch he wishes, society regulates the general production, making it possible for me to do one thing today and another tomorrow, to hunt in the morning, fish in the afternoon, breed cattle in the evening, criticize after dinner, just as I like, without ever becoming a hunter, a fisherman, a herdsman, or a critic.[95]

Thus, for Marx, the utopia promised by communism was not to be a replication of that classical utopia of the Greek gods, the sloth-bound community of Mount Olympus. In fact, Marx rejected such notions as infantile, but he was genuinely ambivalent about—and, indeed, not a little nostalgic for—the Olympian paradise. Marx admitted to the fascination and allure that Greek mythology held out to his own age.[96] "A man cannot become a child again, or he becomes childish," warned Marx. But he admitted that "the historic childhood of humanity," by which he meant classical Greece, exercised "an eternal charm." "The Greeks were normal children," Marx allowed, and their epics "afford us artistic pleasure and . . . they count as a norm and as an unattainable model." Marx concluded wistfully that "The charm of their art for us . . . is inextricably bound up . . . with the fact that the unripe social conditions under which it arose, and could alone arise, can never return." Yet Marx was to experience this childlike desire to return to a world without labor in his own family. His son-in-law, Paul La Fargue, was to write some of the finest odes in praise of "idleness, mother of the arts and noble virtues," and with *The Right to Be Lazy*,[97] his important book published the year that Marx died, he set in motion a great debate among socialist utopians that would last to the present day.[98] In choosing between adoption of an ancient ideal of idleness or a grand march into the utopia of socialized and humanistic production, man must elect to believe in either a myth of eternal return or a linear chain of being and becoming. In one case he opts for sloth and *acedia*; in the other he hopes for release and redemption.

Staging the Drama of Leisure: Space

Writing the scenario and setting the scene for the supposedly pleasant drama of leisure turns out to be no easy task. Even if we confine our attention to the last two centuries the playwrights of this pre-text argue with one another fiercely over just what leisure might look like. What is now considered the debate over leisure and how to employ it had its beginnings in the struggles for the ten-hour workday in the nineteenth century.[99] In crystallizing the workday, the movement to shorten the workman's daily period of labor also established a time for leisure. This, in turn, generated questions about how and where that time should be utilized by the person freed from work. A new drama of leisure required not only a scenarist but also a stage, a set of props, and actors trained to use them. The human roles were filled by means of intense competition, but the scenario, the stage, and the props remained the main problem.

Let us consider the problem of space, that is, the stage on which the drama of leisure would be enacted.[100] For the two hundred years prior to the onset of the Industrial Revolution, the stage for enacting leisurely dramas of everyday life was the commons, that green space especially set aside in rural communities for peasants and rustics to rest and recreate themselves. Enclosures and the rise of cities put an end to this hitherto protected place, and also to many of the activities that occurred upon it. When, after decades of social movement and popular outcry, factory and other social legislation decreased the hours required for labor, the space for the newly created leisure time had disappeared. Moreover the enclosure of public territories was followed by the diminution of private domestic space. In the cities of England the cottage gave way to the tenement flat and these in turn to the smaller apartment. What spatial reorganization had begun, religious movements sought to complete. Warning of the evils attendant upon the release from work, religious bodies not only preached against idleness but persuaded civil authorities to enforce the laws on the matter. As Sunday became the single most important day of leisure, it also became the day most hedged about with restrictions—on circuses, sports, and shows and, later, on sales, cinemas, and salubrious celebrations. And yet, as leisure became an item on which profits might be turned, products and property were reconverted to meet the demand for leisure activities and the objects necessary to carry them out. At the present time the stages of leisure are many and varied and sportsman or spectator, reader or writer, filmgoer and stagedoor johnny are counted among the legions of recreational actors.

But what is the *proper* stage for leisure? One answer is that it is any place convenient for private pleasures. Here the demon of sloth appears to grin—for he supposes that what is offstage is also literally so, that is, *obscene*. Removed from public scrutiny, the argument runs, the leisurely person will sink into lust and gluttony, and insofar as he has private space on which to practice his evil vices, he will indulge himself without restraint. However, privacy does not ensure sensuality, and despite the fears of moralists, a world of enriched eroticism continues to elude even those dedicated to the pursuit of pleasure.

There is still another aspect of the private stage: its size and, with that, its opportunities for various kinds of activity. Typically, modern societies think of the private domain as a small theater for miniature dramatics. Hannah Arendt argues that the modern enchantment with small things finds its quintessential presentation among the French and their celebration of *petit bonheur*. Within the space of four walls, "between chest and bed, table and chairs, dog and cat and flowerpot," the French take their pleasure, "extending to these things a care and tenderness which, in a world where rapid industrialization constantly kills off the things of yesterday to produce today's objects," renders such places as perhaps "the world's last purely humane corner."[101] Yet, as a recent wit has observed, the Parisians take the longest vacations away from their homes, throw themselves into indolent idleness more readily than other Europeans or Americans, and are "limitlessly able to rest." The French, concludes Fernando Diaz-Plaja, "take hold of rest as forcefully as work ... They do it better than anyone else."[102] But, regardless of sensual excess, smallness in size, or its conversion of landscape to escape, so long as the leisure stage is exclusively private it will remain socially inconsequential, sacrificing relevance for charm. The latter is the idealized essence of cloistered leisure; the former is the practical exigency of the active *polis*.[103]

To ideologists of leisure, the playwrights of its *pre-text*, the emancipation of man from labor would result in the enhancement of person, culture, and civilization. In the new freedom from the demands of work the human actor would emerge as his nature promised—as a civilized being, creative, active, learned, artistic, and human. Instead of slothful Mount Olympus, there would emerge the Athens of Pericles which, without its slaves—since mechanization would have made slavery, like drudgery, obsolete—would enhance the lives of all mankind and create a higher culture than the world had ever seen before. But as with so many philosophical pre-texts, this one was doomed to be undone by its text, by its actors, their settings and roles. As Hannah Arendt has observed:

> A hundred years after Marx we know the fallacy of this reasoning; the spare time of the *animal laborans* is never spent in anything but consumption, and the more time left to him, the greedier and more craving his appetites. That these appetites become more sophisticated, so that consumption is no longer restricted to the necessities but, on the contrary mainly concentrates on the superfluities of life, does not change the character of this society, but harbors the grave danger that eventually no object of the world will be safe from consumption and annihilation through consumption.[104]

And so leisure gives rise to one of sloth's promised immorality plays—endless greed.

There is also the enervating drama of *acedia*. While one playwright of leisure's drama has defined the good life as that "in which a rich leisure gives direction and meaning to all else we do,"[105] another has defined leisure time as "all time beyond the existence and subsistence time . . . more specifically . . . as . . . all time not spent in sleep, at work, in school, or in necessary personal choices."[106] Between these two scenic ideas there exists a yawning gap—a gap that Robert MacIver called "the great emptiness."[107] The basic source for this much dreaded emptiness is that leisure restores to man a basic element of his humanity; it endows him with the time and the freedom to choose how to spend it. His newly created spare time invites the individual to develop a joyful, fulfilling pastime. However, the choice—the naked fact of having to make that choice—is frightening. Leisure, the blessing of time free from enforced labor, is also the cursed time that seems so out of joint, and many will flee from it rather than set it right. The flight might be into fantasies—like those of great feasts or of Polynesian sensuality imagined by Paul La Fargue—or into action—pleasurable, risky, and exciting sports—or into violence—perilous, challenging, and nerve-tingling dangers—but whatever its form, it usually fails to satisfy.[108] The *text* of its action might provide a momentary titillation, a sudden, punctuated, and exhilarating feeling of much vaunted freedom, and then it is gone. In its place there returns the gnawing loneliness, the ache of unfulfillment, the agonizing desire to be free from the vacuum which leisure man's nature abhors. And once again the escape into dreams, action, or violence beckons.[109] *Acedia* has set in, except that in the modern drama of leisure, he appears not merely as the noontime *daemon meridianus* who haunted the desert fathers, but as the new *daemon universalis*, who haunts the whole of one's existence. This drama takes place in a dark sleep. The bright dreams of a pleasurable utopia become the black nightmares of deadening reality. Leisure has framed the awful inaction in an eternity of sloth and boredom.

SCENARIOS OF CULTURE AND SLOTH

The dramatistic elements in sloth are not exhausted by examining the scenarios of idleness and *acedia*. They also include the special plays, particular dramas of rare triumph, and regular tragedy, whose characters are the victims or by-products of the progressive release of man from labor. In industrial societies they include the involuntarily unemployed and the disreputable poor; in the age of imperialism their numbers were swelled by the thousands of Polynesians who died of contact with western civilization; and in recent politics it finds new terrors in the activation of the apathetic, once somnolent actors who suddenly and inexplicably arise to play unpredictable parts in the dramas of democracy and totalitarianism.

Capitalism: The Unemployed and the Disreputable Poor

The "Three Little Pigs," so Bruno Bettelheim reminds us, is a cautionary tale about a trio of anthropomorphized swine, two of whom suffer ghastly deaths because they will not relinquish the pleasure principle for the reality principle. Unlike the eldest pig who carefully and laboriously builds a secure house out of brick, and who ensnares the wolf and survives, the two younger pigs carelessly throw together their houses of straw and sticks, respectively, and spend the rest of the day—and just about the rest of their natural lives—playing and dancing in the sun. According to Bettelheim the three pigs are in fact one pig, and the monodramatic morality tale tells the child that he must shed earlier and less mature forms of his existence in order to move on up to higher, more responsible ones. Moreover, Bettelheim argues, the three pigs stand not only for a psychological ontogeny but also for socio-historical phylogeny: "the three little pigs represent stages in the development of man." Sloth, according to this perspective, belongs to the early phases of child development and also to the early stages of man's social evolution. The child, Bettelheim assures us, is not traumatized by the horrible deaths of the first two pigs, because, he asserts, "If we survive in only the higher forms of our identity, this is as it should be."[110]

Unfortunately for the supposed cautionary value of such morality tales, historical and social reality reveals that significant numbers of actual persons behave like the first two pigs and yet survive. Furthermore, rather than belonging to childhood states or primitive tribes, the real human sloths are found in nearly all age groups and throughout history and are a part of the most modern of societies. Indeed, they are a recognized set of actors in the morality plays of everyday life, symbolizing by their very existence and behavior that the sin of sloth is always potential and dangerous. It can neither be consigned to early childhood states nor to early stages of prehistoric development. Like the sociological stranger envisioned by Simmel, the slothful seem to come today and remain tomorrow, but in contrast to that hard-working man their method of survival in the face of the rewards given to the fittest is indeed mysterious.

One way of treating this motley cast of characters in the otherwise bright drama of modern progress is to suffer them to participate in a perpetual degradation ceremony, humiliating them at every turn, and yet not permitting them to die out or disappear altogether. A crucial step in the process is their designation as surplus humanity. Robert Park once called attention to the fact that "Our great cities . . . are full of junk, much of it human, i.e., men and women who, for some reason or other, have fallen out of line in the march of industrial progress and have been scrapped by the industrial organization of which they were once a part."

Moreover, the specialized parts of the city, places Park characterized as a "human junk heap," were in effect the theatrical stages set aside for the performance of these peculiar immorality plays. The "slum areas that invariably grow up just on the edge of the business areas of great cities, areas of deteriorated houses, of poverty, vice, and crime, are areas of social junk," Park asserted. But they were also peculiarly well-suited settings—platforms and props for an exciting but forbidden drama of industrial civilization. As Park admitted, "recent studies . . . seem to show that there are no playgrounds in the city in which a boy can find so much adventure, no place where he can find so much that may be called 'real sport,' as in these areas of general deterioration which we call the slums."[111] Settings for sloth and degradation, the slums of the city were also places where the dangerous classes trod and performed,[112] attracting both spectators and imitators.

Who are these creatures of slothful impulse? In fact they include more than those scrapped by an industrial civilization; most important in their number are those who "remain unemployed, or casually and irregularly employed, even during periods approaching full employment and prosperity." And it is "for that reason, and others," asserts David Matza, that "they live in disrepute."[113] In France, according to Fernando Diaz-Plaja, one type belonging to this class has earned a grudging admiration: the *clochard*, or hobo, who never works and never begs, dresses in castoffs and eats discarded food. A champion of sloth, the *clochard* has escaped from civilization's discontents but not departed the world around him. He exploits that world by dramatic deployment of his dress and demeanor: "His walls are his rags; his guards and dogs are the fear that people have that he harbors evil intentions toward them. Nobody bothers him and he generally doesn't bother anyone else."[114]

The disreputable poor are those who seem to have elected sloth in favor of work, who choose to live idly and by their wits, who count the indolence of their condition as a morally superior situation to that of the regularly employed worker. Matza gives a partial inventory of their social types.[115] It includes the *dregs*, "persons spawned in poverty and belonging to families who have been left behind by otherwise mobile ethnic populations"; *newcomers*, recent arrivals in the city or the society, who, though bereft of marketable skills, nevertheless provide color, ethnic diversity, exotic styles, and pleasant traditions to the drama of antilabor reality played out by the disreputable poor; *skidders*, those who have fallen from a higher social standing and continue to slide down the social scale as alcoholism, addiction, perversion, and other disturbances drive them to those sections of the metropolis that house and accept wasted humans; and the *infirm*, those who have aged, been blinded, crippled, or physically incapacitated and find that their income and deteriorating life style can only be accommodated in the areas reserved for broken human junk. Although the disreputable poor are products of a regular social process of pauperization, a process that is neither natural nor inevitable, their numbers are replenished generation after generation.[116] Their tragedies, comedies, and grotesqueries continue from one epoch to another.

The dramatization of their disrepute is the play diligence writes to ward off sloth. The play has both a text and a subtext, a manifest drama and a latent theme that stand in uneasy relationship to one another. On the visible level is the drama of discreditation played out in the ragged costumes, rude furniture, ruined chances, and wretched language of those who will not or cannot work. On a subliminal level another drama lurks. This is one of temptation. The disreputable poor, like the mythological savages,[117] live closer to man's imagined primordial nature, enjoying the fruits that nature provides, indulging in sensual perversion and promiscuity, and basking in an unearned indolence that the workingman publicly condemns and secretly envies. It is precisely in the semisecret ambivalence the so-called dangerous classes arouse that their danger presents itself. The modern counterpart of the savage, the supposedly lazy black "sambo" as well as the beggar, the bohemian, the gypsy, and the hippie, constitute a special kind of monastic—public hedonistic ascetics, who withdraw their labor and service from the world and yet remain in it.[118] Visibly present but socially unaccounted for, they challenge by their existence and example all who work at ordinary pursuits to leave them and take up a life of indolent vagabondage.[119]

A special play in the American drama of disrepute contrasts sloth proper with acedic melancholy. The former is represented in the cruel caricature of the lazy Black, who idles away the days in frivolous pleasure, worthless chatter, and forbidden sensuality.[120] Imagined to be constitutionally incapable of serious work and temperamentally unsuited to diligent labor, the Black was also accused of being an enemy of civilization itself. He supposedly benefited from its progressive developments, and yet he opposed its construction; worse, he inspired others by his example to be as slothful as himself. By contrast the Chinese laborer was hated and envied because of his alleged melancholic indifference to his own welfare.[121] Supposed to be willing to work for the longest hours at the most difficult and dangerous tasks for the lowest wages, the Chinese were accused of being enemies of labor since they helped to construct civilization but did not demand that its benefits be equitably apportioned.[122] Contrasting conceptions of the orientation toward work and self, Negroes and Chinese suffered for decades the ignominy and injury of countless ceremonies of degradation. Although their putative characters and behaviors were quite different, the opposed conceptions designated the poles of sloth: laziness and *acedia*.

Imperialism: The "Giving-up Syndrome" Among Oceanic Peoples

The desert fathers and the cloistered monks knew the dangers of *acedia* when it crept upon them in the heat of the midday sun or in the world-weariness that struck after long periods of meditation and self-doubt. But the nineteenth century was to witness a more terrible and more incomprehensible case of the dreaded sin. In Oceania the native population of the Pacific islands was literally decimated in the century after European contact.[123] Melanesians, Polynesians, Micronesians, Hawaiians, New Hebrideans, and Solomon Islanders, to name but the most well-known peoples, died, seemingly without cause.[124] The mysterious killer of nearly a whole race has never been fully detected, but from the available evidence and the commentary and analyses of both experts and on-the-spot observers it appears that the Oceanic peoples died because they had lost *the will to live*.[125] Felled by a fatal despair, they gave up their lives quietly and stoically. They withdrew from a world that no longer made any sense, and then ratified their withdrawal by dying. Their life-sustaining culture had already been killed; they followed it to their own graves.

Contact with the West introduced a number of fundamental, indeed cataclysmic changes in the lives of Oceanic natives.[126] Most of the changes were inadvertent, by-products of the contact situation itself. Diseases introduced new and horrible forms of death; influenza, whooping cough, measles, tuberculosis, dysentery, and venereal infection took a frightful toll on a population that had built up no physiological defenses against even the mildest of European illnesses.[127] The introduction of new industries and labor practices—sandalwood cutting, whaling, guano gathering, sugar refining, pineapple farming, and cattle raising; "black-birding," impressment, contracting, and indenture—reorganized life almost entirely and made traditional ways almost instantly obsolete.[128] New ideologies and new religions—the Protestant ethic and the Christian god—challenged the prevailing belief systems and subverted traditional ritual practices. In a matter of a single century the peoples of Oceania experienced the wholesale destruction of their culture, social organization, economy, polity, religion, and personal life.

The scenario of existence had been rewritten. Not only had the players not been consulted, but they had been pushed and pulled against their wills onto an unfamiliar stage, with strange props pressed into their hands, unusual backdrops built up behind them, alien lines put into their mouths, and an uncertain ending promised when the curtain fell on their lives. The drama of a once-familiar social reality had been turned into a grotesque comedy of the absurd. As a result, most players refused to perform. They would not take up their places on this imperialist stage. They would not—or to be more accurate, a great many of them would not—play the parts of household servants, peasant serfs, plantation laborers, guano gatherers, woodcutters, and whalers. As exciting being turned into enervating nothingness they languished. Despair set in. A terrible malaise swept over the formerly magic isles of the Pacific.[129] Depressed, despondent, and deprived, the once proud natives lost interest altogether in living. When the most trivial disease struck them they took it up with relief and resignation. They let the sleep of death rescue them from the sloth of life.

The "giving-up syndrome," as anthropologists like to call the malaise that overcame the Oceanic peoples is, it would appear, an aggravated variant of *taedium vitae*, the condition of boredom that Coleridge credited to Hamlet.[130] That condition certainly encourages suicide, as Hamlet's famous soliloquy so eloquently shows. However, Hamlet did not kill himself, and despite his lethargy, he did, as Freud pertinently points out, rouse himself to action.[131] The question, then, is why the *acedia* of nineteenth-century Oceania led to such fatal consequences. One answer suggested by the evidence of culture contact is that all significant elements of a once vital life had been destroyed or rendered meaningless as a consequence of European encroachment. As individuals watched their kin and friends die of disease, depart for the whaling, sandalwood, or guano grounds, or descend into alcoholism or melancholy, they felt, rather than understood, a fundamental loss of identity and the death of their own civilization. As individuals discovered that other men—strangers from strange lands—could come, conquer, and convert their own people, they sensed—rather than knew—that whatever they had always believed, whatever they had always done, would not be believed or done again. As individuals saw new mores, new social arrangements, and new institutions replace the old familiar ones to which they had been once so familiarly attached, they experienced, rather than analyzed, the creation of a void in their lives which could never again be filled. With kinsmen dead or gone, civilization dying, social and personal identity lost, beliefs undermined, practices eroded, and institutions abandoned, the very components of human life had been subverted. The Oceanic peoples experienced the awful sense of having an obsolete past, an unknown future, and an unintelligible present. Theirs was the condition of near absolute absurdity. A life without meaning, promise, or sense, they must have concluded, was no life at all. Those who could not acculturate in fact ceased to exist, ratifying a death that had already occurred. Thus did *acedia* make corpses of them all.

POLITICS: APATHY AND
AFFECTLESSNESS

The *acedia* that overcame life in nineteenth-century Oceania may have overwhelmed significant portions of civilization in the twentieth-century Occident. However, *acedia* need not lead to physical death; indeed, its worst terrors and most dangerous potentialities are to be found in the deathlike life that it imposes on its victims. There is an accelerating trend toward *affectlessness* among Europeans and Americans in this century. Its various forms and qualities have been recognized in the writings of Kafka and Camus; in the discovery of the apathetic voter, a new creature of enervated impulse who, when activated, can bring into power the most terrible of regimes; and in the recognition that modern societies tend to engender asocial formations of strangers, marginal men, disaffiliated persons, lonely crowds, and uprooted masses who have in common, despite differences in their respective categorizations, a real or potential attenuation from the feeling states appropriate to human existence.[132] These people are not dead in the conventional sense, nor indeed are they very likely to kill themselves in acts of release from a dreadful ennui. However, they might form corps of living corpses, legions of zombies, who, because of their defection from living, prey upon those who have not yet fallen into the cavern of contemporary despair. In this trend of attenuation there is revealed the real horrors of *acedia*, horrors that were only glimpsed by the desert fathers and cloistered monks who first encountered its demon.

When Camus designated Meursault, the acedic French clerk in Algiers, as *The Stranger*,[133] he captured much of the complexity and most of the terror that the affectless type holds in store. Weak in response to intrapersonal or interpersonal stimuli, detached from both events and environment, Meursault constantly subsumes his intimates under general life-destroying categories. He rejects the relevance of value judgments, abstains from moral reactions to others, and minimizes overt actions. Seeing no difference between alternative projects, perceiving like outcomes in any set of choices, and conceiving of death as the goal of life, Camus' stranger is open to any possibility precisely because his indifference frees him from all moral constraints.[134] It is as if the twentieth century had surrounded man with a terrifying danger—feeling—against which he has armored himself with an almost impregnable coat of mail—affectlessness. So powerful is this armor that affectless man is even indifferent to his own indifference, neither ashamed, guilty, nor roused to action or emotion by the calm discovery that nihilism rules his heart. In place of his heart the affectless man substitutes his value-liberated senses.

He becomes an incarnation of the ideal positivist, able to count the number of people present, note the color of their clothes and skin, and finely attune himself to the atmospheric temperature. Like a parody of the much vaunted scientist, the affectless man sees everything and feels nothing. The stranger, having been removed from the world of affect, is prepared to enter the world—as a destroyer.

Camus presented his theme of the terrors of the stranger by having Meursault murder an Arab for no apparent reason. However, historical reality gives us even more deadly and frightening examples. In the revolutionary philosophy expounded by Sergei Nechayev (1847–1882) in *The Catechism of the Revolutionist* (1869, probably written by Bakunin) will be found an ideology of affectlessness and murder pressed into service for the overthrow of the social order.[135] According to the *Catechism* "The revolutionist is a doomed man," who precisely because he accepts his death in advance is capable of every action without regret or guilt. "In the very depth of his being," the *Catechism* observes, "not merely in word but in deed, he has broken every connection with the social order and with the whole educated world, with all the laws, appearances and generally accepted conventions and moralities of that world which he considers his ruthless foes." The revolutionist is doomed, by the society in which he lives, the *Catechism* repeats, but "Should he continue to live in it, it will be solely for the purpose of destroying it the more surely."

The subscriber to the *Catechism* despises doctrinairism, all forms of science except the science of destruction, and is "merciless toward the State and toward the entire system of privileged educated classes." Since he must be merciless to his foes, and severe with himself, he must also renounce all affectionate ties: "All tender, softening sentiments of kinship, friendship, love, gratitude and even honor itself must be snuffed out in him by the one cold passion of the revolutionary cause." Since the inexorable destruction of the prevailing order is his only aim, the revolutionist "must be ready to perish himself and to destroy with his own hands everything that hinders its realization." Ultimately the revolutionary must become part of a desensitized cadre, and that is possible only when revolutionary passion has become a normal phenomenon, that is, with the routinization of affectlessness. "The nature of a real revolutionist," the *Catechism* concludes, "precludes every bit of sentimentality, romanticism, of infatuation and exaltation. It precludes even personal hatred and revenge." Nechayev's affectless philosophy of revolution still leaves room for the cold zeal of insurrectionary action, but we need only to turn to the carefully planned slaughters committed by the Nazi regime to see how feeling disappears altogether, leaving absolute indifference to murder. In Adolf Eichmann is incarnated the postrevolutionary indifferent ascetic, whose countless murders of Jews and other arbitrarily designated victims has produced, in Hannah

Arendt's mordant phrase, the banality of evil.[136] Here is the quintessence of indifference, the nadir of humanity.

SLOTH AND SURVIVAL: CHEKHOV'S DRAMATIZATION OF INERTIA

The single most significant drama that captures both the essence and attributes of sloth is Anton Chekhov's *The Three Sisters*.[137] Every element mentioned thus far in our discussion is distilled to a fine purity in that play, with sloth and *acedia* combining to produce a cultural, social, and moral destruction that is complete, unbearable, and terrifying. The *daemon meridianus* has taken over an entire family and, like a disease, promises to infect an already decaying civilization and to visit both tedium and terror on generations to come. Presented as representatives of the defenders of culture, the Prozorov family and their officer friends are too far sunk into indolence and indifference to protect the life-giving art and philosophy that gives meaning to their existence. As their world crumbles around them they can only worry and wonder, unable to resolve their opposed philosophies, only capable of anger, frustration, boredom, and despair—alternating moods that punctuate and interrupt their daily existence, confounding every conversation and canceling each other out. Idleness and melancholy feed upon one another, producing paralysis of word and deed. One by one the Prozorovs and those close to them are undone by the compound corrosiveness of inner inertia and outer decay. And as they each disintegrate, their home is slowly sucked up, a domicile overwhelmed by the personified force of darkness against which an intensified sloth has no defenses. Ultimately the drama poses the most terrible consequence of *acedia*—the conversion of the world into a meaningless void, full of sound and silence, smoldering feeling and affectless neutrality, meaningless actions and uncertain outcomes. One can neither wait nor hope, move on or give up. Life becomes pure existence.

The plot of *The Three Sisters* is simple on the surface. The Prozorovs, three sisters and a brother, live in shabby gentility in a remote town in the provinces. They have resided there for more than a decade, since their father, now dead, was posted to this provincial town to command a regiment. In the year following their bereavement, the Prozorov sisters have grudgingly adapted themselves to their environment—Masha has married a local schoolmaster, Olga has become a schoolteacher, and Irina works in the telegraph office. As the drama proceeds their brother Andrey, on whom so much depends, abandons his once promising studies, marries a local girl, and joins the Rural Board. Their home, once a salon, is now the meeting place of the remnants of culture in the town—a drunken, cynical doctor, who once loved the three sisters' mother, military officers on temporary duty, and the deteriorating nobility. The hopes of the family are bound up entirely with their dream of returning to Moscow, a dream that will never be realized. Paralyzed by their own despairing inertia, the Prozorovs cannot move. Masha falls hopelessly in love with an officer from Moscow, but their affair breaks off when he and his regiment are transferred to Poland; Olga earns promotion to school headmistress, trapping herself forever in a job she loathes and a government-financed apartment she cannot abide; Irina, her hopes for romance and release in Moscow dashed by events and apathy, reluctantly agrees to enter into a loveless marriage with an ex-officer and nobleman who believes in the salvation of work, only to be denied even this measure of solace when her fiance is killed in a duel. And, all the while these events are taking place, Andrey's wife, the ambitious parvenu Natasha, is deceiving her husband and dispossessing the Prozorovs of their home. In the end the three sisters are left huddling together, stunned and staggered by their fate. Life has lost both meaning and savor. Bereft of love, bereaved by incomprehensible deaths and arbitrary departures, and bewildered by the meaninglessness of all that has occurred, they cling to the faint possibility that the future will provide answers to the questions that haunt their existence.

Like the Oceanic peoples who lacked immunities from and defenses against the destroyers of their culture, the Prozorovs' isolated island of gentility, intellectuality, and *politesse* is also undermined from within and assaulted from without. Indolence has weakened the cultural and personal strengths of the Prozorovs and their friends, sapping their strength, and eroding their skills. Masha, once an accomplished pianist, has not touched the instrument for years; when a benefit concert is proposed her relatives and friends must pretend that she still possesses sufficient talent to perform. An incipient hysteric, she is haunted by the words of a poem that tortures her incessantly. Andrey, regarded as "our intellectual" by his doting sisters, sinks into sloth and gluttony, gaining weight, suffering from shortness of breath, giving up his studies, forsaking his violin except in moments of hysteria (he literally fiddles while the town burns), and ceasing to carve the frames and other *objets d'art* which endear him to his siblings and establish his artistic talent. Olga suffers from constant headaches, is utterly worn out, and between bouts of pain can only ancitipate the weekend and the possibility of free time. And Irina longs for the rescue and release of work, but cannot find any job that gives expression to her feeling for poetry and imagination; she too is always tired, but even in the end, with her fiancé killed in a duel the day before their wedding, she looks forward to relief through selfless devotion to her new-found career in teaching. But the quintessential sufferer from *acedia* is Dr. Chebutykin, an army medical officer who has forgotten what he once knew about medicine and receded into murky alcoholism and melancholic indifference. So remote is he from human affairs that only distant newspaper reports compel his hazy attention, and not even the death of Baron Tusenbach, his young comrade, can rouse him from his apathetic lethargy. The effects of absolute *acedia* are personified in this doctor, who espouses the nihilistic thesis that nothing exists, and that everyone, himself included, is not really here. And even if existence is real, Chebutykin concludes, it doesn't matter. Nothing matters at all.

However, it is not merely their own idleness and melancholy that is doing the Prozorovs in. Their environment is decadent, dreary, and deep in the sloth of despond. Chekhov probably modeled the rural provincial capital of his play after Taganrog, his birthplace, which he once described as "dirty, drab, empty, lazy, and illiterate,"[138] and this aspect of his play represents a gloomy view of Russian cultural life prevalent among intellectuals in the late nineteenth century. In a story written in 1897, four years before he produced *The Three Sisters*, Chekhov had expressed the idea that the Russian cultural environment had decayed so much that the basic education for living could not be acquired from any of its citizens: "How is it" [he wrote] "that in not one of these houses has there been anyone from whom I might have learned to live? . . . Our town has existed for hundreds of years, and all that time it has not produced one man of service to the country—not one. . . . It's a useless, unnecessary town, which not one soul would regret if it suddenly sank through the earth."[139]

Chekhov's mournful theme that life was losing its cultural and environmental supports is repeated through the voice of Andrey in the final act of *The Three Sisters*. Here there is described an entire civilization sunk irredeemably in sloth. There is nothing to look forward to except boredom, gluttony, lust, and sleep.

> "Our town . . . has one hundred thousand inhabitants, not one of them but is just like all the rest. There isn't a single one capable of real achievement, now or in the past, not one learned man, not one artist, not a single one remarkable enough to excite jealousy or eager emulation—they just eat, drink, sleep, and then they die; others will be born and they, too, will eat, drink, sleep . . . and in order not to be drugged by boredom, just for a change, they fill their lives with prurient gossip, vodka, cards, lawsuits; and wives are unfaithful to husbands, and the husbands pretend not to hear anything or see anything, and its devastating triviality suffocates the children, and the divine spark in them is extinguished so that they, too, become pitiful husks—exactly like one another, exactly like their fathers and mothers."

Seeking a break from the creeping ennui that seems about to overwhelm them, both Irina Prozorov and Baron Tusenbach hope to escape through work. In Act I Irina is enraptured by the general promise that work holds out for redeeming a meaningless life:

"People must work in the sweat of their brow—whoever they may be. And only in *this* is the meaning and the goal of their existence, their happiness, their fulfillment. How good to be a workman who gets up at daybreak, breaks stones in the street; or a shepherd; or a teacher who teaches children, or an engine driver."

Irina extends her belief in the wonders of work to the animal kingdom, preferring the draught animals to those that do not labor: "My goodness, not just human beings—it's better to be an ox, even an ordinary horse, so long as you work." In contrast to the workman, who achieves meaning and reaches the goal of his existence, stands the lazy and indolent person whom Irina fears to imagine. Thinking of the hard-working ox or horse, she declares: "Ever so much better than being a young lady who gets up at noon, has her coffee in bed, and then spends two hours getting dressed—oh, it's frightful."

But despite her beliefs, or perhaps, because of them, Irina cannot find any work that is meaningful. Little more than a year after her ode to the joyful fulfillment of work she is complaining: "I'm tired. No, I don't like that telegraph office. I really don't. . . . I think I must look for another job. This one isn't right for me. What I wanted, what I dreamed of, well, that's exactly what this job doesn't have. Work without poetry, without imagination." And a moment later she has shifted her attention from the much-vaunted labor to a longing for escape to Moscow: "Oh my goodness! I dream of Moscow every single night. I'm simply obsessed. [She laughs.] We're going to move there in June and before June comes round we have to get through February, March, April, May . . . almost half a year." Much more than half a year passes but the Prozorovs still do not move to Moscow. They never will. In Act III Irina admits to her failure:

"I can't work, I won't work. I've had enough of it! I worked at the telegraph office, now I'm working in the Town Hall and I loathe and despise everything they give me to do. I'm almost twenty-four. I have been working for ages. My brains are drying up, I'm losing weight, I'm losing my looks, I'm aging and for what? Nothing. I get no satisfaction out of it, time passes and it seems that one is moving further and further away from any real full life—further and further toward an abyss."

In Chekhov's aesthetic of work and sloth, both are associated with somatic changes and suicide. Andrey gains weight after he gives up his father's imposed regimen of scholastic study and Irina loses weight when she works at soulless tasks. When her dreams of work dissolve in dreadful boredom, Irina cries out, "I'm *desperate*. I can't think why I'm still alive, why I haven't killed myself." But Irina's suffering does not end in her own suicide. She agrees to marry Tusenbach, and when he is killed in a senseless duel, she renews her faith in redemptive work, but now work is perceived as related to the worker's living death: "There's work to be done—work. Tomorrow I shall go away. I'll teach in the school at the brickworks. I shall devote my whole life where it's needed. It's autumn now. Winter will soon be here—the world will be buried under snow, and I shall work—and work."

Irina's desire to be buried alive under the avalanche of schoolteaching evokes the formidable image of that same occupation by her sister Olga. Work has not proved fulfilling for her. Her promotion to headmistress constitutes the final nail in the coffin of her dream to escape to Moscow. "Nothing turns out as you hope," she exclaims. "I didn't want to be Headmistress. But here I am; and so I can't be in Moscow."

In Chekhov's dramatic philosophy work is often regarded as absolution for the sin of sloth: occupation will rescue a decaying civilization from its own internal rot. However, in *The Three Sisters*, sloth's inexorable corrosion of Russian civilization has proceeded so far that work's capacity for rescue and redemption can be of little avail. In the naive but touching character of Baron Tusenbach, Chekhov has created the personification of one who wishes to be saved and fears the awful onslaught that will occur if nothing is done. Yet Tusenbach is still so committed to the gallant mores of the nobility that he lets himself be killed in a foolish duel on the eve of his own wedded and work-committed salvation. As *acedia* and boredom begin to work their deadly weal, Tusenbach expresses his longing for a workingman's existence, a kind of life that his lofty station in the nobility has denied him:

> "The longing for work, oh, my God, how I understand that. I've never done a stroke of work in my life. I was born in Petersburg, cold, idle Petersburg, into a family which knew neither work nor the need to work. When I came home from military school, I remember, there was a footman to pull off my boots. I would behave like a spoiled brat, but my mother worshiped me and was astonished if other people didn't. I was sheltered from work of every kind."

Tusenbach is a pessimist, believing that social change occurs in accordance with historical laws about which man has no knowledge and over which he has no control. Life has no moral purpose. A melancholic who resignedly accepts the absurdity of human existence, he senses the coming cataclysm that will overtake them all unless individuals take redemptive and propitiative actions. Work is not only a salvation device but also the single future toward which man can look:

> "The time has come; [Tusenbach points out] there is something enormous coming toward us, a tremendous storm is getting ready to break; it's coming; it's already near, and soon the laziness, the callous unconcern, the prejudice against work and all the rotten boredom will be swept away out of our society."

Tusenbach looks forward with grim resignation to a new world in which "I shall work; and in no more than twenty-five or thirty years everybody will be working. Everyone." The baron's prophecy heralds and presages the revolution that will overturn Czarist Russia less than two decades later. However, the work to which all Russians are to be sentenced hardly seems life-fulfilling. It would appear that neither work nor revolution can redeem a civilization that has slipped so far into sloth.

Can sloth halt productive social change? Chekhov's characters are of two minds on the subject, and in this debate the playwright has presented the quarrel between progress and absurdity. In the drama itself nothing can help the doomed Prozorovs. Their dream of escape to Moscow—a city transformed in their desperate illusion into a place of sunshine, flowers, sensibility, refinement, and intellect—comes to nothing. Masha's passionate affair with Colonel Vershinin ends when his regiment departs for Poland, taking with it what little culture exists in the cold, drab, rural town, and leaving her to the ministrations of her foppish schoolmaster husband. Olga's headache-producing job in the local school has earned her a promotion to a life sentence in the headmistressship and a cold furnished room paid for by the government. Irina, deprived of even a loveless marriage and alternating between hope in work and hysterical despair, can only plead that, "a time will come when everyone will know the reason for all this agony." And Andrey, hag-ridden with his dull paperwork job, cuckolded by his employer, dispossessed of his private room, and about to be thrown out of his house altogether, sinks into melancholy, questioning his useless life, used up before it has even begun:

> "What has become of those days when I was young and lively and clever, when I was full of dreams, when my imagination soared, when my present and my future glowed with hope? Why, when we've hardly begun to live do we become dull, gray, uninteresting, lazy, uncaring, useless, miserable?"

The condition of the Prozorovs' lives corresponds to the description of absurdity presented by Camus: a condition of irremediable exile in a universe shorn of both light and illusions.[140] In such a world man proceeds as a stranger lacking both history and hope. Divorcing the man from his life, the actor from his setting, the condition of absurdity leaves him utterly alone, reliant solely on his own psychical and spiritual resources. As we have seen in examining the cases of the Oceanic peoples on the one hand and Meurseault, Nechayev, and Eichmann on the other, the absurdist situation can lead to suicide, the giving-up syndrome, mindless murder, or an indifferent slaughter of the innocents. However, all these are extreme possibilities because they end in the cessation of human existence. In Chekhov's drama a more deadening outcome is realized: the characters continue to live. Two aspects are worth further analysis: the philosophical talk that engages the attention of the Prozorovs and their friends and, in mordant relationship to that talk, the decay of language itself. Both are products of the *acedia* that pervades the whole of their lives.

The Prozorovs and their guests are fond of amusing themselves by what they call "philosophizing." Some of it is mindless, a game of words to pass the time while waiting for the end, as in the silly comments of Captain Solyony and his worthless argument with Dr. Chebutykin over the nature of two foods, "chehartma" and "cheremsha." However, also running throughout the drama is the debate between Colonel Vershinin and Baron Tusenbach over the future of civilization. The baron believes that progressive material changes will bring about no change in the existential dilemma of life:

> "Well . . . after us, people will fly in balloons, will change the cut of their coats, maybe they'll discover a sixth sense and develop it; but for all that, life will still be exactly the same—a difficult life, full of mystery—and happy. And in a *thousand* years, mankind will still be sighing in the same old way, 'Oh, how hard life is.' And he'll still be afraid of death, just as he is now; still be reluctant to die"

But the colonel accepts the unhappiness of today as the price man must pay for a realization of a more perfect happiness in the future. For the present time, Vershinin insists, "I do wish I could prove to you that there is no such thing as happiness; that there ought to be no such thing and won't be—for us. We must just work and work." In lieu of present-day happiness, the people of today must live in their faith that

> "In two hundred, three hundred years—or even a thousand—the time is unimportant—a new, happy life will come into being. We shall have no part in such a life, that's certain; but all the same we are living for it now; working for it; suffering for it; we are creating it; This, and only this, is the goal of our existence; and only in this way can we approach happiness."

Vershinin's own life reflects his philosophy. Trapped in a hollow second marriage to a suicidal hysteric and burdened with two forlorn daughters, he finds some solace in his affair with Masha, but ultimately believes that "Happiness will only be achieved by those who come long after us." Vershinin's tragic but hopeful vision haunts the play like Banquo's ghost. Just as the sorrowful Scottish knight could only look forward to being the founder of a line of kings but not becoming a king himself, so Vershinin consoles himself with his belief that "If I am not to enjoy it, then at least my children's children will."

Chekhov's two philosophers do not differ in their belief in the positive function of work, only in the scope and extent of that function. For the baron, humble work in the service of his contemporaries promises to provide a modest release from the enervating *acedia* of his own existence; for the colonel daily work builds civilization and prepares the way for a happiness consigned to a distant future. However, set against the indolence and sloth of their own actions, all this talk acts as a moral substitute for and a social evasion of work. In the end Tusenbach accepts Solyony's challenge to a duel from which he is hardly likely to emerge alive. As a civilian about to be married, he might have honorably declined this murderous meeting with a man he knows to be unhinged. Instead, presented with the choice between the meaningless gallantry of his peers and marriage to a woman who refuses to return his love, he selects the noble death. And Vershinin? His philosophy permits him to indulge himself in his own self-pitying sloth. Unwilling to abandon his miserable wife and unhappy children, he dallies with Masha and then moves off to Poland and, presumably, another officers' town with its evenings of philosophy and music that while away his existence. The opposed "philosophies" of Vershinin and Tusenbach are not resolved by Chekhov. They need not be. Dedicated to presenting life as it really is, the Russian playwright has given us a glimpse of the best of conversations among the bored men inhabiting a decadent civilization. As Dr. Chebutykin observes throughout the play, it doesn't matter. Nothing does.

Chekhov's drama places all its characters in almost suffocating contact with one another. Huddling together they form a bored, frustrated, lonely little crowd (". . . here you know everybody," Andrey observes, "everybody knows you, and yet you *are* a stranger—a stranger . . . a stranger and lonely.") Dante painted a picture of a similar kind of intimate proximity, observing the close connection that exists between boredom, hatred, and violence. He also suggested that boredom eventuates into an impoverishment of language as its enervated victims lose the capacity even to frame whole words.[141] The Italian poet's imaginative vision of sloth in some ways startlingly resembles Chekhov's study. All too often the principals are at a loss for words. They are sunk into melancholy, lost in reverie, or just too somnolent or dumbfounded to say anything. "Say something [pause]. Say something," Tusenbach pleads with Irina just before he departs for his fatal duel. "What? What shall I

say? What?" she replies. Tusenbach: "Anything." Irina: "No, I can't."
And turning on his heel to go, Tusenbach stops and turns around once
more. "Yes?" asks Irina. But Tusenbach, not knowing what to say, blurts
out an irrelevancy—"I didn't have any coffee this morning. Ask them to
have some ready"—and quickly departs for his appointment with death.
And this form of exchange, or rather the lack of it, is common among
most of the characters. Speechlessness becomes the first sign of their
inevitable destruction. Hollow men and women in an age that has passed
them by, the Prozorovs and their friends become mute and helpless
witnesses to the seeds of slothful destruction they and their class have
sown.

The villain of Chekhov's play is sloth. It would be a mistake to
differentiate between individual and environmental causes for the destruction of the Prozorovs, and, by extension, Czarist Russian culture.
The Prozorovs have both character and culture but lack any capacity to
activate either. They can neither move to their dream city nor help
themselves to meaningful lives in the town they now inhabit. Vulnerable
to both the creeping *acedia* of their condition and the conniving villainy of
the avaricious classes, the Prozorovs languish and decline. Their languid
existence in a world devoid of meaning or promise is a fate not too
different from that of the Oceanians who *survived.* The corrosion of sloth
has been completed when the sisters are not only subtly evicted but also
socially eviscerated. Ennui has triumphed.

CONCLUSION

The sin of sloth, like all the others, is still with us. Indeed in its twin
forms—indolence and *acedia*—it may be more threatening today than in
earlier eras. Western civilization has in the last two centuries witnessed
an intensification of a twofold despair—a deep feeling of the worthlessness of work coupled with an apprehensive dread of the deadliness of
leisure. Work no longer holds out its magical charm that could, in an
earlier time, beckon man to seek through his own efforts the discovery of
his godly merit. And leisure, although not yet realized even for most
Occidentals, threatens with its boredom more than it invites with its
pleasures. The demystification of everything—a promise made by rationalism to justify its destruction of its predecessors—has torn away the veil
not only from the workaday world of daily reality but also from the
utopian dream of the happy world that was to come. As a price for his
liberation from tradition and superstition, man is unbreakably linked to a
linear history, traveling on a unidirectional time track with neither
possibility of return nor chance to stop. Denied both the myth of eternal
return and the promise of an utopian tomorrow, he becomes chained to

his unromantic disillusion—a lonely stranger in his own world, a hapless victim of his past, a mindless Sisyphus toiling in behalf of an unknown future. In such a condition paralysis and enervation set in. The sloth of despond and the inertia of *acedia* take hold of the spirit and kill it, while the individual is permitted to live.

The responses of this seemingly modern situation are not too different from earlier reactions to a similar if less widespread condition. They take form as the sometimes desperate quest for fulfilling community.[142]

Edward Gibbon's mordant description of the rise of monasticism among the Christians of the fourth and fifth centuries bears a striking resemblance to certain developments in the current age.[143] That earlier era produced a host of exiles from social life who, outwardly moved by a publicly proclaimed religious zealotry, chose to withdraw from common pursuits in order to take up a life of cloistered asceticism. In that era the proselytes who entered monasteries felt much like young people of the 1960s, who entered communes to find a path to eternal happiness. Just as the early Christian ascetics were strengthened in their desire to leave worldliness by secret remorse, accidental misfortune, and personal considerations of vanity and self-interest, so also the hippies and disaffected youth are aided in their experiments in release and redemption by sorrowful experiences, real or vicarious tragedies, enhanced pride, and occasional opportunism. There are other parallels: the elevation of certain ascetics to positions of leadership in both cloistered and worldly society; the subjugation of penitents to an authoritarian regimen that flagellates body and spirit; the corruption of religious monasticism by self-interest, quackery, and the conversion to commerce. But the point is this: when worldly pursuits lose both promise and savor, withdrawal into seemingly slothful asceticism looms up as a likely alternative.

However, there is more. The Christian ascetics equated pleasure with guilt. They forbade any move toward Olympian hedonism among the penitent monastics and urged a pietistic service of labor and prayer. Yet even they relaxed occasionally and lifted some restraints. "The rules of abstinence which they imposed, or practised," Gibbon points out, "were not uniform or perpetual: the cheerful festival of the Pentecost was balanced by the extraordinary mortification of Lent: the fervour of new monasteries was insensibly relaxed; and the voracious appetites of the Gauls could not imitate the patient and temperate virtue of the Egyptians."[144] The modern ascetics, on the other hand, equate pleasure with liberation. They discourage the practice of puritanical inhibitions and hope to establish a pleasure dome on earth. But variations exist among them, and the ideology of pleasurable release which they espouse is neither consistent nor pervasive: the erotic delights of irreligious sensualists contrast with the passive expressivism of pseudo-Buddhist practitioners; the slothful commitment to a vulgar savagery *manqué* stands over against the arduous peasantry required of the once-urban communard-removed-to-the-countryside. However, in almost every case the withdrawal from the world does not achieve its promise. Sensuality gives way to jealousy and fatigue; ascetic prayer leads to boring ritualism, contemplative self-doubt, or melancholic *Weltschmertz*; imitation savagery produces not excitement and joy but impoverishment and disease; and the new farmers find little promise in the agricultural labor that, a century earlier, Marx had seen as the misery of the French peasant pitted against nature. Withdrawal from the world leads to malaise and melancholy. And when this is combined with unquiet frustration, an aggressive spirit arises in search of an outlet. The search for peace leads to petrification, and petrification finds release in pugnacity. Sloth remains both sin and danger.

TWO

Lust

The Eros of Death and the Eros of Life—each conjures up the other, and each has no true end or ending but the other, which it has been striving to destroy!

*Denis de Rougemont**

Of all the seven deadly sins lust seems to be the longest recognized, the most well known, and always prevalent. Defined as an overmastering appetite or craving for something, it is almost always associated with uncontrolled or uncontrollable relish of and yearning for sex. As Venus it appears in the third zone of the astrological soul drama depicted in a volume of the *Corpus Hermeticum*, the collected wisdom of the Egyptian neo-Platonists ascribed to the mythical Hermes Trismegistus. Servius, a Vergilian commentator writing at the end of the fourth century, pointed to the belief among astrologers of his day that descending souls attract to themselves certain divine qualities, including the torpor of Saturn, the anger of Mars, the money hunger of Mercury, the power desires of Jupiter, and the lust of Venus—each of which, in turn, becomes a source for evil and trouble on earth. The idea of the soul journey and its connection to sins, including lust, is found in a passage by Origen, who among his contributions to the reconciliation of Greek, Hellenistic, and Christian thought, describes the departure of any soul from this world as being met by "aerial powers [who] seek if they can find anything of theirs in it; if they find avarice, it belongs to them; if anger, if lechery, if envy or if they find any similar [sin], it belongs to them and they protect it for themselves and draw it to themselves and turn it to the side of the sinners." In still another soul journey, that described in the *Vita sancti Joannis eleemosynarii*, a revelation of the seventh-century monastic St. Simeon Stylites, the soul that departs from the body is met by troops of demons, each representing a sin, who inspect it for unrepentant misdeeds including fornication. That lust, lechery, fornication, or *luxuria* would emerge from the first as one of the seven sins in Judeo-Christian thought is understandable when we recall the nature and significance of the Fall and when we realize that the seven cardinal sins were products of the ascetic and monastic Jewish and Christian communities in Egypt, communities that absorbed both the neo-Platonist and Gnostic views that flesh and matter are evil.[1]

Lust is everywhere described as embracing and confronting the mystery that governs the relations between the thinking, willing, feeling mind on the one hand, and the active, energetic, and spontaneous body on the other. Precisely because lust seems to be independent of the will, and because the (male) sex organ activates itself independent of desire, the responsibility for and control of lust are difficult to establish. Theologians, philosophers, psychologists, and sociologists have all treated aspects of this difficult and complex question of etiology and control. Worry and wonder over the mastery of lust have generated a host of accounts, explanations, proposals, and precautions. In the process, the culpability of those who lust has been mitigated, if not removed altogether. Attempts at social control have from the beginning been in the direction of a combination of homiletic exhortations and institutionalization and channeling of behavior. Marriage became the only proper locus for coitus; abstinence was held out as an (equivocal) ideal; and postponement of satisfaction of sexual desire was encouraged for all those who had not yet married. However, these proposals have foundered on the ease with which lust burst the bonds of societal restraint. Lust could be sublimated in creative works or secreted in the clandestine arenas of human existence. And for some its evil could be desublimated: a claim was made in behalf of the pleasureful life that was denied by all those who spoke of the sin of fornication, the evil of lechery, the weakness of concupiscence. In treating lust society may have met its match.

LUST IN CHRISTIAN THOUGHT: AUGUSTINE, AQUINAS, LUTHER

The "Anthropology" of Augustine

Of the Christian thinkers, Augustine stands out for his remarkable analysis of the nature of lust, for his pseudohistorical and anthropological account of its origins, and for his proposals for its control. In the process of explaining lust, Augustine appears to accept its inevitability among men, and his thought implicitly hints at the mitigations which later thinkers would employ to release men from guilt about their transgressions. As theology gave way to psychology, sin was reduced to symptom and lust became either an illusion, an inconvenience, or a temporary obstacle to an otherwise healthy existence.

For Augustine the specific evil entailed by lust was its mastery of the whole man.

> This lust [he wrote] assumes power not only over the whole body, and not only from the outside, but also internally; it disturbs the whole man, when the mental emotion combines and mingles with the physical craving, resulting in a pleasure surpassing all physical delights. So intense is the pleasure that when it reaches its climax there is an almost total extinction of mental alertness; the intellectual sentries, as it were, are overwhelmed.[2]

The truly remarkable feature of lust, as Augustine so pointedly noticed, was that although it subdued the whole of man, it was not itself subject to direction by the will. Lust appears as a kind of malevolent trickster sometimes arousing the body at a moment when the impulse is unwanted, improper, or embarrassing; other times abandoning the eager lover's body while it is at its greatest intensity in his mind. "Thus strangely does lust refuse to be a servant not only to the will to beget but even to the lust for lascivious indulgence; and although on the whole it is totally opposed to the mind's control, it is quite often divided against itself. It arouses the mind, but does not follow its own lead by arousing the body."[3] Although Augustine does not say so, his description permits a peculiarly sociological interpretation to be made of lust. Anthropomorphized, it is a mysterious stranger who lodges in us but remains alternately unpredictable, cunning, foolish, and knavish. Always it moves or fails to move without notice or apology. Such a phenomenon was truly wondrous as well as troublesome; it required an explanation.

Augustine locates the problem in the disconnection of the sexual organs from the control of the will. At one time, Augustine argues, the original pair, Adam and Eve, lived naked but without shame. Nakedness and the visibility of the aroused male organ were not then shameful to Adam and Eve "because lust did not yet arouse those members independently of their decision." It was only after they had sinned that they recognized they were naked—"stripped, that is, of the grace that prevented their bodily nakedness from causing them any embarrassment, as it did when the law of sin made war against their mind." Thereafter, Adam and Eve and all mankind were afflicted by what Augustine refers to as "the insubordination of their flesh, the punishment which was a kind of evidence of their disobedience."[4] Mankind was punished, hence, by having lust released from the dominion of the will. Because of Adam and Eve's sin lust was let free to plague or pleasure spontaneously.

From his explanation of the liberation of sinful lust from human will Augustine is also able to account for the origin of modesty in dress, the requirement of privacy in sexual intercourse, the grudging necessity of marriage, and the impossibility of true happiness in the present life. Indeed, although he anticipates Gregory the Great in placing pride at the fountainhead of sins, Augustine develops a veritable universal anthropology out of his understanding of the peculiar power of lust. The presence of lust becomes in effect a personal and social fact prescribing customs, institutions, and possibilities for all people, modifying the nature and continuation of human existence, and forming the basis for the contrast between earthly life and paradise.

Prior to the autonomy of lust asserted by Augustine, nakedness was a natural state, and neither the organs of man nor the bodily functions were shameful. "The flesh did not yet, in a fashion, give proof of man's disobedience by a disobedience of its own." However, after the Fall, the genitalia became shameful precisely because they might be activated without decision. "It is right, therefore, to be ashamed of this lust, and it is right that the members which it moves or fails to move by its own right, so to speak, and not in complete conformity to our decision, should be called *pudenda* ('parts of shame'), which they were not called before man's sin."[5] From the attribution of shame to the sex organs grew modesty and the decision to cover the pudenda. "Thus modesty, from a sense of shame, covered what was excited to disobedience by lust, in defiance of a will which had been condemned for the guilt of disobedience." Adam and Eve "sewed together fig leaves and made aprons for themselves" (Gen. 3:7). These aprons were the first clothing, Augustine infers, "and from then onwards the practice of concealing the pudenda has become a deep-rooted habit in all peoples, since they all derive from the same stock."[6]

Augustine's theory of the lust-shame origins of clothing permits him to account for the type of clothing that is necessary for essentials and to observe the variations in style and practice that have grown up as the practice of dressing diffused over the various peoples of the world. Augustine points out that the Latin term for "apron" in the Genesis account is *campestria*, a word best translated as "loincloths." The word is derived, Augustine observes, from the custom of young athletes who when stripped for exercise on the playing fields nevertheless covered their pudenda. Persons who wear loincloths are thence called *campestrati*. The shame-oriented requirement that the genitalia be covered sometimes takes extreme form. Augustine points to the instance of "some Barbarians [who] . . . go so far as to refrain from exposing those parts even in the baths" and who "keep their covering on when they wash," and to the modest habits of the "gymnosophists" of India, "who practice philosophy in nakedness . . . [but] nevertheless have coverings on their genitals, although they have none on the rest of the body."[7] Lust and the attendant shame over the uncontrollable genitalia have thus originated the universal practice of hiding the pudenda, and in turn have given rise to variations in the practice of modesty and the usages for clothing.

The liberation of the sexual urge from willful control has also led to the institutionalization of privacy during sexual intercourse. Augustine here notes that the basic reason for seclusion during the sex act is that "the genital organs have become as it were the private property of lust, which has brought them so completely under its sway that they have no power of movement if this passion fails, if it has not arisen spontaneously or in response to a stimulus." Man, unable to assure himself of control over his sexual passions, is thus ashamed of his reliance on them even for lawful sexual practices such as procreating children in marriage. Even where prostitution is legal, or where fornication is not punishable by earthly law, Augustine observes, the sexual practices associated with these acts are carried on in seclusion and secrecy. "A natural sense of shame," Augustine argues, "ensures that even brothels make provision for secrecy; and it was easier for immorality to dispense with the fetters of prohibition than for shamelessness to abolish the furtive dens of this degradation." If all sex acts—those prohibited by custom, permitted by law, or necessary for the continuation of the race—are carried out in secret, it is not because of the rightness or wrongness of the kind of sex act, Augustine argues, but because of the inherent shame in the nature of the act itself. Speaking of lawful marriage and the procreative act attendant upon the fulfillment of its purpose, Augustine again points to the universal practice of the seclusion of the conjugal pair and asks why such a right action that "craves for recognition in the light of the mind's understanding" is nevertheless carried out in private "to escape the light of the eye's vision." Augustine's answer is to point to the peculiar necessity of lust to activate the organs necessary to perform a righteous act—"something by nature right and proper is effected in such a way as to be accompanied by a feeling of shame, by way of punishment."[8] The shame of man's dependence on lust leads to his insistence on seclusion when in the grip of this passion.

Without the ability to govern his concupiscence, Augustine observes, man's nature is changed from that of the original dwellers in Paradise. "Human nature . . . is, without any doubt, ashamed about lust, and rightly ashamed."[9] Before their sin, Augustine insists, Adam and Eve would have been able to fulfill God's blessing to "Increase and multiply and fill the earth" (Gen. 1:28) without the intervention of lust. It was only after the sin that man "lost the authority to which the body had been subordinate in every part,"[10] and thus developed a shameful attitude toward the sexual organs and the acts associated with them. Those who deny the ubiquity of this shame—Augustine specifically had in mind the

Cynics who rejected civiliation, lived as beggar philosophers, and advocated public performances of sexual intercourse—are guided by error and ulterior purpose.

Augustine is sure that man, created good and spoiled by sin, would prefer, if he could, to carry out the righteous command of filling the earth with his own kind without the aid of lust. However, man is now in a state of dis-grace because of the original sin committed by Adam, "committed when all mankind existed in one man." The retribution imposed on man, snatching the sexual organs from the authority of the will, is, according to Augustine, "entirely fitting" because it manifests itself "in that part which effects the procreation of the very nature that was changed for the worse through the first great sin." This metamorphosis in human nature, in turn, will last, "and no one can be rescued from the toils of that offence, which was punished by God's justice, unless the sin is expiated in each man singly by the grace of God."[11] Thus did Augustine see lust affecting fundamentally both the nature and culture of man.

It is worth noting the sex-specific theory of lust that Augustine presented. Throughout his discussion of *luxuria* Augustine concentrates on loss of control over the male sex organ. Specific to the manifestation of lust is the erection. Whether women were affected by lust in a manner similar to men is left ambiguous by Augustine's silence on the question. That women may participate in coitus without arousal is well known. It would seem to follow, then, that for Augustine, lust with its mysterious power to activate or deactivate the penis was a peculiar and one-sided retribution visited on Adam and his male descendants.

In addition to its presumptive one-sidedness, Augustine's theory permits males to excuse but not to justify their lust. An excuse is an exculpatory statement that admits that while the act in question is bad, wrong, inappropriate, or immoral, the actor is not completely responsible for its commission. A justification, on the other hand, denies the evil alleged to be in the act but takes volitional responsibility.[12] Under the Augustinian view the authority of the will is severed from sexual activity. Hence, a man unable to get an erection after having bedded the woman of his choice can plead that he is a victim of one of lust's impish tricks; a man whose concupiscence is upbraided can claim to be a victim of the bitter legacy of his descent from Adam; and one who refuses to consort with women can argue from his unwanted but inescapable obligation to expiate the sin of the original pair. Lust becomes an ever-present but unpredictable element in social life, a clandestine factor in all social and interpersonal situations, and yet one whose effects can be mitigated by appeals to the argument of a theological anthropology that Augustine insists is man's fate.

Thomas Aquinas and the Sociology of Sexual Deviation

The temptations into which lust led mankind evoked considerable interest in the development of moral and social controls.[13] For Christian thinkers the maintenance of sexual purity was of paramount importance. The problem was how this purity might be institutionalized and protected against the pollution of sin. Christian thinkers distinguished three ways to ward off or control lust: virginity, denial during the single state and widowhood, and, for those who could not conquer their concupiscence, marriage. Paul put the matter succinctly (1 Cor. 7:79):

> For I would that all men were even as I myself. But every man hath his proper gift of God, one after this manner, and another after that. I say therefore to the unmarried and the widows, It is good for them if they abide even as I. But if they cannot contain, let them marry: for it is better to marry than to burn.

The distinctive third place given to marriage in the Christian tripartite division of sexual purity is confirmed in the less than enthusiastic discussions of that institution among early Christian thinkers. Paul had declared, "It is good for a man not to touch a woman. Nevertheless, to avoid fornication, let every man have his own wife, and let every woman have her own husband" (1 Cor. 7:1-2). Tertullian (160?-230) went beyond Paul in asserting that it was better neither to marry nor to burn but modified his stand with respect to marriage, asserting "not as if we superseded a bad thing by a good, but only a good thing by a better; for we do not reject marriage, but simply refrain from it."[14] Jerome (320?-420)[14], the translator of the Bible into Latin (Vulgate), emphasized the burdensome aspects of matrimony, including the difficulties of pregnancy, the interminable wailing of infants, the pain of jealousy, and the dull drudgery of household chores. In contrast to the wife's devotion to her husband, Jerome celebrated the dedication of Mary, the virgin mother of Jesus, who devoted herself to Christ.[15] John Chrysostom (347-407), Patriarch of Constantinople, echoed these views when he wrote that "marriage is good, but virginity is better than marriage . . . I consider virginity to be as high above marriage as the heavens are above earth."[16] Jesus is credited by sociologist Emory S. Bogardus with supporting the family as a social institution above all others, "even above the church and the state."[17] However, as Jay Haley has observed, Jesus required that his followers give up all family ties as a price for their discipleship.[18] "He that loveth father or mother more than me is not worthy of me: and he that loveth son or daughter more than me is not worthy of me" (Matt. 10:37). It is noteworthy, however, that Jesus does not mention wives in this admonition nor in his later more bellicose threat (Matt. 10:34-36):

> Think not that I am come to send peace on earth: I came not to send peace, but a sword. For I am come to set a man at variance against his father, and the daughter against her mother, and daughter in law against her mother in law. And a man's foes shall be they of his own household.

Marriage was to be encouraged over fornication, incest, and homosexuality, but took a lower place than virginity in the hierarchy of Christian virtues. That lust was inextricably attached to coitus in marriage, as well as outside it, led to the painful ambiguity of Christian thinkers about matrimony. Augustine was not only sure that men would reject lust if they could procreate without it, but also assured his readers that before the Fall Adam and Eve had been able to copulate without the agency of lust, since the will then exercised authority over the sexual passions.

> When mankind was in such a state of ease and plenty, blest with such felicity, let us never imagine that it was impossible for the seed of children to be sown without the morbid condition of lust. Instead the sexual organs would have been brought into activity by the same bidding of the will as controlled the other organs. Then, without feeling the allurement of passion goading him on, the husband would have relaxed on his wife's bosom in tranquillity of mind and with no impairment of his body's integrity.[19]

John of Damascus, an eighth-century divine, went further than Augustine, holding that Adam and Eve had been created sexless and that sexual reproduction was part of the retribution for their original sin. If the original pair of sexless creatures had been obedient to God, John continued, procreation would now take place without sin.[20]

Despite their doubts about marriage, however, Christian theologians could not recommend universal virginity as a warrant against lust.[21] Encouraged by the monastic sect of Essenes, some early Christians came to consider all pleasure as evil and rejected marriage; others discouraged reproduction of Christians because of the Roman persecutions of them; still others, sure that the Last Judgment was at hand, found no necessity for marriage or procreation; and finally a general sense of contrition and penitence among early Christians led to a widespread rejection of sex. Virginity was much praised, called the ornament of morality and the crown of concord by Cyprian of Carthage, a third-century ecclesiastical scholar; something supernaturally great, glorious, wonderful, and the noblest way of life by Methodius, at the opening of the fourth century; and the term was rederived from the Latin *viror* (freshness) by Thomas

Aquinas, who stressed the life of reason as superior to that which had been burned by the fire of sexual passion. Tertullian went so far as to proclaim, "The Kingdom of Heaven is thrown open to eunuchs."[22] Eusebius praised those who "have made themselves eunuchs, for the kingdom of heaven's sake" (Matt. 19:12), and Origen and others accepted this injunction and castrated themselves.

Nevertheless, a policy of virginity for all Christians would have led to dependence on continuous conversion for the propagation of the faith. Jerome grudgingly consented to the necessity of marriage, since it made possible the production of virgins.[23] Procreation assured continuance of the church, especially if children born to Christians attached themselves to the religion of their parents. Observing that Jesus had shown a special affection toward and interest in children, though he had had none of his own, Christians emphasized their founder's words, "Whosoever shall receive one of such children in my name, receiveth me" (Mark 9:37). Children born of Christian parents, they argued, should be attached to the church rather than their families. Despite the claim of later writers, such as Bogardus, who aver Jesus' priority of family over church, some early church fathers pointed to the fact that two of the apostles, John and James, "left their father Zebedee in the ship and went after him [that is, Jesus]" (Mark 1:20), and to the harsh rebuke that Jesus gave to the disciple that asked permission to return to his home and bury his father: "Follow me, and let the dead bury their dead" (Matt. 8:22). Despite Jesus' admonition that no one was exempt from the obligation to "Honor thy father and mother," and his dreadful judgment immediately following, "He that curseth father or mother, let him die the death" (Matt. 15:4), Jerome concluded that "Great is the reward for forgetting a parent."[24] With necessarily passionate sex connected to procreation even in church-blessed matrimony, and children pledged to the church, marriage became merely an acceptable management of lust.

However, the sin of lust still found expression in serial marriages and mixed unions. The *Apostolic Constitutions*, an early handbook of doctrine and practice, held that a second marriage was wicked, a third indicative of unbridled lust, and a fourth of fornication.[25] Athenagoras, a second-century Christian apologist, said "a second marriage is merely a specious adultery."[26] And Jerome scoffed at the pleas of widows for a man to provide them with financial aid, a spokesman in court, a responsible supervisor of estate and taxes, a breadwinner, and a disciplinarian for household slaves and children.

Why these pretexts of property and arrogant servants? Confess your vileness. No woman marries with the idea of not sleeping with a husband. If you are not spurred on by lust, surely it is the height of madness to increase your wealth, and for a paltry and passing gain to pollute that precious chastity which might endure forever.[27]

The original marriage might be a grudging concession to lust and concupiscence, provided that the wife obeyed the husband, the husband loved his wife, and the children born therefrom were reared in the faith. However, marriages after death or desertion were signs of unwarranted acquiescence to the sexual passions.

Widows, however, presented a special problem for the opponents of lust. The status of widow was lodged uneasily between the glorified virgins who were at the apex of virtue and the barely tolerated wives, who, while virtuous, could not be held equal to those who had resisted the temptations of lust altogether. Paul urged a distinction based on age and moral character. Widows sixty years of age or older who qualified might be admitted to holy orders, but those below that age ought to be refused entry,

> for when they have begun to wax wanton against Christ, they will marry; having damnation, because they have cast off their first faith. And withal, they learn to be idle, wandering about from house to house; and not only idle but tattlers also and busybodies, speaking things which they ought not. I will therefore that the younger women marry, bear children, guide the house, give none occasion to the adversary to speak reproachfully (1 Tim. 5:9-14).

Paul concluded that widows might remarry (Christians), ruling that "The wife is bound by the law as long as her husband liveth; but if her husband be dead, she is at liberty to be married to whom she will; only in the Lord" (1 Cor. 7:39).

Precisely because marriages between Christians and nonbelievers might alienate the Christian spouse from the faith, or result in the birth of children who were not reared in the Church, such unions were proscribed as products of lust. Tertullian treated such marriages as tantamount to fornication. The Church took direction against this aspect of what it regarded as lust when in 306 at the Synod of Elvira it declared excommunication for five years to Christian parents giving their daughters in marriage to Jews or heretics, unless the unbeliever were willing to convert to Christianity. Constantine the Great (280-337) added the force of imperial Roman law to this ban, making Christian-Jewish marriages illegal, and in 356 the law was changed to declare such marriages adulterous. The fear of the sin of lust, with its complex relationship to precreation and familism, became an agency for ensuring marriage within the faith as well.

The many debates over the management of lust—disputes over the acceptability of marriage, the status of children, the rights of illegitimate offspring, the problems of abortion, infanticide, prostitution, incest, homosexuality, and divorce—led to something of a crisis in the Christian world during the thirteenth century. In 1164 the church had declared holy matrimony one of the seven sacraments, but this only raised the question of when that sacrament began—at the time of betrothal, when the wedding ceremony had been performed, or after the consummation of the marriage—and continued the debate over whether marriages should be arranged or approved by parents or entered into freely by choice of the partners. Thomas Aquinas (1225–1274), writing largely in the tradition of Aristotle, sought to resolve many of these issues and to separate lust proper from those forms of sexual intercourse that were acceptable and righteous.

Although not covering all matters that had troubled the moral opponents of lust, Aquinas directed his attention to carving out a place for licit sexuality that would be secure against the charge of sinful lust.[28] Foremost in what amounts to a veritable theology of sexual deviance is his thesis that "not all sexual intercourse is sinful."[29] Aquinas follows the mode of Aristotelian teleological argument in insisting that, since the end or purpose of carnal union is generation, the preservation of the species, and the upbringing of offspring, unions so contracted and consummated are not sinful. He also asserts that because bodily organs are instruments of the soul, each organ's end is found in its use. The efficient use of the sex organs is carnal union, but since the use of any natural thing cannot be evil in itself, carnal union cannot be evil in itself. With these and related arguments Aquinas concluded that he had disposed "of the error of those who say every act of carnal union is illicit, as a consequence of which view they entirely condemn matrimony and marriage arrangements."

However, it was one thing to establish the logico-ethical propriety for certain sexual unions and quite another to locate them in the morally correct institutional setting. Aquinas was aware of this difficulty and sought a teleological basis for assuring monogamy as the single appropriate locus for carnal union. To accomplish this task, Aquinas had to refute the arguments that fornication among consenting adults was sinless, that polygamous, polyandrous, and homosexual unions were not tainted by forbidden lust, and that marriage among close relatives was permissible.

Aquinas' battle to establish once and for all the appropriate form for permissible sexual union was twofold. Unlike later cultural revolutionaries who sought to liberate a pulsating, free-floating *life* from all *forms of life*,[30] Aquinas sought to oppose both certain forms of sexuality and a liberated ubiquitous lust. Among the forms that he opposed were those modes of sexual union that his contemporaries had begun to justify as without sin, such as fornication by a man with an unmarried woman under conditions of mutual consent wherein no other party (for example, parents or fiancés) would be injured by the act. Aquinas admitted that the justification put forward by the proponents of this type of fornication was reasonable in asserting that neither God nor one's neighbors was harmed by such conduct. Nevertheless it was inescapably a sin.

Aquinas argues teleologically once more that the natural purpose of semen is the propagation of the species. The sexual act is carried out, then, for the purpose of procreation and all that it entails—including the nurturance and rearing of the offspring under conditions appropriate to human development. Included here are both proper nutrition and the education of the soul, tasks to which a woman alone is not adequate. Bringing up children requires the presence of both a man and a woman, Aquinas observes, especially because in matters of prudence and education a husband, "in whom reason is more developed for giving instruction and strength is more available for giving punishment," is prerequisite. "Hence," he points out, "since among all animals it is necessary for male and female to remain together as long as the work of the father is needed by the offspring, it is natural to the human being for the man to establish a lasting association with a designated woman, over no short period of time." The only form appropriate to that lasting association is matrimony. "Therefore," Aquinas concludes, "matrimony is natural for man, and promiscuous performance of the sexual act, outside matrimony, is contrary to man's good. For this reason, it must be a sin."

If fornication was a sin because man's natural purpose was to propagate and preserve the species, and this purpose could only be accomplished through sexual acts performed by persons joined in wedlock, there nevertheless remained those arrangements "for the emission of semen apart from the proper purpose. . . ." Proponents of the position that masturbation, homosexuality, bestiality, and adultery were either slight sins or no sin at all challenged Aquinas to prove otherwise. He disposed of these matters in short order. To the argument put forward by his unnamed antagonists that there is only the slightest of evil or none whatsoever for "a person to use a part of the body for a different use than that to which it is directed by nature . . . because man's good is not much opposed by such inordinate use," Aquinas replied simply, "the inordinate emission of semen is incompatible with the natural good; namely the preservation of the species." Homosexuality was rejected by reminding its proponents not only that "the emission of semen under conditions in which offspring cannot follow is illicit," but also citing scriptural authority. Aquinas invokes *Leviticus* 18:22-23: "Thou shalt not lie with mankind as with womankind . . . neither shalt thou copulate with any beast," to dispose of both homosexuality and bestiality. To drive home the moral injunction against transvestism and sexual acts among persons of the same sex, Aquinas reminds his listeners of the bar to such conduct in 1 *Corinthians* 6:9: "Nor effeminate, nor abusers of themselves . . . shall possess the kingdom of God." Adultery is even more quickly rejected by citations of the admonition that "There shall be no whore of the daughters of Israel" (Deut. 23:17), and scriptural warnings against fornication. Not even pausing to prove that an adulterous wife is a whore, Aquinas sums up his thesis by an abrupt closing: ". . . we refute the error of those who say that there is no more sin in the emission of semen than in the emission of any other superfluous matter, and also of those who state that fornication is not a sin."

However, having raised up and rescued marriage from its competitive alternatives *without*—temporary, consensual unions, homosexuality, bestiality, and autoeroticism—there still remained restrictions against lustful sin *within* the matrimonial form. Aquinas dealt with three—divorce, polygamy, incest.

Divorce, although permitted to the ancient Hebrews as a limited right accorded to husbands, was opposed by most Christian authorities. Wedlock was secured against human intervention by the warning that "What therefore God hath joined together, let not man put asunder" (Matt. 19:6). Nevertheless, an absolute prohibition on divorce was difficult to establish in light of the sins of lust and other evil acts that might be committed by either husbands or wives.[31] Scriptural authority seemed to permit divorce in the instance of fornication (Matt. 19:9: "Whosoever shall put away his wife. except it be for fornication, and shall marry another, committeth adultery"), but some theologians advocated other grounds as well. Hermas, a well-known Christian thinker of the first century, favored granting divorces not only in cases of fornication but also when a wife was guilty of apostasy, covetousness, or idolatry. Origen permitted husbands to divorce their wives for fornication or any other crime of equal or more serious nature. Although there was a grudging tolerance for husbands divorcing their wives on established grounds, the reverse case was most strenuously opposed. The Council of Elvira (306) threatened excommunication to any women who divorced their husbands. However, wives were permitted to divorce their husbands under the edicts of Constantine (331) if it could be shown that the accused party had committed murder, poisoned someone, violated sepulchers, or not communicated with his wife over a period of four years of military service. For the church fathers, recognition of grounds for divorce tended to reside in lustful practices. Augustine insisted on the indissolubility of marriage, except in cases of "unlawful lusts" on the part of either spouse. Jerome shared the expanded view on the subject presented by Hermas. And John Chrysostom regarded adultery as sufficient ground for severing the marital tie. In 407 the Council of Carthage ruled that marriage was absolutely indissoluble, but eleven hundred years later the Council of Trent (1545-1563) permitted two forms of solubility that were not complete breaks in the marital tie—*divortium a vinculo matrimonii*, that is, annulment on the grounds of belief that the original marital vows were tainted, and *divortium a mensa et thoro*, separation from bed and board on grounds of adultery, apostasy, heresy, and cruelty, However, remarriage was not permitted in either case.

Writing three centuries before the ruling by the Council of Trent, Aquinas sought to prevent any dissolution of marriage whatever. Remarkable for its omission of the problems of sinful, criminal, or heretical activity on the part of spouses, Aquinas' argument appeals to the solicitude for and needs of offspring, the inequities of divorce, the sincerity of long-lasting friendships, and the teleological necessity of both human and divine laws on the indivisibility of marriage. Holding that "generation is the only natural act that is ordered to the common good," since "generation" [pertains] to the preservation of the species," Aquinas reasons that "those matters which pertain must, above all others, be ordered by laws, both divine and human." Human laws, in turn, should stem from the prompting of nature. "So, since there is a natural prompting within the human species, to the end that the union of man and wife be undivided, and that it be between one man and one woman, it was necessary for this to be ordered by human law." However, human law does not supply sufficient reason for indissolubility. Divine law provides the example of the union between Christ and the Church, which Aquinas observes "is a union of one spouse with another." He concludes that since "disorders connected with the act of generation are not only opposed to natural instinct, but are also transgressions of divine and human laws, . . . a greater sin results from a disorder in this area than in regard to the use of food or other things of that kind."

Permanent unions provided a kind of insurance against evil behavior, argued Aquinas. Not only did it satisfy husbands' "natural solicitude to know their offspring" throughout the entirety of life, but it also prevented husbands from sending away their wives after the latter had lost their beauty and fecundity. Marriages that could not be terminated before the death of one of the partners guaranteed faithfulness, protected joint property, reduced tensions with relatives, and removed the "occasions for adultery which are presented when a man is permitted to send away his wife, or the converse."

If, for Aquinas, the sin of lust was removed from permanent carnal unions dedicated to procreation, there still remained the question of the number of such unions a person might enter at the same time. Aquinas addressed himself to both the questions of polygyny and polyandry. The latter practice of having more than one husband at a time was disposed of by invoking the need for a man to know, nurture, and bring up his own offspring. "[F]or, as we said, man naturally desires to know his offspring, and this knowledge would be completely destroyed if there were several males for one female." The issue of polygyny, however, could not so easily be opposed. Aquinas reasons that because "every animal desires to enjoy freely the pleasure of the sexual act, as he also does food," the freedom of a woman associating with her husband is abridged when the latter has several wives. Aquinas seems to sense the danger of this recognition of the "pleasure of the sexual act." He goes on to argue that only among animals that have no concern for the rearing of offspring is promiscuity on the part of the male common. Therefore, "since, of all animals, the male in the human species has the greatest concern for offspring, it is obviously natural for man that one male should have but one wife, and conversely." Still not convinced that he has refuted the case for polygyny, Aquinas adds that for one man to have many wives would relegate the friendly relations requisite to matrimony to that of servility, would render the condition of wedlock inequitable, and would be contrary to moral customs, good order, and the concord required of domestic society. Invoking the scriptural text, "They shall be one flesh" (Gen. 2:24), Aquinas closes the case with the order that "the custom of those having several wives is set aside. . . ."

Sinful lust was likely to arise in the household among persons closely related by blood. Paul had observed incestuous practices and issued a dire warning against them. "It is reported commonly that there is fornication among you, and such fornication as is not so much as named among the Gentiles, that one should have his father's wife. And ye are puffed up, and have not rather mourned, that he that hath done this deed might be taken away from among you" (1 Cor. 5:1-2). Nevertheless incestuous unions had been encouraged among wealthy Christian families in order to protect and extend the wealth and property of the family and preserve it against aspiring upstarts.[32] Aquinas condemned incest as a serious sin, but one ranking below bestiality, pederasty, and sodomy.

In his assault on incest, Aquinas is less than absolute in his condemnation, noting that if some good purpose could be recognized for a marriage between close relatives, human law, which is always subject to qualification and modification, might provide a dispensation in the particular case. Nevertheless Aquinas objects to incestuous unions on the grounds of the excess of sinful pleasure that their open recognition would encourage. As Aquinas sees it, if a man were permitted to have sexual relations with those members of his family with whom he lives, "excessive indulgence in this pleasure would result, for the occasion for sexual relations with such persons could not be removed." Moreover, incest, by conflating the love that arises from common origin with the love that arises to chasten lust, would corrupt the soul and ultimately lead to its domination by sinful pleasure. Marriage should be a union of "diverse persons," whose fleshly union is not confounded by the feelings of shame natural to coitus and those of respect requisite to family members. Finally, Aquinas appeals to the necessity for friendship to arise among many people in human society, a necessity that is inhibited when related persons are bound in matrimony, but increased when marriages are contracted among strangers. Although his argument is much hedged about with qualification and admittedly subject to legal modification and dispensation, his comments on the dysfunctions of incest provide the basis for a societal theory of lust. Rooted in the recognition that the loving pair have obligations to others beside themselves, Aquinas' analysis of lust and incest prepare us for the social arrangements that people and communities of later centuries would employ to limit the power of lust to harm their own society.

Martin Luther and the Psychology of Lust

When a president of the United States confessed in a popular magazine that he had lust in his heart, he was echoing an interpretation of sin that had found earlier and more complete expression in the writings of Martin Luther (1483-1546). Prior to Luther, much of the significant discussions of lust had been devoted to designating the deeds properly associated with that sin and defining the modes of carnal union that were chaste. Luther participated in such discussions himself, but he prefaced his interpretations of sin in general and lust in particular with an analysis of flesh and spirit that redefined both. Here we will be concerned with his discussion of the former and with his reconceptualizations of the chastity in marriage, the rights of divorce, the place of women in society, and the abominations of prostitution and homosexuality.

Foremost in Luther's argument was the redefinition of sin, extending it beyond the acts of the body. "The word *sin* in the Bible means something more than the external works done by our bodily action," wrote Luther. "It means all the circumstances that act together and excite or incite us to do what is done; in particular, the impulses operating in the depths of our hearts."[33] Unbelief and lack of faith encourage the appetite for sin, according to Luther. "[U]nbelief is the sole cause of sin," thundered the first Protestant; "it exalts the flesh, and gives the desire to do works that are plainly wrong, as happened in the case of Adam and Eve in the garden of Eden." Having recast the original sin as one of unbelief rather than disobedience, Luther goes on to enlarge the scope of the fleshly appetite. Flesh, he argues, invoking the authority of Paul and Jesus, "means everything that is born from the flesh, i.e., the entire self, body and soul, including our reason and all our senses." Luther included among "carnal" acts the gibberings about spiritual matters of a man without grace, and in a rather ambiguous phrase implied that lack of faith was a matter of fleshly rather than spiritual weakness. In general, however, Luther expands the meaning and span of the term "flesh" so that in his words it "applies to a person who, in thought and in fact, lives and labours in the service of the body and the temporal life." Moreover, faith does not free men from the temptations and subversions of sin. "Throughout our whole lives, we shall be kept fully employed with our own selves, taming our body, killing its passions, controlling its members till they obey, not the passions, but the spirit." Thus Luther's position leads to hope for and prediction of an ultimate reversal of that descent of man described by Augustine. Augustine located lust precisely in man's loss of willful authority over his sexual organs. Luther not only speaks of the lifelong struggle to obtain spiritual control over the fleshly members, but also proclaims the final outcome of this war on sin: "The final goal is that we should be entirely liberated from sin, rise again in the body with Christ, and live for ever."

The struggle against sins of the flesh was interminable so long as men lived. Toward those engaged in the struggle Luther offered both comfort and encouragement. More than this, however, Luther reviewed the papal laws governing marriage and offered some remarkable liberalizations. Marriage was removed from among the sacraments. In addition, turning to Angelus de Clavassio Chiavasso's *Summa Angelica*, a popular fifteenth-century handbook of casuistry discussing all possible matters of conscience in alphabetical order, Luther opposed the eighteen impediments to marriage enumerated therein.[34] These impediments had not only worked to the disadvantage of many of those who wished to wed, but also played into the hands of the more unscrupulous or clever of those who sought to end unwanted marriages. Church control over annulments, argued Luther, led to the degradation of the priesthood, turning them into "market-stall holders" selling "male and female pudenda"; for, as Luther acidly announced, "there is no impediment to marriage nowadays which they cannot legitimize for money." Luther proposed, first, that all papally declared obstacles to marriage that were not authenticated by scripture be dispensed with immediately. Among these were the expansion of the incest taboo which the Fourth Lateran Council in 1215 had enlarged to the fourth degree. "The scriptures forbid only the second degree of consanguinity," Luther reminded the supporters of Rome, and thus had declared only twelve familial statuses to be beyond the pale of chaste marriage. Marriage hence was rightfully prohibited to one's mother, stepmother, full sister, half-sister, granddaughter, father's sister, mother's sister, daughter-in-law, brother's wife, wife's sister, stepdaughter, and uncle's wife. But all other relatives were eligible for chaste and lawful unions, including the daughter or granddaughter of a sibling. In a related instance the taboo against marriage to one's godchildren was also to be set aside.

Beyond new rules governing incest, Luther proposed that marriage between Christians and unbelievers be permitted, that persons who had committed murder or adultery at some earlier time be free to marry so long as both were unencumbered by marital ties, that a man who has had sexual relations with another woman after his betrothal be permitted to marry his fiancée, that priests and deacons not be bound by oaths of celibacy, and that persons whose fiancé(e)s die before marriage, and widows as well, be permitted to marry.

In addition to enlarging the freedoms of those who wish to marry, Luther dealt with that adverse punishment of tricksterish lust and carnality—impotence. Here he becomes quite concrete, presenting a hypothetical instance in which a woman, desirous of having child, is married to an impotent man but unwilling to hail her husband into divorce court because of the notoriety and embarrassment that would ensue. Luther favors her right to divorce, but if her husband refuses to consent to a decree, Luther advises that the woman obtain her husband's consent to have intercourse with another man, preferably her husband's brother, for purposes of procreation. This second "marriage" should be kept secret, Luther suggests, and all children born therefrom should be ascribed to her lawful husband, the putative father. However, should the husband withhold his consent from this secret liaison, Luther counsels the woman to contract a (presumably bigamous) marriage with some other man and to flee "to some distant and unknown region." This advice, Luther argues, is better than letting the unhappy wife "burn or commit adultery."

Having thus suggested divorce, bigamy, and secret liaisons with other men as a remedy for the victim of a man's impotence, Luther insists that his proposals do not put the woman in jeopardy of salvation because of sin. The woman remains eligible for salvation if she follows his suggestions because "in this case a mistake due to ignorance of the man's impotence created a false situation which impedes the marriage proper; the harshness of the law does not allow divorce; yet by the divine law the woman is free, and so cannot be forced to remain continent."

Luther also directs his attention to the problems of child support and inheritance that his new perspective would create. Addressing himself to the charge that it would be unfair for the offspring of a secret liaison to be heirs of their putative father, Luther argues that there is no evil or injury if the husband has given prior consent for his wife's conduct. If, on the other hand, the wife carried on with a potent man behind the back of her husband, Luther urges Christian charity toward the woman, and he reminds her accusers that she has been the victim of a prior fraud: her husband's impotence was not known to her at the time of the marriage. "Does not the man commit the greater sin by wasting the body and life of his wife, than the woman in alienating a quantity of temporal property?" Luther waxes hotly against the claims of the husband as he continues on—the cuckolded man becomes a "bully," likened to a man who keeps another man's wife in prison separated from her husband. He concludes that the impotent husband "ought to be compelled either to accept divorce, or support his putative child as his own heir. . . . For it is his own fault, and not his wife's, that she labours under this wrong."

Luther's attitude toward divorce was far more ambivalent than on other matters. Limited by the passage in *Matthew* 5:32 that permitted divorce only in cases of fornication, Luther recognized other instances where he deemed divorce reasonable. He admitted that for his own part he had "such a hatred of divorce that I prefer bigamy to divorce," but he was quick to add, "I do not venture an opinion whether bigamy should be allowed." Luther opposed the additional grounds for divorce allowed by papal dispensation, since they lacked scriptural authority and proceeded from what Luther denounced as "presumptuousness." Rather than pronounce any conclusions on the right of divorce, Luther preferred to return to the impediments to marriage—this time concentrating on the bar to remarriage instituted by the Catholic Church against all those who had been deserted or divorced by their spouses. Claiming to have witnessed or heard about numerous "cases where wives or husbands have run away and deserted their partners, to return perhaps ten years later, or even never," Luther acknowledged that "This kind of thing distresses and depresses me, for there are instances day by day, whether due to some special piece of wickedness of Satan's, or to our neglect of God's word." Luther's distress and depression did not lead him to enunciate any new rules or regulations. He hoped, rather, that the principle behind 1 *Corinthians* 7:15 would be interpreted to permit the spouses of nominal believers to remarry if deserted, and a returned penitent not to resume the former marriage but to marry another. Unable to come to any fixed conclusions, however, Luther hoped for a settlement of these matters outside papal authority.

Luther's attitudes toward marriage and impotence and his ambivalence about divorce seemed to espouse a special sympathy toward women and, as in the analysis of impotence, a greater contempt for men. In one sense Luther's discussions continue the thesis implicit in Augustine's argument that the retribution for the original sin had been visited upon man directly, denying him authority over his sexual arousal and subjecting him to the whims of an insubordinate and wicked lust. Nevertheless, the association of women with evil in general and lust in particular had developed from other interpretations of the Fall. As the sin of lust gained prominence among the evils against which Christians must contend, women's status declined because of their association with carnal attraction or with the deception of Adam. Paul had argued (1 Tim. 2:14) that "Adam was not deceived, but the woman being deceived was in the transgression." As the first woman, who thus contained all women in herself, Eve became the organ of the devil to Clement of Alexandria, the "devil's gateway" to Tertullian, and a "necessary evil" to John of Chrysostom.[35] Clement had insisted that "every woman ought to be filled with shame at the thought that she is a woman," and others referred to the descendants of Eve as scorpions, vipers, and other fearsome and detested animals. Augustine, it should be noticed, as less harsh in his judgment.[36] He insisted that "woman . . . is the creation of God, just as is the man." And, he added "her creation out of man emphasizes the idea of unity between them." Women as well as men will keep their sex at the resurrection, Augustine insisted. "For in that life there will be no sexual lust, which is the cause of shame. . . . However, the female organs will not subserve their former use; they will be part of a new beauty, which will not excite the lust of the beholder . . ." In the interim, however, women were subject to the retribution for original sin, in that their sexual organs would arouse the carnal lust of men.

The relation of women to the devil, arising out of Eve's original response to the serpent, led to the association of their sex with demonology and witchcraft. Although men as well as women were designated witches, the tendency was to identify demonology and witchcraft with femininity and especially with carnal unions with demons or devils.[37] Typically the devil is personified as masculine, and the original scene in Eden is one in which the essentially masculine Evil One, transformed or entering into his agent, the serpent, nevertheless retains his masculine hold over Eve. So recent an interpreter as Ruth Nanda Anshen insists on this interpretation, on the still outstanding debt the devil owes to Eve for starting the process of history, and on the important role women play in the diabolic world.[38]

Luther's sympathy for women was purchased at the price of their reduction in status and power in relation to men in general and their husbands in particular.[39] Luther thought he observed in women's physiognomy the natural basis for their proper estate—as wives, mothers, and caretakers of infants. "It has often been a great delight and wonder to me," he exclaimed, "to see how the whole body of a woman is adapted and formed for the care of infants." Doting on the anatomical conformity of women to their maternal duties, Luther goes on to warn that women are unexcelled so long as they stay in their spheres of bedroom and nursery. If a woman presumes to rule over her husband, however, "she . . . engages in a work for which she was not created, a work which . . . is evil." Arguments opposed to these restrictions are, according to Luther, either false or pernicious. Women are born to an eloquence on domestic matters, Luther observes, but "they do not rate when they talk outside the domestic field, about political matters." "From this it appears," Luther concludes, "that woman was created for domestic concerns but man for political ones, for wars, and the affairs of law courts. . . ." "A woman," Luther writes, "should either be subjected to her husband or should not marry. If she does not want a master, then let her keep from taking a man; for this is the order God has prescribed and ordained through His apostles and Scripture."

Luther's argument for a fixed and natural place for women depends ultimately on their relation to sin and lust. "Without women," Luther points out, "marriage would be impossible." However, that seemingly obvious point depends on the definition of marriage, which, according to Luther, is "the God-appointed and legitimate union of man and woman in the hope of having children or at least for the purpose of avoiding fornication and sin and living to the glory of God." Since the guarantee of children cannot be given, marriage requires that a man live with his wife in contentment, and that he "avoid all lewdness with others." Thus, "Taking a wife is a remedy for fornication." This remedy is aided by woman's "natural inclination to be desired and loved," and man's inability to "get along without women." Men are inextricably attracted to women because they "have been conceived in the bodies of women, have been nourished in them, borne by them, nursed and reared by them." Woman's duty, then, was to assuage man's carnal lust through the institution of marriage.

Since mankind could not escape the demands of the flesh, it required marriage as a relief for lust. "Flesh and blood remain flesh and blood," Luther insists, "and the natural inclination and attraction run their course without let or hindrance, as everyone sees and feels." God has commanded marriage, Luther observes, so that it may be easier to avoid unchasteness.

However, there were other "remedies" for the cravings of a carnal appetite, and Luther knew and opposed these—premarital intercourse, fornication, legalized prostitution, and homosexuality. The first three of these concerned the sexuality of women outside of marriage. But, Luther pointed out, God "did not create man and woman alike . . ." These differences were established "not for lewdness, but [rather that] they should live together, be fruitful, beget children, and nourish and rear them to the glory of God." Luther inveighs against what he calls "sowing wild oats" before marriage. To the authors of justifying proverbs that encourage premarital experimentation—"A fellow must be a fool some time"; "a young angel, an old devil"—Luther replies with the *argumentum ad hominem*: "Heathen they are; like heathen, nay, like devils they speak . . ." As for simple fornication Luther asserts that it is a mortal sin and those who commit it will not "possess the kingdom of God." Legalized prostitution is not a remedy for fornication, argues Luther, but an encouragement to licentiousness and the raping of girls. Governments should not only outlaw public brothels, argued Luther, but also punish fornication and adultery, "at least the cases that are public." However, he reserved his most severe assaults for homosexuality. Carnal unions between persons of the same sex are "inhuman" and "satanic." Indeed, Luther accounts for the onset of homosexual desire by asserting that it arises when a man "has once turned aside from the fear of God." The "devil puts such pressure upon his nature that he extinguishes the fire of natural desire and stirs up another, which is contrary to nature . . ." Homosexuality "departs from the natural passion and desire, planted into nature by God, according to which the male has a passionate desire for the female." Thus, Luther's essays on morals conclude that women were created for the use of men and to contain their lustful passion through the institution of marriage.

Luther's most important contributions to the understanding of lust was his distinction between obedience to holy law and the doing of righteous works and the cheerful obedience to right conduct that transcends and in fact requires no external law or effort to be effected.[40] Conscience became the battleground for Satan and God. A man, regardless of his conduct, might experience the lust in his heart as a gnawing anguish. His struggle against the sins of the heart—now included as part of the sins of the flesh—would last throughout his life. Without "works" to measure his righteousness, he could never be sure; he must ever suspect his conscience, inspect his thoughts, respect holy virtues.

Puritan Attitudes Toward Lust

Painful examples of the operations of the sin of lust on the hearts of men are found among the Puritans. The consciences of these men of divine election were plagued by thoughts of sin—especially those of lust. Michael Wigglesworth (1631-1705), both a paragon and prig of Puritan virtue, provides a diary that testifies throughout to the torments of the heart that accompanied even a relatively modest and abstemious life. Worrying whether God does indeed love him, Wigglesworth looks into his deepest emotions: ". . . when I look upon my vile ungrateful impenitent whorish heart I am ashamed to think that god should love or owne me. I abhor myself o Lord for these renewed incurable distempers. I could even take vengeance of my cursed heart that is so deceitful and desperately wicked in impenitent departure from god."[41] The involuntary nocturnal ejaculations that came upon him occasionally caused considerable anguish and prayer for relief: "I found myself much overborn with carnal concupiscence nature being suppressed for I had not had my afflux in 12 nights. Friday night it came again without any dream that I know of. Yet after it I am still inclined to lust. The lord help me against it and against discouragement by it and against temptations of another nature and disquietments." Devoting a special section of his diary to "Considerations against sensuality, and delighting more in the creature than in god," Wigglesworth gave vent to the scope of apprehensions that afflicted him: "The formidable face of this sin sometimes makes me a terrour to my self." Sensuality and lust "argues a Carnall, fleshly, sensual, spirit debasing it self below the sphear of a reasonable creature, much more of a son of God." Holding a fellow human in greater love in one's heart than God was, to Wigglesworth and other Puritan divines, a traitorous offense. "This is spirituall adultery," wrote Wigglesworth, "and it provokes the Lord to Jelousy . . ." Wigglesworth went on to detail a hierarchy of offenses of this kind and to excoriate himself for his guilt:

> . . . I can intertain dalliance with strange lovers and shut christ my Lord out of dores . . . I can let the creature into my affections, but find no room for the god of glory. Not to love christ were an amazing prodigious sin, but to love the creature with that affection which is due onely to christ this were spirituall adultery and falsness in the covenant; but to have love to the creature and communion therewith, and not to have love to christ and fellowship with him: Heaven and earth may be astonished that such a thing should be found in a heart that had ever tasted the sweetness of christ. doth falseness in the Covenant with man deserv both temporall and eternal death? oh then the guilt that this falshood leaves upon me!

Although the struggle to maintain the Christian virtues against the assaults of lust and other sins was not simply a sublimation of sexual and filial experiences, much of that struggle functioned to divert sexual energy and impulse to a higher goal. Regarding both God and sex as natural and subject to their respective obligations, the Puritans suspected human affection of being a rival to that for God.[42] Puritan ministers warned their flocks not to love one another too much, for the highest love was reserved for God himself. The conflation of *eros* and *agape* in Puritan thought no doubt proceeded from the difficulties ordinary individuals had in sorting out the nature and objects of their emotions, feelings, and yearnings. So devout a divine as Cotton Mather was suspicious and guilty about the love he bore for his children, the indulgence of his sexual impulses in three marriages, and the corruptions of his own body. He sought solace in the intensity of his worship of God, prostrating himself six and later seven times a day in his study, begging, beseeching, and pleading. "The diseases of my soul are not cured until I arrive to the most unspotted Chastitie and Puritie," he wrote at the age of fifty-five, having already buried two wives and married for the third time two years earlier. Yet he hastened to add "I do not apprehend, that Heaven requires me uterlie to lay aside my fondness for my lovelie Consort."[43]

Historians and sociologists have recently made much of their findings that the Puritans were less ascetic and abstemious than later generations had supposed.[44] Significant as these discoveries are, they tend to overlook the brooding conscience and consciousness of sin that characterized Puritan life. Faced not only with their unwillingness to rely on "works" for salvation but also by the challenge of the Indian civilization and its even more naturalistic and seemingly hedonistic attitude toward sensuality, the Puritan conscience could hide its inner turmoil over sin from public view.[45] Lust might invade the heart, subvert the love of God, direct its yearnings and cravings toward a fleshly being. Even if no evil conduct were to follow from this forbidden appetite, it was sin nonetheless. Constant prayer, the exhortation to continue the struggle, and the confinement of one's sinful confessions to a secret diary are adequate testimonies to the vitality of lust and the agonizing self-appraisals it cost.

THE SOCIAL ORGANIZATION OF LUST

Sociology has not advanced very far beyond the Puritans in the understanding of lust. Indeed, much of American sociology conceals a concern for the sinful aspects of lust beneath an amoral analysis of the positive effects (*functions*) of monogamous marriage, nuclear family formations, and heterosexual activity for modern industrial societies. Sociologist William J. Goode provides a fine example of sophisticated current sociological thought on the subject. A foremost authority on love and marriage in American, European, and non-Western societies, Goode observes that what he calls "love patterns" are fitted in various ways into the practices of mate selection in almost all societies. Love itself is defined by Goode as "a strong emotional attachment, a cathexis, between adolescents or adults of opposite sexes, with at least the components of sex desire and tenderness."[46] Lust is hidden below the surface of this definition and chastened by feelings of attachment and tenderness. Moreover, love, in this definition, not only compounds sexual desire with a softened affection but also limits its expression to persons of the opposite sex. By ignoring the term lust altogether, and concentrating attention on love, Goode and other American sociologists avoid a most important issue—the social organization of erotic attachments and sexual expression.

Love is in fact but one of the elements in the societal organization of controls over lust. The emphasis on love rather than lust and the direction of romantic attachments toward members of the *opposite* sex are socially contrived modifications of an otherwise free-floating and potentially promiscuous sexuality. Left to govern itself, lust might shatter social relationships, sabotage societal continuity, and subvert society altogether. In terms of the current jargon of the sociology of the family: love is functional, lust is dysfunctional. In the discussion that follows four basic questions, each concerned with the social organization of lust are answered: (1) What are the general dysfunctions of lust? (2) How are these dysfunctions mitigated by channeling lust into acceptable structural arrangements? (3) How do these dysfunctions vary in society, culture, and social setting? (4) Can lust be halted altogether, successfully sublimated, or, on the other hand, liberated from any inhibitions with societal and personal impunity?

The Asocial Consequences of Lust

Lustful cravings are likely to arise anywhere, anytime, and toward any object—human, animal, or ideal. The Christian theologians, convinced that man's affection should be primarily expressed in the love of God, worried, wondered, and warned about the affections toward fellow humans. Societies organized on a basis of traditional clan systems, such as that of prerevolutionary China, believed that a man's primary obligations were to his lineage brothers and suspected the subversive power of love, accusing it of undermining suprafamilial duties and rebuking those who fell under its sway. American marriage counselors, concerned over the possibility that a man's affection for his wife might interfere with his duties to his career, urge that marital love be confined to conjugal relations and domestic interests. In each case, the general point is the same: lust, whether ennobled by love or not, can consume the totality of interests, activities, and energies of those overwhelmed by it. Once this has occurred, the contributions to society, or to that part of it to which the parties are attached, are diminished by the loss of the lustful parties' services. In the most general sense the various methods of social control employed to curb or channel lust are directed toward securing society against the losses entailed by lustful withdrawal.

Incest

Edward Westermarck was among the pioneers of sociological thought on familism and kinship who supposed that the taboo against inbreeding arose because of its negative biological effects. However, biological degeneration has not been proven.[47] It would seem more reasonable to look for the origins of this taboo in general societal needs. Augustine was among those who recognized the societal interest in preventing incest. As this fifth-century bishop observed, the fact that the offspring of the original pair took each other as mates was "a completely decent procedure under the pressure of necessity." However, in subsequent generations brother-sister marriage was outlawed in order to facilitate the enlargement and betterment of societal ties. "The aim was that one man should not combine many relationships in his one self, but that those connections should be separated and spread among individuals, and that in this way they should help to bind social life more effectively by involving in their plurality a plurality of persons." Fifteen hundred years before the functionalists had approached an explanation of the incest taboo, Augustine had outlined their argument. Augustine delineates the problem of role specification by concrete examples. The bar against sibling marriage began with the grandchildren of Adam and Eve, when for the first time cousins were available as spouses. Cousin marriage, rather than that of brothers and sisters, began the division of roles and the uniting of increasingly disparate elements in kinship.

> For marriage of brothers and sisters would at this stage mean that one man would be father, father-in-law and uncle to his own children. Similarly his wife would be mother, aunt and mother-in-law to the children she shared with her husband. And the children of the couple would be to each other not only brothers and sisters and spouses, but also cousins, as being the children of brothers and sisters.[48]

By encouraging their own children to seek mates from among their cousins rather than their siblings, the offspring of Adam and Eve began the process of establishing societal networks through kinship and of individuating the labors that pertain to familial and other relationships. Speaking of the particularity in avuncular relations, cousinhood, brotherhood, sisterhood, and parenthood, Augustine observes, "If those relationships were distributed singly to different persons they [that is, the marriages of Adam's and Eve's grandchildren] would have connected nine people, instead of three, to each of these persons. For then one man would have one person as his sister, another as his wife, another as his cousin, another as his father, another as his uncle, another as his father-in-law, another as his mother, another as his aunt, another as his mother-in-law." Nonincestuous marriage, then, rather than constricting the responsibilities of the wedded pair into an ever-diminishing circle, would widen their connections to diverse and discrete others, and bind their services to these others through the obligations of kinship. As Augustine concludes, "Thus the social tie would not be confined to a small group but would extend more widely to connect a large number with the multiplying links of kinship."

The prohibition on intrafamilial marriage is supposed to aid in the inhibition of lust. Some recent theorists have supposed that the familiarity of a joint and common upbringing within the same household would dampen sexual arousal, but this depends on the sexual or asexual character of that familiarity.[49] Augustine allowed for "a certain mysterious and inherent sense of decency" which he said existed "in human conscience." This sense is, in turn, applied to those women who are related to men by kinship, and by that fact alone owed a certain measure of honor and respect. Such a woman, Augustine concluded, "is shielded from the lust (and lust it is, although it results in procreation) which, as we know, brings blushes even to the chastity of marriage."[50] However, neither Augustine's mysterious sense of decency nor Westermarck's reliance on the asexual functions of familiarity have proved fully effective against carnal cravings. Despite the fact that sexual aversion is encouraged among siblings in most Occidental cultures, incest—brother-sister coitus, and parent-child sexual relationships—is still to be found, if rarely.

The modern functional theory of incest is dependent on the resolution and sublimation of lustful desires among all members of the nuclear family. According to this theory, which seems most applicable to middle-class families in urban, industrial societies, both boys and girls develop erotic attachments to their parents and might also become aroused by one another as well, but these lustful trajectories can and usually are inhibited, suppressed, and ultimately rechanneled into interests in and the development of attachments to nonfamilial members of the opposite sex.

The societal interest in coopting the education, labor, and skills of males and ensuring the domestic and maternal duties of females finds repeated and varied expression in the popular culture and mass media. Sons and daughters are encouraged in countless ways to seek romantic love and erotic satisfactions among the strangers whom they encounter in school, neighborhood, church, and recreational facilities. Parents and especially mothers are urged to gradually relinquish their affectionate attachments to and controls over their own children. In reciprocation children learn to seek recognition for their personal attractiveness among outsiders and rewards for their intelligence and skills among teachers and employers. Discouraged from incest and homosexuality by positive incentives and negative sanctions, young people are chastened with respect to these two modes of lustful conduct. That at any rate is the societal ideal. However, as Parsons points out, this ideal will be realized only if the family members are not given free reign over their own erotic impulses. Specifically, Parsons points to the necessity for a mother "to control her own regressive needs," and for siblings to find objects of sexual gratification outside the family and of the opposite sex.[51] Failings in these arenas of emotional attachment and conduct leave room for incest and homosexuality to arise, that is, for forbidden patterns of lust.

Dyadic Withdrawal

As Parsons points out, "Incest is a withdrawal from [the] obligation to contribute to the formation and maintenance of supra-familial bonds on which major economic, political and religious functions of the society are dependent." However, incest is not the only form of withdrawal injurious to society. The involvements of loving or passionate couples with each other, their sense of exclusive obligation to one another, their constant and secluded intimacy, their isolation from all others, threaten all those collectivities, organizations, and interests to which each member might contribute.[52] Erotic attachments, with their potential to monopolize and control the entire economy of energy and interest, bid fair to drive out all other linkages or to so dampen a person's ardor for anything but his or her paramour that all social value is lost. For this reason societies with quite diverse cultures have sought to weaken the opportunities and inhibit the passions that lead to such departures from duty.

Societal regulations about dyadic withdrawal arise from the fear that, left to themselves, individuals would respond to their impulses and needs without regard to the social consequences. Carnal cravings of each person for the other and concomitant feelings of exclusivity and sexual monopoly are prime causes for the lovers to fall back on one another. In Occidental industrial societies where free choice of mate, relative privacy in the period of premarital courtship, and neo-local residency have only recently come to prevail, the chances for this to occur are frequent. On the other hand, the onerous demands of making a living in a society that is at least nominally a meritocracy, requiring individual exertion and rewarding ambitious effort, militate against a considerable amount of exclusivity. Sexuality and its demands tend to be sequestered in the household, scheduled in accordance with other demands on time and energy, or snatched from free time in affairs and "one-night stands." In addition, individuals are hedged about with a peer group subculture and its watchfulness during adolescence and young adulthood, married in a public ceremony that testifies at least implicitly to their social obligations, permitted a temporary withdrawal from society in a "honeymoon" that by its very special status reminds them of its singularity and invites their return, and intruded upon by in-laws, relatives, the birth of their own children, neighbors, and, in varying degrees of intensity and activity, the community at large.

In those societies where an individual is bound to suprafamilial sodalities such as a clan, there is a tendency to separate lust, romantic love, and family obligations. Lust might be satisfied by an open or grudgingly tolerated acceptance of the male's right to visit prostitutes, have concubines, or consort with a mistress. Irrational and uncontrollable love is officially scorned, ridiculed, and feared for its potential subversion of clan solidarity. Rational self-controlled affection is desirable but not necessary. Procreation for the benefit of lineage continuity is satisfied by the birth of children from arranged marriages. Where patriliny, patrimony, and patrilocality prevail, women are especially suspect for their seductive powers and danger to clan solidarity. Loveless marriages are encouraged—the parties may not even have met before the nuptial night—and husbands are warned about the dangers of excessive intimacy with or domination by their wives.

The dangers of lust-dominated dyadic withdrawal are the same whether the loving couple are of the same or opposite sex. The "marriages" of homosexual males or females constitute a threatened withdrawal of the services of one or both men from the workaday world and of both females from procreative maternal duties. Of course none of these possibilities will necessarily come to pass. Both parties to a homosexual union might hold down full-time jobs, lesbians might still bear and rear children, and women who work can also carry on a marriage of any kind. Nevertheless, it is noteworthy how much the availability and employment of male or female prostitutes, the temporary liaisons of a single or a series of one-time passionate encounters and widespread if clandestine promiscuity promote and reinforce the societal opposition to dyadic withdrawal.

EXCURSUS: THE DRAMA OF SIN AND DYADIC WITHDRAWAL IN DANTE'S *INFERNO*

That lust might lead to overwhelming craving for the body and soul of the other, and to suspension of all other duties, occupations, obligations, and services, serves as one *leitmotiv* in the drama of netherworldly reality presented by Dante in the *Inferno*.[53] Presented as a "soul journey" through hell, purgatory, and paradise, the *Divine Comedy* provides a unique theatrical tour and an unusually prescient sociological and historical commentary on the sins and virtues. It is beyond the scope of the present discussion to examine the entire structure and analysis of sin in that great work.[54] Suffice it for the present to discuss certain elements of lust as they appear in the *Inferno* in relation to the issues of societal obligation and libidinal withdrawal. Our cases are drawn from the tales of Brunetto de Latini, a renowned teacher and sodomite, residing in the third ring of the seventh circle of the inferno—that reserved for sinners against God, nature, and art—and of Paolo Malatesta and Francesca da Rimini, slain lovers, sentenced to the second circle of hell—that reserved for sinful sensualists—and to an eternal buffeting in the whirlwind of lust. In both instances, instances that by no means exhaust Dante's discussion of lust, a specific element of departure from duty accompanies the lustful activities for which the sinners are punished.

Brunetto de Latini, a teacher of Dante and a much-honored man of letters in his day, is presented with sympathy and respect by the author, even though he is found among the sodomites. That this teacher should be so placed by his respectful student has long been a matter of wonder to scholars who examine the poem. A related question also arises: why is sodomy, a sin against nature, located together with the sins against God and art several circles *below* the sin of unrepentant heterosexual lust but *above* the first ring of the eighth circle of hell, that reserved for panders and seducers of women? One answer is possible from interpreting the reply given by Brunetto to Dante's question about the background of his companions in Hell:

> Know then in brief, all these were scholars bred
> And clerks, and upon earth great fame they knew,
> And all by the same soilure forfeited.
>
> *Inferno* XV:106-108

Historically, the charge of sodomy was quite commonly brought against teachers and clerics in Dante's day. Their close association with boys and youths, their awesome manner and outward morality, and their required celibacy and dedication to church and learning put them into a position where sexual seduction was very possible—and even more likely suspected.[55] Roger Bacon is reported to have complained of teachers' homosexual seductions of students in Paris; the preface to *Wyklif's Bible* laments similar practices at Oxford; and Philip le Bel accuses the Templars of sodomy above all his other charges against them.[56] That education might subject pupils—especially boys—to all manner of debauchery, licentiousness, excess, and lust was a common fear after the establishment of academies and colleges in Europe and America.[57] Perhaps Dante's familiarity with the facts of student life kept him from too great an outrage at this particular sin; perhaps, as some critics have hinted, he harbored similar feelings toward youths himself, but these suggestions alone do not explain the precise location of sodomy in hell or Dante's sympathy toward his teacher's plight.[58]

Recalling that sodomy resides together with sins against God and art, it is not unreasonable to note the significance of its practitioners' occupations. Dante's poem speaks to the degradation meted out to persons who have fallen away from a cognitive and higher calling in order to pursue and be consumed by a fleshly and lower craving. Unrepentant sinners sentenced to an eternity in hell, they now lament the particular retribution for their sinful lust—their banishment from intellectual life and pedagogic service. Brunetto de Latini gives poignant expression to this pitiable exile when he parts from Dante with a final request for remembrance:

> But let my Treasure (and I ask no more)
> Wherein I live still, be commended thee.
>
> *Inferno* XV:119-120

The reference is to Latini's greatest work, *Il Tesoro* (*The Treasure*), an encyclopedia of history, ethics, and rhetoric. Thus, in his works of scholarship from which he derived his earthly fame—and, incidentally, that same source of fame from which he gave instruction to Dante— Brunetto had a claim to honor and even virtue. Moreover, he had an honorable claim on others, who would obtain enlightenment and guidance from his teachings. All this, however, was sacrificed to lustful impulse. What arouses sympathy tinged with horror in Dante, and mitigates the damnation, is the fact that Brunetto and his companions in hell combine in themselves the apex of reason and the nadir of fleshly desire. Sodomy to Dante is a vice that expels the best of men from human nature, but more practically it also exiles them from that human association wherein the better part of their character might find room for service and even valor. But for Brunetti it is too late to do any more than lament his own sinking to such a base and worldly vice. To Dante he gives a piece of advice obtained from his own experience:

"If thou follow thy star,
  Thou'lt fail not glorious harbour at the end,
  If in the beautiful life I did not err.
And had Fate chosen my own years to extend,
  Seeing Heaven did on thee so benignly look,
  I had been with thee to hearten and befriend . . ."

Inferno XV:55–60

Brunetto and his companions are spared from the eighth circle of hell where panders and seducers are tormented by demons, perhaps because the higher calling of these former teachers elevates them above the mean viciousness of those who derive financial gain from catering to the lust of others. However, Paolo and Francesca are above both the sodomites and the seducers. Theirs is not a crime against nature, but rather a milder felony in Dante's hierarchy—the sin of simple lust and ordinary sensuality.

Briefly, the story of this tormented couple is this: Francesca, the daughter of Guido Vecchio da Polenta, Lord of Ravenna, is given as wife to Gianciotto Malatesta, a deformed cripple, in order to end a feud between the two houses. Paolo, the handsome brother of Gianciotto, is sent as proxy to secure the marriage contract. Francesca, mistaking him for her intended husband, falls in love with him right away. After the forced marriage of Francesca to Gianciotto, the now devoted lovers continue their illicit affair. Several years later they are discovered together by the cuckolded cripple, who, enraged at this betrayal by both wife and brother, kills them.[60] For their sin, Francesca and Paolo are sentenced to the first circle of hell, where, together with Semiramis, Queen of Assyria, Dido, lover of Aeneas, Helen of Troy and her lover

Paris, Achilles, Tristram, and "More than a thousand pair . . . whom love had power from life to tear," they must forever whirl

> corrupted spirits . . . rapt in air
>   To and fro, down, up, driven in helpless plight,
>   Comforted by no hope ever to lie
>   At rest, not even to bear a pain more light.
>
> *Inferno* V:42–44

Still we must probe further to learn the precise nature of their sin, its special location in hell, and the reason for its peculiar mode of punishment. Although Paolo and Francesca have betrayed Gianciotto, it is he rather than they who is punished for that particular sin, for as Francesca tells Dante:

> He that sought
> And spilt our life—Cain's hell awaits him now.
>
> *Inferno* V:106–107

Gianciotto has been sentenced to the first ring of the ninth and lowest circle of hell—that reserved for traitors to kin. Since Francesca and Paolo might have been charged with a betrayal equal to that of Gianciotto and in fact the one that enraged the poor hunchback into committing the murder for which he is eternally damned, Dante must have had some very different idea in mind when he placed the pair of lovers at the gateway to hell's deep cavern.

The second circle of hell is reserved for those who have committed crimes of *sensual* incontinence. For Dante incontinence might take form in gluttony, miserliness and prodigality, anger and sullenness, and heresy. For each of these a circle is reserved in the inferno, but they all rank below that of sensuality. Apparently it was the peculiar sympathy he had for *amor* that led Dante to place it so near the entrance to the eternal home of the damned.

Dante had been in his youth one of the *fedele d'amore*, a cult of young poets who had pledged themselves to be "love's lieges," faithful to their mistresses and to the sentiments and illusions that love inspires.[60] Crucial to Dante's reasoning, and to the argument presented in this interpretation, is the relation of love to reason. Vergil, Dante's guide through the inferno, represents the Aristotelian ideal of reason in the drama. In the second circle of hell, love blinds man to reason. It is precisely this aspect of libidinal withdrawal—departure from reason and the higher cognitive faculties—that condemns love at the very moment that it also excuses man, or at least some men, for succumbing to it.

The pathos and power of love dominate the story of Paolo and Francesca. When Francesca is asked to tell her story, she relates it exclusively in terms of Paolo's and her own bondage to love.

> Love, that in gentle heart so quickly wakes,
>> Took him with this fair body, which from me
>> Was torn: the way of it still hurts and aches.
>
> Love, that to no loved one remits his fee,
>> Took me with joy of him, so deep in-wrought,
>> Even now it hath not left me, as thou dost see.
>
> Love led us both to one death.
>
>> *Inferno* V:100–106

Francesca and Paolo have been blindly obedient slaves to the love that moved them, neither thinking about or worrying over the consequences. Lust whirled them out of their senses; in retribution they are sentenced to the whirlwind that their particular sin has reaped. Pander to their unquenchable appetite for one another was the medieval romance about the love between Lancelot and Guinevere. Dante here speaks to a situation and materials that permit lust to appear, take charge of the lovers' lives, plunge them into a passion that soon overwhelms them, and ultimately hurl them into an infernal hurricane. The situation is unchaperoned isolation of young people, precisely those subject to lust's seductive powers; the materials are fictional romances, poetic and rhapsodic works that entice their readers to imitate idealized lovers and experience rapture. As Francesca explains to Dante, when he asks her "How did Love vouchsafe proof of what he is, And of the obscure yearnings make you wise?"[61]

> One day, together, for pastime, we read
>> Of Launcelot, and how Love held him in thrall.
>> We were alone, and without any dread.
>
> Sometimes our eyes, at the word's secret call,
>> Met, and our cheeks a changing colour wore.
>> But it was one page only that did all.
>
> When we read how that smile, so thirsted for,
>> Was kissed by such a lover, he that may
>> Never from me be separated more
>
> All trembling kissed my mouth. The book I say
>> Was a Galahalt to us, and he beside
>> That wrote the book. We read no more that day.
>
>> *Inferno* V:127–138

Dante's analysis of lust, love, adultery, and sodomy both anticipates the sociological understanding of love's subversive power and hints at the several modes by which that power might be curbed. The lust that is ennobled by the feeling of love holds its fallen victims in servitude to itself. It makes their all-consuming passion a personal affair. But it is precisely this potential for departure from worldly matters that makes such involvements a danger to society. Paolo and Francesca, finding opportunities to be alone together, give into the sentiments of the moment. Their affair ripens into a passion. They remove themselves from the mundane and ordinary activities that worldly life requires. (The real Francesca neglected her daughter; Paolo, his two sons, and perhaps his occupational duties as well.) Even when they resume the daily routines that circumscribe and shield their illicit adventure, they do so with less alacrity, interest, and purpose. Lust has drained them of their energies for ordinary life. Paolo and Francesca have obligations to the families to which they belong. The marriage of Francesca and Gianciotti was contracted in order to seal a truce between these families. Paolo's and Francesca's affair threatens this interfamilial peace; moreover, it incarnates the lovers' wanton disregard for matters outside of their own immediate happiness.

"Left to themselves," writes Philip Slater, "human beings would mate entirely in response to instinctual demands and psychological affinity."[62] The attraction of youths for their older teachers, the romance that ripens between a nubile maiden and the handsome courtier who comes to represent his brother's matrimonial suit are two examples of the combinations of lust's "instinctual demands" and "psychological affinities" that endanger the social order. Everywhere, in fact, attempts are made to inhibit lust's drive for libidinal withdrawal, to channel lust into safe waters, to ensure that however lust arises, it will not conquer. The policy of censoring literature that flows from Dante's hostility toward medieval romances is but one type of societal weapon against lust. Unbridled lust is the gateway to hell, and that is precisely where Dante has placed those who commit that sin.

THE DESUBLIMATION OF LOVE

Lustful cravings appear to be ubiquitous among humankind. It is no wonder then that attempts are made to restrain, hinder, or arrest its development; direct, supervise, and control its objectives; sublimate, enhance, ennoble, or hide its inequities. Among the modes by which lust is thus controlled are two general directives—the first seeks to treat the exalted state of love as an illusion, denigrating it as a product of weakness of mind or arrested character development; the second seeks to push that element in the population most inclined to lustful passion, that is, youngsters, into appropriate role behavior and status slots so that the discharge of their libidinal energies will occur within socially acceptable channels. The first directive aims to check libidinal withdrawal; the second to assure societal members that lust is not undermining the social structure.

The Denigration of Love:
Sociological and
Anthropological Views

Love patterns include but do not exhaust all possibilities in the romantic love complex. The latter is said by Goode to be found in the modern urban United States, Northwestern Europe, Polynesia, and in a special form known as "courtly love" among the European nobility of the eleventh and twelfth centuries. Whereas *love patterns* exist wherever popular ideology and social custom hold that love is a permissible and expected prelude to marriage, a *love complex* exists wherever it is believed shameful to marry without being in love. In societies characterized by a love complex, "falling in love" is the most desirable precondition for marriage, and romance is expected to arise out of and accompany courtship.[63] Put another way, in a society where the romantic love complex reigns supreme, a couple who did not marry on the basis of love would be expected to provide an excuse or justification for their conduct; in a society where love has a more variable pattern such a marriage would likely go unremarked.

We should expect that where unbridled lust might arise spontaneously and frequently, or where romantic involvements are likely to result in disastrous consequences for the social structure, that there will be movement and policy to dampen its ardor. Hence in clan societies like that of China, romantic love is often an object of ridicule, especially when it arises between a man and his wife, or as a part of a supervised and arranged courtship. In societies like that of the contemporary United States, where young people are formally free to find their own mates, where romantic love is a popular ideal celebrated in song and story, and where—in the minds of elders—its free-floating operation bids fair to undermine careers, wreck family relations, and damage the psyche, it is remarkable how much expertise has been brought to bear on checking its flow and denying its reality.

Occidental anthropologists, sociologists, and psychologists have felt it necessary from time to time to speak disparagingly of romantic love. Thus Ralph Linton reduces it to "occasional violent emotional attachments between persons of opposite sex, . . . psychological abnormalities to which our own culture has attached an extraordinary value . . ."[64] Margaret Mead extolled the virtues of sexual culture on the island of Manu'a, where premarital sex was permissible and fun, but where young people completed their period of experimentation by willingly accepting an arranged marriage bereft of romantic attachment. In contrast to the sometimes frenetic situations faced by romantically involved young people in the United States, in this Samoan society "adolescence represented no period of crisis or stress, but was instead an orderly developing set of slowly maturing interests and activities." If the romantic love complex idealizes a single love object, whom one hopes and aches to meet, fall in love with, and then marry, to live happily ever after, the Manu'an "girls' minds were [by contrast] perplexed by no conflicts, troubled by no philosophical queries, beset by no remote ambitions." Instead of longing for romance and adventure, for the female Manu'an it was enough to "live as a girl with many lovers as long as possible and then to marry in one's own village, near one's own relatives, and to have many children . . ."[65]

Geoffrey Gorer, a British anthropologist, has proposed a reorganization of society and social values so that "the physical changes of puberty and adolescence will not entail either social or psychological disturbance."[66] In his thinly veiled assault on the evils and excesses of lust and romantic love, Gorer calls for the rearing of children in "conjoint or extended households," so that "ambivalence which is almost inevitable when children are raised in nuclear families" will be avoided. For Gorer it is the oedipal complexes and incestuous ambivalence that nuclear families inadvertently foster and encourage. "In . . . nuclear families it is almost inevitable that the father or mother is the focus of both intense love and hate—for young children must inevitably be thwarted . . ." The remedy for this excessive discharge of libido is the division of paternal and maternal roles among a wider network of persons. Such a respecification of roles would have the effect of diminishing the intensity of emotions; "and when the child grows up it is much less likely to expect an intense romantic relationship with potential lovers or spouse." By diffusing adolescent emotional energy over a range of kin-connected persons, Gorer hopes both to suppress parent-child revolt and dampen affective and sensual feeling in general. Adolescents "should not be treated as though they were different sorts of creatures from adults," he continues. Opposed to conceptions of children as either innocent or wicked, Gorer urges that sexuality be treated as enjoyable, "as a good meal is enjoyable," but "basically not very serious." Not quite an advocate of "the easy sexuality of the Samoans and Lepchas," he proposes instead a general "lowering of emotional intensity throughout the whole society." Stressing the need to reduce emotionality in general, Gorer in fact suggests a policy for the containment of lust.

Sociologists have also found ways to denigrate love. Typically their reasoning is like that of Dante, who observed that love is accompanied by a flight from reason. However, rather than showing concern for societal damage because of excessive romantic commitments by the young and able-bodied, sociologists have been agitated about the unstable effects of love on marriage. Mowrer comes closest to relating love to lust when he insists that "All the 'love' elements have their origin in sex . . ." He goes on to apply a "Freudian" interpretation to love objects, suggesting that individuals fall in love with persons who are either parent substitutes or personal projections. Regardless, however, Mowrer holds that "love develops suddenly and tends to burn out in a short while," and that therefore it is a poor foundation for lasting marriage. The seductive subtleties of women in attracting men and arousing sexual interest in themselves are spoken of scathingly by this representative of the "Chicago School" of sociological thought. And Mowrer confesses that he is baffled by the "loyalties . . . of a wife to the man with whom she has had all her sex contacts and for whom she has borne children even though he may have deserted her for another woman."[67]

That the idealization of romantic love is but a youthful response to a recent popular ideology is the position taken by Martinson in his denigrative sociological approach. Romantic love is treated as an element in one of America's several "sexual revolutions." As part of a revolt against tradition in the 1920s there appeared a "full flowering of a folk belief in romantic love." Prior to the Great Depression, Martinson argues, there was a brief "period of innocence" during which "America provided fertile soil in which romantic love could thrive."[68] Romantic love is contrasted with the bonds of fidelity called for in the "Judaic-Christian marriage model." The latter ensured a lasting relationship, but romantic love only required remaining together while the passion lasted. Those gripped by "passionate love" became slave[s] of love," devoted to their "soul mates." "Whether soul mates remained true to each other," Martinson continues, "was not within the control of the lovers; they could not predict whether their love for each other would flourish or die." Moreover, lovers enslaved to their passions might not marry, but only carry on with one another in rapturous pursuit of pleasure. Martinson concludes that "the notion that man is a slave of love is inconsistent with a view of man as rational and has its roots in romantic love, not in humanism." Clearly preferring that marital form wherein "God's presence in the marriage resulted in a mysterious union, making the two 'one flesh,'" Martinson hardly disguises his belief that sociology should identify with "Persons in positions of leadership [who] have felt constrained to support a traditional conservative sex code."

Whether romantic love is love at all or something else entirely is a much debated question in sociology. The debate itself helps cast doubt on the phenomenon. According to Willard Waller love is a kind of propulsive force that results from a blocking of the sex impulse.[69] Kephart insists that "sexual love is *not* romantic love," wishing to reserve the latter for strong emotional attachments to a person of the opposite sex, the idealization of that person, and a masked physical attraction to that person, "the fulfillment of which is reckoned by touch."[70] And

Farber, who points out that in "American society love is supposed to be a prelude to marriage," finds it difficult to explain just what love is. He goes on to note how much of a part chance plays in romantic love, and he urges long courtships before marriage so that individuals might learn to come to terms with one another on matters that transcend romance. A brief period of premarital intimacy is dangerous, he argues: "Following a telescoped courtship, the couple may or may not develop a workable mutual accommodation."[71]

Still another approach that seeks to subordinate passion to reason, and thus resolve any difficulties in marital adjustment, requires the rationalization of love and courtship. Prominent here is the work of Ernest W. Burgess and his followers, who treat love as an orientation that should emerge gradually out of a long and carefully conducted courtship carried on by persons of equal status, common social backgrounds, and similar personalities.[72] Romantic love, on the other hand, "has been glorified by the mass-communication media. . . . At the same time, romanticism has been decried as the cause of many incompatible marriages."[73]

The strategy followed by Burgess and his followers is first to distinguish love, affection, and sexuality from one another, and then to reintegrate them in a carefully plotted appropriate course toward a stable marriage. Having disposed of romantic love as a product packaged and publicized by the mass communications industry, Burgess and his followers remind their readers that there "have been no systematic investigations of the relationship between love and sexual drives . . ." Affection, different from love, is then introduced as "an emotion involving liking, being fond of, having a firm attachment to, and desiring to be in the presence of the object of one's affections." Accordingly, affection is more rational than love because "the physical expressions of an affectional feeling, such as kissing, embracing, and caressing may be associated with either a nonpassionate or passionate sexual desire." However, since a "feeling of love and affection is possibly the most important feature of the courtship process," love is readmitted to the premarital process, but this time under sociocultural chaperonage. Heterosexual love is redefined as the outcome of a relationship involving six interrelated processes—establishment of rapport, self-revelation, mutual dependence, the reciprocal meeting of personality needs, idealization of the other, and the development of adequate sexual behavior. There is a hint but not a direct statement that these processes occur as a sequence of orderly stages, culminating in the emergence of love. The six processes are said to be "interdependent and [they] tend to reinforce each other. Together they result in the development of love and affection." Thus lust and passion are chastened by a rationalized developmental model calling for a slow and gradual growth of love. At the finale of this lengthy process "adequate sexual behavior" becomes "socially approved sexual behavior," a transformation that requires integrating "the biological sexual drive with cultural definitions of sexual expression." Curbed by culture and leashed to a prescribed courtship cycle, passion is inhibited, reason is consequently restored, and marriages are assured of greater stability. Thus does sociology provide a remedy for lust.

The Denigration of Love: Psychoanalytic Views

Psychoanalysis has also desublimated the exalted image of love. Most notable is Freud's discussion of degradation in erotic life, ostensibly an explanation of psychical impotence in men, but in fact a much broader analysis of civilization and its sexual discontents. Central to unraveling the etiology of male impotence, Freud argues, is an understanding of the process whereby "normal" heterosexuality emerges. Part of this normal development is love for the sex object. Love, Freud points out, unites two currents of feeling—the tender-affectionate and the sensual. Thus love is a compound of lust and tenderness, elements that do not readily or easily fuse. Impotence, according to Freud, results when the current of sensual feeling in a man remains attached in the unconscious to incestuous objects or is fixated on incestuous fantasies. Product of an arrest in libidinal development, the man has been either frustrated in his choice of sexual object during early phases of adolescence, or excessively attracted to the objects of his infantile eroticism when he should have relinquished them, or both. However, this condition need not result in total impotence. Often enough, it finds expression in the liberation of lust from all ties to tenderness. Then the unfortunate victims are plunged into a hellish life on earth. "The erotic life of such people remains dissociated, divided between two channels, the same two that are personified in art as heavenly and earthly (or animal) love."[74] The fate of these unfortunates could not have been more painfully described: "Where such men love they have no desire and where they desire they cannot love."

Freud's explanation of impotence does not halt at the individual level. Rather, he sees an extension of psychic impotence in a condition he believes to be quite common in the Occident-psycho-anesthesia, the incapacity to take pleasure in the sexual act even when it can be performed, a condition, he believes, that arises from the same cause as impotence. Moreover, Freud attributes the prevalence of this condition to civilization itself. The "behavior in love of the men of present-day civilization bears in general the character of the psychically impotent type." The matter is this: the fusion of tenderness and sensuality into a single strain is accomplished by but a few "people of culture." For the others sexual satisfaction can only be achieved when the sex object is degraded, subjected to perversion, and regarded as of little worth. Hence, men's search for women of a low and inferior status for sexual satisfaction, their chaste idealization of wives, and women's association of sexuality with forbidden behavior. Both psycho-anesthesia in men and frigidity in women "are the consequence of the long period of delay between sexual maturity and sexual activity which is demanded by education for social reasons."

Freud has no institutional solution to offer. To those who look to psychoanalysis for aid "in the strenuous efforts being made in the civilized world at the present day to reform sexual life," he points out that psychoanalysis "cannot . . . predict whether other, perhaps even greater, sacrifices may not result from other institutions." Although the problem is civilization-wide, Freud believes that the fundamental issue is contained in the nature of sexuality itself. "However strange it may sound," he writes, "I think the possibility must be considered that something in the nature of the sexual instinct itself is unfavourable to the achievement of absolute gratification." Just as the genitals have not undergone any change in the direction of beauty over the long course of evolution, "so . . . today love, too, is in essence as animal as it ever was." Lust cannot be suppressed. "The erotic instincts are hard to mould; training of them achieves now too much, now too little." Culture acts on lust, but only at the cost of pleasurable sensuality, and the erotic instinct remains. The "persistence of the impulses that are not enrolled in adult sexual activity makes itself felt in an absence of satisfaction."

Social Controls Over Lust

Lustful stirrings arise in all people, and erotic attachments might focus on anyone. Everywhere marriage is a link not only of the wedded couple but of families, lineages, and status groups. And precisely for that reason, not only marriage but sexual expression in general is an objective of societal control mechanisms. Illustrative of the many ways in which lust can be circumscribed, channeled, or even closed off are such institutional arrangements as stigmatization, selectively enforced castration, child and arranged marriages, chaperonage, and controlled assortative mating (that is, mating on the basis of likeness).

Stigmatization and Degradation Ceremonies

Sexual practices considered reprehensible are likely to be censured in song, story, homiletics and counsel. In addition, practitioners are likely to be objects of scorn, ridicule, and prejudice. Thought is also fueled by actions: exclusionary practices, isolation, occupational and housing discrimination, legal restrictions, and police surveillance are likely modes of control and limitation. The obvious case is that of homosexuality, although other forms of erotic expression—such as group marriage and foot fetishes—have also been objects of popular prejudice and official repression.[75]

Homosexuality is a form of eroticism that tends to isolate sexuality from the network of social relationships to which it is intimately connected.[76] Only by fictive measures can the homosexual couple have relationships with in-laws, offspring, and the larger family structure. Because of this fact—and because of the sanctions against it that reinforce social ostracism—homosexual relationships all too often tend to be brief, secret, and filled with anguish.[77] Except where homosexuals are singled out for special purposes, or where they form an exclusive community outside of but symbiotically attached to the larger society, these liaisons are likely to take on the character of commercial transactions, impersonal relationships, a purely physical relief of a lustful urge.[78] Studies of the "tearoom trade," the prostitution ring involving the "boys of Boise," and the asocial relationships between "queers and peers" all speak to this double separation of sensuality from love and affection and of sexuality from social relationships.[79]

The social controls and sanctions against homosexuality follow the pattern of a continuous collective degradation ceremony.[80] Foremost among these is dehumanization. By treating homosexuals as persons who commit crimes against "nature," societal elites and opinion leaders have in effect provided justification for inhumane treatment. But it is by no means clear that homosexuality meets the requirements of sin.[81] The attribution of mental illness to homosexuals does not of itself reduce them to subhuman proportions, but it does stamp their attitudes and conduct with an indelible stigma.[82] Moreover, the stigma of mental illness—especially when combined with fears about pederasty[83]—provides the organizational grounds for official sanctions against them. As persons who might commit crimes because of their "uncontrollable" and "abnormal" passion, or who might "infect" the morally untutored if given the opportunity, homosexuals become subjects for surveillance, incarceration in prisons or asylums, and therapy designed to reorient their sexual perspective. The individual effects of widespread ideas about the "immoral," "unnatural," or "pathological" nature of homosexuality include a general fear among troubled young people that they might somehow be homosexually inclined. Thus, Mirra Komarovsky reports on cases of shy, rural, and introverted college men who confess to apprehensions about homosexuality when their heterosexual dating life is unsuccessful.[84] Such fears both indicate the status of homosexuality in the everyday world and also act often enough to push the young man into a more aggressive effort to assure himself of his own "masculinity."

However, the attempt to root out homosexuality not only fails to eliminate the practice but also inspires a reaction. The contemporary attempt to convince public opinion that homosexuality is a "life-style" deserving of recognition, protection, and civil rights is a case in point. Employing tactics of persuasion, reeducation, and public pressure, homosexual defense groups also utilize organizational strategies and political pressure to lift both social stigma and institutional discrimination.[85] The discovery, revelation, and composition of heretofore undisclosed histories and biographies aid in the attempt to legitimate homosexual status.[86] And, in some cases, efforts are made to effect a rupture and reversal of the linguistic universe of repressive rhetoric by taking over the hostile language of the heterosexual majority and employing it with self-approval, group pride, and aggressive display.[87]

Eunuchs, Celibates, and Castrati

Men who are potent and virile are eligible either for exploitation as counters in interfamilial courtship bargains or for independence as founders of families of procreation. They are, then, the subvertible objects of unbridled lust as well as the agents of continuity and stability in the social structure. Those who cannot or will not participate in coitus or procreation, on the other hand, constitute a class of men supposedly removed from the world of eroticism and specifically disobliged from family obligation. Their peculiar condition as outcasts makes them eligible for recruitment by those seeking undivided allegiance and absolute loyalty. The classic cases are court eunuchs appointed by ancient and Oriental despots to counteract the independence of state bureaucracies.[88] Once the opportunities open to eunuchs as pawns of imperial rulers became recognized, however, parents considered castrating sons in order to advance the social, economic and political interests of their family, and the value of eunuchs as unfailingly loyal servants of kings and emperors was compromised.[89] China provides a case in point. Offered a choice between continuing the lineage of an impoverished family or surrendering his "manhood" in return for a chance at wealth and status, many a poverty-stricken Chinese youth elected castration over starvation.[90] At times the number of castrated men applying to the Chinese imperial court outnumbered the available administrative positions by many thousands.[91] Those rejected for official positions returned to the countryside, where, bereft of kin and the butt of jokes, they became robbers and wastrels— vivid testimony to the outcast status of those who could not serve or procreate.

However, neither eunuchism nor impotence is an absolute bar to lust or eroticism. In traditional China, where studies of both the theory and technique of sensuality far exceed in number and quality those in the Occident, the "Tao of love and sex" explained how a "soft entry" method would permit coitus for those who could not have an erection.[92]

Among the eunuchs eroticism still found an outlet. Youthful guardians of the imperial seraglio became the playthings of the women; older eunuchs took wives and adopted children so as to continue their family line. Some men surrendered their genitalia only after forming a family and siring sons.[93] In India, eunuchs formed a separate band of commercial prostitutes that included transvestites and hermaphrodites, but it distinguished itself from the organizations of noncastrated male prostitutes and that of female women of the night.[94] By far the most interesting form of lustful craving occurred among certain Chinese eunuchs who sought magical and technical means to restore their virility. Lao Ts'ai, eunuch tax collector in Fukien, had virgin boys killed so that he could eat their brains and thereby regrow his lost genitalia. Wei Chung Hsien, who is among those eunuchs who reportedly did not lose his sexual potency after castration, committed the same act, devouring the brains of seven executed criminals. In addition to erotically inspired necromantic cannibalism, eunuchs employed artificial devices to replace their penes, and some were said to be still potent as a result.[95]

The attempt to eliminate lust and create a body of stigmatized, kinless lieges, eager to serve anyone who would reward their services, had one other unexpected effect. Castration tended to increase the appetite for the other deadly sins. Chinese eunuchs are uniformly reported to be proud and arrogant, gluttonous, melancholic, quick to take offense and become angry, envious of the condition of other males and jealous of their own perquisites, and greedy beyond measure.[96] And, as we have seen, the severing of scrotum and penis did not put an end to carnal craving; it only enhanced the search for innovative ways to give it expression.

Castration in the Occident occurred among some divines who sought purification, as a punishment for fornication, and as a pathological act of self-mutilation.[97] A milder, less visible remedy against fornication—sexual sterilization—has been employed to put an end to diseases or conduct alleged to be hereditary. Perhaps the most celebrated instance of punitive castration is that of the cleric and philosopher Peter Abelard (1079-1142) in twelfth-century Paris. Having seduced Heloise, an adolescent pupil into whose uncle's house he had been invited as a teacher, and fathered a child by her, a contrite Abelard offered her uncle a compromise wherein he would marry the girl if his marriage could be kept secret. The uncle accepted; Heloise, however, refused this proposal, reciting as grounds not only the offense to the Church involved, but also echoing, it would appear, the perspective on marriage and children of John Chrysostom—that parenthood was incompatible with philosophy, Abelard's real talent and his profession as well. Marriage and its attendant duties of father and husband, Heloise argued, would turn Abelard away from both devotion to God and his own calling. "And if you do not regard the privilege of cleric, at least uphold the dignity of a philosopher," she abjured him; "If you despise reverence for God, let the love of uprightness at least restrain your shamelessness." Abelard withdrew his suit for marriage with her, the child was given to his sister, and the devout lovers resumed their affair but much more discreetly and with less frequent visits. Her uncle, enraged at the breach of Abelard's promise, hired thugs to castrate Abelard.

Reflecting on his fate, Abelard came to see it as punishment appropriate to his sin. Before meeting Heloise, he recalled, he had been chaste and naive: "I had always detested unclean harlots and my constant attention to my books had kept me from frequent association with women of nobility and I knew little of society among women in the world."[98] At the height of his fame as a teacher, proud of his accomplishments, revered by his students, and envied by his rivals, Abelard believed he was cast down by both pride and lust: "I then enjoyed such renown and was so outstanding for my charm of youth that I feared no repulse by any woman whom I should deign to favor with my love." After he had been mutilated, Abelard bitterly reproached himself for succumbing to carnal pleasure and losing virility, fame, career, respect, and reputation thereby:

> I fell to thinking how great had been my renown and in how easy and base a way this had been brought low and utterly destroyed; how by a just judgment of God I had been afflicted in that part of my body by which I had sinned; how just was the betrayal by which he whom I had first betrayed paid me back; how my rivals would extol such a fair retribution; how great would be the sorrow and lasting grief which my mutilation would cause my parents and friends; with what speed the news of this extraordinary mark of disgrace would spread throughout the world; what course could I follow; how could I face the public to be pointed at by all with a finger of scorn, to be insulted by every tongue and to become a monstrosity and a spectacle to all the world.

Abelard attempted to retire to cloistered teaching, but neither his fame as a teacher nor his shame as a eunuch would give him peace. Accused of still harboring carnal lusts—and of consorting too much with nuns—he was the victim of innuendo, gossip, and plots for most of the remainder of his life.[99] Here again is an instance where castration did not bring to a close the carnality that the knife was supposed to cut off forever.

The famous *castrati* of Italian opera, internationally renowned during the eighteenth and nineteenth centuries, are a singular instance of institutionalized eunuchism in the Occident. These men did not surrender their sex organs to lower their sexual urges but rather to raise their vocal range. Following Paul's interdict—"*mulier taceat in ecclesia*"—women were forbidden to sing in church, and this prohibition extended itself to theater after opera began to flourish in Italy. Boys, male falsettists, and male sopranos might be employed to substitute for the required female voices, but the first were mischievous and untrustworthy, the second unavailable after the last of the renowned Spanish singers of that style died, and the third difficult to find outside the ranks of the mutilated. The emergence of an operatic form that employed the upper ranges of the musical scale put *castrati* in demand. A secret commerce in their creation and sale emerged, and until the middle of the nineteenth century—when a more masculine and vigorous musical style overwhelmed them—*castrati* were the toasts of the operatic world.

Carnality and eroticism haunted the lives of these singers. They were accused of perversions, denounced as homosexuals, and also charged with providing an abnormal but safe form of eroticism for wanton wives. Casanova, on a visit to Rome in 1762, describes the near irresistible attractiveness of one well-known *castrato*:

> In a well made corset, he had the waist of a nymph, and, what was almost incredible, his breast was in no way inferior, either in form or in beauty, to any woman's; and it was above all by this means that the monster made such ravages. Though one knew the negative nature of this unfortunate, curiosity made one glance at his chest, and an inexpressible charm acted upon one, so that you were madly in love before you realized it. To resist the temptation, or not to feel it, one would have had to be cold and earthbound as a German. When he walked about the stage . . . his step was majestic and at the same time voluptuous; and when he favoured the boxes with his glances, the tender and modest rolling of his black eyes brought a ravishment to the heart. It was obvious he hoped to inspire the love of those who liked him as a man, and probably would not have done so as a woman.[100]

Heterosexual love did not forsake *castrati* either. Women found them both fascinating and useful—since a sexual dalliance could not lead to pregnancy. Although some *castrati* desired to marry, both the Catholic and Lutheran churches forbade unions with eunuchs or impotent men, and those that persisted in their quests for lawful and holy matrimony were doomed to disappointment and heartbreak. Much discussed and lionized, the *castrati* of Rome and Milan suffered the outrages of a cruel fortune that had severed their sex but not their sensuality.

In the United States, castration, vasectomy, and salpingectomy (excision of the fallopian tubes) have been employed at various times as restraints on lust, hereditary conditions, and procreation. Fearful of what they believed were the uncontrollable lusts of black men for white women, white mobs murdered and mutilated blacks throughout the South from the close of the Reconstruction period to the middle of the twentieth century.[101] Thousands of men and boys were killed in these fear-and-hate-inspired orgies, almost always characterized by brutal acts of castration.[102] So overwhelming was the movement and cause for castration murder in the South that one sociologist sadly confessed to his belief that it must be part of the mores of the area.[103] Racial pride found its evil reflection in racial prejudice, and in the fear inspired thereby— namely, that blacks harbored a sinful and savage lust within themselves that could only be stamped out by a greater savagery that would overwhelm and kill both man and sin.

The eugenics movement and its supportive claims from biological and criminological sciences found expression in movements to sterilize allegedly unfit persons or populations. "Three generations of imbeciles are enough," said Justice Oliver Wendell Holmes, Jr., in upholding the order to sterilize one Carrie Buck, a feebleminded woman incarcerated in an asylum, who was both a mother of and a daughter to mental defectives.[104] The first proposal to sterilize criminals by vasectomy was made in 1899, the severing of the vas deferens being held superior to castration, since the aim of the procedure was to put an end to hereditary criminality, feeblemindedness, and carnal abuse. By 1915, thirteen states had enacted sterilization laws.[105] Most of them were later declared unconstitutional. Voluntary movements toward sterilization have been a feature of population control movements, but it must be noted that vasectomy and salpingectomy do not destroy the sexual urge, only the potentiality for issue that might arise from intercourse.

Chaperonage

The sexual urges that arise among the young might find any kind of outlet. Where marriages depend on female chastity and on status considerations among families, marriageable females are supervised and watched over, especially on those occasions when they might be alone with men. Especially appointed functionaries—the duenna, governess, or adult escort—chaperone such women whenever they appear in public places or when men come to court. In late nineteenth-century America, sisters were expected to set good examples of chaste womanhood for their brothers, to stay home in the evenings, and to watch over and instruct siblings. More particularly sisters were to guide and lead their brothers from the pathways of lustful temptation. Where chaperones were unavailable or formally free choice of mate recognized, self-controls were urged by adult leaders and mass media.[106] Thus in *fin de siècle* America, boys and girls were warned by manuals and ministers about the evils and terrors of the "solitary vice"—masturbation. Girls were urged never to encourage men in courtship, to consort with strangers, or to engage in careless and animalistic passions. The reading of novels was strongly opposed, as was "silly letter-writing" between adolescents, dancing, and the display of "unnatural affections" for persons of the same sex. Unchaperoned young people were expected to have absorbed an enormous dosage of fear and horror about their own bodies as well as those of other persons. They were also expected to appreciate the moral and medical dangers of unbridled sexuality, and to shun premature worldliness, erotic eccentricity, or sensual passion in their private and secluded moments. The degree to which such secondary chaperonage prevented lustful excess is unknown. That it inspired fear, ignorance, and emotional troubles is assured.

Assortative Mating

The objects of lust or love can be controlled by restricting the association of marriageable people to those whom they are eligible to marry. Two related patterns are relevant—isolation and segregation. The former is often a concomitant of sexual abstinence or postponement; the latter, of mating patterns that are limited to specifically designated population aggregates. In either case the blockage or channeling of lust is partly effective.

A fine instance of isolation as a group sanction against sexual expression is found among the celebrated heroes of the Chinese classical tale, *The Water Margin*.[107] A band of dedicated fighters and rebels, the Chinese heroes live according to a code emphasizing brotherhood and camaraderie, absolute devotion to the martial arts, social generosity, appetite for food and wine, and sexual puritanism.[108] However, since they are usually destitute and quite willing to commit robbery, arson, and murder, their only proof of having spiritual virtue above that of ordinary men comes from sexual abstinence.[109] They live in isolated areas apart from females, scorn to associate with prostitutes, ridicule any loving attachments toward women that arise among their compatriots, and gorge themselves on wine and meat when they are not fighting. Homosexuality can only be imputed to these men by prurient minds. Occasionally, however, one or another takes a mistress or a wife. But precisely because of their earlier vows to gymnastic training and the ascetic philosophy associated with it, these wives and sweethearts take second place. The elements of control here include the *sifu*, or martial arts master, who counsels his students against losing strength and energy through intercourse, and the peer group, who monitor each man's conduct.

Social segregation proceeds more efficiently when it is accompanied by spatial separation or enclosure, as is the case in South Africa's system of apartheid, the so-called separate-but-equal schools that flourished in the American South before they fell before judicial scrutiny, and the racially separate recreational facilities, YMCAs, dances, and clubs that characterize so much of America. Here the attempt is to reduce the chances for sentimental feelings, romantic encounters, and sexual relations to develop among members of distinctive racially endogamous groups. Accompanied by a folk knowledge that characterizes the other race as unworthy, inferior, and dangerous, these practices have never proved invulnerable to the flow of love or the expression of lust.

During the slavery period white masters forced their attentions on black slave women. As a result the so-called Negro race in America is largely a population of mixed bloods, only a few of whom have been designated as mulattoes. The coercive sexual intercourse between masters and slaves and the procreation of so-called "Negroes" is vivid testimony to the linkage of a primordial lust to an even more primordial racism. Libido seldom remains caged in socially approved channels.

A combination of isolation and segregation is revealed in the treatment of Chinese immigrants to America.[111] Barred first by village custom and later by American law from bringing wives and sweethearts to the overseas venture, they were also kept apart from white women by ghetto restrictions and miscegenation statues. From 1882 until 1930 it appeared that the entire Chinese presence in America would be obliterated by these concerted preventives of procreation. Nevertheless, carnal cravings and romantic attachments found expression in the hundreds of brothels that dotted the cramped and crowded Chinatowns. Homeless men hoping to return to China after they had made their fortune, the lonely Chinese sojourners turned to prostitutes for solace and relief and, less often, to opium for release from their dreary lot. Occasionally love blossomed in the brothels, and tragedy ensued when the love-sick man attempted to make the "sing-song girl" his concubine or wife. Jealous of the value that women had in a sex-starved community, brothel keepers employed secret-society thugs to recapture or kill any girl who escaped. The excessive restrictions on sexual expression are among the most important factors accounting for the social characteristics of the Chinese community in America.

Child and Arranged Marriage

One way to secure marriage against the effects of love is to establish the former before the latter has had the chance to express itself. Betrothing children in marriage is the favored method. Arranging marriages also serves to prevent love's blind arrow from lodging permanently in the wrong target. However, closer attention to the dynamics of arrangements reveals that romantic attachment and parent-determined marriage are by no means incompatible. Thus, where neighboring villages act as wife-trading organizations as well, young people might meet, signal to each other surreptitiously, or have clandestine assignations, and then hint, wheedle, or cajole parents into selecting their paramour as spouse.

Whatever barriers are put up to hold back or halt lust, or its sublimated form, love, they are never proof against it altogether.

THE MORAL EQUIVALENT OF LUST

Max Weber was the preeminent observer of the fact that Christian asceticism, once confined to the monastic cell, had escaped and become a ubiquitous force for the building of civilization based on rational conduct and on the idea that there was a calling for each man to follow. Once freed from its cloister, Christian asceticism had become judge, sentencing its own penitents to a lifetime of renunciation. It called upon its followers to turn away from the fullness and beauty of life and to devote themselves instead to their respective vocations. Christian asceticism did its part, as Weber pointed out, in building the monumental economic order known as capitalism.[112] However, the price for this construction has been great and the casualties high. Among the victims have been truth, beauty, love, and the *élan vital*. Certainly lust had been caged for a historical moment when capitalism was born, and if, as we now suspect, both lust and the spirit of religious asceticism have escaped from the iron cage that encloses man's dreary workaday world, a yearning for the salvation given by the former is accompanied by a dread of the hell inflicted by Eros' deviltry. Man's pleasure-loving spirit longs for a fresh, exhilarating, and satisfying outlet, a dionysian delight that is at the same time spiritual and promises no scourging in the inferno in return.[113] Man wants, in short, *a moral equivalent of lust*.

The struggle to liberate *life*, free, pulsating, and vibrant, from the *forms of life* that seem ever to constrain its exotic flights is a theme looming darkly over the twentieth century. The nineteenth century was haunted by the specter of communism; the twentieth has already seen its form and darker shade. What is required—and not to be, as Georg Simmel observed so presciently—is a revolt in behalf of *life* itself, a revolt opposed to all *forms of life*.[114] After the triumph of such revolutions no iron cage will ever again enclose mankind—a mankind liberated for the first time from the shackles of culture. Hedonist, dionysian, and bacchic, this new world promises life acting in its own behalf. And yet it will fail: there is no life without form—every destruction and every utopia begets its own constructive restraints. In the paradise envisioned by this new revolt, there will be neither marriage nor prostitution, for both are merely forms of the erotic, and this revolution will seek to establish the erotic for itself. Is it possible? Gregory the Great had warned: "From lust are generated blindness of mind, inconsiderateness, inconstancy, precipitation, self-love, hatred of God, affection for this present world, but dread or despair of that which is to come."[115] If the erotic is to be freed from lustful iniquity, a morality of its own will have to accompany and exalt its liberation.

The Theater of Cruelty of Antonin Artaud

Among those committed to the revolt against form Antonin Artaud (1896–1948) stands out as a most prominent *engagé* in the struggle.[116] Actor, playwright, director, essayist, poet, and critic, Artaud was also a mad genius who strove to reconstitute both life and theater.[117] His single most important contribution is a proposal for a "theater of cruelty," a new theater that would transcend the old forms of dramatic performance, descend into the hearts, and salvage the souls of the audience.[118] Designed to dissolve the barrier that separates actors from spectators, "the theater of cruelty" aspired to plumb the depths of man's existence. It would burst the shackles of language, break apart the proscenium that separates the actor from his existence, and give vent to the emotional screams, grunts, and yelps that make up real living. It would tear at man's soul. And yet it would commit no evil; it would be lusty but not commit lustful acts. It would be the moral equivalent of lust.

That Artaud saw himself as a protagonist in the revolt against culture is clear from his own writings. At a time when life itself was at stake, Artaud pointed out, there was too much talk about civilization and culture.[119] There is not so much a need to "defend a culture whose existence has never kept a man from going hungry, as to extract from what is called culture, ideas whose compelling force is identical with that of hunger." Rather than continuing to build up systems of philosophy, culture, and civilization, Artaud proposes "the idea of culture-in-action," a kinetic synthesis of existentialism and phenomenology, a civilization that is built literally on *"presence of mind."* "If our life lacks brimstone, i.e., a constant magic," he observed, "it is because we choose to observe our acts and lose ourselves in considerations of their imagined form instead of being impelled by their force."

Life has lost its adhesive strength in the contemporary world. Echoing ideas that had already found expression in the writings of Weber and Simmel, Artaud explained that "this painful cleavage . . . is responsible for the revenge of things." Man no longer experiences poetry within himself, nor does he find it in possessions. Suddenly, however, there is a sort of *élan* that appears "on the wrong side." "[C]onsider," Artaud challenges us, "the number of crimes whose perverse gratuitousness is explained only by our powerlessness to take complete possession of life." Life must be possessed independent of the forms into which it has been cast. "It is good that our excessive facilities are no longer available, that forms fall into oblivion: a culture without space or time, restrained only by the capacity of our own nerves, will reappear with more energy." For Artaud the vehicle of this revolution of life for itself was theater, for the theater was not caged like man, not confined to a fixed language and a firmly established form, and not stunned into awed silence before the false shadows of contemporary culture. Theater "not only destroys false shadows," Artaud thundered, "but prepares the way for a new generation of shadows, around which assembles the true spectacle of life."

Artaud believed himself to be an inmate in the "prison house of language,"[120] and, indeed, he spent many years in that prison house reserved for those whose expressions earmark them for exile from the ordinary world—the asylum. In fact Artaud appears to have been struck by a true alienation from role capacity, by an inability to enter into any ordered sequence of writing or conversation.[121] In a screenplay prepared in 1925-1926, Artaud captures the essence of this peculiar sickness in modern civilization. The central character is an actor, like Artaud himself, who

> has been stricken with a bizarre malady. He has become incapable of reaching his thoughts; he has retained all his lucidity, but no matter what thought occurs to him, he can no longer give it external form, that is, translate it into appropriate gestures and words.
>
> The necessary words desert him, they no longer answer his summons, he is reduced to watching a procession of images, an enormous number of contradictory images without very much connection from one to the next.[122]

Like man after the Fall as envisioned by Augustine, Artaud's actor suffers from an unexpected impotence caused not from the insubordination of the *pudenda* to the will, but rather of language to thought. As a result he is rendered "incapable of participating in the lives of others, or of devoting himself to any activity." He can neither enjoy life as a hedonist nor reject the world for his calling. Relief from this form of alienation can be found not in an admission of literary incompetence or poor development of verbal skills, as Artaud's critics jeered, but rather in a daring accusation against language itself—and in a refusal to remain incarcerated within a restricted form of communication that could not express thoughts and feelings adequately. To burst the bonds of language that stifle man's expression of basic emotions and ideas was the goal that Artaud sought to realize in his unique theater.

However, language was not the only problem. The other was the body and its relation to the mind. Theater had followed the path of Occidental philosophy and subordinated man's body to a lofty mind that both controlled it and denied dramatic presentation to its natural functions. Artaud was deeply impressed by Freud, and, like the founder of psychoanalysis, he also noticed the close physical and emotional proximity of the sex organs to those used for excretion and the elimination of waste products.[123] Artaud sought to give full expression to the body and to its exaltations and degradations of man. Justifying a woman's role he had directed in Roger Vitrac's bedroom farce, *Victor ou les enfants au pouvoir*—that of a lovely and voluptuous heroine with an irrepressible urge to break wind—Artaud "explained ... that this character represents the intrusion of the sordid side of matter into the realm of spiritual beauty."[124] When he was in the throes of opium addiction, Artaud had opposed all attempts to suppress the drug because he believed that it held out no danger whatsoever to society. What misfortunes occurred in the world, he argued, resulted from the fact that "We are born rotten in body and soul, we are congenitally maladjusted ..." If society were to do away with opium, Artaud argued, it would still be faced with what he called the "cancers of the body and the soul." These included "the propensity to despair, inborn cretinism, hereditary syphilis, the instability of the instincts."[125] Opium, Artaud pleaded at another time, was a remedy against sins of the flesh. "All sexuality and all eroticism ... are a sin and a crime against Jesus Christ and the antidote to eroticism and the spells of the Demon is opium ..."[126]

By 1947 Artaud had abandoned spirituality and resolved the difficulties of the body by ascribing them to mind.[127] In his poetic farewell to a commitment to spiritual, religious, or drug-induced salvation, *Chiote à l'esprit*, Artaud argues that the Cartesian dualism is false:

> For we know what the body is,
> but who says
> that the spirit is the principle from which all that is living gushes?
> . . .
> For one can very well invert the problem and say that the spirit and its values and data might never have existed if the body, which at least sweated them out, had not been there, . . .
>
> . . .
> For the body doesn't ever need us to define what it's done.
> . . .
> And it was right there that the big bully, the big coward, that buggerer of the tide of pure essences, was knocked out . . .
> Too cowardly to try making it to a body, the spirits . . . roam around in the empyrean where their emptiness, their nuls and voids, their downright laziness keeps them spiritual.
> By virtue of having seen the body of man underneath them, they came to the conclusion that they were going to be superior to the body of man.[128]

There remains the sublimation of body, or rather of man as an integral being, a transcendent move that would provide a moral equivalent to the entire actuality of human existence. That would be realized in the "theater of cruelty."

It is remarkable how much of Artaud's dramatic language is redolent with the words and phrases associated with lust, *eros*, and procreation. Anticipating his later manifesto in behalf of the theater of cruelty, Artaud had already developed some of its basic principles by 1925. The quintessential scenario for theater, according to Artaud, was a police raid on a brothel:

> The dismal sound of police whistles tears the air. Little by little the circle closes in. . . . It is an ordinary-looking house whose doors suddenly open, and from inside the house there emerges a group of women walking single file, like beasts to the slaughter. The plot thickens: the police net was intended not for a gang of criminals but only for a group of women.[129]

Artaud contended that this scene would bring emotion and amazement to a peak: "For surely we are just as guilty as these women and just as cruel as these policemen." Such a drama was not only a "complete spectacle" but also "ideal theater." And the description of ideal theater is much like the complex of feelings associated with sex itself: "This anguish, this feeling of guilt, this victory, this satiety give the tone and feeling of the mental state in which the spectator must leave our theater." In terms of our thesis the spectator will have vicariously experienced many of the elements, feelings, and orientations associated with sexuality, but not have committed a sex act. Artaud did not put it this way; instead, he said simply, "The spectator must have the sense that what is being performed in front of him is a scene from his own life, and an important scene at that."[130] But is this enacted raid on a brothel not the *moral* equivalent of lust?

Artaud's theater of cruelty seems to fulfill the promise of bringing together audience and actor in a spectacle that exalts life over its constraining forms. More to the point here, its very description is in a rhetoric of erotically determined words. "The theater," writes Artaud, "must give us everything that is in crime, love, war, or madness, if it wants to recover its necessity."[131] The images for such a theater already exist, Artaud tells us, in the paintings of Grunewald and Hieronymus Bosch, and the spectacle created thereby will "recover from the cinema, the music hall, the circus, and *from life itself* what has always belonged to it."[132] The elements of *eros*, or as Artaud puts it, of "Creation, Becoming, and Chaos," are the base from which the new "metaphysics of speech, gesture, and expression" are to be built up. The new language will be a "language in space, a language of sounds, cries, lights, onomatopoeia [which] the theater must organize into veritable hieroglyphs." The symbolism and interconnections of the hieroglyphs, in turn, will affect "all organs and on all levels." Through an "Oriental means of expression, this . . . concrete language of the theater can fascinate and ensnare the organs." Artaud describes the sensual effect of this new means of expression:

> It flows into sensibility. . . . It utilizes the vibrations and qualities of the voice. It wildly tramples rhythms underfoot. It pile-drives sounds. It seeks to exalt, to benumb, to charm, to arrest the sensibility. It liberates a new lyricism of gesture which, by its precipitation or its amplitude in the air, ends by surpassing the lyricism of words.

And ultimately it achieves its objective, liberating man from his subjugation by language and providing him with a new and deeper way of knowing. "What is important," concludes Artaud, "is that by positive means, the sensitivity is put in a state of deepened and keener perception, and this is the very object of the magic and the rites of which the theater is only a reflection."[133]

Artaud's allusion to magic and rites hints at a complex new morality that infuses his theater and that will overcome its audiences. The presentation of this morality is veiled in Artaud's comparison of the actors in his theater to victims of a plague and to persons about to commit murder. Just as a plague covers the outer skin with hideous sores and boils but does not affect the physical state of the inner organs, so the new theater requires that an actor present the external character of a murderer, a rapist, a sadist and a hundred other kinds of villains without becoming one in deed or in his inner being. Moreover, the spiritual force of dramatic poetry is much stronger than that force that compels a criminal to commit a crime. "Once launched upon the fury of his task," Artaud observed, "an actor requires infinitely more power to keep from committing a crime than a murderer needs courage to complete his act."[134] The actor commits a murder on the stage, but of course no one is actually killed. And the powerful drama of murder committed on the stage has a moral and cathartic effect on the audience because "the action and effect of a feeling in the theater appears infinitely more valid than that of a feeling fulfilled in life." The theater envisioned by Artaud would imagine a pure criminality without carrying its action into the reality offstage, and would reveal an intention and a determination to do evil, which Artaud believed was the distilled essence of cruelty. It is in the drama of intended evil and staged crimes that Artaud commits theater to the moral equivalent of sin in general and—as we shall see presently—of lust in particular.

The theater of cruelty combines enormous dramatic force with enormous emotional release. It takes up the burden and represents the sins of mankind and simultaneously bares and negates them on the stage. It provides a vicarious enactment of man's moral dilemmas and a curative release from his sins:

Compared with the murderer's fury which exhausts itself, that of the tragic actor remains enclosed within a perfect circle. The murderer's fury has accomplished an act, discharges itself, and loses contact with the force that inspired it but can no longer sustain it. That of the actor has taken a form that negates itself to just the degree it frees itself and dissolves into universality..

For Artaud a true theater is one that disturbs the repose of the senses, liberates the elements repressed in the unconscious, and incites a virtual revolt. But, as he insists, the revolt "can have its full effect only if it remains virtual," imposing on the "assembled collectivity an attitude that is both difficult and heroic."

For Artaud the theater fulfills for man's spirit what the plague does for man's physicality—it drains a great abscess. For the theater that abscess is the evil in man, which corresponds to that revealed in "the dark hour of certain ancient tragedies." The theater provides "the revelation, the bringing forth, the exteriorization of a depth of latent cruelty by means of which all the perverse possibilities of the mind, whether of an individual or of a people, are localized." In theater, observes Artaud, there is "a kind of strange sun, a light of abnormal intensity," that illuminates the darker areas of freedom. Artaud holds that "all true freedom is dark,

> and infallibly identified with sexual freedom which is also dark, although we do not know precisely why. For it has been a long time since the Platonic Eros, the procreative sense, the freedom of life vanished beneath the somber veneer of *Libido* which is identified with all that is dirty, abject, infamous in the process of living and of throwing oneself headlong with a natural and impure vigor, with a perpetually renewed strength, upon life."

Artaud's morality subscribes to the thesis that "life as it is and as it has been fashioned for us provides many reasons for exaltation." The theater drains the abscesses of man's evil, and it does so collectively. By illuminating the dark caves of carnality and other evils, it acts like the scourge in a plague. "It invites the mind to share a delirium which exalts its energies; and we can see . . . that from the human point of view, the action of theater, like that of plague, is beneficial, for impelling men to see themselves as they are, it causes the mask to fall, reveals the lie, the slackness, baseness, and hypocrisy of our world."

Rudolf Bultmann is among the theologians who believe that "man is incapable of redeeming himself from the world and powers which hold sway in it." For Bultmann these powers are preeminently "the flesh, sin, the law and death."[135] Artaud's resolution of man's irremediable guilt provides a moral equivalent of fleshly desire and with it the virtuous stance appropriate to the endless struggle of lust with life: Artaud concluded that theater shakes off the asphyxiating inertia of matter which invades even the clearest testimony of the senses; and in revealing to collectivities of men their dark power, their hidden force, it invites them to take, in the face of destiny, a superior and heroic attitude they would never have assumed without it.[136]

CONCLUSION

Lust is ever with us but mysterious. It resides in that limbo between mind and body, and seems independent of will, custom, and law. It rules over man not so much as an authoritarian tyrant but rather as a malevolent trickster. It undermines the soul, enervates the will, overturns the flesh, and wreaks havoc on sociability. The theologians sought to understand it, trace its origins back to the fall of man, and warn against its treachery to life and salvation. However, their moral authority could not overcome the lustful desires that crept in everywhere. Moreover, practical issues of social and personal life—problems of marriage, divorce, desertion, widowhood, and remarriage; problems of propagation, inheritance, child support, and lineage; problems of celibacy, concupiscence, homosexuality, and illicit sexual liaisons—plagued the church fathers and defied solutions that squared clearly and unambiguously with religious doctrine.

The social sciences sought to control lust by splitting its facets into those that seemed worthy of support, such as love, rationality, affection, companionship, and those that crippled the social order, such as romantic illusions, erotic escapades, and sexual practices deemed deviant. However, the moralistic preachments underlying this social science were not easily concealed behind the inauthentic jargon of objectivity and scientism; moreover, precisely because it was rooted in a system of morality and in encouraging the institutions that would foster and enforce that morality, this social science provides a perspective that is ineffective against lust's overmastering disregard of morally based restrictions. Faithful to the cultures of its subjects, the social sciences would fail to provide a wall strong enough to hold back the pressure of an acultural, supracultural lust.

If lust could not be overcome, perhaps it could be bypassed. A substitute for it, a force or a spectacle so powerful that it might provide catharses for man at the very moment that it burst the chains that bound him to his lust, is proposed at least implicitly in Artaud's theater of cruelty. A moral equivalent of lust that provides erotic satisfaction without shame, degradation, or the disruption of the social order, this unique theater has yet to be tested in the crucible of life wherein it must prove effective or ring down the curtain on a failed ethical imperative.

Meanwhile, we live with the devil. He is our companion in sin and everyday life. Perhaps, if we get to know him better, comprehend the nature of lust and the forms it gives to life, culture, and society, we will pass more wisely through the vale of tears that is ever with us— civilization and its discontents.

THREE

Anger

Sing, goddess, the anger of Peleus' son Achilleus and its
devastation, which puts pains thousandfold upon the Achaians,
hurled in their multitudes to the house of Hades strong souls of
heroes, but gave their bodies to be the delicate feasting of
dogs, of all birds, and the will of Zeus was accomplished since
that time when first there stood in division of conflict Atreus'
son the lord of men and brilliant Achilleus.

The Iliad *of Homer**

When Homer designated anger as the driving force which set in motion
the troubles and tragedies that would overtake the Greek forces at Troy,
he gave dramatic expression to the puissance of this primordial sin. Of all
the sins anger is perhaps the most dangerous, certainly the most volatile,
and all too frequently the source or cause for crime, rebellion, and
revolution, the disintegration or destruction of the social order. "From
anger," wrote Gregory the Great, "are produced strifes, swelling of
mind, insults, clamour, indignation, blasphemies."[1] In speaking of the
acquisition of mortality by the soul journeying to earth, Arnobius, a
North African church father, lists but two of the sins—lust and anger—as
"causes" which "pursue [us] from the world's circles, through the
working of which we become bad, aye most wicked." These are the
principal sins with which mortals burn, and the reasons they spend their
lives "in shameful deeds . . ."[2]

In some versions of the natural history of the seven deadly sins, the
primordial, base, and basic significance of anger is attested to by locating
it in childhood as "tempestuousness." However, in a perhaps Mithraic-
originated drama of the soul journey, anger, redefined as unholy daring
and rash audacity, is surrendered after reaching the fifth zone of the
heavens; only after that sin has been lifted can the soul proceed to give up

greed and falsehood in order to enter the final and supreme eighth celestial sphere.[3] In an early fifteenth-century sermon by the Augustinian friar John Gregory, anger, together with pride and envy, is pointed out as the weapon of the devil, while gluttony, lechery, and sloth are agencies of the flesh. Man, portrayed here as an elephant, is required to fight off the world, the flesh, and the devil, but clearly the latter with his tripartite arsenal of evils is the most powerful of the three foes.

That anger is related to indignity and esteem and threatening to the moral order is indicated in the sculptured imagery of the seven deadly sins at Amiens Cathedral, where Anger is depicted as a woman with a sword threatening a monk who is reading. And that the ultimate effect of anger is to separate man from himself, creating a true and fundamental alienation, has been asserted by St. Edmond of Pontigny, who, in his *Speculum ecclesiae*, observes that although sloth torments, lechery enslaves, and avarice and gluttony beguile and deceive man, the other three deadly sins are essentially alienating: pride separating man from God, envy from his neighbor, but anger from himself. To some students of the sin—reflecting perhaps on its self-alienating character—anger is the gateway to all of the others. Man departs from himself and, angered, is often pictured as a snarling wolf; the angry man is to be avoided as one would fly from a ravenous dog, a mad hound, or a raging lion. Yet to others, anger is a neutral and justifiable passion, while the indulgence of it, in *wrath*, is a freely chosen sin of the will. Undeniably a sin, yet still a conundrum, anger invites sociological scrutiny as to its causes, construction, and cure.

Anger is the first passion that must be domesticated if social order is to be secured and maintained. It is anger, in the form of the beast at one's throat, that describes the state of nature which the social contract will replace. Hostilities among men were endemic, according to Simmel, and could only be curbed by customary controls, legislative limits, and enforced judgment. "The entire history of social life," wrote Simmel, "is permeated by this process; the positively antagonistic motives of individuals, with which their social life begins, grow up into separate and independent organisms. Thus, from the regulations for preserving the group-life there arise, on the one hand, the law which codifies them, and, on the other, the judge whose business it is to apply them."[4] Thus it is that anger is not only the first and foremost of man's passions, but, through its sublimation and social control, a foundation stone of the social order itself.

Yet anger will show itself. At best curbed and corraled, it will erupt, leap over the walls of psyche and society that hem it in, and bare its ferocious face. What will evoke its display? Anger arises as a defense of self in the face of actual or impending loss of esteem. Anger is the response to humiliation.

Consider the most famous case in epic literature, that of Achilles.[5] (Indeed Robert Graves and I. A. Richards have gone so far as to entitle their translations of the poem *The Anger of Achilles*.) Homer makes clear that the sole cause of the entire action of the *Iliad* lies in Agamemnon's selfish mistake—his humiliation of Achilles. The Greek king has appropriated for his own a prize of war, a girl, won by Achilles. Achilles accuses his commander of greed, but Agamemnon denies the charge, claiming that his royal status not only entitles but requires him to enjoy the best prizes of war. Nevertheless, Achilles persists, pointing out that he himself has no quarrel with the Trojans, that he has volunteered his services to Agamemnon, and that he deserves the prizes that he wins in battle with his own hands. At length he denounces Agamemnon for the latter's cruelty, heedlessness in recklessly sending brave Greeks to their deaths, and, most significantly, for humiliating those who fight on his behalf. Outraged by his own humiliation, Achilles withdraws his services from the Greek cause and sulks disconsolately in his tent. Here we have a confluence of three sins: Agamemnon's greed has injured Achilles' pride, resulting in a remarkable display of resentful anger. A resolution of the dilemma might start with any one of the sins. Agamemnon could renounce his avarice, Achilles forget his loss of self-esteem, or set aside his ire. In fact, however, in an effort at reconciliation Odysseus seeks to redirect the savage pride and sinful wrath of Achilles, perhaps because he believes that Agamemnon is beyond reach or redemption. But Odysseus is unsuccessful; Achilles' hurt is too great.

However, Achilles' retirement from the battlefield serves to humiliate him even further. The Trojan hero Hector, taking advantage of the absence of Achilles, kills the latter's dearest companion, Patroclus. A numbing injury has been added to a needless insult. Achilles' self-mortification at first knows no bounds. There is but one way for Achilles to restore his shattered self-esteem. Whereas he feels guilt for having deserted his friend in the face of death, he can only restore his moral worth by an act of vengeance. Achilles passes through the phases of remorse, self-pity, and shame. With each passionate development, however, there grows a burning fury. His self-recriminations and accusations are gradually transformed and, in the form of enraged anger, find a new target in Patroclus' killer, Hector. Achilles, knowing that he himself will die soon because of his faithlessness to his friend, must expiate his own sin before death makes its claim on him. His shameful guilt, transformed into terrible anger, provides the emotive backdrop for the final chapter of this great morality play. Internalized, his guilt, shame, and hostility toward himself can only fester and corrode his already deeply scarred dignity. But projected as justified anger toward Hector, his wrath, activated in revenge, will restore him. Turning on the Trojan warrior, Achilles first heaps insults upon him and then kills him in a most cruel and barbaric manner. Having not only dispatched but also degraded his enemy, the embodied form of his own guilty self, Achilles is once again restored to honor and in the end reconciled with Priam, the father of his victim. The dignity of Achilles, lost by humiliation, is regained by an act of violence, and the social order has once more been salvaged. The price of degradation is great, the argument seems to be, for it unleashes an anger so great that only the most bloody outcome will cause it to relent.

Homer's epic thus unveils the nature of anger as a phenomenon both terrible and commonplace. The wrath of Achilles is a response to dishonor. Endowed with godlike capacities for self-esteem, human beings nonetheless live in a world where the possibilities for injury to self-esteem are ever present. Everywhere lurk the persons and situations that might degrade and dishonor. Although often less dramatic than the Greek epic, ordinary life may nevertheless present instances and ceremonies of degradation that evoke awesome anger. The consequences to self and society of anger invite individuals either to find ways wherein the dignity of all persons might be preserved or, failing that, to invent ways to curb and control the scope of anger that dishonor and loss of self-esteem evoke.

ANGER AND THE DEFENSE OF SELF

Anger, the aggressive defense of an injured self, takes a variety of forms. When the self is so esteemed, so admired, and so loved that no other can replace it in the ardor of ego, psychologists speak of narcissism. The narcissistic self will brook no assault upon its expansive dignity. Those who challenge its estimate, criticize its stature, or cut down its size are sure to arouse the hostility if not the rage of the owner. Harry Stack Sullivan, distinguishing between serious dangers to survival that bring out "the fury of the cornered rat" and milder threats to self-esteem that evoke "irritation, bad temper, and frank anger," argues that the latter arise from apprehensions about whether "we are worthwhile and respected." Defense of the self, hence, need not be defined as a narcissistic neurosis. Some measure of self-love seems to be required for ordinary life and mutual cooperation. The arsenal of self-esteem is protected not only by the egoist but also by all those who defend their own human dignity. And, as Sullivan has argued, the perverse refusal to guard against any assault on one's own esteem may have physiological as well as psychological consequences. "I said years ago," he writes, "that if one swallows much resentment it will ruin one's belly; there are few better established hypotheses than that which sees in unrecognized recurring resentment the prime factor in troubles from the stomach onward in the alimentary canal."[6]

In seeking to illustrate the forms of self-defensive anger, let us first turn to the realm of the child.[7] Typically anger is experienced as a response to punishment, although it is not likely to develop into rage except under the most extreme of provocations. At a later stage of child development, however, punishment, especially punishment for activities whose prohibited aspect or dangerous features are not foreseeable by the child, is likely to produce a more complex reaction. Knowing that a direct expression of anger will not restore his injured ego, and in fact is more likely to engender even further punishment, both physical and emotional, the child will feel or even express *resentment*. In an even more complicated process the child will feel his need to manage all the more the emotional information that he communicates to his oppressors. Hence, he will conceal not only his anger but his resentment as well. Insofar as these activities involve repression they might also have psychosomatic aspects, wherein physiological mechanisms help distribute tensions created by psychosocial situations.

Just as Achilles' anger must find an outlet, so also the repressed anger of the wounded child will eventually show itself. According to the perspectives developed by psychoanalysts and certain psychiatrists, repressed anger and concealed resentment may bury themselves below the surface of visible behavior, congealing in a long latency period, only to emerge in later years as malevolence, hatred, prejudice, hostility, or, in pathological form, as paranoia. Those analysts who reject both social contract theories and assumptions of the innate evil in man tend to argue that certain kinds of early childhood experiences are likely to provoke a later expression of malevolence. According to Sullivan, children who are thwarted in their search for needed tenderness, who are punished not for their transgressions but rather for their good and lovable deeds, experience a deep psychic hurt, a wound to the core of their self-esteem. Repeated experiences of this kind are likely to result in the displacement of the feeling for tenderness and the substitution of an openly hostile attitude whenever sympathetic response is offered. The malevolent person illustrates the antisocial element of the sin of anger. "[W]hen the juvenile makes it practically impossible for anyone to feel tenderly toward him or to treat him kindly, he beats them to it, so to speak, by the display of his [hostile] attitude."[8] Having been denied a sense of his own emotional worth, the person presents an outwardly angry self, making it impossible for him to be loved except by the most obtuse, persistent, or, indeed, perceptive observer. The ultimate expression of this attitude is misanthropy.

Anger and Group Defense

However, interesting as these child-centered theories of the etiology of anger are, they do not cover all, or even the most interesting of cases.

Anger develops out of concrete situations in which prestige, dignity, or esteem may be lost. Some of these may be institutionalized and culturally specific. Consider the instance of secret society mercenaries in America's Chinatowns.[9] Hired to protect and defend the illegal operations of the clandestine associations, these angry and violent thugs were recruited from among the more melancholy and misanthropic members of the Chinese community. A few were frustrated suitors for a prostitute's hand in marriage or concubinage who, unable to obtain by consent or purchase the exclusive services of their sweetheart, sank into despair and, generalizing and projecting their loss of face, took up arms against the more respectable elements of society. Even more were victims of Chinatown's traditional *kadi* justice, which, serving an oligarchy of clan and mercantile interests, publicly humiliated them by stripping them of their businesses, impugning their family names, and denying them the dignity afforded to more favored elements. Enraged over their loss of self-esteem, group worth, and economic opportunity, the dispossessed joined in the criminal and rebellious opposition to community authority.

One patterned form of status loss is occasioned by downward mobility. That this can lead to anger, rage, fury, and, indeed, the institutionalization of these emotions in the form of bureaucratized agencies of terror is no doubt illustrated in the case of Nazi Germany. Many of the analyses of the Hitler phenomenon refer to the significant role played by the downward mobility of large numbers of persons and families in the two decades preceding the advent of the National Socialist regime.[10] Perhaps even more important for the onset of rage were fear of the humiliation attending downward mobility and shame over having lost World War I. Although studies showing similar amounts of downward mobility in other countries during the same period cast doubt on the sufficiency of that factor for explaining the support for Hitler, the role of collective aggressive reassertion of lost self-esteem cannot be discounted altogether.[11] According to Harold Lasswell the German lower middle classes suffered from psychological impoverishment, and this emotional penury led to massive protests and large-scale support for movements through which the petit bourgeoisie might revenge themselves.[12] And Frederick L. Schuman pointed out that the brutality of the *Sturmabteilung* (storm troopers) stemmed from the same source as hate-generated anti-Semitism, antipacifism, and antirationalism. "These men," he wrote, speaking of the uniformed, youthful corps of early Hitler supporters,

> had been punished—wounded, tormented, twisted, and warped by the unkind forces of defeat, depression, and collapse. . . . Nazi terrorists tortured and killed literally for the sake of torturing and killing—that is, for the subjective satisfactions, the inner release of tensions which these activities afforded. . . . Terrorism was not a political necessity, but a psychological compulsion. The victims

were but incidental instruments of self-gratification upon whose
bodies inverted Nazi egoism could recover sanity and security.[13]

Schuman is of course quite incorrect in referring to the "incidental"
character of the Nazi targets. The victims were as precisely chosen as
Achilles' choice of Hector; what makes up the unique horror of the Nazi
system was its bureaucratic mobilization of terrifying anger for a war
against the Jews.[14]

Downward mobility, however, does not always result in the
expression of anger toward others. Hatred can turn inward on itself and
become grief, sorrow, and bitterness. Defeated, depressed, and dejected,
those who have suffered a deep narcissistic wound sometimes sink into an
irredeemable apathy and a despairing melancholia. Unable to summon up
the energy for angry response, they remain in a state of absolute
disesteem. Such a sad condition was uncovered by the sociographers
Jahoda, Lazarsfeld, and Zeisel in their last year at Marienthal, an
Austrian town in the throes of unrelieved poverty.[15] The first shock
waves of mass unemployment later gave way to resignation for many,
loss of the capacity to cope for others, and a general lethargy in the entire
community. Removed from the opportunities, joys, and sufferings of
worldly competition, their illusions and hopes irremediably dashed, the
people of Marienthal gradually settled into despair. Denied the chance
for dignity, they seem also to have been spared the sin of anger.

The explosive quality of long-repressed anger and resentment has
been given vivid expression in what Horace Cayton calls "the psychology of the Negro under oppression."[16] Having first discovered his own
hatred of white people through the revelations of psychoanalysis, Cayton
perceived that his particular condition was not unique but rather a
psychosocial product of his membership in the much-beset black race.
According to Cayton's theory of the "fear-hate-fear complex," American Negroes suffer an especially deep psychic wound, intensifying and
reinforcing their normal insecurities, because they live in a world
wherein punishment—violent, psychological and physical injury—might
leap out at them from every side, at any time, for any reason, or for no
reason at all. The Negro's personality is brutalized and humiliated at
every level of an unusually harsh environment. Ordinarily such persistent
and irrational assaults on one's self-esteem would evoke anger and
resentment, and this is certainly true in the case of blacks. However, the
certain knowledge that he will be punished if he reveals these feelings
produces a fearful response, a suppression of both anger and resentment,
and a profound sense of apprehension and guilt for having these emotions.
"Fear leads to hate; but the personality recoils with an intensified and
compound fear," writes Cayton. "This is the Negro's reaction to his own
brutalization, subordination and hurt. It is this vicious cycle in which the

American Negro is caught and in which his personality is pulverized by an ever-mounting, self-propelling rocket of emotional conflict."[17] Yet this deep internal conflict might find one route to resolution in a violent and effective expression of what two recent Afro-American psychiatrists call black rage.[18] Just as Achilles transformed his own inner emotional hurt and confusion into wrath projected against an external enemy, so also the Negro occasionally experiences a terrifying yet exhilarating catharsis in an act of enraged revenge on his white enemies. Richard Wright, novelist and intellectual colleague of Cayton in the development of an understanding of the psychology of oppressed peoples, presented a powerful example of the restorative function of activated rage in *Native Son*, his fictional account of black urban life in Chicago.[19] Bigger Thomas, a young black man of the streets, experiences the excruciating emotional terrors of the ghetto mind-life until, quite by accident, he unintentionally kills a white girl who has seduced him but whose cries, he fears, would betray him to the white world as a rapist. The remarkable thing, he later explains to his lawyer on the eve of his execution in the electric chair, is that he never felt so alive until he felt things hard enough to kill for them. The message of the theories and the realities of black rage seems to be that unbridled wrath might indeed be a terrible sin, but the oppressive humiliation that evokes and ultimately unleashes it is as terrible an evil. More broadly, a similar theme is adumbrated in Frantz Fanon's haunting analysis of the problems of racism and colonialism in the contemporary world.[20] Insofar as oppression and humiliation create whole categories of people who feel they are the wretched of the earth, they also excite the moral indignation of the disesteemed. This indignation threatens to ripen into rage. A collective wrathful response, a response that could engulf the entire world in blood, might explode from an aroused anger that knows no bounds.

Anger and Sexual Property

A nearly unbounded wrath is sometimes aroused by the appropriation of another's sexual property. Treated in the classical sociological essay by Kingsley Davis as jealousy, this emotional state and its attendant response are also understandable as an angry reaction to lost self-esteem. Indeed, Davis himself points this out, characterizing jealousy as "apparently a fear or rage reaction to a threatened appropriation of one's own or what is desired as one's own property."[21] Of all the types of properties over which dominion is sought, sexual property seems to evoke the most intimate connection to self-worth. The bonds of love or affection express not only one's feelings toward the other, but also an implicit reciprocal image of these feelings toward oneself. The lover feels that his love is a part of himself and inextricably bound up with his own existence and being.

Sexual property above all others is likely to engender vanity and pride in, and satisfy a fundamental need of, its possessor. Accordingly, an attack on one's sexual property usually cuts a deep wound in one's self-esteem. The objects of one's jealousy are rivals for or trespassers on the affectional grounds of one's own acquired sexual property. Where a competition for sexual possession precedes ownership or control, as in the courtship phase of the romantic love complex in Occidental societies, rivalry tends to be hedged about with norms and rules, and losers in the competition are expected to retire gracefully from the field. However, some rivals will not accept defeat since it demands acquiescence to frustration of a strong emotional desire. Violating the approved monopoly of possessive ownership over fairly won sexual property, the rival becomes a real or potential trespasser, continuing to compete, perhaps in secret or employing subtle stratagems after the contest is over. A jealous regard for one's own dearly purchased prize in the marketplace of love may arouse the most intense fears, deepest insecurities, and ultimately the most ferocious wrath as a threatened possessor fights to preserve his pride, passion, and property. And precisely because jealousy arises out of the more significant elements of self-esteem, its fury might know no bounds. An outraged husband might murder the man he suspects of seeking the favors of his wife or, perhaps believing that his rival has a competitive advantage over him, might kill his wife, thus robbing his rival of a prized property that the murderer anticipates he himself is likely to lose should the contest for affection proceed.

The outrage engendered over real or imagined trespass on sexual property is not confined to the microcosm of scorned lovers and rivals. Indeed in the rules, norms, customs, and violations that obtain in caste-dominated or racially organized societies we find a cultural and organizational expression of the anger that jealousy and wounded pride can evoke. Consider the special form of racial and caste prejudice that prevails over marriage and sex relations in such societies.[22] Typically, marital forms are morally dichotomized into those that are *agathogamic*, in accordance with accepted norms for choosing a spouse, and *cacogamic*, or in opposition to such norms. The latter are strongly discouraged.[23] Low-caste orders and racially disprivileged groups are prohibited by law or barred by custom from marrying members of the higher castes or dominant race. Yet in fact some liaisons across forbidden lines do occur.[24] More significantly, apprehensions about secret or savage assaults on their sexual property tend to loom large in the thought of the societal elites, who guard their sexual preserves with a mixture of fear and pride, insecurity and boastfulness, that clearly portends jealousy. As Herbert Blumer has observed, race prejudice is at bottom a preservationist ethic toward one's own group position, coupled and animated by the fear that the other races have designs on one's own group's privileges and perquisites.[25] Fears about the possibility and consequences of the sexual trespass of Blacks in the United States, to take an outstanding example, have aroused the most bloody and violent expression of outraged fury. In the southern states lynchings, burnings, and castrations characterized more than eight decades of life after the Civil War, whenever a black was so much as suspected of looking appreciatively at the face or body of a white woman.[26] And, on occasion, the humiliating indignity of caste prejudice provoked an angry black man to take revenge in precisely the manner that the whites feared—sexual assault.[27] A vicious cycle of enraged jealousy, evoked in the first place by insecure feelings of misgotten group privilege, took collective vengeance on a race whose victimization resided solely in its hardly deserved reputation as a poacher on the sexual property of its oppressors.

ANGER AND THE BEHAVIORAL AND SOCIAL SCIENCES

The rise and proliferation of the sciences of man since the 1850s have been attended by the fall and contraction of the idea of sin.[28] Perhaps most significant in this movement has been the philosophical victory in the minds of most educated persons of determinism over freedom. Once man was relieved of full responsibility for his deeds, once dark forces of the mind, of history, of heredity, or of culture were found to shape his thoughts and shackle his reason, sin with its insistence on the freedom of the will to choose between good and evil had to retreat into the recesses of a suspect theology; at the same time dire punishment as a deserved retribution for the willful commission of wrongful deeds had to give way to remediation and rehabilitation.[29] The establishment of social-scientific determinism paved the way first for a scientific authorization for the distrust of human reason and, ultimately, for the triumph of the therapeutic.[30] Through the bloodless language of the new sciences the sins are neutralized: sloth becomes "affectlessness"; lust changes to "sexual deviance"; envy shows up as "*ressentiment*"; greed reforms itself as "the spirit of capitalism"; gluttony fades into "addiction"; and pride is reduced to "mental illness." Anger, however, resists the expurgations of scientific and lexical sublimation; typically, we find it characterized as "aggression."

The tendencies in modern thought are to shift man's responsibility away from himself and to relieve society from having to depend for its security solely on a combination of repressive force and reliable conscience. Moreover, the emergence as objects of study of the forces of history, the darker landscape of the mind, and the fateful features of environment—each said to be the cause of a variety of human miseries—has turned attention away from sin. The general trend in the moral philosophy underlying social and behavioral science has been to set man adrift somewhere between the shores of humanism and fatalism, and to argue that for most of mankind the tides flow toward the farther shore of unfreedom. Sin has been thrown overboard as a useless and burdensome cargo of the mind, but together with it went much of human reason and freedom, dragged down into the sea of determinism through whose murk only the scientist can peer with his ever-sharpened devices for behavioristic vision. For the rest of us, the argument seems to run, control and understanding of our own conduct is colored by perceptions through a darkened glass. Fated to experience what the forces of destiny have in store, we can only wait for the end or hope for a benevolent and general liberation through improved science.

Let us follow the sin of anger down the road of scientific progress on its will-destroying journey to near oblivion. Psychoanalysis, social psychology, ethology, and sociology seek to drown the will to anger in a sea of scientific refutations of human freedom. However, the will to anger does not expire altogether. In phenomenological sociology it shows certain signs of revival.

Psychoanalysis and Anger

Despite his penetration into the darker corners of the mind in pursuit of the sources of sin and evil, Freud confessed to having overlooked anger and its attendant expressions for a rather long period. "But I can no longer understand," Freud admonished himself and his followers in 1930, "how we can have overlooked the ubiquity of non-erotic aggressivity and destructiveness and can have failed to give it its due place in our interpretation of life."[31] Perhaps one cause for Freud's oversight is to be found in the fact that the Europeans experienced no major war or upheaval between 1871 and 1914. Buoyed by their good fortune, European intellectuals accepted the grand illusion that mankind, or at least the European segment of it, had risen above the need for destructive action, progressed so far in the development and application of human reason that large-scale violent aggression had become not only unnecessary but also obsolete. Whatever the reason, however, the fact remains that until 1915 Freud had confined his observations about the expression and etiology of what we are calling anger to an understanding of sadism. Even on this limited aspect of anger, Freud vacillated between identifying sadism as an aggressive component of the sexual instinct or as an impulse to cruelty that was independent of sexuality but capable of being united with it.[32] Indeed, for a long time Freud resisted believing that there could be "a special aggressive instinct alongside of the familiar instincts of self-preservation and of sex, and on an equal footing with them."[33]

However, in 1915, Freud changed his mind. Hate, he argued, "derives from the narcissistic ego's primordial repudiation of the external world" and "always remains in an intimate relation with the self-preservative instincts." The vehemence of an ego activated by hate, Freud continued, was such as to unleash the most destructive of deeds: "The ego hates, abhors, and pursues with intent to destroy all objects which are a source of unpleasurable feeling for it, without taking into account whether they mean a frustration of sexual satisfaction or of the satisfaction of self-preservative needs."[34] Continuing the pursuit of the ego's primordial repudiation of the external world, Freud eventually turned to a biological account. In *The Ego and the Id* the death instinct, which in an earlier work he had described as working against the life instinct (*eros*) to destroy the ever-enlarging preservative units,[35] is located in the human cells and expresses itself "as an instinct of destruction directed against the external world and other organisms."[36] The libido had the duty of rendering this instinct harmless, and it accomplishes this task by directing its expression outwards toward objects in the external world. There the instinct expresses itself as an urge to destroy, the will to mastery, or the will to power. Some of the libido is not transposed, however, and should the external aggressiveness be blocked, it is aggravated by the re-introjected, or internalized, destructive instinct to form an enlarged masochism.[37]

By the end of his life Freud had become convinced that the death instinct, originating in the biological nature of the human organism, is not only ineradicable but also most dangerous. In one of his final papers he warned that the death instinct is beyond control.[38] As Freud put it in 1933, "It seems as though it is necessary for us to destroy some other thing or person in order not to destroy ourselves, in order to guard against the impulse to self-destruction."[39] Freud was quick to see the profound implication for ethical prescription in his discovery. It was, he said, "a sad disclosure indeed for the moralist!" Thus Freud acknowledged the grim nature and terrifying consequences of anger in the very moment that he absolved man from willful sin.

Social Psychology and Anger

Of the many theories in social psychology, none is so apparently clear and direct in stating the origins and onset of aggression than that developed by John Dollard and his colleagues in 1939 and pretested, so to speak, in a community study carried out in 1936-1937. The argument of Dollard et al. is that all aggressive behavior is a response to frustration and any condition of frustration leads invariably to aggression.[40] With this theory Dollard and his co-workers liberated the study of aggression from a multicausal etiology, permitting social scientists to eschew the analysis of other suggested antecedents to aggression. At the same time they presented frustration as an all-encompassing but vague cause of the inevitable generation of aggression.

In his investigation of the reciprocal aggression of whites and blacks in "Southerntown," Dollard provided a broad framework within which a variety of frustrations ensued.[41] Blacks, for example, were not only blocked in almost every path to economic achievement, educational advancement, free choice of mate, political office, social probity, and public respect, but also had to swallow these insults, conceal their resentments, and adopt a front of amicable and cooperative accommodation to their miserable condition. Their frustrations were endemic to their existence first as slaves and then as the lowest of caste members in a rigidly stratified and segregated society. Their reported reaction to this condition, however, belies the more simple statement about the consequences of aggression that Dollard and his colleagues were to make in 1939. Blacks do occasionally rebel against the self-abnegation required by their white overlords, and they assault, rob, or kill representatives of the hated oppressor class as well. But this is done rarely and often secretly, while several other responses seem to detour, deter, or deny altogether the aggressive reaction that the frustration-aggression theory predicts. In fact, blacks sometimes shift their hostile responses to members of their own race, retire from competition with whites and sink into melancholic despair, or set aside their resentments and redouble their efforts to win the laurels and plaudits of white society despite the obstacles of caste.[42] However, the implication of Dollard's case study and theory seems to be that the conditions of aggression are endemic to the cultures and communities that exhibit them. Product of a synthesis of history and mores and the mental anguish that they produce, aggression will only be alleviated when the drift and direction of culture and custom change. Anger is thus detached from sin, as the will of man waits upon the weal of history.

Ethology and Anger

In the philosophies and sciences of man, humans have always been located somewhere between earth and heaven, between corporeal being and incorruptible bloodlessness, between carnal knowledge and conscience-bound reason. During the nineteenth century the rise and popularity of Darwinism threatened to bring man down closer to the animals, and in the early decades of the twentieth century a "Social Darwinism," emphasizing the natural and efficacious functions of life lived by a barely sublimated tooth and claw, almost succeeded in justifying a kind of bestiality.[43] But beginning in the 1920s and continuing until recently challenged by the new science of ethology, psychoanalytic, social psychological, and sociological theories did much to combat the deleterious aspects of *Social* Darwinism while preserving most of Darwinism's philosophical and natural scientific underpinnings.[44] What the social-scientific counterattack began, the horror at the brutality of Nazi Germany completed. But three decades after the defeat and destruction of Nazi Germany, a state unique in that it had built part of its antisocial system on perverted forms of race and heredity theory,[45] the science of ethology is saying that much of human evil is innate. Man is not really very close to God, the argument goes. He is much closer to the ape, the wolf, and the rat. He is not a sinner but a beast.

That man is a killer because killing is part of his nature is an idea all too easy to accept, according to Ashley Montagu.[46] In recent years not only has it received the support of scientists including Niko Tinbergen, Raymond Dart, Konrad Lorenz, Desmond Morris, and Marston Bates, but it also has been disseminated in the mass media by novelists such as William Golding and Anthony Burgess, film makers like Stanley Kubrick and Sam Peckinpah, and actors such as Malcolm McDowell.[47] Moreover, the idea of man-as-killer is a peculiarly comforting rationalization, excusing the varieties of violence and bloodletting reported all around, and encouraging, perhaps, a furtive belief that contemporary men should be even more aggressive than before in their day-to-day dealings with others.

However, one thrust of the animal studies which have been the basis for the ethological thesis about human aggression has emphasized the mechanisms of control that nature has supplied to restrict and restrain the most terrible consequences of animal nature.[48] Thus, part of Lorenz' study of aggression shows that love and friendship, and other bonds of strong personal attachment among mates and packs, tend to limit the aggressive instinct to an expression only against outsiders.[49] Other ethologists have emphasized how little actual overt fighting there is among animals of the same species. Real aggression is rare, they argue, because behavioral controls reduce anger to rituals of display, threat, submission, or appeasement.[50] And when violent conflict does ensue, it tends to be defensive, usually parried easily, or even an expression of a merely passive defense.[51]

The real value of animal studies for the science of man and the understanding of the sin of anger is in their provision of clues to the nature and expression of dramatic and ritual display mechanisms. While the proof for innate or species-specific aggressive tendencies is unimpressive and in fact largely nonexistent, the illustrative materials provide a veritable "theater of the animals." That theater, announced and anticipated a half century ago by Nicolas Evreinoff,[52] describes the dramatic quality of the body movements, facial features, and vocalized gestures that both incite and define the action of every kind of animal—cats, dogs, elephants, lions. Ethology has given precision and exactitude to Evreinoff's hypotheses. Rather than insisting on the ethological inversion of the "pathetic fallacy," sociologists might better employ the results of investigations of animal behavior to sharpen their own understanding of the theatrical basis of human life. Then sin, rather than being pushed into the primordial ooze by evolutionist ethology, would be produced before the proscenium of dramatistic sociology.

Phenomenological Sociology and Anger

Recent developments in sociology have focused on a frequent error of earlier approaches—mistaking the topic of study for the resource for understanding or explaining it.[53] Many of the older major theories have treated societal arrangements and social actions as if their existence flowed directly out of values preestablished, or violated, in the society. Certain newer schools—especially ethnomethodology and the sociology of the absurd—regard arrangements and actions as social accomplishments carried out by actors competent in the skills necessary to assemble the social order.[54] In this light the seven deadly sins may be seen as aspects of everyday life when they become part of the architectonic procedures by which people carry out and comprehend their own daily existence.

Anger is capable of being restored to its sinful proportions by such perspectives while it still may be studied dispassionately. The issues of freedom and determinism lose their status of philosophical absolutes and become instead existential possibilities on a continuum, with each individual and group enjoying variable but determinable experiences of humanistic self-control and fatalistic domination. Responsibility and guilt for choosing to do something that either is known in advance to be evil or becomes such as a product of the interpretive process are assessable in terms of the degree of experienced freedom of the will that prevails.[55] From this point of view the aggressive delinquency engaged in by a portion of America's male (and increasingly, female) youth is explicable partly as an idiosyncratic variant of the cultural encouragement to masculinity but much more as acts attempting to release individuals from the mood of fatalism. Believing that they are like balls on a pool table, that is, their motion is possible only when pushed or struck by powerful agents, the young people convert their unfreedom to a "humanistic" liberation by making others act: they assault symbols of power, deviation, or weakness, they rob, rough-house, or wreck. In the very acts of violence they invite the authorities to come after them; they have pushed the authorities to action by their own infractions.[56]

Dramatistic sociology not only helps understand the relation of anger to sin, guilt, and human freedom but also comprehends the social control of aggression as well. The fundamental cause of aggression, we have argued, following Homer, is damage to or loss of self-esteem. Modern societies provide a remarkable number of institutional and noninstitutional degradation ceremonies that unintentionally or by design deprive individuals and groups of their sense of personal and moral worth as well.[57] Sending people to social death while leaving them physically alive is a dangerous move, since, like Achilles, they might strike out in enraged fury. As a matter of social fact, however, arrangements are often made to lessen the loss, teach the degraded not only to accept defeat but also to suffer humiliation in silence.[58] A drama of moral resignation is enacted by persons, personnel, or personification. Moreover, anticipating societally induced loss of esteem, some individuals hedge their bets by avoiding commitment to perilous roles and statuses, by multiplying their statuses and diffusing their involvement, by engaging in role-distancing devices to ensure against future losses. The dramatic ploys, the chances for relief and retribution, the joys of victory and the mortifications of defeat are all part of the sociocultural scenario in which the sin of anger plays a vital but variable part.

ANGER AND TERRITORY

Although it is doubtful that an ethological imperative to occupy and defend territory can be demonstrated for humans, it is nevertheless the case that territoriality is a significant dimension of human endeavor.[59] The precise relationship of anger to territorial defense and aggression resides in the fact that space confers status and esteem upon its owners and occupiers, while its loss carries with it a concomitant humiliation. Distinguishing among the several types of territory, we have already discussed anger and defense of its most intimate form under the heading of sexual property. There is also the defense and aggression toward public territories in the form of war, patriotic nationalism, and population expansion; the protection of home territories against defacement and desecration; and the guardianship of interaction territories against interlopers. In each case of territorial challenge there is the potential for anger, the palliative of social control, and the possibility of chaotic outrage. Herein we will consider the relation of anger to loss of esteem in public and home territories.

Public Territories

Anger expresses one of its most terrible faces in the conduct of war.[60] In what passes for the international order, the spaces of the world are divided up into landed sovereignties that compartmentalize territory, create states, and certify collective esteem. Several consequences flow from these social facts. First, the macrocosmic order recognizes a social control that affects self-determined and institutionalized aggregates but not human individuals. Not only does occupation of land confer collective prestige but also, and of equal importance, control over land transforms the state created thereby into a fictional being, empowered to speak for individuals and anthropormorphized with a will, sentiments, and memory. Among its endowed qualities is the capacity for dignity and, with its loss, rage. Second, precisely because the boundary lines of territories mark off political units embodying ultimately the charisma of the dominating peoples, trespass of those lines constitutes a prima facie case for armed defense. Ironically, the instrumental character of terrain that makes its occupation necessary for military tactics also constitutes the casus belli that necessitates the employment of those tactics. Geographic considerations help engender the establishment of peaceful relations *within* territorial units; they also imply hostility as encroachment, rivalry, and international competition erupt in conflict. Third, the territorial state or portions of it becomes a *stake* in bellicose struggle, an *environment* for basic hostilities, and a *theater* of belligerent operations. Territoriality and aggression are complements in man's never-ceasing attempt to come to terms with nature, culture, and self.

As a *stake* in the international game of diplomacy and war, territory holds no equal. Pieces of territory are all too often endangered by threats of invasion, occupation, secession, or reconstitution. Good examples are found in borderlands, where two sovereign powers claim ownership or control of the strips of land or water that separate and connect them. A massing of troops along the border is usually signal enough that an invasion is expected, and the organized anger of both parties to the dispute will be aroused. Homelands are often stakes in the struggle for prestige engaged in by diasporic peoples. Zionism has found both its moral sustenance and its material fulfillment in the establishment and maintenance of Israel against the claims of Arabs and Palestinians and within the wider power games of the international cockpit. And, as the geographer MacKinder observed, the control of heartlands and rimlands is sufficiently important that areas designated as such are stakes on whose diplomatically wagered outcome world peace and human survival might depend.[61]

As an *environment* conditioning the expression of collective anger and resentment, territory provides a varied landscape. It is an exaggeration to say with Montesquieu that liberty is likely to be better defended in mountainous, sparse regions than in flat, fertile ones. But his central point comes close to our own, namely, that where the terrain itself, rather than its products, is the source of prestige, an angered response to encroachment upon it is likely. Older geographical thinkers used to say that climate and topological conditions determined the destinies of peoples and states. But, as Teggart and others have pointed out, while everywhere the beginnings of political organization have been determined by the physical disposition of the land, these dispositions in turn have been determined by peoples who, in their movements over the face of the earth, have paused to take stock, designate, describe, and organize territory.[62] Once a point of land or sea has been established as a significant terminus of a trade route, Teggart argued, it continues to be regarded as such despite successive waves of conquest and resettlement. Although many heartily subscribe to Teggart's corollary theory on climatological causes for population movement,[63] Teggart's own emphasis on the fact that certain points of land tend to remain fixed in purpose and definition reinforces the conservative element in territorial processes. Such fixity tends also to be enhanced and legitimated by the emotional attachments that develop around such territorial points. Territorialized emotion, in turn, becomes the threatened representation of dignity and worth in defense or destruction of which wars erupt.

When territory is perceived as a *theater of operations* we come closer to seeing the role of anger and aggression in the scenario of human life. Here we recognize that terrain has just those endowments that man chooses to recognize and employ as stakes in or as environments of action. The military science and martial art of geopolitics becomes a form of the pre-text, that is, the written scenario, from which real action may flow. However, just as the text of action differs from the pre-text of scenario in the production of a play, so also the texts of war and aggression differ from the pre-texts of the geopolitical playwrights who encourage them.

It was Karl von Clausewitz (1780-1831), perhaps the greatest writer on war, who reluctantly recognized this distinction. This Prussian student of belligerency wished war not to be considered in terms of the many varied, chaotic, and absurd events that composed it, but rather as "great decisive events which must be dealt with separately."[64] Lamenting that most wars "appear only as an angry feeling on both sides, under the influence of which, each side takes up arms to protect himself, and to put his adversary in fear, and—when opportunity offers—to strike a blow," von Clausewitz attributed the failure of total war to develop to the "number of interests, forces, and circumstances of various kinds, in the existence of the State, which are affected by the War, and through the infinite ramifications of which the logical consequence cannot be carried out." In effect, von Clausewitz grudgingly conceded that the state is a great and varied theater of actions, a plethora of scenarios, plots, subplots, and characters, each of which is moving in accordance with the text of its own or its group's drama. The result, and von Clausewitz could only bemoan his discovery, is that "man, who in great things as well as in small, usually acts more on the impulse of ideas and feelings, than according to strictly logical conclusions, is hardly conscious of his confusion, unsteadiness of purpose, and inconsistency."[65] It is precisely in this conception of territory as a theatrical stage that we understand the onset, the control over, and the conclusion of aggression. Endowed with the human capacity to suffer disesteem through encroachment on its life space, the territorial state erupts in war to defend itself or to aggrandize its prestige. But composed of an infinite variety of real dramas, the state must occasion the enactment of its own "grand guignol" in recognition of the other plays that go on around and within it. The staging area of war, the territorial state, is also the theater for escape from, opposition to, or subversion of belligerency.

Home Territory

Once an area has been marked out by some population so that it bears their special insignia, their personal charisma, or their particular identity pegs, it becomes especially significant to those who have endowed it with their own unique qualities. The translation of territorial states into national entities constitutes the current extension of this phenomenon in the macrocosm. But on a lesser level, "home territories" can be noticed in the variety of niches, recesses, ornamented places, and carved-out spaces that humans furnish with their own special character. Precisely because these places have become virtual extensions of the group that inhabits them, they also absorb the dignity of that group. To damage or destroy their architecture and artfulness, their symbols and substance, or their material and moral matter is to assault the dignity, esteem, and worth of those who occupy them. Thus it is that home territories are also fortified castles. They habitually enjoy the peace and tranquility that their inhabitants find in private communion. But once encroached upon by invasion, violation, or contamination the inhabitants are likely to turn on their depredators in rage and even frenzy. The sin of anger is aroused by the defilement of someone's domestic habitat.

Perhaps the finest illustrations of angry defense against encroachments on home territory are to be found in the reactions to imposed reconstructions and forced reorganizations of those domesticated niches created under conditions of stress, strife, or sequestration. The jealous guardianship of small spaces taken over by British families in the crowded London Underground tunnels during World War II bombings, the seizure and protective defense of window seats and other prized territories by inmates in insane asylums, the sometimes rigid housekeeping rules and hostile reactions to outsiders that prevail among inmates in their small cells all testify to the moral worth and mental anguish incarnated in home territories. Perhaps the extreme reaction to encroachment is found in concentration camps, where, stripped of every other source for self-esteem, prisoners cling to the small spaces out of which they have carved a rude "home." Consider two examples: the internment camps for Japanese Americans during World War II, and the civilian detention camp in Shantung, China, during the same war.

From 1942 until 1945 approximately 120,000 persons of Japanese descent residing in the United States were ordered to move first into evacuation centers and then into barbed-wire-enclosed camps.[66] A population composed of all ages, both sexes, a wide range of classes, occupations, and professions, varied social outlooks and political orientations—65 percent of whom were citizens of the United States— suddenly discovered it had become outcast, tarred with the prejudicial brush of race and ancestry, and ignominiously degraded by incarceration. Cries of moral indignation, however, were also accompanied by practical efforts at making a way of life under harsh and unpromising conditions. Once removed from their homes, jobs, familiar surroundings, and friends, Japanese Americans found it physically necessary and morally advisable to domesticate the barren wasteland of the barely constructed camps to which they had been exiled.[67] Dormitories were decorated, eating places established, a wide variety of former activities reconstituted, and new practices developed. Artwork flourished in some camp areas, creating what one observer called "beauty behind barbed wire."[68]

While no one who lived there would call these intensive accommodations to an unjust imprisonment the creation of a home, nevertheless home territory orientations grew up around the niches and crevices of private life that were created.[69] But because these were prison camps, operated by a self-arrogating racial caste superior in strength and armament, fears and apprehensions about these private arenas interfered with whatever small joys they might provide in an otherwise unredeemed vale of sorrow. This was especially the case in those camps, such as the one at Poston, Arizona, where tar-paper shacks badly needed the lumber that did not arrive, where stoves were in short supply, where the bitter cold of the night was matched by the blazing heat of the midday sun, and where camp informers, spies, FBI agents, and constant surveillance made each individual feel less than secure even in the recesses of that small space engineered for personal solace.[70] The hurt and anger that festered swelled into ugly incidents. Inmates suspected their fellow prisoners of harboring designs on their few possessions and privileged places, of being spies or slaves of the white camp management, of conspiring with both other inmates and the *hakujin* bosses to heap even more indignities on the already demoralized inhabitants of the camps. In some cases, an altercation between a few angry men or the breaking of a government promise was all that was needed to evoke a violent riot. And at the end of the war, when the Japanese Americans were at last permitted to leave the camps and return to their former homes, a few had developed emotional attachments to the little havens within the barbed-wire enclosure. Fearful of what would greet them in their former habitats, some were reluctant to leave the shacks and barracks that had housed them for three years.[71]

During the same war, the Japanese occupation forces in China established a detention camp in Shantung for over 2,000 British and American civilians who had not escaped from the war-torn area. Crowded together in a very small space, and often enjoying not even a subsistence existence, these inmates also founded tiny colonies of special purpose which they guarded against every type of encroachment. Langdon Gilkey, one of the prisoners who organized and participated in the self-help "housing authority" inside the compound, was at first astonished at the difficulty in obtaining consent for equalizing housing conditions, dividing up sleeping quarters according to reasonable needs, or taking care of orphaned or wayward children. Eventually, however, he began to understand that the angry and occasionally violent responses to any suggestion that the private organization of domestic property be reapportioned stemmed from the sop of psychic support and shred of self-esteem that ownership or control of space gave to humiliated individuals and despairing families. The great fear, he noticed, arose out of an apprehension that one did not belong anywhere, that one existed only in a "free and faceless air." "Everyone, having lost his 'place' in his home and club porch in the treaty ports, and thrown into cramped quarters with insufficient room to establish himself, felt less than real until he had made some small corner of space his own."[72] Gilkey further observed that the "lonely and isolated people in our dorms would cling to every inch of space as if it were the very foundation of their being—as indeed it was." Individuals and groups attached markers and memorabilia to a special place. "They would lavish on it and its sacred dimensions the same fanatical love that a nation will lavish on the boundaries of its territory." And in this regard the colonizers and establishers of these tiny home territories in effect vowed to protect and defend them against all enemies. In their refusal to share bedroom space, provide more play areas for young people, or take in other people's children, Gilkey began to see what for him had been a hitherto unnoticed feature of human nature. Ultimately he concluded that "in the wider world, each of us, driven by this fear of never 'being' at all, is eager to 'make a place for himself' by almost any method available. And it is for that reason that we will defend our present status with all our ferocity if we should feel it threatened."

THE DRAMA OF ANGER

As the studies of aggression in animals have already indicated, anger is very much a matter of display and the management of expression. It partakes of the dramatic art. Indeed, again taking a clue from the discoveries in ethology, we may take note of the fact that the *display of anger* is often a deterrence to the doing of violence. The wolf bares its teeth, and the opposing wolf turns and slinks away. So, often enough, is the case with anger in human beings. Anger is expressed as an orientation within a role played by an actor before an audience. And the display of anger does or ought to have an effect. Its visual and aural presentation becomes part of what George Herbert Mead called the conversation of gestures in which all individuals engage and from which they understand the meaning and value of a situation.

However, like any dramatic effect, anger must be recognized as such. Here we are concerned with the presentation and interpretation of man's artful practices such that a consensus on their definition is possible. In dramatic parlance we are concerned with the physical, behavioral, and gestural techniques in which an actor engages in order to indicate to others that he is in the ritual state appropriate to the scenario. Anger requires a patterned range and modulation of voice, a limited and more or less specified employment of the face, arms, and hands, and a stance that distinguishes the perturbed state from others. In situations of collective anger and crowd hostility, there are other techniques that express the same sentiment. And, as with so many elements of human display, cultural variations may dictate alternative modes; thus it is that an expression of anger derived from the codes of one culture may go unrecognized as such before an audience from another.

Let us first consider the face and body. As Georg Simmel once observed, the anatomy of the face constitutes the small space on which most people depend for the communication and understanding of the entire repertory of human emotions.[73] By the artful manipulation of the skin of the forehead, the arch of the eyebrows, the movement and intensity of the eyes, the flaring or closing of the nostrils, the curvature of the mouth, the color of the cheeks, and the jutting of the jaw, humans indicate to others (and to themselves when looking in a mirror) their own interior emotional state. The reading of "other minds" is not only a problem of analytic philosophy but also a practical process of everyday life. States of mind express themselves in the first instance as states of body.

Nature has assisted man in developing a set of anatomical props useful for the display of anger and the threat of aggression.[74] Thus the chin with its forward projections provides the possibility for jutting which is everywhere taken as a sign of anger and defiance. Where the chin is too weak to be jutted, hair in the form of a thick and full beard can be shaped to indicate strength and superiority. Voice modulation also serves to indicate anger, either in low registers as a growl or a snarl or in the upper pitches as an enraged scream or shout. The fact that children and women tend to have moderate voices, little or no facial hair, and modest jaw development restricts their capacity to appear angry to others and in turn protects them in some measure from the bullying aggression of a jut-jawed, shouting adult male.

Skin and mouth are also parts of the dramatic arsenal of aggression. The skin changes color in rage, so that a reddening of the cheeks and forehead (in Caucasians) is a fairly sure sign of rising anger. The facts that in humans there tends to be a much greater baldness in the forehead than in other primates and that hair style and cosmetics often compress the bare forehead space on females tend to increase the strength-anger display possibilities of males, providing more area for exposed redness. Teeth, of course, are typically associated with expressions of anger, and the cosmetic presentation of teeth, such as the practice of *ablation* (knocking out certain teeth), can assist in shows of ferocity. Thus, where the upper incisors are removed as a puberty rite, the gap is framed by the two lower incisors, giving off an aggressive biting look, such as is found in the makeup Hollywood gives to vampires. Mottling the teeth and making their edges jagged or rough produce a similar effect. The mouth, together with the tooth display and voice production, also expresses anger through lip curvature and pursing or opening.

Height and weight increase the look of menace such that very big people are also taken to be very aggressive or capable of ferocious response when aroused. A good example of how the combination of voice, height, and physique can inadvertently produce an attitude of aggression is reported by body builder Arnold Schwarzenegger. On a beach in Santa Monica, California, a girl heard him talking, thought his Austrian accent sounded like that of Dracula, and turned to face him. Wide-eyed and terrified at the sight of his mammoth proportions, she ran screaming across the sand, shouting, "It's a monster, it's a monster."[75] Where persons are short and scrawny their shouts, reddenings, and gestures might be taken less seriously or even as a matter for mirth. Indeed the potential for humiliation with which nature endows some of her subjects is itself a source for rage, as an original expression of hostility is subverted by anatomical and physiological handicaps over which the actor has no control.

The gestures and stance associated with anger are also more or less ritualized and patterned. A woman might express displeasure with a man by slapping him in the face, a move that adds slight injury to serious insult. Men typically raise the arm, clench the fist, and sometimes shake the extended limb vigorously. In some cases these same acts are taken as aspects of tension management holding back an even greater threat of violence, as when the upraised arm or the clenching and unclenching fists are recognized as a self-restraining drama of indignation in lieu of a knockdown fight. Stature and stance tell much about one's emotional state, so that humans who walk in a bowed position look much less offensive than those who carry themselves straight and upright. And the gross, tall person towering over a sitting group, as some large and overweight college teachers have discovered, can cause the seated ones literally to cower in fear.

However, the drama of anger is not confined to the anatomy of its actors. There is also the scene. Anger is an appropriate expression in certain types of scenes. The central plot line of these scenes is the rupture of relations. Elsewhere we have outlined the framework for understanding these phenomena in terms of game analysis.[76] Here it is sufficient to note that a tactic in the breaking of relationships that once were comfortable is a display of anger. Thus it is that the strategic research site for studying the scenario of anger is any situation where individuals or groups must break up in opposition to one another. The ending of intimacy and courtship among lovers, the collapse of negotiations between the representatives of workers and management, the onset of feud, and beginning of rebellion are all theaters of angry display. In every case what might begin as a reasonable discussion among rational parties will prove unproductive. Perhaps one party wishes to withdraw from the relationship while the other does not. Or perhaps one party has an outstanding difference with the other, or is exploiting the other, or threatening the other. Whatever the case, there often comes a moment when, all else having been of no avail, or else to punctuate the intended rupture, anger is openly expressed. When Hamlet breaks with Ophelia, when blood feuds break out in the Mediterranean area, when peasants rise in revolt, or when working men go out on strike, a ritual of angry drama usually precedes the separation of parties.[77] Moreover, should the break be followed by open conflict or war, ritual displays of anger will be continued as part of the struggle.

Moreover, the drama of anger finds ritual expression in certain occupations and sports. Football players are sometimes reported to work themselves into a rage before leaving the locker room; boxers sometimes display hostility by heaping abuse upon their opponents, snarling, and baring their teeth; exponents of the Chinese martial arts utter guttural noises, shrieks, and shouts, go through an elaborate and artistic display of body and hand movements, and then attack their opponent. On the other hand note how one must distinguish between the imitation of anger necessary to communicate a hostility that is only pretended, the contrivance of anger that is calculated for improving aggression or ensuring a break, and the outbreak of uncontrolled anger that occurs when the insult or injury to one's dignity is too overwhelming to bear. While each type of anger is recognizable analytically, each bears a different moral valence. The mock anger of the professional wrestlers that everyone who knows the game takes to be only a pretense is a source of fun in a harmless and "fixed" encounter. The contrived anger of the businessman, who has rehearsed his part and knows just when and how to explode in rage, is recognized as a useful and sometimes effective tactic in ongoing commercial relationships. But the spontaneous uncontrolled rage of the truly angry person is often taken as a weakness, a defect in character, and, in an older parlance, a sin.

FOUR

Pride

To be God is to be all that there is to be and to be impeded by
no restraint whatsoever. . . . The vision of Prometheus returns
in each age to tempt men with the hope that they can be more
than they were created to be. The rabbis were well aware of
the yawning abyss of nothingness which the apocalyptic
promise of Prometheus barely disguised. . . . The preference
of rabbinic Judaism was always for limitation and life rather
than perfection and death.

*Richard L. Rubenstein**

Although pride has often been designated the first sin and even as the root
of all others, it has an ambiguous status, even containing positive
elements that negate its sinfulness. Its synonyms reveal the possibilities
for contradictory, or at least euphemistic, evaluations—self-respect, self-
esteem, self-confidence, arrogance, conceit, haughtiness, dignity, gratifi-
cational identity or association, egotism, and vanity. The absence of
sinful pride is called humility or modesty, but these apparent virtues hide
their own faults and failings. Humility can give way to servility and
obsequiousness—an exaggerated enhancement of the other's and a slavish
devaluation of one's own worth. Modesty can lead to extremes of self-
effacement, denials of one's existence and value that threaten social
withdrawal or personal extinction. Poised somewhere between sinful
vanity and self-destructive submissiveness is a golden mean of self-esteem
appropriate to the human condition. Straying too far from it in either
direction leads to active evil or passive victimization. Discovering the
proper stance for oneself or identifying the sin of pride in another is
difficult, and opportunities for exculpation are many.

Early Christian Views of Pride

In the development of the seven deadly sins, pride did not always take first place. The earliest reference to seven chief sins, in the "Testament of Reuben," a part of the pseudepigraphical *Testament of the Twelve Patriarchs* (109-106 B.C.), lists vainglory and pride as separate sins in the fourth and fifth positions.[1] Evagrius of Pontus (died c. A.D. 400), one of the earliest orthodox Christian writers to employ a schedule of cardinal sins—he listed eight—designates vainglory and pride as the sixth and seventh sins. Although Leontius of Neapolis, a seventh-century divine, named pride as the leader of the first troop of demons that accosts the soul on its journey to heaven in his *Vita sancti Joannis eleemosynarii*, Abba Isaias had much earlier insisted that all sins were derived from *desidia* (that is, *acedia*). John Cassian (died c. A.D. 435), whose list of seven sins was eventually superseded by that of Gregory the Great, observed the evil superiority of pride when he wrote "How great is the evil of pride, that it rightly has no angel, nor other virtues opposed to it, but God himself as its adversary."[2] The Cassianic list placed gluttony first among the sins and *superbia* (arrogance) last, an order based on the belief that each sin grows out of the previous one, but also directed as a warning against the vices to which monks were especially vulnerable—gluttony, lust, and *acedia*.

The elevation of pride to first place in the sins was proposed by Gregory the Great. In fact Gregory set aside *superbia*, as the root of all sins, and began his list of seven sins with *vana gloria* (vainglory). Later *superbia* and *vana gloria* were combined and a compound "pride" came to head the conventional list. Despite a proffered reordering of the sins by Henry of Ostia (died A.D. 1271), one that still left *superbia* in the prime position but put *avaritia* (greed) second, the order proposed by Gregory the Great has remained the most popular.[3]

Gregory's analysis of pride is particularly astute. For him pride was "the queen of sins," which, having "fully possessed a conquered heart . . . surrenders it immediately to seven principal sins . . . to lay it waste." "[P]ride is the root of all evil," Gregory continued, "the beginning of all sin." The seven principal vices that "spring doubtless from this poisonous root" and become, in effect, its "first progeny" are "vain glory, envy, anger, melancholy, avarice, gluttony, [and] lust." But each of these has its own army of vices which it leads. In the case of "vain glory there arise disobedience, boasting, hypocrisy, contentions, obstinacies, discords, and the presumptions of novelties."[4] The essence of pride, in Gregory's terms, was an arrogance wherein man "favours himself in his thought; and . . . walks with himself along the broad spaces of his thought and silently utters his own praises."[5]

Arrogant, isolated, and full of his own praises, the sinfully proud man wrongs God, himself, and society by his haughty withdrawal and voluntary removal from the blessings of God and the vigilance of the world. Pride alienates man from God, but it separates him from society as well. He departs from devotion to and the grace of God—and he exiles himself from the company of and cooperation with his fellow humans. He becomes the ever-flattering companion of himself. Just as lust shuts off the couple from holy chastity and removes them from the constraints imposed by companions and codes of conduct, so also pride alienates its solitary victims. Pride militates against the theocentric world view and the mundane community at the same time. Its awesome vice is *monadic withdrawal.*

Gregory traces the evolution of its tyranny over both soul and society. Pride conquers step by step.

> He who with enslaved mind admits this tyranny within himself suffers the first greatest loss, for the eye of his heart being closed, he loses calm of judgment. Then it comes about that all the good things of others become displeasing to him, and the things he has done himself, even when they are mistaken, alone please him. Now he always looks down on the doings of others and admires only his own actions; because whatever he has done, he believes he has done with singular skill . . .[6]

Gregory's commentary brings Christian thought together with that of Aristotle. The orientation of the theological writings on sin pointed toward the vices likely to affect monks and anchorites, but the Greek philosopher had been concerned with a more worldly and mundane problem in ethics.

Aristotle on Pride

Aristotle envisioned a social type or ideal, *megalopsychos*, the magnificent or great-spirited one, the man who in the words of Robert Payne was a "magnanimous devotee to culture, the man who dares to live alone in the secret worship of his own soul."[7] Plato had said that the man who lived alone would partake of the character of either a god or a beast, but Aristotle identified the individual alone with his carefully cultivated honor as the soul of lofty indifference. *Megalopsychos* possesses a complex attitude that centers on honor and dishonor.[8] Devoted to perfect virtue, it "is chiefly with honours and dishonours . . . that the proud man is concerned." Among the honors that will moderately please him are those that are great and conferred on him by good men, "for there can be no honour that is worthy of [his] perfect virtue." Since the greatest honor to be conferred by good men is the best that can be had, but is still not quite good enough, "he will at any rate accept it." On the other hand, this magnanimous magnificence will not allow an honor to be bestowed on him for a trivial act or by "casual people," since "it is not this that he deserves." Nor will he accept dishonor either, "since in his case it cannot be just." Concerned equally with the quality of the honors he receives and the character of those who bestow them, *megalopsychos* accepts the accolades of the worthwhile multitudes with a public show of moderation. He treats honors as if they were not so great a thing, and by extension, his bearing communicates a similar indifference toward other valuable things of this world, such as power and wealth. Since all such things seem to be regarded by him as of little value, "proud men are thought to be disdainful."

For Aristotle *megalopsychos* is a man of perfect virtue—some have uncharitably thought it was a self-portrait—distinguished from the unduly humble or the foolishly vain, and deserving of respect and emulation. Yet there is something dark and foreboding about his innerworldly indifference. His cultivated sense of faint ennui at the world and all it has to offer allows him to be the sole arbiter of his expenditure of energy and wisdom. He not only chooses his benefactors but also the recipients of his bounty—and incidentally puts the latter in his debt, "for he who receives a service is inferior to him who has done it, but the proud man wishes to be superior." He selects his acts with an eye to their honorableness and chooses the conditions surrounding his social contributions: he is "a man of few deeds, but of great and notable ones." *Megalopsychos* is open in hate and love "except when he speaks in irony to the vulgar." But when it comes to hazards he does not leap into those that are trifling, "but he will face great dangers, and when he is in danger he is unsparing of his life, knowing that there are conditions on which life is not worth having." This man of proud virtue seems ever to assume the mask of disinterest in matters central to life. Essential to his character is an attitude of lofty detachment and unconcern that characterizes a smug spectator at the amusements that the theater of life has to offer. But Aristotle treats *megalopsychos* as having realized a golden mean of pride that neither demeans nor defames him.

In the analysis of that mean Aristotle points to the dilemma that makes characterization of pride as a sin so difficult. The "mean has not received a name." Men desire both more and less than they deserve. Hence, when a man is criticized as "ambitious," what is meant is that he seeks more than is rightfully his and, perhaps, goes about that quest wrongfully; when criticized as "unambitious," that he is not willing to undertake what would be his for the right reasons. However, sometimes the ambitious man is praised for "being manly and a lover of what is noble," and the unambitious man is lauded for "being moderate and self-controlled." It is the combination and synthesis of these two praiseworthy character traits—a combination that has no recognized name (and therefore, perhaps, no mode of calculation)—that are found in *megalopsychos*. That unnamed synthetic compound of virtue can be realized by discovering and living in accordance with the mean that separates a host of vices from their virtuous counterparts. Among these are anger (appropriate from inappropriate); humility (obsequiousness from modesty); boastfulness (mock-modesty or bragging from truthful self-reports); tastelessness (vulgar humor or unpolished sobersidedness from tactful and convivial ready-wittedness); and shame (proper disgrace from blushing false modesty).

Buried beneath the distinctions that Aristotle draws is a latent dramatistic argument. *Megalopsychos* relies as much on the recognition of his virtuous estate as on its existence. To be sure, Aristotle insists on the actuality of virtue in this ideal man. But the indicators of that internal virtue are external, visible signs given off to others. The open display of virtue is insurance that the honor appropriate to the virtuous will be bestowed. Therefore, it behooves all those who are virtuous to endeavor *to appear to be so* as well. They must understand not only the nature of the expressions of their virtue but also how to reveal them to others. Without this knowledge of the tactics of self-display the virtuous might go unrecognized and unrewarded. By the same token, however, these outward appearances of virtue might be learned by anyone, whether he possesses the righteous character or not. Unscrupulous and mischievous persons hence might appropriate the symbols of *megalopsychos* without possessing any of his substance. The problem for those seeking to discover the truly worthy, then, is one of ascertaining authenticity. Prideful sin might be masked by modest dignity.

Adam Smith on Pride

A further specification of the sinful aspect of pride is to be found in Adam Smith's elaboration of the original Aristotelian argument.[9] Smith wishes to locate vice in those who are excessive in their estimation of themselves. Nevertheless he equivocates, calling some of those who are extravagant in praise of themselves "spirited, magnanimous, and high-minded," while others, in whom "we can discern no such distinguished superiority," are difficult to pardon or even to keep in close company. The intoxication with self among the latter is either pride or vanity. But Smith wishes to distinguish between these two terms of culpability: vanity is always blameworthy, but pride is only so "for the most part." The terms "vain" and "vanity" can never be taken as complimentary, Smith argues; even when such a description is made about another's character in good humor, it remains a "foible" and a mark of ridicule. The terms "proud" and "pride," on the other hand, sometimes evoke virtue, and this is properly the case when they refer to a characterization like that of Aristotle's *megalopsychos*.

The proud, for whom we might grant greater forbearance than the vain, can be distinguished from the latter both in character and in manner. A veritable theater of hubris is opened up by Smith's distinction and subsequent discussion. Both pride and vanity are enacted in dramatic displays that the discerning eye can see, classify, and evaluate. The tokens of each vice comprise that which is directly given in the presentation of self and that which can be inferred. The proud are ill at ease among their peers and their superiors, comfortable only when they are in the company of their inferiors, whom they patronize in return for flattery. The vain, on the other hand, court their superiors, basking in the latter's reflected image, and presenting themselves as candidates for preferment and fortune. The proud are grave, sullen, and intense, quick to see the insolence in others and adamant about the injustice of the world that denies them a superior place; the vain person, by contrast, is sprightly, gay, good-natured, but annoying. The proud person tells black lies designed to denigrate his competitors and superiors; the vain tell white lies, innocent falsehoods meant to raise their own status at no one else's expense. The proud is sure of his own worth and worthiness; the vain more likely a precocious usurper of glory yet to come. The proud person is tormented by the indignity he suffers at the hands of unjust superiors who refuse to recognize his value and reward his talent; the vain lives in dread of the shame that he would suffer were his actual state to be revealed.

The proud and the vain are both dissatisfied with their lot. When pride and vanity are combined in the same person the character is flawed so severely that close human association is made almost impossible. Afflicted with both pride and vanity, the unfortunate victim of sin comes to suspect his peers and friends. "He feels that they see through, and suspects that they despise, his excessive presumption; and he often suffers the cruel misfortune of becoming, first the jealous and secret, and at last the open, furious, and vindictive enemy of those very persons whose friendship it would have given him the greatest happiness to enjoy with unsuspicious security."[10]

Smith's proud and vain man corresponds to the prideful sinner that Gregory the Great had in mind. His private torments and public fury isolate him from the sociable company of others. Moreover, his superiority to and aloofness from society are likely to temper his judgments, weakening his sense of justice and charity. A haughty spectator at the trials and tribulations of mankind, the prideful sinner is likely to respond with neither sympathy nor understanding. Filled with absurd conceit, he holds all others in disdain; from him they can expect no mercy, not even a fair hearing. Hence, the proud man not only is outside the grace of God and removed from the good fellowship of men, but he is also dangerous. As a supremely self-sufficient ego, he blasphemes God; as a being superior to the rest of mankind, he behaves arbitrarily. Standing above, beyond, and in disregard of heaven and earth, he is law and lover unto himself.

Alanus de Insulis on Pride

The particular evil in the sin of pride—its removal of man from sacred and communal constraints—is fully depicted in *De Planctu Naturae* (*On the Complaint of Nature*), by the twelfth-century writer Alanus de Insulis.[11] Alanus had available more than one thousand texts on the subject—but his single theme is monadic withdrawal, the divorce of man from his kind, the separation of the haughty ego from those who might restrain its excesses. For Alanus, the proud are those who "violently exalt themselves above themselves," and because of that "descend in ruin beneath, detract from themselves in their very arrogance, sink while they bear themselves aloft, [and in the end] destroy themselves in their self-elevation." The sin of pride leads to a self-selected departure from society so that the proud "take pleasure in individualising their actions, try everywhere to be lonely in a crowd, peculiar among the general, opposed to the universal, diverse in the midst of unity." These sinners "give themselves up to the pleasure of silence" while others engage freely in conversation, are overly involved in serious matters when others take up leisure, and enjoy "wanton pleasures" while the virtuous are engaged in religious devotions. But everywhere the issue for Alanus is isolation, disdain, aloofness. The prideful sinners "reveal, by a silence merely external, what the pride of inner indignation keeps close-shut." They care not a whit for the ordinary exchanges of everyday intercourse that betokens good-naturedness. "For they disdain to grant a share of mutual conversation to others, whether these lie in the lower walks of life, or resemble themselves in the equality of worth, or sway in more exalted eminence or dignity." Alanus concludes his description with a stunning denouement, distilling the sin of pride into three pithy phrases: "With them, being is a moment, life is a shipwreck, the world a banishment."

Pride and its concomitant, disdain for the world, are indicated in modes of speech and mannerisms of silence and also in the vanity expressed in fashionable dress and cosmetic beautification. Alanus is never so pointed as when he describes how the proud spurn even the most conventional talk. "They speak," he says, "either with a solemn pomposity or they keep silent, . . ." And their haughty disregard of all other associates shows itself in the span of time they take to answer even an ordinary inquiry: "If one requests [a] word from them, the reply is separated from the question by such a great interval of silence that it seems unrelated to it by any tie." Inner pride reveals itself as outer contempt: "their countenances present a very tempest of malevolent severity."

Alanus' discussion of adornment treats it as the very token of pride. According to Alanus the human frame itself is pressed into service in behalf of arrogance: "[A]s if they despised everything earthy, with heads thrown back [the prideful] look up to the things of Heaven, indignantly turn aside their eyes, lift their eyebrows markedly, turn up their chins superciliously, and hold their arms as stiff as a bow; their feet graze the ground on tiptoe only." What Alanus called their "external peculiarity of deportment" signifying "an inner demeanour of pride," was set off by the careful and exaggerated attention they paid to cosmetic camouflage and tonsorial display. To Alanus such adornment bespoke a wrongful identification with feminity. Some of the proud ones "make their bodies too effeminate by means of woman's attire." Alanus was not here referring to actual cases of transvestism; rather he is referring to such allegedly feminine practices as dressing "the assembly of their hairs in such peace that no breeze can lift them," clipping, plucking, or rooting out altogether "the fringes of their dense eyebrows," bringing "to bear on the stripling beard the frequent treachery of the razor," wearing excessively light gloves, and imprisoning their feet in narrow shoes. Alanus cries out against "this arrogance, this pride in men." He concludes with a solemn, even fearsome pronouncement on the life of the proud. "Their birth is fraught with sorrow, trouble and pain consume their life, and the still more painful necessity of death ends even that pain."

Georg Simmel on Pride

Alanus' treatment of adornment emphasizes the peculiar and isolating functions of dress and deportment. However, Georg Simmel, seven centuries later, while still recognizing the element of pride involved, sees these affectations as social in character.[12] The attention paid to haute couture and fine jewelry has behind it both a "kindness, a desire of the individual to give the other joy" and "the wish for this joy and these 'favors' to flow back to him, in the form of recognition and esteem, so that they [will] be attributed to his personality as values." Pride, in the form of enviable and admirable adornment, requires others as both audience and respondents. They are the company that ego requires to assure itself of its own sense of exaggerated worth. "Adornment," observes Simmel, "is the egoistic element as such: it singles out its wearer, whose self-feeling it embodies and increases at the cost of others (for the same adornment of all would no longer adorn the individual)." Yet this pride in adornment is also altruistic—"its pleasure is designed for the others, since its owner can enjoy it only insofar as he mirrors himself in them." For the proud person, then, the others act as the pool that captured the image and captivated the soul of Narcissus. But Simmel adopts a modern metaphor. Adornment, Simmel notes, "intensifies and enlarges the impression of the personality by operating as a sort of radiation emanating from it. . . . One may speak of human radioactivity in the sense that every individual is surrounded by a larger or smaller sphere of significance radiating from him; and everybody else, who deals with him, is immersed in this sphere." Writing before radioactive effects were understood, Simmel is nevertheless prescient: "The radiations of adornment, the sensuous attention it provokes, supply the personality with such an enlargement or intensification of its sphere: the personality, so to speak, *is* more when it is adorned." And that radiation, Simmel might have added, similar to the latent effects of radioactive poisoning in the body, leads to a corrosive destruction of the soul.

A MEDIEVAL EXCURSUS: CHAUCER'S "PARSON'S TALE" AND THE WASTE AND OBSCENITY IN PRIDEFUL DRESS

It is in the Parson's Tale, that unversified epilogue to *The Canterbury Tales*, that Chaucer adds to our understanding of the sin of pride by perceiving it in terms of material waste and immoral obscenity.[13] For Chaucer, as for most medieval thinkers, *superbia* is the principal sin, cause of all the others. However, his analysis of pride departs from that of earlier writings and introduces three strikingly modern notes—first, a concern for wasted material, an evil that arises from the excesses of personal adornment. Related to this is a second, obscenity, or rather an unconcern for modesty in dress and appearance, that the prideful affect as part of their general impudence. Standing apart from these visible forms of pride is yet another kind altogether—the pride that resides but cannot hide altogether within the heart. Certainly excesses in costume and immodesty in dress betray this heart of darkened pride, but so also does speech and manner itself. The proud sinner falters in both presentation of and emanations from self.

Chaucer's Parson begins with a distinction between two kinds of pride—one that is within the heart of man and thus hidden from direct inspection, and the other that is external, contained in man's appearance, but nevertheless a sign of the first. Heartfelt pride finds its expression both in evil speech and in falling victim to the "sin in clothing." Chaucer's Parson presents an extraordinary catalogue of lexical misconduct in his discussion of sinful speech. Overweening pride reveals itself in malicious *disobedience* to the commandments of God, *boastfulness* about the harm, or the good, that the sinner has done, *hypocrisy* in concealing the bad and pretending to the good, *maliciousness* in scorn for neighbors and also for the precepts governing righteous conduct, *arrogance* in beliefs about his own good nature and high station, *impudence* in a disdain for moral instruction and a complete lack of shame over sins, *insolence* in refusal to acknowledge the judgments of others, *elation* in a refusal to submit to a master or recognize an equal, *contumacy* in an indignant hostility to every authority, *presumptuousness* in undertakings, *irreverence* in withholding honor where it is due, *pertinacity* in defense of follies and overconfidence in wit, and *babbling* in an ever-constant stream of ego-inflating conversation.

From pride there arises not only these thirteen evils of vocative commission, says the Parson, but also one "secret kind of Pride." The latter is exposed in acts unaccompanied by speech wherein "a man waits to be greeted before he will give greeting," "waits or desires to sit, or else to go before [a worthier person] on the road, or to give the kiss of peace, or to offer incense, or to bring an offering in before his neighbor, and such things." In effect, to use language familiar to readers of Erving Goffman, Chaucer's proud sinner is one who elects to dominate, disregard, or dismiss altogether the tie signs, and the supportive and remedial interchanges that make social relations in public possible.[14] And why does the prideful one violate public order in this way? The Parson answers that "he has set his heart and his purpose on a proud desire to be magnified and honored before men." Pride here goes before the fall of society itself.

Like Alanus de Insulis, whose *Complaint* inspired his own discussion of pride, Chaucer speaks of excessively ornate clothing as the outer sign of pride. However, Chaucer's discussion takes a different turn from that of Alanus. For the latter, adornment of the body served as a makeshift emblem for the naked evil of the soul. Chaucer certainly shares this view, but goes a step further to treat the uneconomic waste required in such dress and to rail against the immodesty practiced in revealing clothing. Chaucer's Parson begins by asserting that "if there had been no sin in clothing, Christ would not have noted and spoken of the clothing of the rich man in the Gospel." The Parson links pride to dress, dress to wealth, and wealth to waste. Following Gregory the Great, the Parson argues that costly clothing is responsible not only for an immodesty in dress, but also for "soft living, . . . strangeness of manner and elaborate ornamentation, and for superfluity, or for great honor." There is an ambivalence here, as the last phrase shows, and the Parson follows it with a sigh— "Alas!" Honor and superfluousness are so mixed in the dress of man that sorting out the sinful from the select is almost impossible.

However, the central argument of Chaucer's Parson is that the proud man does not care to perceive the sinful expense of such finery or to notice its encouragement of both ornamental excess and sinful scantiness in dress. On the economics of waste the Parson speaks in detail, becoming, in effect, a critic of haute couture. The costliness of clothing is increased by the money spent on "embroidery, the elaborate indenting or adorning with bars, the use of waved lines, or upright stripes, twisting or curving, and the like waste of cloth in vanity." But there is more. The

Parson inveighs against "costly furring in . . . gowns, so much punching of holes with chisels, so much cutting with shears; and also the unnecessary length of the aforesaid gowns . . ." Rather than pay such a costly tribute to their own vanity, the virtuous should give the extra cloth to the poor, "who suffer great loss for the want of it." Even in his encouragement of charity, however, the Parson is checked by his understanding that stylized clothing exists as a sign of status. Even if the chastened proud ones were to give some of their own costly raiment to the poor, it would not be suitable for the poor since, as the Parson points out, such sartorial splendor is at the same time above their station and beneath their basic needs. And so, as the Parson sees it, the sin of vanity leads to an insoluble economic problem. The large amount of fabric used in the manufacture of finery drives the price of cloth up by creating a scarcity in material. The poor cannot afford even the mean garments suitable to their condition and necessity. And yet a charitable donation of the excess clothing would neither reduce the price of cloth nor rescue the poor from the cold.

Vain dress and adornment also find outlet in shameful immodesty, according to the Parson. If wasted energy and material are employed to add beauty and length to the gowns of the proud and wealthy, a wicked purpose is also served by making other garments too short and too revealing. Vanity here is closely connected to lust and to invitations to forbidden sensuality. The Parson's moral concerns permit us to note the differential effects of fashion on moral concerns about the sexes. In Chaucer's time men's fashions were far more refined and much more revealing than those of women.[15] Hence, the Parson reserves his most severe criticism for the immoralities inherent in men's clothing. Echoing Augustine on the shame appropriate to the pudenda, the Parson speaks of "the horrible and unseemly scantiness of clothing, such as these loose garments or short jackets, that on account of their shortness, do not cover the shameful members of men . . ."

It was especially in its display or exaggeration of the primary sex organs and secondary sexual parts that medieval fashion outraged decency and betokened a more than unseemly pride. "Alas!" cried the Parson, "some of them show the curves of their shape and their horrible swollen members, that have the appearance of hernia, in the wrapping of their hose." Both the color and the cling of their stockings and codpieces called an insolent and dangerous attention to men's carnality. The "wretched, swollen members that show through the ornamentation, where their stockings are separated in white and red, make it seem that half their secret organs are exposed." Other color contrasts used in fashionable men's hose—such as black and white, blue and white, black and red—exacerbated the sinful display, making it appear "that the half part of their private members were corrupted by the fire of St. Anthony, or by cancer, or by some other affliction." The attention that medieval haute couture paid to the buttocks also sinned against nature and propriety. Dazzling finery made these fleshy protuberances "look like the hind part of a she-ape in the full of the moon." The Parson was sure that this dernier cri in style exaggerated a part of the human anatomy that was "horrible to see." It was "in scorn of modesty" that impudent men called any attention to "that part of their body where they purge themselves of their stinking ordure." It was not in their fastidiousness but rather in the ornamental excess and immodest scantiness of their clothing that arrogant men—and some haughty women—"give notification of lecherousness and pride."

Pride and Dress: Later Variations

The medieval concern with the morality of men's fashion faded with the effects of the Reformation on male attire.[16] The Calvinist emphasis on the calling to which each man must hearken, the hard work that each man must undertake with respect to a vocation, the postponement of worldly gratifications, and the search for the signs of divine election led to a conservatism in taste in general and a puritanism in men's sartorial style in particular. The rise of an at first ascetically inclined bourgeois class in the cities shifted social orientations from noble courtesy to public civility. And the latter—separating itself from both the ragged vulgarity of workers and peasants and the courtly mode of the nobility—emphasized moderation in dress and manner. Bourgeois civility called for an inhibition of natural functions and an activation of a new modesty with respect to the organs of the body associated with those functions.

Naturally the changes in the direction of "decency" in manly attire did not occur all at once. According to the psychoanalyst J. C. Flugel, the "great masculine renunciation" of the claim to be considered beautiful in bodily form and elegant in dress occurred in the late eighteenth century.[17] The triumph of the French Revolution evoked egalitarian uniformity and plebeian simplicity in men's dress. Beautification and adornment of the body were given over to women, who, in exchange for the protected and presumably sought-after status of wives and sweethearts, contented themselves with a monopoly on the claim of bodily beauty and lovely and revealing costume. After this remarkable reversal and exchange of sartorial style between the sexes, women were more likely to be accused of immodesty and lustful excess in dress and adornment, and men judged as modest and altogether indistinguishable from one another in their attire.

The problems of pride have remained, but in different form and with quite different consequences from those imagined by Chaucer's

Parson. Women, having become the human repository of both beauty and the sinful pride and lust associated with it, have defended themselves with an excuse. If their own sex is unduly immodest in dress and adornment, women respond, it is only because men have forced them to be so. Courtship, marriage, and attractiveness in general have been fastened onto women, and desirability is expressed through revealing dress. Women might be temptresses, but they are not altogether guilty. Responsibility for their seemingly sinful state belongs to the men who have placed them in the path of sin. Men in turn might reply that this attempt to obviate their own guilt is a female projection. Feeling guilty about their own sinful desires, women attempt to relieve themselves of their nagging sense of culpability by blaming the opposite sex. Pride, lust, guilt, and shame thus continue to weave their complex mesh of anguish.

Men in turn, having given up the chance for that ego enhancement derived from dress, turned to other arenas to assuage and build up their pride. Most important of these is work. After the diffusion of the Protestant Ethic into nearly all aspects of Occidental culture, a man's moral and social worth became a function of his work. Competition for desirable and rewarding occupations and professions became so regular a pattern that those who chose to avoid, postpone, or show indifference to the world of work became chargeable with the sin of sloth. Clothing became less a measure of man's inner self or a source for body or ego display than a uniform that indicated occupational status.[18] Work tended to inhibit the individual ego's tendency to show itself off by resort to sartorial splendor.

However, if outwardly men were no longer enviable and desirable, they were still able to perceive these same prideful aspects in women. According to Flugel, males changed from passive exhibitionism in dress and physique to active sexual pleasure in the visualization of women's figures and of revealing fashions. The erotic pleasure in selective sexual perception might be sublimated through a generalized desire to see much of everything and know more than others. However, for many men it retains its pristine form, finding outlets in a sensual contemplation of women, fantasies, or active voyeurism. In addition, a man may bask in the reflected beauty of the woman on his arm. In such a case he enjoys a vicarious pride by keeping company in public with beautiful and voluptuous women. In more extreme cases the vanity that men once monopolized in dress and adornment is recaptured in "effeminate" manners and fastidiousness, or in transvestism.

Chaucer's Parson feared for the evil that would follow man's susceptibility to vanity in dress and demeanor. Presumably, the medieval courtier's show of his own anatomical contours indicated an excessive involvement in bodily beauty and too much concern for personal sexual attractiveness. However, the enforced puritanism of modern men's clothing seems to have produced a humiliating overreaction.[19] Flugel argued that modern men (that is, of the early twentieth century) suffer from exaggerated shame about exposure of their own bodies. Men's fashions represent "an ascetic reaction-formation." Moreover, judged "both by the satisfaction given and by its ability to adapt to real situations, men's clothing must be pronounced a failure; the wholesale inhibitions that underlie it are so severe that they cannot but cause much suffering and much loss of efficiency." According to Flugel, both unlearning and relearning are needed in order to restore men's wounded egos. First men must be convinced that neither their respectability nor their virility is dependent upon a clogging coat and a choking collar. At the same time both men and women must not only tolerate but come to admire the male body for its own sake. Men must give themselves more freedom to exploit the natural beauty of their own bodies for self-confidence and for attracting women. Flugel, however, was just as concerned about what earlier moralists considered certain evil conse-quences of vanity—homosexuality and narcissism. Somehow, men's fash-ions and men's orientations must be kept away from these deviant trajectories. In addition, Flugel argued, an increase in masculine beauty consciousness would relieve women from the "enormous temptations in the direction of an exaggerated indulgence in Narcissism." Other sins, such as envy and jealousy, are also associated with present-day sex-distinctive fashions. However, Flugel is sure that it would be possible "to devise garments that would be comfortable, hygienic, and attractive without arousing any high degree of sexual jealousy or social emulation . . ." Humility and asceticism in dress have not ended man's conflict with the protean sin of pride.

Since Flugel wrote, another revolution in attire and adornment has gone some way to dissolve the distinctions between the sexes. Although the "unisex look" has only affected a small portion of the population in the Occident and is inspired by both the student and feminist revolts of the 1960s, it challenges the division in dress that separated men from women. Accompanied by marked attempts to "dress down," to adopt styles evoking exotic and minority group identities, and by hirsuteness in men, the couture of the youthful rebels and revolutionaries nevertheless produces its own vanities.[20] Among these are all those aspects of arrogance-in-humility that occur as affectations among middle-class youth. A certain interest in hiding, playing down, or disowning their own physical beauty occurs among college women, who vie with one another to look plain and dowdy. Long hair and tonsorial carelessness seem to be encouraged by the movement; some men compete with one another to carefully stylize their hirsute commitment to nonconformity. Anti-fashion, or "Funky Chic," as Tom Wolfe calls it,[27] retains its own peculiar style, adornment, body imagery, and is a fashion of its own.[21] As such it evokes pride and shame, vanity and embarrassment, envy and contempt.

PRIDE AND THE INDIVIDUAL

Our discussion of the tortured history of pride's effects on fashion is but a particular aspect of a more general problem. Pride most frequently enters the heart and soul of the individual through egoism. The habit of valuing everything in relation to one's personal interest constitutes not only an instance of unwarranted self-centeredness but also a denial of the relevance and value of the other and a self-proclaimed exaltation of oneself. Recognition of the common humanity of mankind is supposed to deny the egoistic claims of this arrogance, while the practice of all established social hierarchies presumably permits elevation of persons or groups only for already specified and legitimated reasons. Egoism proper, then, is the usurpation by the self of illegitimate centeredness. Its expression in haughtiness, selfishness, conceit, and disdain for all others is the hallmark of egocentrism.

Egoism and Evolutionism

Undoubtedly the philosophical and cultural recognition of the individual as a discrete unit provides a basic impetus for the development of egoism. Yet the ideology of individualism has rarely been challenged on these grounds in the West, even by those who proclaim themselves advocates of pluralism or collectivism, group structures that are put forward with little more to recommend them than a collectivized projection of an ego ideal. An exception to this celebration of the individual is found in the critical commentaries of Louis Dumont.[22] Taking his cues from Max Weber's suggestion that a study of the unanalyzed elements in the expression "individualism" would be thoroughly in order for the development of comparative social science,[23] and from his own studies of India's culture and social structure, Dumont argues that Occidental sociology has failed to grasp the conceptions of society and of man as a social being that Durkheim had tried so valiantly to introduce. Dumont is at pains to make us realize that the apperception of man as a social being is more than an academic outlook—although the latter is certainly his central concern. It also holds out the possibility that man will become aware of himself as a social being, will come to understand that what he conceives and senses as his own unique personality is in fact inextricably connected to the language, attitudes, and gestures reflected in the conduct of his neighbors. Even more directly, the proper apperception of social humanity will chasten that tendency in man to suppose that a thought new to him is in fact original with and, indeed, had originated in him. All too often, Dumont points out, a general idea presents itself to an individual as a personal idea when it becomes realized in him. Man's need to claim uniqueness for himself requires him to appropriate his experiences as peculiarly his own. There is indeed a person, Dumont tells us, and for him his experiences are both personal and unique, but socially conceived; both his individuality and his experiences are made up in large part from common elements. Such an understanding might act as an antidote to unwarranted pride.

Rather than treat the individual as the starting point and a basic resource for sociological theory, Dumont proposes that the idea of the individual be considered a *topic* for investigation and individuation a *problem* for comparative historical sociology. It is unnecessary and beyond the scope of our own investigation to pursue Dumont's brilliant and challenging analysis further. One example illustrates the direction of his thought and calls attention to the institutionalization of pride in social-scientific thought. Dumont argues most persuasively that Marx, often credited with being the single most important founder of Occidental sociology, is as much affected by an unanalyzed normative commitment to the idea and the emancipation of the individual as subsequent non-Marxist sociologists.[24] As Dumont sees it, the nineteenth-century socio-logical ideal of the individual found its most pervasive representation in the Victorian gentleman. This type, as well as the scholars and intellectu-als who apostrophized him, indulged in a special variant of the sin of pride, one rooted in evolutionary historical science. Locating Victorian man at the upper end of a unilinear line of development, the evolutionists supposed that other peoples, although equal in their "humanity," were nonetheless "lower" in their development of individuating institutions and emancipatory culture. Hence, by accepting the "laws" of evolution-ary development, these scholars combined an arrogant hierarchy of peoples and cultures with a vision of humble humanistic equality. Marx was no exception to this kind of thinking. In his treatment of non-Western civilizations, Dumont argues, Marx followed the evolutionary lead and placed certain types of society on the borders of mankind, or on the lower steps of the evolutionary scale. "When Marx considers India," Dumont points out, "his strict idea of History and his perception of a fundamental difference as compared with the modern West leads him to see not a development, but a stagnation. In some manner, India is kept out of history as he understands it."[25] The egocentrism that welled up from the bowels of individualism led to ethnocentrism.

Marx's unanalyzed commitment to individualism and to an emanci-patory science in service to it is not unique. Men of science far less revolutionary than Marx have accepted the notion of the linear development of humans or of society, always treating a confidently proud and splendidly isolated Occidental type or society as the measure and ideal toward which all history is headed. As these conjectural histories of humankind take on general cultural currency, they admit just those occurrences that fit the preconceived line and expel all the rest as accident, epiphenomena, or obstacle.[26] There is in this product of Western individuation a peculiar arrogance, a disdain of the actual and the factual in the lives of "lesser" humans, a refusal to accept the complexities and surprises of lived histories. Having placed itself in the forefront of the growth of history and presented itself with the gift of its own societies' development as crowning social achievements, Occidental humankind demotes all other beings and cultures to lower rungs on the ladder of destiny and progress. The pride of the West provides an arena for prejudice against all other peoples and cultures.

Egoism, Redemption, and Revolt: The Ascetic as Redeemer and Revolutionary

Egoism entered modern social science through the evolutionary elevation of Western man above all others. It enters history in a decisive way when the introjected ego ideal comes forth as a leader of men, a maker of revolution, a giver of laws, and a commander of collective adulation. Of course not all leaders, revolutionaries, lawgivers, or objects of servile devotion are active narcissists. However, according to Bruce Mazlish, there has come to the fore in the last few centuries "a new version of the god-like legislator, a special kind of modern political type, the revolutionary ascetic . . . functionally endowed in a unique way to perform certain historical tasks."[27] Growing out of "a spirit of revolution" that Mazlish believes can be connected to the "ascetic ethos" in much the same manner that Weber showed the latter's connection to the spirit of capitalism, the revolutionary ascetic appears as a special instance of narcissism that has been given an unparalleled historical opportunity. Such figures as Oliver Cromwell are classic cases. In modern and secular eras the revolutionary ascetic appears as Lenin and Mao Tse-tung.

It is not necessary here to recapitulate the entirety of Mazlish's argument. Our concern is with the sin of pride, and in the case of the revolutionary ascetic, we discover still another sublimation of that sin. Such a person comes to believe, on the one hand, that he embodies the highest ideals, greatest virtues, and most wondrous powers and, on the other, that he must follow an inner calling to employ his gifts and talents to rescue humanity.

The Reformation, Weber has reminded us, carried ascetic isolation out of the monastic cells, bringing with it a continuing estrangement of man from the very world into which he was plunged. Imbued with his exalted sense of piety, Mazlish tells us, the Calvinist or his modern avatar might succumb all too easily to the pride growing in his saintly yet secular heart. However, a calling might redirect and channel that pride into secular revolutionary or sacred millennarian activity. No longer in conscious service to his overweening pride, the committed revolutionary comes to see his own conduct as altruistic service to God, man, or destiny. Obedient to the inner voice that tells him he alone is worthy of leadership, he leaps to the forefront of the fray that social unrest and intellectual developments provide. Or, in the absence of propitious objective conditions and ideological imperatives, he channels his creative genius into the social construction of just those elements of reality that would invite his leadership. In a secular age the calling to what otherwise might remain thoroughly introjected pride or a highly localized narcissism comes not from religious obedience but rather from history's ineluctable dictates. Thus, if history promises the end of class exploitation, the release of oppressed masses, or the liberation of humiliated minorities, then the proud ascetic can find outlet for his self-proclaimed talents and virtues by leading men into history's promised land. Whether he serves God or history is insignificant in comparison to the fact that such seemingly selfless service to an awesome impersonal authority absolves him from the sin of pride.

Asceticism adds another salvation device to the armament of the proud man who would lead others in a holy or historical cause. In one sense, asceticism involves sacrificing hubris for the benefit of nemesis.[28] The former arises from the overweening demands men make on themselves while wide awake and socially visible to others; the latter comes from below the levels of consciousness and exists in the secret protestations of the proud heart. Nemesis finds its usual outlet in fantasies of triumph. The narcissistic servant of nemesis experiences the completion of his ordinarily frustrated acts of victorious self-enhancement in imaginings of incest, sodomy, paternal emasculation, and other obscene manifestations of his supposedly enormous potency. For the revolutionary ascetic, however, fantasy is transposed. Guilt-ridden dreams are converted into soul-relieving realities of victory, or at least of its inevitability. By disavowing worldly pleasures hubris is surrendered: the revolutionary demonstrates his worthiness by concentrating all his efforts on the single, overriding, altruistic aim. Abstaining from the pleasures that leadership usually appropriates to itself as a matter of course and station, the revolutionary ascetic ostentatiously avoids sexual license, alcoholic excess, and a show of finery. In return nemesis is freed from the confines of the heart and the unconscious and given a chance to realize its erstwhile nightmares in the world at large. The revolution thus permits the darkest variant of the sin of pride to come forth, while at the very moment of its liberation the sinner is absolved from his crime.

Still another version of the exalted leader whose potentially sinful pride goes unchallenged is the ascetic redeemer. What is required for his presence as savior is the belief that a basically good society or an essentially worthy people cowers helplessly in the face of an overpowering evil, unable or unwilling to repulse it. There enters a stranger, a sympathetic but estranged outsider, who repels the terrible evil and then—in final evidence of his absolute purity—disappears, taking no reward for his services. Variations on this mythic theme are more or less commonplace, but what is significant for our purposes is the relation of such incidents and characters to sin.

The Ascetic Redeemer in American Culture

A modern version of the myth of the ascetic redeemer is played out over and over again in the popular culture and mass media of the United States. Indeed, so pervasive is this myth that two scholars, one a theologian, the other a philosopher, have dubbed it "the American Monomyth" and warned against its encouragement of civic passivity, antidemocratic irresponsibility, mass celebration of moral holidays, and, in the end, authoritarian rule.[29] Nevertheless, the modern version of the monomyth expresses the following particular morality matrix. In its ideal form, a community (village, town, or a whole nation), inhabited by a joyous and for the most part good-hearted people, is enjoying a paradisiacal existence, untroubled by the general social evils to be found elsewhere. Law, order, and social control seem hardly necessary—until evil menaces the town. However, the particular evil does not strike until it is triggered by some sinful excess among the townspeople. Typically, the sin that invokes this punitive response is lust, although greed, gluttony, and sloth are not uncommon. Corruption in the Edenic community provokes a kind of terrible, arbitrary, and excessive retribution (attack by outlaws, foreign invasion, assault by a murderous shark, whale, or gorilla, tidal waves, earthquakes, and so forth). But the complacent citizenry is so inured to evil that it refuses to believe in or take concerted and rational action against the threatening menace. Moreover, the civic and social institutions prove helpless—unable to function because of callousness, corruption, or cowardice.

Enter the redeemer. Often enough he is a resident of the community, and, although a permanent outsider to its social relations, he shares in its beliefs in peace, harmony, and joy. His initial condition of moral equality with the rest of the community fails to set him sufficiently beyond and above them. All too often his early warnings and his advice on what to do about the threat go unheeded; sometimes they are even derided. However, the assumption of redemptive obligations requires social distance from and moral elevation above the population and especially from its sins. Hence, the would-be redeemer cuts himself off from sexual pleasure, eats and drinks sparingly if at all, works hard on acquiring the knowledge and skill to overcome the great enemy, tempers his anger at the complacency of the others, neither seeks nor envies the worldly rewards that go to his less worthy companions in the struggle, and humbles himself in the face of the terrible task that his inner calling has compelled him to carry out. Having driven off the temptations to sin, he overcomes the evil that endangers the others, rescues the community, and then retires from public life. No one accuses him of exercising an overweening pride.

The ascetic redeemer appears as the stranger, but, in order to assure us of his lack of pride, often enough he ends up as a wanderer, or he disappears altogether. However, the helplessness of the populace remains. Hence, in the absence of any new social order, his or some substitute's services will be required again. "There must be a Lone Ranger," as LeRoi Jones once said.[30] There are alternatives, however. The redeemer can set aside his humility, accept the plaudits of the crowd, and translate his conquest of evil into command over the community. Presumably, nemesis is not sinful in this case because populist legitimism justifies the redeemer's authoritative control. In such a manner can pride go before a rise.

Narcissism: Sin and Sublimation

There can be little doubt that egoism has been given greater opportunity for outlet in the Occident because of the emancipation of the individual from the several solidarities that at one time circumscribed and checked its expression. The general process that demolished these solidarities can be summed up by the term "individuation." The emancipation of the individual from the kindred, the clan, and the family, and the individuating functions of a money economy, private property, religious individualism, demographic diversification, and intercultural contacts are among the most recognized forms of that process.[31] In the variety of emphases that social scientists and philosophers have given to it, the individuating process is noticed as part of the transition from status to contract (Maine); from mechanical to organic solidarity (Durkheim); from Gemeinschaft to Gesellschaft (Tönnies); from traditional to rational-legal law (Weber); from Stand- to Klassen-individuum (Marx); from sacred to secular social organization (Becker); and from folk to urban societies (Redfield). Concomitant with all these sociocultural developments in the Occident is the emergence of the formally free individual as an entity in its own right. That entity had rights, claims, and demands; it also had fears, needs, and worries. One problem that arose was how the emancipated individual would find and sustain the psychic strength to secure its newly won status. One solution was enhancement of self-confidence. Egoism was given a new lease on moral life—as a basic resource for psychic security. By the same stroke, however, egoism was threatened by nemesis and its positive effects were negated by narcissism. Once again pride was caught between sin and salvation devices, between unwarranted pride and required self-confidence.

Narcissism is perhaps the quintessential form of monadic withdrawal. First identified in psychopathology by Näcke and Ellis, it remained for Freud to define it and explain its etiology. Narcissism, Freud wrote, denotes "the attitude of a person who treats his own body in the same way as otherwise the body of a sexual object is treated; that is to say, he experiences sexual pleasure in gazing at, caressing and fondling his body, till complete gratification ensues upon these activities."[32] The term derives from the Greek myth about an incredibly handsome youth, Narcissus, the son of the river god Cephisus and the nymph Liriope. The seer, Tiresias, warns Liriope that her son will live to a ripe old age "if he will not have come to know himself." Narcissus grows up to become at sixteen so comely a youth that he is the love (or lust) object of boys, girls, and the nymph Echo. However, he will give himself to no one. Eventually he is inveigled to look into a pool wherein he sees himself for the first time and promptly falls in love with his own image. Nothing can draw him away from the pool and the wonderful image he beholds in it. Unable to consummate his love, Narcissus dies at the bank. In the underworld he is permitted to gaze once more at his own reflection in the river Styx. Where his body lay on earth there grows a yellow flower with a circle of white petals in its center.[33]

Psychoanalysis has selected elements of the myth of Narcissus to develop the symptomatology of a perversion. Central to the psychoanalytic thesis is narcissistic withdrawal. Freud found narcissism among paraphrenics (schizophrenics), who characteristically display intense megalomania coupled with a withdrawal of interest from the people and things of the external world. What distinguishes the paraphrenic from the obsessional neurotic or the hysteric, Freud insisted, is that while the latter two have abandoned their relationship to reality, they have not broken off erotic relations to persons or things. The paraphrenic narcissist, on the other hand, is a true isolate: "He seems really to have withdrawn his libido from persons and things in the outer world, without replacing them by others in his phantasy." Just as the beautiful Greek youth would not let boys, girls, or even the nymphs touch him and eventually fell under the fatal spell of his own beauty, so the true narcissist takes no object for his own love except himself.

When the narcissist is totally absorbed in himself, Freud continues, so that his self-love takes up the whole of his sexual life, his orientation "has the significance of a perversion."[34] Moreover, Freud is at great pains to show us, narcissism is a likely part of the orientation of homosexuals and is a central element in an entire class of illnesses, including hypochondria, neurasthenia, and anxiety neurosis. Indeed, a common thread of libidinal withdrawal from others to the ego is found in sleep, illness, and narcissism. However, the central theme that informs the first part of his analysis derives from a disease or medical model. What is important for our purposes is that in Freud's first approach to the subject, narcissistic pride is classified as a disease, or as a symptom of a disease. Because of this diagnosis the proud person is transfigured. Once the culpable party to a sin, he has become the pitiable victim of an illness.

Freud's explanation of primary narcissism is peculiarly sociological and ultimately rooted in an unstated and perhaps unrealized cultural definition of parent and child peculiar to the modern age. Essentially, Freud argues, primary narcissism arises in the child as a product of the revival and reproduction of the long-since-abandoned narcissism of the parents. Taking the form of loving overestimation, the aroused but latent narcissism of the parents impels them to ascribe to their child all manner of perfections, to overlook and forget all his shortcomings, and to pretend to themselves that their child has no sexuality about which they should be concerned. Furthermore, parents are inclined to suspend or repeal altogether the cultural constraints and social controls to which they themselves are subject in favor of the child's gratification and privileges. Freud sums it up nicely:

> The child shall have things better than his parents; he shall not be subject to the necessities which they have recognized as dominating life. Illness, death, renunciation of enjoyment, restrictions on his own will, are not to touch him; the laws of nature, like those of society, are to be abrogated in his favour; he is really to be the centre and heart of creation, "His Majesty the Baby," as once we fancied ourselves to be.[35]

The reader who is familiar with the history of childhood in the Occident, or who has a knowledge of attitudes toward children in various cultures, will at once understand that it cannot be taken as universally valid. Rather, Freud has by this analysis unwittingly opened our eyes to one more effect of the long and as yet incomplete process of individuation in the Occident: the psychic consequences of emancipation of the child from the limitations imposed by kinship, condition, culture, and nature itself. Freud's argument shows in effect that this emancipation reveals and indeed requires a new source of confidence to replace all those once-powerful others that offered security to the enclosed individual. Once the individual is institutionally freed from the many cocoons that traditional cultural configurations and customary social sodalities provided, he is naked, alone, and unprotected. He can rely on no one but himself. But what is this "self" upon which he must place so much reliance, and whence comes its strength and security? Narcissism provides no answer to the first question but it does supply a resource for the second. The projected narcissism of the parents wraps the child in a psychic cocoon seemingly of his own making, and secures that barely established self from the onslaughts of a society that once protected and preserved it. The pattern of parental overestimation and excessive indulgence helps establish the psychic institution that must replace the now defunct social institutions of human conservation. Emancipation of the individual requires him to abandon his dependence on social security in favor of a hardly developed psychic self-sufficiency. The personal character appropriate to this liberating social structure is one in which pride must hold an important place. Less a sin than a necessity in the modern lonely age, pride is absolved from much of its guilt as the individual is freed from most of his constraints.

Moreover, at the generational level Freud's description of the onset of primary narcissism addresses the temporal direction of the antitraditional age. Man in this era must face not backward to his predecessors for support and identity but forward to his successors for hope and eventual triumph. Freud makes the point directly in his discussion of the parental expectations added to the narcissistic pride in the baby: "He is to fulfil those dreams and wishes of his parents which they never carried out, to become a great man and a hero in his father's stead, or to marry a prince as a tardy compensation to the mother."[36] Ultimately, however, this projection of the wishes of the parents onto the duties of the child goes too far. The ego ideal of the parent, in its transferral to the ego of the child, seeks nothing less than everlasting life. "At the weakest point in the narcissistic position, the immortality of the ego which is so relentlessly assailed by reality, security is achieved by fleeing to the child." Such a flight, we might observe, is not only a psychic process but also a blasphemous act. The immortality of the ego, purchased at the price of intergenerational narcissistic projection, seeks to imitate God and appropriate God's powers. Freud does not make this point. Rather, he concludes with an ambivalent coda: "Parental love, which is so touching and at bottom so childish, is nothing but parental narcissism born again and, transformed though it be into object love, it reveals its former character infallibly."[39]

Narcissism has yet another paradigm. Freud treats it in terms of love objects. Originally, he writes, every human has two sexual objects—himself or herself and the woman who takes care of him or her. The first named indicates that a primary narcissism is part of every person's makeup. Primordial narcissism thence becomes a feature of the human condition itself, and excusable on the grounds that humanity cannot escape the fundamental conditions of its existence. Of course this last argument is not part of Freud's discussion, but rather it is interjected here to show that psychoanalytic theory provides a groundwork for mitigating if not removing altogether the culpability for narcissistic pride.

The culturally approved sublimation of the second love object—the mother or the mother surrogate—is expressed in the form of dependent erotic interest in persons of the opposite sex. For women the matter is more complex, and heterosexual orientations are products of a search for security and protection. However, narcissism finds outlet directly or indirectly in erotic interest in persons of the same sex. Thus Freud points out that a love object of a narcissistic type takes as its model not the mother but the self. This occurs, as Freud says, "in persons whose libidinal development has suffered some disturbance, as in perverts and homosexuals." The narcissist, moreover, is not confined to a single model of his own self as love object, for as Freud observes he might take as his love object (1) what he is himself, (2) what he once was, (3) what he would like to be, (4) someone who was once part of himself.[38]

There is a sense in which narcissism takes a form of what might here be called "antisocial social interaction." Normal adults, according to Freud, subdue both their earlier megalomania and their infantile narcissism. The process by which this is accomplished involves creation of an ego ideal and the expenditure of ego-libidinal energies on it. The infantile narcissism is not given up; rather the individual projects it ahead of itself and onto the ideal. The ego ideal, in turn, is idealized, that is, aggrandized and exalted in the mind. Idealization, however, does not necessarily include sublimation, or deflection as an object of sexual gratification. Narcissistic love of the ego ideal is not uncommon. An unsublimated ego ideal may, however, find external outlet in the love felt for another who embodies that ideal and becomes thereby an erotic object. Whether that ideal is nostalgic, serving a love for a self once possessed, or futuristic, serving a love that embodies a self that is desired, is irrelevant with respect to its externalization. Indeed the finding of another to love seems to be the narcissist's favorite "cure" for his ailment. Having announced and felt his love for the other, he has outwardly given up the sign that he lavishes his affections on himself alone. He enjoys the gratifications of his own narcissism while seeming to have transcended it. "This is the cure by love," Freud observes, "which he prefers to cure by analysis."[39]

From the point of view of pride's principal evil, megalomaniacal social withdrawal, such love for another appears to be indeed an improvement and something of a departure from sin as well. But Freud is pessimistic about this curative. "We might be satisfied with this result," he writes, "if it did not bring with it all the dangers of an overwhelming dependence upon this helper in his need." Caught between the lonely isolation of social withdrawal on the one hand and his excessive dependence on retrojected self-love on the other, the proud narcissist suffers in anguish; his life becomes a hell on earth, perhaps more terrible than the hell imagined by the theologians and the poets.

PRIDE AND KNOWLEDGE

Pride is not exhausted by an exclusive ardor for the body or the self. It also is found in persons or groups as an expression of their condition or their achievements. It is now a commonplace of sociology to treat man in relation to two sorts of potential for worthiness—those that are ascribed and those that are achieved.[40] The former are those that are independent of individual qualities or capacities and arise out of an arbitrary assignment of sociocultural importance to universal conditions of human existence such as sex, age, or kinship. Achieved status, on the other hand, arises out of the individual's capacities, talents, accomplishment, knowledge, or his failures therein. Part of the history of the Occident is the still ongoing struggle to overthrow those systems of human worthiness based on birth or involuntary condition and to attach value to all those accomplishments that test and display the talents and mettle of an individual. To the extent that this has occurred we may speak of a meritocracy being developed in place of or in challenge to aristocracies of birth, kinship, race, sex, or age.

Once status is a function of acquisition, the individual is put on his guard to learn, train, practice, and seek out instruction in all those kinds of knowledge for which there are social and economic payoffs. Knowledge and knowledge institutions in turn provide the opportunities and certify the qualifications for individuals, who later must display whatever degree of capability, talent, skill, and originality they have acquired. It is almost always supposed that the distribution of innate abilities and the chances to acquire proper education will be less than equitable, so that meritocracies are not devoid of aristocracies and hierarchies. Such phrases as "the talented tenth" (associated with W. E. B. DuBois' approach to the establishment of a Negro leadership class) and the "aristocracy of talent" refer to the potential for elitism in societies dedicated to rewarding individual achievement.

Pride becomes both precarious and precious in meritocracies. Ideally the individual in such a society should not only take personal credit for his accomplishments but also personal responsibility for his failures. Getting ahead in such a society seems to require socialization for achievement. Those persons and groups that succeed are alleged by sociologists and by their own spokesmen to possess and encourage competitiveness, individuality, responsibility, and self-confidence, while the less successful are accused of cooperative, group-oriented, dependent, and personally insecure attitudes. The facts are no doubt more equivocal than such pronouncements and evaluations would indicate. Rather than risk the pangs of culpable failure alone, individuals are likely to invoke the claims of age, sex, race, or lineage that still prevail in their situation or society to account for their lack of success. At the same time individuals are just as likely to claim sole credit for their own successes, denying the roles that accidents of family, race, sex, or creed might have played in gaining them their eminent position. Proud of their accomplishments and excused from their failures, the successful citizens of the modern near-meritocracy enjoy more self-proclaimed entitlement than their own society actually permits, while they suffer less humiliation than they might deserve. The sin of pride is transformed into the virtue of self-confidence.

Pride, Knowledge, and Sin in Jewish Thought and Practice

Max Weber sees a remarkable instance of anxieties about self-confidence in the unsafe world of Jews in Babylonian exile and in the Diaspora. According to Weber, Jews habitually meditated upon their own religious obligations and the relation of these to their wordly condition. God (Yahweh) would look favorably on their own efforts only if they in turn were fastidious in observation of religious law. In the post-Exilic era this took the form of a theodicy of disprivilege "which expressed despair at finding any meaning in this world of vanity, submission to the chastisement of God, anxiety lest one sin against God through pride, and finally a fear-ridden punctiliousness in ritual and morals."[41] This combination of fear, acquiescence, and despair led to a desperate struggle for self-respect and an anxious search for a sense of personal worth. Self-confidence became a scarce and valuable psychic resource, and eventually success in one's occupation became the tangible evidence of God's favor. However, unlike the Puritan ethic that combined self-fulfillment in a calling with inner-worldly asceticism, Jewish economic ethics retained their traditional, nonascetic, and particularistic elements, and ultimately "produced within the realm of Judaism itself a strong component of the morality of *ressentiment.*"

The several systems of ethics that developed out of debates over Jewish thought led to a distinctive if ambiguous orientation toward knowledge. One concern here is with the relationship of a prohibition against pride to limitations in the search for knowledge. Religious justifications of deprivation retained much of the Yahwistic orientation toward God's anthropomorphic status, even after Elohistic anti-Yahwist intellectuals had tried to dislodge it. Specifically, the older Yahwistic tradition had had Yahweh regret his acts and resolutions. The most that later attempts at revision of this theme could do was "have the prophet intercede to assuage Yahweh's wrath." "Yahweh changes his mind," Max Weber goes on to observe, "either upon intercession or upon repentance and penance." It is precisely the character of anthropomorphic unmysteriousness in the Yahwistic conception of God, his binding relation with the Hebrews through a covenant, that permits dialogue, debate, and disagreement with him. Although Jews were constrained to beware of God's wrath, to obey each and every stipulation in the covenant to the letter, and to be humble, they were not in principle barred from investigating the nature and content of God's laws or of discussing the meaning and interpretation of them with God and with their fellow Jews. To be sure these discussions and hermeneutics often took place through the medium of spokesmen—charismatic leaders, prophets, priests, and rabbis—but in principle, and in the encouraged practice of universal education among Jews, they might be taken up by any Jew. The secularization of this attitude toward education found expression in a willingness to investigate taboo topics, to pioneer new and unorthodox ideas, and to seek intellectual preeminence in a world that had denied them political power, cultural authority, and social respect.

Institutionalized in Johanan ben Zakkai's school established at Jabneh in the immediate aftermath of the destruction of the Temple in Jerusalem, the celebration of learning and the measure of a man's worth by learning, testing, and a life of scholarship were both universalized and democratized. The practical demands for the "cure of souls" became secularized over the many centuries since that time in the forms of codification and study of Jewish and later other systems of law, and of application of scientific knowledge to medicine and social and psychic amelioration.[42] More important for our general theme is the fact that the pursuit of knowledge, independent of wealth or station, became the preeminent ideal. According to the historian of the Diaspora, Werner Keller, the acceptance of the leadership of scholars established at Jabneh became both characteristic of and unique to Jewish life. Keller goes on to point out that "neither origin nor title, neither connections nor material wealth henceforth decided a man's prestige, nor gave him entry to the circle of the rabbis, but solely his intellectual qualities. Any man of the people, no matter what his descent or occupation, could become a scholar, a rabbi, and hence a holder of authority."[43] Moreover, the early scholars set an example by their own occupations for distinguishing the higher worthiness of learning from whatever labor or job a man might perform. The *tannaim* (teachers) who gathered at Usha near Galilee in A.D. 135 to reconstitute Jewish life after the bloody but abortive revolt of Simon bar Kochba included Rabbi Meir, a copier of documents; Judah ben Ilai, a cooper; Jose ben Halafta, a tanner; Rabbi Johanan, a sandal maker; and Simon ben Yohai, a man so destitute—and so persecuted by Emperor Hadrian's soldiers and under constant surveillance by informers—that he and his son had lived for twelve years in a cave eating wild fruits but absorbed in their studies. Pride in learning and skill in disputation became a characteristic feature of Jewish life and one source for self- and group-confidence in the face of seemingly endless waves of gentile persecution.

However, the extent to which this Jewish search for and acquisition of knowledge has been limited by censorious controls over heresy, heterodoxy, and human hubris remains problematical.[44] On the one hand, Jews are encouraged by Scriptural authority to learn as much as they can and to study diligently; on the other hand, they are constrained by the prophet Micah (6:8) to always "do justly, and to love mercy and to walk humbly with thy God." Over the centuries, instances of unusual knowledge or esoteric wisdom, accompanied by actual or putative claims to leadership or hints of heterodoxy, have aroused censure by and, occasionally, excommunication from the Jewish community. The ambiguous fate of the kabbalistic mystic Sabbatai Sevi (1626-1676), whose messianic movement engulfed nearly the whole of Jewry from England to Persia and then was suddenly and irrevocably smashed by its leader's conversion to Islam, is one case in point. The vast majority of his once loyal followers withdrew in chagrin and amazement, treating the conversion as a shocking indication of apostasy and false messianism. That Sabbatai Sevi had been threatened with death by torture if he did not convert did not matter to most of his outraged followers. What outraged them was his rejection of Judaism. A few, however, saw his conversion as the fulfillment of his mission, a mystery wrapped in a paradox, ultimately the basis for continuing sectarian development.[45] However, to most of those who rejected him, Sabbatai Sevi had gone too far. He had failed to walk humbly with God; rather, proud of his doctrine and frightened for his life, he had rejected God for an alien and false religion.

The seventeenth century also witnessed two cases of excommunication for heresy from the Jewish community of Amsterdam.[46] Settled by fiercely pious former Marranos from Portugal, the "Dutch Jerusalem" became a cockpit of both free thought and pietistic censoriousness, whose quarrels were exacerbated by the arrival of German Ashkenazim, refugees from the Thirty Years' War. The suicide of the brilliant but erratic Uriel da Costa, who had been twice subjected to the dreaded *cherem*—excommunication—followed directly upon his acceptance of penance and submission, consisting of a thrashing of thirty-nine blows and prostration before the synagogue while each of the congregants stepped over him. Humiliation, however, had proved too much for this one-time Catholic who had left the canonship of a Jesuit university to rejoin the faith of his fathers. Upon completing a stirring vindication of his life and thought, *Exemplar humanae vitae*, and unable to reconcile his freethinking commitment to a rationalist view of religion with the pietistic requirements of his heritage and community, he shot himself.

Baruch Spinoza (1632–1677) suffered a similar fate at the hands of the Amsterdam Jewish community in 1656. Having studied both the Jewish philosophical works of Maimonides and Hasdai Crescas and the gentile rationalism of Descartes, Spinoza elevated reason above all other sources of knowledge, attempted to rationalize ethics on mathematical foundations, and developed a new epistemology. Fearful that another da Costa had arisen in their midst, the Amsterdam rabbinate tried to dissuade the youthful philosopher and, when that failed, urged upon the potential apostate at least outward conformity to Jewish orthodoxy. All was to no avail, however, and on July 27, 1656, the twenty-three-year-old genius was excommunicated. Neither frantic nor frustrated, Spinoza retired to The Hague, took up the humble craft of lens polishing, and continued to write. His quiet, scholastic search for philosophical knowledge sought neither power nor patronage. Spinoza refused a professorship at Heidelberg, published only one work under his own name before his death (his *Treatise on Religion and Philosophy* was published anonymously in 1670), and died at the age of forty-four, leaving "a bed, a bolster, two blankets," and the unpublished manuscript of his *Ethics*, a work which transposes the Jewish belief in God into a reconciliation of God and nature. Pride in knowledge, humility, and acceptance of lonely and impoverished isolation were so mixed in Spinoza that the sin in his outlook is difficult to discern or even to disentangle from the virtue.

Christianity, Heresy, Knowledge, and Pride

The Christian was under even greater threat of succumbing to the sin of pride than the Jew. The evil consequences of pride included a dual alienation—that of man from his fellow man and from God. The latter evil was of course the greater to the religious man and might also include heresies and announcements of unbelief. Augustine regarded pride as the first sin in a temporal sense, holding that an arrogant will preceded the original sinful act.[47] Pride, wrote Augustine, is "a longing for a perverse kind of exaltation," an exaltation that encourages man "to abandon the basis on which the mind should be firmly fixed" and to take up in its stead a complacency based on self alone. Turning away from God leads to a partial loss of man's own being, Augustine urged. "Yet man did not fall away to the extent of losing all his being; but when he had turned towards himself his being was less real than when he adhered to him who exists in a supreme degree." Rather than lose a part of his being,

Augustine exhorts mankind to seek ever after humility, for "in a surprising way, there is something in humility to exalt the mind, and something in exaltation to abase it." This apparent paradox is resolved by Augustine's recognition that "humility makes the mind subject to what is superior," that "[n]othing is superior to God," and, thus, that "humility exalts the mind by making it subject to God." Exaltation, on the other hand, abases the mind, "derives from a fault in character, . . . spurns subjection for that very reason," and hence "falls away from him who has no superior, and falls lower in consequence." Moreover, this sinful exaltation is an assault on God. It exercises its dominion in the devil who seduces man with the offer to be like God. "This then is the original evil," Augustine concludes: "man regards himself in his own light, and turns away from that light which would make man himself a light if he would set his heart on it."

Regarding oneself in one's own light, losing part of one's being, meant also giving up one's faith.[48] Aquinas pointed out the connection between pride and unbelief.[49] Pride consists in an insubordination to God "in that one lifts himself above the limit prefixed for him according to the divine rule or measure." Aquinas sees this insubordination as a direct outcome of the unlimited quest for knowledge; "for the proud man subjects not his intellect to God, so as to gather the knowledge of the truth from him." Proceeding from his overweening arrogance, the sinful seeker after knowledge countenances abandonment of faith and heretical opinions—and for these reasons his "sin is rendered more grievous than it would be if it arose from ignorance or infirmity." Although Aquinas acknowledges that "Heresy is relegated by the saints outside the number of sins which occur among the faithful . . . and . . . is not reckoned among the capital sins," he argues that "if it must be reduced to some one of the seven capital sins, it may be brought under Pride."[50]

The Christian suspicion of the pursuit of knowledge as susceptible to pride is dramatized in Dante's *Inferno*.[51] It is possible to see the entire *Divine Comedy* as a literary celebration of its author's own unquenchable intellectual pride, as well as an allegory on his own search for release from exile. In one sense Dante presumed on God's knowledge to walk through and describe hell, purgatory, and paradise. Dante in life as well as in literature was a man who tried almost everything and flinched at nothing. His love of Beatrice did not prevent him from having other romances. His visions of hell are blinding. The bounds of his pride in his own intellectual powers seem unlimited when he peoples hell and purgatory with popes, politicians, and his own peers as well as the famous and infamous characters of legend and history. His assignment of so many to the various regions and circles of the underworld—a veritable mythopoetic architecture and moral demography of hell and purgatory—betrays such a sense of superiority about himself that it embodies the

Italian *terribiltà*, a remorseless, cold audacity, capable of the most terrifying violence, the most remarkable and incomprehensible tenderness, the absence of any feeling of sympathy, and the lofty refusal of all understanding. Dante appears to Robert Payne as a "demon of pride, rejoicing in the heights of his genius, . . . contemptuous of man and deliberately separate from God . . ." And yet this critic forbears from absolute condemnation of the poet, for he too is caught under his spell: "If we accuse him of pride, it is at some peril, for he may have possessed more than a consciousness of his own significance to the world; a divinity seems to flow from him; when he rages, it is as a god rages."[53] However, despite Payne's unwillingness to damn Dante altogether, there is nevertheless revealed the most terrible aspect of the sin of pride—the presumption upon the character of God.

Dante's *Divine Comedy*, especially cantos VIII to X of the *Inferno*, presents a dramatic analysis of pride's assault on the intellect.[54] In Dante's moral and physical architecture of the inferno, the City of Dis is located in the sixth circle of hell, the last of the circles of the upper tier, all of which are devoted to the sins of incontinence. For Dante the deepest, most spiritual, and worst form of incontinence is heresy, the refusal to bring "every *thought* into captivity to the obedience of Christ." However, Dante's sense of heresy reverses the Augustinian thesis and links incontinence of flesh to incontinence of spirit as the former eats its way into and corrupts the latter. Below the upper tier of incontinence are all those tiers imprisoning sinners against others. In Dante's division of evils the crimes against mankind are more despicable than those that the individual inflicts on himself. Thus, Dante's netherworldly architecture displays a moral hierarchy in the order of sin. Incontinence in the form of lust, gluttony, miserliness, prodigality, anger, and, finally, heresy is but a lighter set of sins that lead to a terrible consequence, abandonment of faith; lack of faith, in turn, leads to the far greater evils of violence, fraud, and treachery against one's fellow men. Dante's moral thesis places six of the seven deadly sins in the upper tier of hell, leaving only envy beneath those seemingly lesser sins that upon closer inspection lead to graver and more insidious consequences.

However, the relationship of pride to intellect is not exhausted until Dante's guide, Vergil, faces the guardians of the City of Dis. Vergil is the representative of human reason, and the powers and limitations of that reason are the problems explored in this section of the *Inferno*. The deep moats, iron walls, and garrison of fiends that surround and defend the city against Dante's and Vergil's entrance are metaphors for the dangers and difficulties involved in examining the relationship of reason to faith and doubt. Vergil is at first turned back from the gates by the guard of fallen angels, exemplars of pride's abandonment of faith in God. Human reason, this incident seems to say, is not able in itself to surmount the questions of the universe, the challenges thrown at it by unbelief. Moreover, the insubordinate and fallen angels possess an intelligence that is far above man's puny reason. The sinful pride of unbelief, accompanied as it always is by obstinacy, is both great and terrible, and the arch-heretic rebel angels are more active and more clever than the heretical human souls that Dante portrays as impotent and dead in their tombs. Vergil's encounter with the guardians of the city gates unfolds the three appeals of heresy to human reason—rationalism, mysticism, and despair. Rationalism assaults faith by accusing it of having no reasonable ground and calling on man to discard it; mysticism undermines by introducing those feelings, instincts, and intuitions that are beyond rational comprehension; despair opposes all justifications of God's ways and all hope for salvation. Human reason is insufficient in the face of these assaults, but when it is led by divine grace, symbolized in the poem by the heavenly angel who descends to open the gates to Vergil and Dante, it understands its limits and may prevail. In Dante's comedy, human reason, doubt, and intellectuality are approved, but only within the limits imposed by the prior and superior grace of faith.

The Reformation did not put an end to pride's danger to intellect. Although Robert K. Merton has shown how Puritanism encouraged the development of an empirical and experimental science that would employ human reason and diligent efforts to glorify God in all his works,[55] there still remained those rationalistic doubts, mystic flights, and fits of utter despair that Dante had recognized as challenges to belief and saboteurs of faith. A Puritan had ever to be on guard against the pride in his heart or in his head that might be a token of Satan's subtle subversion.

The diary of Michael Wigglesworth, a seventeenth-century Puritan of New England, accurately reflects the anguish of Puritan conscience. Hardly a day passes in the five years (1653-1657) recorded by Wigglesworth that he does not notice the sinful effects of his own intellectual, spiritual, or incontinent pride. Ultimately he writes an epilogue entitled "Considerations Against Pride," wherein he sets down his objections to that sin. Among these are its many modes of arrogance: of ingratitude that fails to recognize God's freely given gifts of love, protection, and bounty; of impudence that rates man's puny skills and intelligence above that of God's incomprehensible intellect and glorious wonders; of impertinence that frustrates God's ultimate purpose, for which he gave his son, his own glorification; of idolatry that adores the self and its vainglorious excellence rather than God; of proud satanic emulation that adopts the orientation of the fallen angels rather than that away from whom they fell; of wantonness that converts God's gifts of grace into gods of lust; of sinful imitation of all the dreadful examples that pride has already caused. Moreover, Wigglesworth goes on, pride is "a sin against the place and persons where I live . . . a grievous sin against myne owne soul . . . [a sin that] shuts god and all his grace from my soul." The Puritan conscience worried because God "dwels with the humble and contrite, but he holds the proud afar off . . ." Ultimately Wigglesworth recognizes God's active resistance to the proud:

> he crosseth my contrivances, and blasteth my indeavors, and disappointeth my hopes and expectations, and feeds me with the Torment of emptiness, with vexation and rebuke where I hoped to have met with comfort, so that my soul overwhelmed with trouble, and I could even roar or make a noise for the disquietment of my heart, but how little kindly melting is there for this my iniquity which causeth it, as 'tis committed against my god?[56]

Wigglesworth's exhortations toward humility become themselves a threat of sin as he protests almost too much. But even this is in a sense testimony to the limitations on man's intellect and the preternatural power of God. As Wigglesworth plaintively concludes: "This is my pride and the fruits of it and if I see so much god sees much more evil in it."

The Christian assault on unlimited intellect is not only to be found in Catholic and Puritan homiletics; it is also present in an essay of Kierkegaard (1813-1855) that distinguishes between genius and apostleship in accordance with the divine authority that is the sole justification for the latter. The decisive thing about a statement, according to Kierkegaard, is not its content, which might be repeated by any other person, but the authority of the speaker. Hence, Kierkegaard urges, when Christ says "There is an eternal life," a Christian priest is foreclosed from discussing that statement in terms of its profundity; rather he must simply say, "We have Christ's word for it that there is an eternal life; and that settles the matter."[57] Kierkegaard insists on the authoritative legitimation of God's, Christ's, and the apostles' pronouncements, and goes on to assert that an acceptance of them based on any other quality—for example, their wit, cleverness, profundity, or aesthetic quality—is a mockery of God, a blasphemy that arises from intellect's presumption upon holy authority. "Doubt and superstition," writes Kierkegaard, in effect echoing Dante's story of Vergil before the City of Dis, "which make of faith a vain thing, have among other things also made men shy of obedience, of bowing before authority." Priests who preach faith in Christ on grounds other than his divine command, who speak of the profundity of Christian doctrine, who philosophize about it, or who ponder its deeper meanings are guilty of an affectation. Obedience on the basis of reflection, or doubt of apostolic authority, is to Kierkegaard a kind of rebellion. "This rebelliousness worms its way even into the thought of better people, perhaps unbeknown to them," he observes, "and so begins all the extravagance, which at bottom is only treachery, about the profundity and the beauty which one can but faintly perceive."

Pride of intellect thus bids fair to become the worm of a skeptical consciousness, boring its way into man's soul, undermining his faith, and leading to treachery against God.[58] The moral architecture of Dante's inferno is still to be seen in the edifice of Kierkegaard's Christian philosophy of intellectual subservience. Intellect must give way to God's inscrutable authority.

PRIDE AND INTELLECT IN THE SECULAR AGE

In the modern age of secularism religious faith has fallen by the wayside, not to erode as an illusion whose unreality has been demonstrated, but rather as a kind of moral economy of energy whose marginal utility to inspire has been reached. Hence, from time to time charismatic movements and exotic sects rise up to capture the spiritual longings of people starved by reason or steeped in ennui. At the same time, intellect, freed from the constraints of religion, peers into the depths of the natural, physical, and social worlds. Mind reaches farther than the body that encases it and suffers from a kind of homelessness.[59] Bereft of the honor that once clothed its representatives in holy, royal, or patron-designated robes, intellect is the resident stranger at the modern university and at best seeks to salvage some dignity in its isolation. Genius and talent struggle for recognition in a new world in which personal authenticity has become the supreme morality.

Intellect must always battle for its place in the realms of the wise and the powerful. The precise relationship of knowledge to wisdom is unknown. Because of that unanswered and perhaps unanswerable question, accumulations of knowledge, and honorific status for those who possess such accumulations, are suspect. At bottom, the fear is that unencumbered intellect is a demon of pride, an avatar of the devil that has possessed man and will lead him into evil. Hence it is that J. Glenn Gray, a man of intellect and wisdom, who has written an agonizing but brilliant philosophical portrait of modern war and warriors, and who has the deepest empathy for the sickness of the soul in a secular age, warns against the danger of contemporary intellectual pride to democracy.[60] "No pride," writes Gray, "is so insidiously dangerous to democratic society as intellectual pride." Modern democracies such as that in the United States have proscribed pride of birth and accommodated themselves with some measure of control to pride of wealth, Gray observes, but "intellectual pride is more divisive in its effects and harder to eradicate in its possessors." Americans, Gray believes, are particularly susceptible to acquiescing to the sinful pride of intellect because they believe they have already freed themselves from it by scorning "the

egghead." Gray believes, however, that there still exists an "overestimation of intellect divorced from social responsibility and a feeling of
common humanity with average human beings." And thus he specifies
the character of worldly sin in the modern pride of intellect—its
tendency to encourage lofty and disdainful disregard for ordinary people.
Pride of intellect "creates resentment in the soul of man," observes Gray,
and he adds that this resentment is "a much underestimated vice that acts
like an acid to destroy the sense of community among people." One
solution to this problem of secular vice, Gray believes, is to yoke talented
intellect with human character. "When gifts of intellect are joined with
those of character," he writes, "there is always a proper humility."

Character's control of overweening intellect cannot be guaranteed.
In fact the likelihood of vicious arrogance in intellect overcoming
virtuous humility in knowledge is very great indeed. Gray foresees this
difficulty when he warns against entrusting policy and programmatic
development to proven but unfettered intellectual talent. The brilliant
are not likely to be the responsible, for "nothing is less ambiguous than
the evidence that intellectual brilliance can and does co-exist with
egotism, selfishness, and indifference to the common good." Given that
humble character and social responsibility cannot be counted upon to
neutralize the evil pride in intellect, democratic societies must strengthen
the critical and judgmental powers of the average citizen. Just as prideful
intellect raises doubts about the existence of God and undermines
religious faith, so also that same intellectual pride casts doubt on the
opinion of the general public and undermines faith in popular government. "Faith in the democratic process," writes Gray, "is quickly lost
once one begins to doubt the capacities for judgment of the ungifted
majority." Democracy rests on the assumption that the collective
judgment of the people is superior to that of any aristocratic oligarchy,
whether of blood, race, or talent.[61] Intellect threatens to create such an
aristocracy and to employ its talents to convince the populace of its right
to rule. As a counter-measure, improving the capacities for criticism and
evaluation in the general public might prevent proud intellect from
becoming too potent a power.

However, there is another aspect to this argument. The process of
Western individuation has recently reached new heights. In general that
process had an effect on pride by shifting its form from *honor* to *dignity*.[62]
The former links pride to the identity that is circumscribed by institutional roles; the latter links pride to identity that is independent of these
roles. What has happened in the sociological history of pride is that it has
become more and more detached from institutional moorings—from
both ascribed and achieved statuses—and has become linked to a radical
individualism that at one and the same time celebrates and searches for
the basis of personal dignity. In the case of pride in intellect the problem

is quite complex. On the one hand, the as yet incomplete emancipation of the individual from aristocracies of birth, kinship, race, ethnicity, and sex succeeds in liberating individual intellect to find its own level and to seek pride in its own accomplishments. On the other hand, the emphasis on authenticity that is the hallmark of the new radical individualism deprecates intellect as a one-sided and therefore distorted indicator of bad faith. In the midst of this anguishing reconstitution of self and self-confidence, new struggles for dignity and honor have emerged out of the claims of disprivileged and disenfranchised minorities.

The emergence of intellect in its own right, unprotected by the shibboleths of church, nobility, race, or sex, leads in turn to its homelessness. Intellect is rarely satisfied to remain a hermit phenomenon, an isolate suffering a lonely existence in order to serve itself alone. Rather, in the guide of altruistic service or in the will to power, intellect becomes a social and a political force of unpredictable potency. Typically, intellect is institutionalized in universities, where, warned to serve an impersonal god of science, truth, or art, its potential for social change is harnessed.[63] Moreover, institutions of higher learning house not only individuals of genius and talent but also a good many mediocrities as well. The latter all too often outnumber the former and, employing the politics of majorities, do much to degrade and dishonor both the house and the persons of intellect. Intellect feels trapped in what has become the prison house of knowledge and, unable to rescue the institution from its usurpers, sinks into despair, rages at its shackles, or seeks a new world to conquer. Modernity has all too often made intellect a refugee and turned mind into a wanderer seeking if not a kingdom at least a home.

The New Shibboleth: The Quest for Authenticity

Radical individualism strikes another blow at intellect or, at least, its Cartesian incarnation in a mind that is superior to and separate from the body. Central to this new liberated individuation is the realization and display of authenticity. Not only can authenticity no longer be anchored in traditional statuses or institutionalized roles, it also cannot be located in an emphasis on any single element of human existence such as the cognitive or the cathectic (the latter signifying the emotionally invested). Authenticity, as the moderns define it, requires the self-conscious discovery and the absolutely truthful revelation of the *whole* of one's existence.[64] Whereas earlier, unemancipated honor consisted in the display of escutcheon, uniforms, and the exercise of perquisites that indicated one's station, modern "authentic" dignity requires the abandonment of all cover and the presentation of a naked self.[65] An ideology that opposes all role-inhibited performance, that insists on total communication, and calls for the abrogation of the institutional separation of private and public life is part of the politics of authenticity.[66] There is indicated here a fall of public man as well as a dislodging of recognized intellect.[67]

Specifically, the "authentic" individual is constrained against taking any undue pride in intellect alone. Over against what is scornfully denigrated as a "head trip," the liberated individual is urged to rediscover the connection between mind and body, to liberate mind from its domination by reason and reintroduce into thought and action elements of mysticism, irrationalism, and sensuality as well as magic, witchcraft, and (exotic) religion. In some versions of "authenticity," there is not only to be a liberation of mind from reason and of body from mind but more significantly an inversion of the old discredited hierarchy: mind will become the servant of body, thought the response to action, reason the servant of feeling. Intellect suffers a double loss. First, its place in the hierarchy of man's nature is challenged and discredited. Second, its private home in the mind is invaded by passion, mystery, and sensualism. To the extent that it is unwilling to accept this double-edged humiliation, intellect experiences a new sense of homelessness. No longer at home in the mind, no longer the patriarch of the person, it must depart to look for new lodgings. Here there is not the homeless mind but rather the homeless intellect, abandoned by mind that takes pride in the "authenticity" realized in the new-found synthesis of body and soul.

There is, however, more than one crisis in confidence created by this revolution against Cartesian dominion. First, the much-vaunted "authenticity" both urged and promised by the ideology of this cultural revolution has by no means been realized among its adherents. Grounded in the vagaries of appropriated mysticism, occultism, sensuality, and underground esoterica, and moved by the morality of Sartre's ethical admonition against bad faith, authenticity finds no precise and proved expression.[68] The revolution of recent years in behalf of a life unfettered by sociocultural constraints is antinomian in character. The revolutionaries, secular saints of a yet-to-be-realized utopia of authenticity, picture themselves as "pilgrims between the dying world and the world not yet born."[69]

Within this perspective there are manifested rectitudinal certainty, moral superiority, and all too often an arrogant self-righteousness that sits in judgment over the validity and degree of others' authenticity. The peculiar quality of this pride, and of the revolution to which it is inextricably attached, is its divorce from both past and future. The dissolution of history, and of the future as history, in this movement converts time into a never-ending series of presents. Without recognition of or responsibility to predecessors or successors, the authentic person feels little humility. Carl Jung captured the disdainful quality of the pride in this attitude when he described it as "always egocentric and conscious of nothing but its own presence." Jung observes the particular connection between this ego's relation to temporality ("It is incapable of learning from the past, incapable of understanding contemporary events, and incapable of drawing right conclusions about the future") and its narcissism ("It is hypnotized by itself and therefore cannot be argued with").[70] Ultimately, this proud advocacy of human liberation and the realization of an ultimate authentic utopia might become a tyranny of the authentic supermen over the yet-to-be-liberated common men.[71] Penultimately, it lends itself to anxiety over the realization of one's true self, anguish over the quest for certain authenticity, guilt over one's own failures at self-liberation, shame over the inauthentic self that still remains, and envy and resentment against those who have already succeeded in becoming "true" to themselves and to others. Pride and fear are here so conflicted that confidence in oneself is not very likely at all.

Second, the revolt in behalf of the unencumbered life coincides with at least three other revolts against the very forces of modernization that spawned the anti-Cartesian revolution. Most important in this regard are the worldwide revolts against colonialism that address themselves to counter-acculturation and to new forms of nationalism, national socialism, and neo-fascism.[72] Next are those revolts of oppressed minority peoples and women within established but limited democracies, such as the United States, that argue for an even greater pluralization of society and a reconstituted ethnic and sex consciousness.[73] In yet another contemporary social movement, there is the revolt against the excesses of industrialization—pollution, waste, ecological destruction—that calls for a diminution of community size and a halt to technological advance.[74] Finally, there is the remnant of the nineteenth-century class struggle, which obtains a new lease on life by trying to absorb all of the other revolts under its own ideological aegis.[75] One strand common to all of these revolts is their hostility to modernization. Neo-nationalism, anti-racist racism, ecologism, feminism, and neo-Ludditism share with varying degrees of emphasis the common view that a better society will be characterized by self-confident group pride, preservation of nature, and pastoral communalism. "Demodernism" militates against the continuing individuation that has produced modern alienated but still inauthentic man. In place of the interdependent but free individual who realizes his unique potential by "being himself" and "doing his own thing," certain forms of demodernization call for the reconstitution of certain tradition-bound solidarities—such as sex, racial, and ethnic groups and kin-related or pseudofamilial clans—and the reconstruction of pride and faith in these collectivities.[76] Individual liberation and revived group consciousness clash with one another.[77] Pride presides benignly over the protracted struggle, knowing that regardless of the outcome it will have a place in the new order.

Third, there is the struggle to gain self-confidence that is part of the general problem created by emancipation and progress. To be sure, the demand for authenticity and the anticolonial and sex and ethnic consciousness revolts speak to this lack of sufficient confidence, but it has its own intrinsic qualities and sources. The claim that modern, urban industrial civilization segments the personality, separates man from other men, and alienates man from himself finds expression in lonely, insecure, and frightened individuals who long for an escape from their terrifying freedom and an end to the tyranny of progress.[78] Somehow man is to be restored, his estrangement from himself to be ended, his fractured social nature to be mended, and his confidence to find outlet in a psychic security that permits realization of human and humane potential. Note here that pride is regarded not as a threat but rather as a need. In the guise of self-confidence it will be both cause and effect of a revolt that salvages too humble a mankind from victimization by its creations. There is also here a potential but not yet a program for a newly reconstituted pride in intellect. Enlightened by humane considerations, pride in intellect becomes a noble servant of those who are less gifted. Submitting itself to the judgment of the populace, dignified intellect finds its own worthiness in its selfless accomplishments. It performs for the general welfare and in the name of the public good.

PRIDE AND THE RELIGION OF SOCIOLOGY

The secular age has made an anachronism of the age-old problem of the *communion* of man with God and raised to central importance the *community* of men in society.[79] Hence, religion has given way to sociology but with a certain similarity in result. Pride is the sin that stands in the way of both communion and community. Although the Jewish and Christian religions have both warned against the alienating consequences of pride, their theological pronouncements have sometimes taken such self-righteous expression as to call into question their own absolution from this sin.

Sociology, beginning with a recognition that scientific truths are neither absolute nor neutral, nevertheless came to believe in the truth of its own message for earthly rehabilitation. Sociologists offer visions of a new world and contribute ideologies to serve specific social and political elements. Moreover, by these contributions sociology makes itself not only an object for later sociologists to study, but also a "religion" in its own right. As a "religion of humanity," setting for itself the task of accomplishing on earth what God would accomplish in the eschatological kingdom of heaven, sociology typically identifies with the disprivileged classes and groups, much as religion provides a theodicy, or defense of God's goodness and power, for these same collectivities. As the late

Albert Salomon observed, "These 'religions' of sociology have been secular religions, in that they have tried to bring about salvation in this world by elaborating schemes that would ensure final harmony and continuity in the social process." Sociology as a religion of humanity and sociologists who profess that religion are certainly vulnerable to being charged with the sin of pride. In the contemporary period, although much of sociology seeks absolution and claims objective neutrality, "the ambition and the pretension are still there," according to Salomon. Currently, the kingdom of this religion of humanity on earth is America, where sociology offers itself as a universally applicable science and yet retains a paradoxically pragmatic, optimistic—in effect, American—outlook.

The combined efforts of social theorists and social engineers to solve social problems have proved less than equal to the task, however, and as a result, faith in this secular religion has decreased considerably.[80] Some sociologists profess "heresies" and "heterodoxies," that is radical reinterpretations of the sociological "gospel"; others deny its melioristic aim and creep behind the protective curtain of positivism and value neutrality; still others sink into despair and inactivity, their once-confident voices silent in the face of recalcitrant social inequities; and a few proclaim that the "new earth" is already here and that the era of prophetic ideologies is over. In each response there is to be discerned a trace of pride or its effects. The sociological intellect might absolve itself from pride by proclaiming no superiority for its own statements over those of its subjects'—that is, over those of other human beings. Faithful to the nature of its subject matter, this new sociology might start by taking seriously its recognition that man is the social animal who symbolizes, constructs, and reconstructs his world, and by renouncing its scientific right to distrust human reason.[81] The sociological task would then be to describe the processes of social architectonics, and not to build the new society in advance of them. The democratic ethos requires a decent respect for the opinions of mankind. A humbler sociology might ratify that ethos without either applauding or opposing the social visions that the reason of ordinary people produces. A "sociology of the absurd," one that recognizes and appreciates man's unending struggle to understand and cope with a world that is ultimately and essentially without meaning, removes the sociologist from his lofty position.[82]

In accordance with the philosophy enunciated by Pico della Mirandola (1463-1494), the sociologist of a humbler persuasion might locate himself side by side with man "at the midpoint of the world."[83] Free to judge, confined by no bounds save those of his own making, man fixes the limits of nature and culture for himself. His position "at the center of the world" permits him to "more conveniently look around and see whatsoever is in the world," while his position above the brute beasts and below the heavenly powers presents him with an ambiguous legacy: "Neither heavenly nor earthly, neither mortal nor immortal, . . . like a judge appointed for being honorable. . . ." Man, continues Pico, is the molder of himself; he is the sculptor who can shape himself as he pleases, choosing to imitate the beast or aspire to the divine. Of course, in correction of Pico, it must be said that man's capacity to carve out his own image and shape his social and natural environment is a function of his power and his opportunities in society, which are inevitably distributed unequally. In addition there are the limitations imposed by sloth, poverty, ignorance and institutional obstacles.[84] A sociology of the absurd recognizes man's potentiality and his frailty; it uncovers power and resistance, acquiescence and rebellion, reform and resignation. It describes the multitude of modes, mores, and manners in malleable society and multivalent man.[85]

A DRAMATIZATION OF PRIDE: DIGNITY IN DEATH

Augustine distinguishes between the death of the body and the death of the soul. Even though the soul is held to be immortal, "it has nevertheless a kind of death. . . . [that] results when God abandons it." The death of the body, on the other hand, occurs when the soul departs.[86] The modern age has been characterized by man's abandonment of God. Secularism and the age of reason, science, technology, and *machtpolitik* have turned attention to this world, left spiritual matters to the structure of private beliefs and religious institutions, and substituted the often mortified self for the immortal soul. With science sentenced to uncover penultimate truths, the ultimate truth and mystery of death remain unresolved. Pride expresses its quintessential presumption not in reaching an understanding of death but rather in overcoming it. Immortality, the ultimate presumption upon God, is man's final arrogance.

The phenomenon of death evokes the absurdity of life. And as Occidental life presents itself in linear form—the present connecting the past with the future—the meaninglessness of any present in its own right, the meaninglessness of contemporaneous life in the face of incomprehensible death becomes the awesome omnipresent absurdity.[87] How to overcome that absurdity becomes the burning question of modern life and thought. Man becomes an aspiring immortalist, seeking to rescue both the self and the body from decline and decay. Miguel de Unamuno captures the essence of this peculiarly modern and tragic theme: "I do not want to die—no; I neither want to die nor do I want to want to die; I want to live for ever and ever and ever." Moreover, this desire to live forever is corporeal as well as spiritual. Unamuno opposes the thesis that immortality of the soul finds expression as submersion "in the vast All, in an infinite and eternal Matter or Energy, or in God." In lieu of this, Unamuno cries out "not to be possessed by God, but to possess Him, to become myself God, yet without ceasing to be I myself, I who am now speaking to you." This "I" is not only sentient but also a fleshly being; as Unamuno, shameless but fearful, states his claim: "I dread the idea of having to tear myself away from my flesh; I dread still more the idea of having to tear myself away from everything sensible and material, from all substance." Unamuno justifies this claim even while admitting it is Egoism ("Egosim, you say? There is nothing more universal than the individual . . . Each man is worth more than the whole of humanity. . . . That will we call egoism is the principle of psychic gravity, the necessary postulate") but denying that it is sinful pride (Pride? Is it pride to want to be immortal? Unhappy men that we are! . . . Only the feeble resign themselves to final death and substitute some other desire for the longing for personal immortality."[88]).

Immortality can be achieved in different ways: by living forever through one's progeny, through one's works, or through the merging but as yet incomplete antithanatological technology. Mention has already been made of the revived and projected narcissism wherein parents hope to achieve immortality through their children. Works provide a similar outlet for immortalist desires. Again it is Unamuno who understands this phenomenon of pride, a pride that leads to "quixotic madness." Don Quixote returns from Barcelona and is on the point of recovering his sanity when he catches sight of a lovely meadow and returns to a reverie of eternal life and immortal fame.

> For this was his radical madness [writes Unamuno], this was the source of his action, this . . . the reason which led him to become a knight-errant. . . . The point is to leave a name through the centuries, to live on in the memory of man. The aim is not to die! Not to die! This is the taproot, the root of roots of all quixotic madness.[89]

The desire for immortality leads some men to make a monument of themselves in their own lifetime. Such a "sculpted" expression of life everlasting conceals a more dangerous purpose. Pride in one's own accomplishments accompanied by the wish to live forever sometimes includes the desire to take revenge on all who live on after one's own death. Just as there are revenge suicides wherein the motive is to punish all those who must live on without the dead party, so also there is a revengeful immortalism that seeks to kill all who are alive after the immortalist's own death.[90] For the man who makes a monument of his life or his works, revenge finds expression in outstripping not only all contemporary competitors for fame and glory but all future ones as well. The dead statue comes back to fetch the living, as in the legend of Don

Juan, only here an unbounded pride seeks preeminence not in the lifetime of the individual but in all lifetimes to come.[91] Furthermore, the same dreadful motive can take as its target for revenge not the successors but the predecessors of a man. Immortal works stand over against all others that do not survive. Just as history flings out a challenge to Toynbee's twenty-one civilizations to survive or die, so the immortalist challenges the living presence of past men's accomplishments to survive in the face of his own achievements. Arrogance and honor are confounded in these revengeful themes wherein sinfully proud men seek nothing less than eternity for themselves alone.

As Unamuno recognized, immortality might take form either as eternal life or as resurrection. In the former there existed only a hope for spiritual or memorial preservation, but the latter promised corporeal permanence as well.[92] Modern technology has lent added possibility to this dream of the immortalist.[93] Employing a newly developed and as yet untested technology, cryonics—an applied techno-scientific spinoff of cryogenics—hopes to freeze dead bodies and keep them in cold storage until such time as medical science can ensure eternal life by finding the cures to all diseases. Held in "cryonic suspension" in "dormantories" until the age of eternal life is at hand, the proud immortalist chooses a temporary departure from inner-worldly concerns until presumptuous science can supplant God's or nature's mysterious law of death. Here we have, perhaps, the quintessence of pride, the nadir of sin—for man seeks nothing less than to overthrow the physical body itself, to halt its cyclical degeneration into old age and death, and to produce a race of gods who will live and enjoy youthful life forever.

The Drama of Death and Dignity

The problem of pride-in-death is not exhausted by the search for immortality. There is also the matter of dying well. To physicians and scientists death is a process imperfectly understood, but to the ordinary mortal death is an event.[94] What kind of event it is or will be, whether sudden or protracted, painful or peaceful, honorific or degrading is a social and personal issue. Of course for some the issue is resolved by chance, accident, or historical intercession. Thus, according to J. Glenn Gray, the modern soldiers' relation to death is that of negation: "For them, death is a state and a condition so foreign and unreal as to be incomprehensible. They reject it with aversion without bringing its reality to the level of consciousness."[95] For others, death holds out the kind of challenge met so well by the ill-fated thane of Cawdor in Shakespeare's *Macbeth*. Accused of treason against his king, the thane went to his death most nobly, as reported, thirdhand it must be admitted, by Malcolm:

... I have spoken
With one that saw him die, who did report
That very frankly he confess'd his treasons,
Implored your highness' pardon and set forth
A deep repentance: nothing in his life
Became him like the leaving it; he died
As one that had been studied in his death,
To throw away the dearest thing he owed
As 'twere a careless trifle.

Macbeth I, iv

For those who wish to exalt or maintain the honor they have in life when they take leave of their own mortality, or who wish to snatch a shred of dignity from the jaws of death, there is a "Cawdorian" possibility. They might be able to carve out some measure of esteem in the craft of their dying. Present-day medical practices make the art and craft of dying far more difficult to manage than in earlier eras. At one time the death scene occurred at home; the dying person was surrounded by his relatives, friends, and a religious ministry. His passing was governed by customs that, whatever their failure in prolonging life, gave to death a dignity that is now difficult to secure.[96] At present, deaths typically occur in hospitals; the advanced and complicated technology applied to preserve life at all costs encumbers the dying patient with wires, tubes, clips, and bodily restraints, making death a humiliating and noisome degradation.[97] The modern mores of medically supervised death have made a shambles of the erstwhile *ars moriendi*.[98]

The art and craft of dying appear not to have been rationalized by a written set of procedures until the fifteenth century in England.[99] In France the religious requirements of the *ars moriendi* had become so debased by the eighteenth century that they no longer commanded respect. For those who had turned away from religion, or who wished to salvage more dignity from death than the church would allow, planning and even rehearsing their final moments of life became imperative. At the other end of the scale of respectability were those condemned criminals who, without a shred of dignity in their lives, wished nevertheless to die in a manner that enhanced, or at least did not lower, the esteem in which they were held. In studying the manners and modes of these secular and self-constructed *artes moriendi*, we are given vivid illustrations of the dramatization of pride. For purposes of this illustration, we select the deathbed plans of Voltaire on the one hand, and the artful constructions of dignity in death by hanging on the other.

Voltaire and the Art of Dying in Eighteenth-Century France

The religious instructions on how to die properly were in great measure aimed at assisting the dying person to resist the temptation to sin at the last moment.[100] The devil was presumed to assault a person on his deathbed and to tempt him into sin against his salvation. Emphasis was placed on faith, on the penitence of confession, on assurance of God's mercy, and on a ritualized mode of interrogation and answer that the dying person should utter before losing consciousness or reason. Friends and relatives were also to participate, not only as assistants at and witnesses to the dying person's maintenance of faith but also in acknowledgment of their own mortality, their own need to attain a state of grace, and their own attestation of belief. Of particular importance at the last minutes of life was the temptation to submit to the sin of pride or to one of its demons: doubt, despair, impatience, or worldliness. In the first tract of the *ars moriendi* the archetypical dying Everyman, called Moriens, is called upon to resist five "most principall" temptations, of which the first is unbelief, the second despair, the third impatience and complaining, the fourth spiritual pride, and the last, avarice. The first four are definite variants of pride and even the last named, the temptation to avarice, summons Moriens to put away all thoughts of worldly concerns—riches, carnality, honors, and the like—and to concentrate on God and his grace. Making a good death, as it was called in that era, required Moriens to engage in a dramatic dialogue with sin in general and pride in particular.

In eighteenth-century France, deathbed rituals had become public performances. The church-sponsored drama of death included confession, absolution, and communion—*le viatique*, extreme unction, and the *prières des agonisants*. A crowd gathered at the bedside. The confessor exhorted the assembled throng as well as the dying penitent. In contrast to the current situation wherein a person all too often dies alone, or in the company of those relatives who manage to make it to the hospital in time, with the instruments of medical science constraining his breath and masking whatever dignity he might have, the French of that era died amidst a crowded scene and according to a prescribed scenario. Indeed the final moments presented a veritable drama of death. According to McManners, the French "lived their lives on a stage, and their concept of the family was broader than ours, bringing in more relatives, and servants and dependents. They died in public, fulfilling and seen to be fulfilling their obligations to family and connexion, their station and its duties."[101]

The drama of death ended an individual's direct participation in the drama of social reality. Up until the end it was Moriens who directed the play. As Ariès points out, death in France from the thirteenth to the eighteenth century "was a ritual organized by the dying person himself, who presided over it and knew its protocol." With scenario prefixed, actors and audience prescribed, and the dying person enjoined to both produce and direct his own death, only delirium, unconsciousness, subterfuge, forgetfulness, or outright refusal on his part could keep the dying person from his performance. "Should he forget or cheat," Ariès observes, "it was up to those present, the doctor or the priest, to recall him to a routine which was both Christian and customary."[102] For the incoherent and irrational, much was forgiven and overlooked by priests and others present; ideally, the *ars moriendi* would be enacted before the dying person had slipped away from consciousness and contact.

Pride played a major and complex role in the drama of death. Not only the temptation of sinful pride was at stake. In the age of Voltaire the honor of the church was also challenged by Deists, Jansenists, rationalists, and unbelievers. A strategic place to stage one's revolt against or ridicule of the church was the deathbed. For some who had lived in apostasy, heresy, Deism, anticlericalism, agnosticism, or atheism, death became the ultimate challenge to their principles. On the other hand, those who wished their deaths not to be accompanied by the denial of absolution or the refusal of burial in consecrated ground sought ways to meet the minimal requirements of church ritual without sacrificing personal beliefs.

Voltaire's death became the arena for a strategic and tactical struggle to preserve the principles of *philosophe* without losing the benefits of a Catholic conclusion to earthly life.[103] The great philosopher had before him the various scenarios employed by others similarly situated, and there is every evidence that he studied these closely in determining just exactly how his own drama of death would be performed. Among the theaters of *thanatos* that Voltaire examined were Rousseau's sentimental deistic scene of the death of Julie in the *Nouvelle Heloise*; the defiant final dramas performed by Jansenists, atheists, and anticlericals who went to their deaths with outrageous jests, impudent refusals of last rites, or condemnations of churchmen and God; the stoical and reserved death scenes performed by quiet and courageous unbelievers who did not wish to disrupt their own peace of mind or to cause a scandal by their deaths; the clever and subtle scenarios planned by unbelievers who wished to make no concessions to society but nevertheless found ingenious ways to evade the sacraments with impunity. Voltaire elected the last course of action for himself.

Pride more than other motivations governed his choice. But it was pride mixed with principle and prejudice. Voltaire shared the sentiments of his age that opposed *l'appareil*, the Catholic ceremonies for dying—the dislike of theological doctrines of hell and purgatory, the contempt for the confession and sacraments, the offense at the clerics' willingness to take advantage over man at his weakest moment, and the deist preference for an unmediated relationship of love between man and God. The fact that the practice of confessors at the deathbed tended to emphasize consolation rather than condemnation, that absolution was rarely refused a dying man, that the desire to confess was often sufficient reason to be absolved, and that even a notorious sinner might be heard if he recanted in public gave little solace to doubters like Voltaire. There were too many incidents of actors, Jansenists, dissident abbés, deists, and others being denied absolution or burial in consecrated ground to give credence to clerical considerations. Voltaire denied the possibility of a hell, but he half-believed, half-hoped for an afterlife. He apparently feared death, spoke to his friends about his desire to avoid either scandal or ridicule because of his manner of dying, and he wanted a civilized—that is, a church-consecrated—burial. Yet he wished at the same time to die a *philosophe*, an honored member of the Academy, and a renowned citizen of his country who departed from it still in "la religion de sa patrie."

Voltaire proceeded to plan his death as a grand *coup de théâtre*. It was in effect a play-within-a-play, the drama of a man who would die a Catholic but not a Christian. The key to his drama was securing absolution, proving membership in and reconciliation to the church. Once absolution was obtained, ecclesiastical burial was assured. Hence Voltaire looked for a confessor who would accept as sufficient for absolution two statements consistent with his outlook—that he believed in God and that he was sincerely penitent—but who would not require him to renounce his writings, recognize the divinity of Christ, or receive the sacraments. Employing his two nephews in Paris, both legal experts, to collect the documents and prepare the briefs should a lawsuit against the clergy be required after his death, Voltaire managed to separate the legal from the ecclesiastical, the duties of the citizen from the observances of a believer, and yet to conceal from the chosen representative of Catholicism his actual state of mind. Confession was given to a naive priest, the Abbé Gaultier, witnesses to Voltaire's confession of faith included two men of impeccable credentials, and higher clergy and his own parish priest were excused from attendance at so great a man's confession on grounds of his own virtuous modesty. Once absolution was given, the Abbé Gaultier was not permitted to see his dying penitent again, except at the last moments, thus avoiding any further questions, clarifications, or additions to the original declaration of faith. When the confessor produced a ready-made confession of faith, Voltaire politely evaded it, pointing out in place of it that "Je meurs dans la religion catholique où je suis né," or "I die in the Catholic religion of my birth." In the religion but not of it, Voltaire sacrificed none of his principles.

Preserving his honor, maintaining his dignity, and giving only latent expression to his pride, Voltaire at 83 years of age gave the performance of his life at the moment of his death. The Abbé Gaultier was permitted to extract an apparent concession when he asked Voltaire if he had made a secret protest against church or clergy and received a carefully contrived ambiguous denial. A flimsy excuse turned out to be sufficient ground for refusing the sacrament. Three months after receiving absolution, Voltaire lay dying, coughing blood and suffering from a painful urinary infection. Gaultier and a curé were summoned, but Voltaire presented himself as too incoherent to receive the viaticum or sign a more complete declaration of faith. Gaultier followed the common practice of setting aside the church requirements because the penitent was "unconscious." The curé insisted on asking the crucial question, however: "M. de Voltaire, vous êtes au dernier terme de votre vie: reconnaissez-vous la divinité de Jésus-Christ?" Voltaire's reply proved to be his last rhetorical masterstroke: "Laissez-moi mourir en paix." The curé chose to ignore the answer, declaring Voltaire no longer in possession of his faculties, and granting him final absolution. Principled, proud, and capable of deft deception to the very end, Voltaire had produced, directed, cast, and starred in his own deathbed scene. In his last drama he ensured in memorial and monument the recognition and honor he thought he deserved without losing the ecclesiastical blessing that his philosophy had threatened. *Sic itur ad astra.*

The Problem of Pride in Public Executions

"Cawdorian" deaths are among the final problems that beset persons about to be executed. Declared by law to be beyond the pale of respect or mercy, those sentenced to death may try to salvage some small remnant of personal respect in their final moments. What counts in such situations is a public display of *savoir faire*, of cool composure or proud detachment. The matter of their dying having been settled, it is the manner of their deaths that becomes important. The place of execution becomes a theater, the weapons or mechanisms of death props, the clothing of the condemned man a costume, and the speech, gesture, inflection, emotion, and gait part of a dramatic display. Honor having been lost, dignity might yet take its bow in the last act of life.

However, the theater of pride in such deaths is not usually under the direction of the person who is about to die. The laws and customs of the state set the terms under which executions are carried out. In general a fundamental shift has occurred in the culture and mores of official executions—from open and public displays to closed and concealed proceedings.[104] No longer does it occur that the convicted prisoner is taken directly from the bar of justice, conducted along a thoroughfare crowded with a motley audience of well-wishers, scoffers, yelling indignants, bloodthirsty sadists, weeping women, dolorous priests, deploring intellectuals, and an assortment of curiosity seekers, children, pickpockets, and prostitutes. Before such an audience the condemned man might make quite a handsome scene, dressed in his own choice of costume, speaking to the assembled crowd, acting the penitent or refusing the solicitations of the clergy, pleading his innocence or defying his captors, coolly accepting death, proudly submitting his mortal body while securing his immortal soul for posterity. To be sure, his show of *savoir faire* was aided by the other members of the official cast—the judge, jurors, police, guards, priest and acolyte, and executioner. Each might do his part to help or hinder the performance.

The modern execution is usually a concealed ceremony. The condemned man must wait months or years between the time the sentence is given and the execution carried out. Appeals to the courts or for clemency ensure a judicial review of the legal matter but are likely to engender a restive and anxious manner in the inmate. In lieu of the public parade, the death-destined prisoner is taken but a few steps in the company of silent, solemn, but passive professionals, and sentence is carried out in the presence of but a few witnesses, none of whom are intimates of the convicted man. Preexecution rites include the services of a religious practitioner, a selected meal, and, perhaps, final appeals for state-sponsored mercy. The Cawdorian death is dependent upon second- and thirdhand reports, since no motley throng can see its hero or villain die. A secondary dramatic rendering, over which the victim can have but little directorial control, celebrates, denigrates, or ignores altogether whatever nobility in death is displayed by those condemned by state and society.

CONCLUSION

Pride comes or goes—after or before a fall. Ever potential in the hearts of men, it nevertheless finds varied opportunity for expression and form. Its sinfulness is by no means sure. Sublimated as honor, dignity, or self-confidence, it serves as a sign of morality, a surety of character, or an incentive to succeed. Honored as patriotism, national prestige, or ethnic hyper-consciousness, it establishes a nonrational basis for state security, restores damaged dignity, and gives additional ground for psychic self-sufficiency. The much-vaunted virtues of humility—pride's remedy and opposition—are by no means established. Taken as weakness, or, worse, as concealed pride, a humble character may win few laurels and open up chances for victimization. Drawing the line between a just pride and vicious arrogance becomes a matter of excruciating ethical anguish. Just wars have been found all too easily. Just pride is more prevalent—more evil and more beneficial, it haunts man's life, preys upon his insecurities, makes and breaks his very existence.

FIVE

Envy

The isle is full of noises, Sounds and sweet airs, that give delight, and hurt not. Sometimes a thousand twangling instruments Will hum about mine ears; and sometimes voices, That, if I then had waked after long sleep, Will make me sleep again: and then, in dreaming, The clouds methought would open, and show riches Ready to drop upon me; that, when I waked, I cried to dream again.

*William Shakespeare**

APPROACHES TO A DEFINITION

Of all the seven deadly sins, envy may seem to be the easiest to define; however, it is a complex phenomenon. To appreciate its potency as well as its potentialities for good and evil envy must be both defined and characterized.[1] Let us proceed with the latter first. Envy qualifies and threatens the whole as well as the parts of human relationships. Universal and ubiquitous, envy expresses itself differently in different epochs, cultures, subcultures, and specific social formations. The pervasive quality of envy enters into any and every sphere of social and personal existence, emerging in the midst of public affairs and thriving in private life. But while recognized everywhere as an evil and a sin, envy is also a goad to action, a resource for personality modification, and, in its sublimated forms, may translate itself into a virtue or become an incentive for social good.

True envy, as Max Scheler has pointed out, emerges out of the joint experience of covetousness and impotence.[2] Thus envy requires a minimum of two social elements for its development—the one who covets and the desired possession (item, object, or character, for example) that is owned or under the control of another. Envy, a truly *social* phenomenon, can only arise in society and indeed in a society where, at the very minimum, some forms or kinds of social differentiation occur and an orientation toward invidiousness prevails. The phrase, "Comparisons are odious," points to the painful process whereby envy begins. The perception of differences in possessions, the attribution of value to that which one does not possess, the inability to obtain a desired object, the designation of the possessors as holding the desideratum against right or justice, and the realization of one's own impotence with respect to acquisition are the steps that result in envy.

The objects of envy might be any thing or character that is capable of social or personal valuation. These include material objects and wealth, culturally and socially ranked characteristics such as beauty and physique, and the virtues that are said to reside in another person or social group such as honesty, honor, courage, and fidelity. Finally, qualities and capacities, demonstrated or anticipated, are enviable, such as motor or administrative skills, business or political acumen, social adeptness or interpersonal perceptivity, fertility, numerous opportunities or favorable luck. The universality and pervasiveness of envy is attested to by the many objects, characteristics, virtues, qualities, and capacities—in effect, both *virtù* and *fortuna*, the twin facets of life itself to the prescient Florentine observer, Machiavelli—toward which it can turn. That the objects of envy might be so various is also an invitation to search out its modes of social construction and the clues to its recognition.

However, before we turn to its social formation, we must take notice of its other background characteristic—impotence. Envy is not realized solely or simply in the desire for that which belongs to another, but also and equally significantly in the belief that one cannot acquire it. Envy emerges out of frustrated desire for possession of the things belonging to another. Hence, envy is inextricably related to the power structures that control the distribution of value and valued items. Once we note the ubiquity of allocative structures and of social stratification, the universal potentiality for envy to arise is clear.

Envy is both a form of and a resource for protest at the injustice of the world. Valuables have not been equitably or rightly distributed. Those who enjoy the prized things do so without right. Those who lack are victims of the denial of equal protections and equal opportunities. The powers that prevail have so organized matters, the argument runs, that some will benefit and others, although deserving, will be denied. A democratized envy, properly transformed into an ideology of group righteousness, is one basis for revolution. In the new world that its egalitarian ideology promises, the envy that both aggravates existing relations and foreshadows the coming conflict will be dissolved in democratic justice.

However, envy is more often experienced in isolation from one's associates, or as a secret sin to be hidden from view. In these situations impotence is felt not with respect to established political structures or social institutions but rather with respect to particular persons or the mysteries of fate. To wish in vain for the beauty that makes one person a much sought after companion while one's own looks go unnoticed in the crowd is to suffer from an outrage of nature's cruel fortune. It is not revolution that emanates from this form of frustration but *revenge*. And when envy's own thrust toward aggression cannot be completed, revenge is replaced by *ressentiment*. Envy is likely to reside in a heart of darkness, a secret sharer as well as a corrosive product of the sorrow and anguish of unrequited desire.

ENVY AND THE SOCIAL STRUCTURE

In a most general sense, envy is related to *scarcity*. Its orientation is toward valued things or prized qualities that have been perceived as *possessions*. The fact that these things or qualities are under the dominion or part of a "property" right of another, that they are not readily available or easily acquired, establishes the factual basis for their scarcity. And, obversely, the fact of their scarcity reinforces, if it has not already established, their value. A strategic research site for the study of envy as a social phenomenon is available wherever scarcity exists, no matter what it is that is in short supply, the only qualification being that the scarce item also be held dear.

Although it is by now clear that any thing or quality might become the object of envy, it seems best to proceed by a division of these into three sorts: (1) basic needs for human existence and survival; (2) goods, objects, and qualities that have emerged as markers in some kind of social competition among individuals or groups; and (3) qualities of an essential human or social character that might be acquired or ascribed.

Envy and Survival

Utopians have believed that they could construct a social order in which basic scarcity would be ended forever, and in consequence that the fundamental human passions would not be directed in envious or other sinful directions. Robert Owen, for example, offered a plan whereby "those who are now a burden to the country for want of employment" would be put to work and hence, "the vicious, the idle, and the pauper shall be virtuous, industrious, and independent." Indeed, Owen, who had already founded cooperative workmen's communities for the relief of the poor, supposed that he had already "succeeded in giving to a population originally of the most wretched description, and placed under the most unfavourable circumstances, such habits, feelings, and dispositions as enable them to enjoy more happiness than is to be found among any other population of the same extent in any part of the world."[3]

Charles Fourier, who sought to harmonize the passions through the agency of planned communities, went even further in remarking on the role of poverty and unredeemed inequality in producing envy and, thereby, social disorder.

> Poverty [he writes] is the principal cause of social disorders. Inequality, so much maligned by the philosophers, is not displeasing to men. On the contrary, the bourgeois delights in hierarchy; he loves to see the bigwigs decked out and parading in their best finery. The poor man views them with the same enthusiasm. Only if he lacks what is necessary does he begin to detest his superiors and the customs of society. This is the origin of social disorders, crimes and of the gallows, that sad bastion of the civilized order. It is easy to prove that all social crimes committed out of ambition proceed from the poverty of the people, from their efforts to escape poverty, from the anxiety which is instilled in society by the presence of poverty, from the fear of falling into it, and from disgust for the odious habits which it encourages.[4]

The aim of *Harmony*, Fourier's utopian scheme, was to achieve such great productivity that scarcity would be eliminated altogether. Thence, indigence and discomfort would be obviated, and "all the sources of discord will be dried up or reduced to very little."

More recent social scientific investigations have noticed a reciprocal rather than a causal relationship between scarcity and envy. In his study of the envy-ridden Dobu, Fortune found it impossible to distinguish cause and effect in the connection of poverty to jealousy: "But here . . . it is not possible to say whether poverty has created the jealousy or vice versa. Either point of view could be put forward. Accordance is all that can be demonstrated, and in truth it is probable that the more accordance there is in the elements of a culture the stronger an intensification of the mutually agreeable elements will result. They will react upon one another."[5] Moreover, the elements of envy may be so complicated with respect to scarcity that a functional rather than a causal relationship prevails. In the Haitian valley communities observed by Melville Herskovits, for example, land is dearly valued as wealth, and "the drive to obtain property is an obsession with the Haitian peasant." Yet wealth is not prized for display or conspicuous consumption. The wealthy dress simply and unobtrusively when in public places because they believe that to make an "undue display of possessions would arouse envy, and envy brings upon a man's household the evil eye."[6]

Perhaps the most intense study of the effects of scarcity upon the dispositions is Turnbull's portrait of the Ik, a hunting people living in the mountainous area where Kenya, Uganda, and the Sudan come together. Driven into the barren wastelands by public policies over which they have no control, prohibited by law from hunting the animals that once were their principal source of survival, and unable to take up farming, the Ik are literally starving to death. The near absence of minimum basic requirements for survival has resulted in the destruction of Ik social organization, the disintegration of the tribe into scattered bands of antagonistic predators, and the deterioration of the conditions of trust, compassion, love, affection, kindness, and concern that are fundamental for social interaction. What survives is envy, contempt, competition, *schadenfreude* (pleasure at the degradation of others), and indifference.

Among the Ik, food is so scarce that individuals try to hunt, forage, and, more to the point, eat alone or in small groups so that they will not have to share with their family or fellow tribesmen. Custom apparently directs that they ought to share food if surprised in the act of eating. Ik typically look over the bush and forest carefully for telltale wisps of smoke, indicating a clandestine cookout. Once they have spotted the smoke, they rush upon the scene, trying to come unaware upon the men eating, and force them to share. In turn the lucky hunters attempt to eat their prized kill as rapidly as possible, jealously guarding the food against the envious eyes of others. Ironically, Turnbull, who believes that the Ik have abandoned such qualities of social life as "family, cooperative sociality, belief, love, hope and so forth," nevertheless asserts that "the Ik clearly show that society itself is not indispensable for man's survival, that man is not the social animal he has always thought himself to be, and that he is perfectly capable of associating for purposes of survival without being social."[7] Perhaps, in the light of Turnbull's chilling analysis, it would be proper to infer that envy is such a great sin because in extremis it can become *the organizing principle* of society—a kind of asocial sociality. When all else is gone, and basic resources are depleted, a veritable state of nature threatens to engulf everyone.

The Ik live on the edge of civilization as well as starvation. In the midst of envy-ridden civilization, mass starvation has effects that go beyond envy. Essentially, as Pitirim Sorokin has observed, the desire for food impels masses to violent actions, social outbursts, and rearrangements of the social order. The basic aim of the starved people is to obtain the food held in reserve or in hoarded rations by the wealthy, the elites, the privileged, or the criminal classes. Sorokin observes that although the methods employed may vary—*direct action* expressed in disturbances, revolutions, and "nationalization" of food stores; *pressures* on the governing elites to feed the hungry at the expense of the well fed; or *demands* that the rich and satiated redistribute food charitably or in return for newly instituted services—the ultimate result is statism. In the dark and forbidding finale envisioned by Sorokin in 1922—compulsory statism—"society is characterized by unlimited interference in safeguarding and regulating life, behavior, and mutual relationships among the citizens, complete lack of autonomy and self-determination, and frequently egalitarian despotism."[8] Absolute scarcity in organized society might lead to the demand for absolute relief—and ultimately to both collective violence and organized actions. In the dismal end imagined by Sorokin, the masses, unlike the isolated asocial Ik, are converted, cajoled, or coerced to accept an antisocial totalitarianism.

TOWARD A DEFINITION OF SOCIAL JUSTICE: ENVY, RELATIVE DEPRIVATION, AND RESENTMENT

Of course envy is not confined to conditions of "absolute" scarcity. Indeed, precisely because some basis for comparison is inherent in the envious orientation, a situation of relative deprivation and putative social, institutional, or interpersonal injustice is sufficient for the onset of envy. In the absence of some operative theory of social justice the resentments felt about inequalities of wealth or condition are incapable of evaluation. When the idea of justice is lacking, all claims might be judged the products of envy, the results of natural differences, the stepchildren of ignorance, or accidents of fate. Thus, to an accusation that they are envious the less well off must answer that the system of distributive justice is clearly unfair and uniformly unjust.

Resentments over inequities may be classified as legitimate or illegitimate. If legitimate, they are related, or at least relatable, to some theory of justice that gives them their impersonal sense of moral and social rectitude. However, illegitimate resentments might be products of some "false" consciousness or incorrect perception of the actual distributive system. Errors that are products of false consciousness, in turn, run the risk of moral denunciation. Signs or products of sin, these resentments against the socially or economically better-off argue that envy has led to an unrighteous and undeserved claim on the wealth, status, or possessions of others. "Whatever meaning is given to 'justice,'" writes W. G. Runciman, "the appeal to justice will distinguish those feelings of relative deprivation which can and which cannot be properly described as a sense of envy rather than the perception of an unfulfilled right."[9]

It is precisely the presence of a single overriding meaning for and theory of justice that discourages societal ambiguity with respect to relative deprivation and diminishes personal ambivalence over feelings of resentment. When, for example, those without money are aroused to anger about others who are wealthy, the central issue is not the former's actual lack of wealth but rather whether their poverty is deserved, their cause worthy, their demand just. The requirement that claims made upon the possessions of another be in accordance with some principle shifts the orientation of the claim outward, from some deep inner frustration to a general idea with which others similarly situated can identify. That principle, in turn, absolves the individual from the charge of unwarranted envy and dissolves whatever guilt he might feel about an equally unwarranted selfishness.

However, the institutionalization of that single principle is by no means easy or immediately at hand. Speaking of that principle as one that predisposes men toward a much prized character, an "affection to mankind," Adam Ferguson inquired: "In what situation, or by what instruction, is this wonderful character to be formed?" Ferguson gives us a clear portrait of this wonderful character and its functions, but he is far less precise about specifying the societal arrangements that might originate and nourish it. A person of "an affectionate mind" would, according to Ferguson, ensure his recognition as a man of unimpeachable integrity by demonstrating those qualities. He continues:

> To love and even to hate, on the apprehension of moral qualities, to espouse one party from a sense of justice, to oppose another with indignation excited by iniquity, are the common indications of probity, and the operations of an animated, upright, and generous spirit. To guard against unjust partialities, and ill-grounded antipathies; to maintain that composure of mind, which, without impairing its sensibility or ardour, proceeds in every instance with discernment and penetration, are the marks of a vigorous and cultivated spirit. To be able to follow the dictates of such a spirit through all the varieties of human life, and with a mind always master of itself, in prosperity or adversity, and possessed of all its abilities, when the subjects in hazard are life, or freedom, as much as in treating simple questions of interest, are the triumphs of magnanimity, and true elevation of mind.[10]

However, as Ferguson shrewdly observes, these operations of an upright, vigorous, and cultivated spirit, these triumphs of magnanimity and elevation of mind, are threatened by the kind of societal arrangements that do in fact prevail. Under existing arrangements envy, jealousy, and malice are likely to rule in place of virtue. "The case, however, is not desperate, till we have formed our system of politics, as well as manners; till we have sold our freedom for titles, equipage, and distinctions; till we see no merit but prosperity and power, no disgrace but poverty and neglect."[11] Thus did Ferguson hint at the encroachment of sin and selfishness on the basic institutions of governance in modern societies.

In those societies wherein no single uniform principle of justice prevails, and in which a variety of principles of justice contend with one another, the moral character of any resentment over conditions of inequality is more difficult to ascertain. Are the poor in modern industrial societies wronged victims of a system over which they have no control, or are they sinful—lazy, lustful, gluttonous, greedy, proud, angry, and envious?[12] That contemporary thinkers have raised complex questions— for example, the merits of equality of opportunity versus equality of result; whether contractual justice requires a test of fairness, righteousness, or hedonism; and the proper priorities of ascriptive and achieved status—serves to indicate how much of current social thought still leaves room for the evocation of sinfulness.[13] And for the pious individual, an apprehension that his or her own sinful envy might evoke the disapproval of others acts as an inhibition: what in the presence of a uniform and clear conception of justice might be put forward without hesitancy is silenced altogether.

Kant regarded envy as one of the vices that arose from the hatred of mankind. Its sinfulness, he observed, derives not only from the propensity of the envious to view with antipathy those who possess or enjoy greater benefits than themselves, but also because the envied, aware of the hostility projected upon them, become jealous of their own possessions, grudging and miserly about charity and mercy, and spiteful about the condition of the less fortunate.[14] It is perhaps a popular and primitive form of this "Kantian" sense of the absolute evil of envy that gives rise to its association with magical practices. According to Sumner, there is a widespread practice of scoffing at the wealthy not merely in order to check and humble them, but actually to protect them from the aroused envy of demons or gods who would like to do them harm.[15] Among some peoples, envy translates itself into malevolent witchcraft, taking as its object the prosperous, the better housed, the very happy, loved persons who are unloving, and all those who seem to be getting more out of life than others. The witch exercises her powers to bring misfortune upon the heads of the envied. In turn, the envied, or those likely to be such, not only take magical precautions against bewitchment but also avoid undue ostentatious display.[16]

The belief in the evil eye constitutes a complex example of this phenomenon. As Sumner has pointed out, belief in the demonological origins and preternatural realm of the evil eye must be distinguished from an anthropomorphized version of envy known in Italy as *jettatura*.[17] A case study by Anne Parsons of paranoid delusion in an immigrant Italian woman reveals the role of envy and *jettatura* in the onset of mental illness. Mrs. Perella, committed to Boston Psychopathic Hospital, believes that she has been bewitched by Mrs. J. According to the patient, Mrs. J. is extremely jealous of her because many friends gave her presents each time she bore a child. Further analysis by Parsons and the medical staff suggests that Mrs. Perella may have guilt-ridden anxieties over a latent homosexual attachment to Mrs. J. and, further, to have conflated these unconscious feelings with ambivalence and guilt toward her own mother. Ultimately, Parsons asserts, "The persecuting agent in a paranoid delusion is either a formerly loved object or a representative of such an object."[18] The attribution of envy and *jettatura*, it would appear, arises in this case out of repression, displacement, and a complex projection, all occurring within a larger psycho-cultural framework that masks spurned and forbidden love with the awesome terrors of the evil eye.

In modern societies, where witchcraft and the idea of the evil eye have little credence, the successful must nevertheless show enough concern about the potential dangers of aroused envy to keep both the general public or their own less fortunate friends under control. Precisely because resentment against social or economic inequities might translate itself into collective anger and social discontent—might, in effect, attach itself to principle and convert its argument into ideology—the enviable are on their guard to protect both their public position and their established virtue. Again, unostentatiousness, modesty, avoidance of display, and charity are encouraged as precautionary measures. But friendships are also at stake.

Perhaps no one understood this so well as Adam Smith, who founded a theory of moral sentiments on his belief that "the chief part of human happiness arises from the consciousness of being beloved." Smith noticed that "the man who, by some sudden revolution of fortune, is lifted up all at once into a condition of life greatly above what he had formerly lived in, may be assured that the congratulations of his best friends are not all of them perfectly sincere." The newly fortunate man, even if he has earned his social promotion by his own efforts, should, according to Smith, try to avoid the inevitable envy that arises among his friends. He should "smother his joy and keep down that elevation of mind with which his new circumstances naturally inspire him." Smith's moral and behavioral advice is quite specific and recalls the folk wisdom on the subject of more primitive peoples: "He affects the same plainness of dress, and the same modesty of behaviour, which becomes him in his former station. He redoubles his attention to his old friends, and endeavours more than ever to be humble, assiduous, and complaisant." However, even Smith was pessimistic about the effect of following his own advice. What is likely to happen Smith said, is a diminution in the number as well as a debasement in the quality of the fortunate man's friendships:

> In a little time, therefore, he generally leaves all his old friends behind him, some of the meanest of them excepted, who may, perhaps, condescend to become his dependants: nor does he always acquire any new ones; the pride of his new connections is as much affronted at finding him their equal, as that of his old ones had been by his becoming their superior: and it requires the most obstinate and persevering modesty to atone for this mortification to either. He generally grows weary too soon, and is provoked, by the sullen and suspicious pride of the one, and by the saucy contempt of the other, to treat the first with neglect and the second with petulance, till at last he grows habitually insolent, and forfeits the esteem of all.

Smith's less than sanguine analysis led him to suggest a different remedy: a restructuring of the *pace* of promotion: "He is happiest," wrote Smith, "who advances more gradually to greatness, whom the public destines to every step of his preferment long before he arrives at it, in whom, upon that account, when it comes, it can excite no extravagant joy, and with regard to whom it cannot reasonably create either any jealousy in those he overtakes, or any envy in those he leaves behind."[19]

Where modesty and self-effacement fail or when the enviable do not wish to deprive themselves of the fruits of their wealth, they rely on armed protection, the use of the police or the army, or—more subtly and pervasively—the establishment of a legitimating counter-ideology that includes emphasis on the sinfulness or pathology of envy.

Because envy is such a stigma, theories of justice are usually constructed with a mind to ward off its taint, prevent its arousal, and deny its efficacy. Hostility toward the better conditions of others, argue the theorists, must not only be grounded in principle but also be derived from some source other than the individual or group psyche. Both Runciman and Rawls, two contemporary theorists of justice, offer an interesting test for such a principle—that the claiming individual announce adherence in advance to the principle even if he might be disadvantaged by its implementation.[20] By putting his claim to the possessions of another exclusively in terms of a general principle, the individual can avoid the accusation that he is envious.

A similar argument seems implicitly to animate the discourses on just legislation presented by George Cornewall Lewis in 1852.[21] Recognizing that just legislation requires a proper relationship to exist between the intent of the law, the mischief it seeks to prevent, and the remedy chosen by the legislators, Lewis proposed a careful, analytical, and objective approach for ascertaining the propriety of each of these.

However, Lewis did recognize that hidden motives might influence legislation. These might include an unwarranted desire to obtain political or economic advantage, hostility to certain individuals or groups, or jealousy of the powers, prerogatives, or position of another. By insisting on the search for a reasonable public intent, the establishment of a rational and clear relationship between that intent and the method chosen by the law to reach it, and by further insisting on the proper categorization of all individuals and groups touched by that method, Lewis hoped to put the matter of public law on a sound social scientific basis. He also hoped that his approach would prove useful for uncovering motives forbidden to law; in our terms these would include envy, greed, lust, pride, and anger.

In a recent discussion of justice in terms of the constitutional guaranty of equality, ten Broek and Tussman offer an approach that also seeks to distinguish the appropriate and just principle from any baser motivations.[22] Arguing that a proper test of the equal protection clause of the Fourteenth Amendment to the United States Constitution requires that a challenged legislative act be shown to have a reasonable relationship between its public purpose and the classification necessitated thereby, the latter authors, in a manner strikingly consonant with that of Lewis, remove the juridical justification of such a law from any possible grounding in malevolent psyches, envious desires, or spiteful interests. More recently, Rawls has put the issue directly: he calls for a distinction between what he regards as the moral sentiment of resentment and true envy. "If we resent our having less than others," he writes, "it must be because we think that their being better off is the result of unjust institutions, or wrongful conduct on their part."[23] In return for and, indeed, as a condition of being released from the charge of envy, resentful claimants are placed under the burden of demonstrating precisely how some institutions are unjust, some classifications improper, and some conduct illegal. If unable to demonstrate such claims, they are open to the accusation of envy.

ENVY, EMULATION, AND COMPETITION

There is one sense in which envy can be benign. Such a situation arises when the sight or knowledge of one person's or group's goods, possessions, or qualities, arouses in another the desire to acquire the same for himself by meritorious effort. The benignity of this form of envy shows itself in the several senses in which it differs from malign envy. First, unlike antipathetic forms of envy which, at the sight of another's goods, wish the owner harm even if nothing is to be gained thereby, benign envy does not direct any hostile attention toward the better off. Rather, it takes the envied person as a role model, admires him, emulates his methods, and seeks by that effort to attain the same kind of goods that the other possesses. Second, precisely because benign envy is emulative rather than aggressive, it lends added support to the existing social order, ratifying its social rectitude by acting in such a manner as to acknowledge belief in its payoffs. Third, benign envy reinforces the channeling of any resentments held by others into legitimate activities, and thus provides a model of behavior for others to follow. Finally, benign envy lifts the sinful orientation from the putative sinner, transmuting it into a legitimate individualistic virtue—ambition.

When the perception of social inequities leads to emulation on a society-wide basis, competition for the valued items is likely to develop. Any system of competition typically establishes a frame of action and sentiment whose borders may not be transgressed. Within the confines of this system are to be found the ethically endowed practices which individuals and groups follow in order to obtain the prized values and items. Hence, it follows that emulation of the better off will be encouraged when that emulation is nonviolent, lawful, and unlikely to engender social unrest. Typically, the admiration of others, from which emulation follows, is grounded in character traits. In turn these traits are the objects of imitation in the hope that development of like traits will produce like successes.

> Emulation [writes Adam Smith], the anxious desire that we ourselves should excel, is originally founded in our admiration of the excellence of others. Neither can we be satisfied with being merely admired for what other people are admired. We must at least believe ourselves to be admirable for what they are admirable.[24]

Among the positive effects of emulation noticed by Smith are enhancement of introspection, improvement in the capacity for taking the role of the other, and a critical, impersonal evaluation of the self. As he puts it,

> We must become the impartial spectators of our own character and conduct. We must endeavour to view them with the eyes of other people, or as other people are likely to view them. When seen in this light, if they appear to us as we wish, we are happy and contented. But it greatly confirms this happiness and contentment when we find that other people, viewing them with those very eyes with which we, in the imagination only, were endeavouring to view them, see them precisely in the same light in which we ourselves had seen them.

Since, as Smith observes, "man naturally desires, not only to be loved, but to be lovely; or to be that thing which is the natural and proper object of love," the goal of ambition, moved to action through the process of emulation, converts the search for love into a careful inspection of the qualifications for it. It turns the desire for praise toward the acquisition of qualification for praiseworthiness. By enhancing his capacities for role playing and observing the self as an object, man discovers that his own praiseworthiness is grounded in the estimation of his fellow men.

> Their approbation necessarily confirms our own self-approbation. Their praise necessarily strengthens our own sense of our own praise-worthiness. In this case, so far is the love of praise-worthiness from being derived altogether from that of praise, that the love of praise seems, at least in a great measure, to be derived from that of praise-worthiness.

However, Smith and other social thinkers confined their sanguine analyses of the effects of emulation and competition to the middle classes. It was in these classes, they supposed, that the issue of social esteem loomed so large that individuals would be on their guard not to offend their good names in the eyes of the law or their peers and would be so vulnerable to mutual inspection that secret motives and illegal practices would be sharply inhibited.

> In all the middling and inferior professions, real and solid professional abilities, joined to prudent, just, firm and temperate conduct, can very seldom fail of success. Abilities will even sometimes prevail where the conduct is by no means correct. Either habitual imprudence, however, or injustice, or weakness, or profligacy, will always cloud, and sometimes depress altogether, the most splendid professional abilities. Men in the inferior and middling stations of life, besides, can never be great enough to be above the law, which must overawe them into some sort of respect for, at least, the more important rules of practice. The success of such people, too, almost always depends upon the favour and good opinion of their neighbours and equals; and without a tolerably regular conduct, these can very seldom be obtained.

Benign envy, hence, generates emulation, and when this is entered into on a society-wide scale, within established limits and under the jurisdiction of a code of conduct, a system of regulated competition is underway. The social order in this situation is regarded as legitimate; promotion in the ranks goes to those who earn it. In such a society, individuals and groups are likely to look one another over carefully. Each rates the other according to his progress in the contest, and each seeks to imitate those who are better off in order to better himself. A contest-oriented mobility system transforms the identity of each individual so that he perceives himself as a competitor and all others as opponents and rivals. So long as a sufficient number of those who agree to abide by the rules of the contest obtain rewards for their efforts, and so long as others, who do not enter the game, or who seek to violate or circumvent its rules, go unrewarded or are punished, the social sublimation of envy engendered by the competitive system will have beneficent results. However, where meritorious effort goes unpaid or undervalued, where crime and corruption are rewarded, where sponsored favorites take precedence in the ranks over those who labor independently and alone, the ambitious and hardworking are likely to resent their own condition, to seek alternative routes to success, to withdraw commitment to the system, or even to contemplate the establishment of new systems that promise to compensate honest effort.

A fine analysis of the structure and dynamics of a competitive and emulative system is contained in Ping-ti Ho's study of the traditional Chinese civil service.[25] A society-wide ladder of success, the Chinese administrative bureaucracies were staffed by men recruited regardless of background through passage of an examination. Admission to the lowest rank in the bureaucracy followed successful performance in a difficult test on the Confucian classics; promotion might be secured by passing still more examinations. Preparation required years of patient study. Since bureaucrats were universally admired and families and whole villages believed that their own advancement might be secured by placing a member in the civil service, emulation of the studious and successful magistrate was quite common. Whenever a village youth showed signs of precocious scholastic aptitude, he was relieved of his agricultural duties and domestic chores and required to study the classical literature. Families would go into debt to fund a studious son, and the hopes and fears of the family's future rested on his scholarship. A successful passage of the first examination was a cause for personal happiness and familial rejoicing; a failure, a cause for the student's remorse, nervous break-down, even suicide, and for his family's disgrace.

So long as the civil service absorbed a goodly number of applicants, there was little complaint. However, precisely because so much depended on passing the examinations, suspicions were aroused when a particularly bright person failed. More seriously, charges of corruption might be leveled when persons of no educational standing were appointed to office, while earnest students were returning to their villages empty-handed. Accusations that the families of degree holders influenced the choices made by examiners, that wealthy merchants could purchase degrees for their sons, or that the standards for successful performance were readjusted in accordance with the number of offices available filled the air when large numbers of unsuccessful candidates emerged. At certain times discontent with the operation of the examination system resulted in wholesale attack not only on the recruitment practices of the civil service but also on the fundamental structures of the imperial government itself. In this regard it is perhaps worth recalling that Hung Hsiu-Chuan, leader of the Godworshiper sect that mounted the Taiping Revolution, was a frustrated student who had failed the imperial examinations three times, and that Mao-tse Tung, an erstwhile student, wrote one of his most telling critiques in order to "Oppose the Party 'Eight-Legged Essay,'" that is, in opposition to the carefully prescribed writing form once associated with the conventional imperial examination compositions.[26]

Envy and Display

Envy may be channeled into emulation and competition for nonmaterial items such as honor, status, and esteem. Perhaps no better analyst of this phenomenon has ever written than Thorstein Veblen. As Veblen perceived social change in advancing industrial societies, an excess of consumption over production and the creation of newer classes of *nouveaux riches* led to an increasing acquisition of superfluities for conspicuous display. Veblen was careful to point out that this chase after display goods and ostentatiously visible leisure was not motivated by any want in subsistence or lack in the basic necessities for physical comfort. Should that have been the case, he argued, "then the aggregate economic wants of a community might conceivably be satisfied at some point in the advance of industrial efficiency." However, the competition was not for wealth, but rather for recognition and esteem. And, "since the struggle is substantially a race for reputability on the basis of an invidious comparison, no approach to a definitive attainment is possible."[27]

One form taken by this contest for status among the *nouveaux riches* was the competition in visible and estimable marks of one's worth. Clothing and adornment became the focus of this struggle in fin de siècle America. Ornamenting the body is, of course, one of the oldest modes by which a person or group can give indications of moral or social status. It has already been noted that modesty in dress and display may be employed to ward off envy. On the other hand, decorative dress is one of the most readily available tactics in the competition for social recognition and esteem.

The general properties of dress and display were perceptively pointed out by Georg Simmel, who treated adornment as the optimal research site for the study of that point where two opposing philosophies of conduct—man's being-for-himself and his being-for-the-other—become mutually dependent as ends and means.[28] The sociological effect of exquisite adornment, Simmel wrote, "which exclusively serves the emphasis and increased significance of the actor, nevertheless attains this goal just as exclusively in the pleasure, in the visual delight it offers to others, and in their gratitude." Adornment of oneself excites the admiration and envy of the other, but as Simmel observes, it is a benign and productive use to which this envy is put. "For even the envy of adornment only indicates the desire of the envious person to win like recognition and admiration for himself; his envy proves how much he believes these values to be connected with the adornment." Adornment, thus, is both egoistic and altruistic, indicating pride in oneself, exciting admiration and envy in the other, and stimulating emulation and the reinforcement of prevailing values. Envy here is sublimated as a support for the social order.

In the age of the American leisure class described by Veblen, a sublimated envy took the form of rating and grading oneself and others with respect to social and moral worth. The index for this contest was pecuniary achievement, and more especially its display. A show of one's purchases and of one's employment of time had to be ostentatious so that it could be measured and compared to others' shows of the same kinds of things. One example of this competitive display occurred in the employment of dress as an expression of an individual's or a family's social and economic station. As Veblen points out, taste in dress acted as a dramatic indication of social and economic distance from the world of productive primary labor. "A detailed examination of what passes in popular apprehension for elegant apparel will show that it is contrived at every point to convey the impression that the wearer does not habitually put forth any useful effort." More particularly, he noticed that an artful and prominent display of costume required enormous care for one's clothing. "The pleasing effect of neat and spotless garments," Veblen observed, "is chiefly, if not altogether, due to their carrying the suggestion of leisure— exemption from personal contact with industrial processes." Furthermore, through their stylish apparel and showy accoutrements, men might indicate to others that they were worthy of respect appropriate to members of the leisure class. "Much of the charm that invests the patent-leather shoe, the stainless linen, the lustrous cylindrical hat, and the walking stick, which so greatly enhance the native dignity of a gentleman, comes of their pointedly suggesting that the wearer cannot when so attired bear a hand in any employment that is directly and immediately of any human use." And Veblen concludes, "Elegant dress serves its purpose of elegance not only in that it is expensive, but also because it is the insignia of leisure. It not only shows that the wearer is able to consume a relatively large value, but it argues at the same time that he consumes without producing."[29]

Pecuniary canons of taste and display are not only excited by envy but, as Simmel observed, may also in turn arouse envy in others. Throughout the era of the leisure class in America, reports of excessive expenditures on superfluous commodities, conspicuous consumption of leisure, separation of wealth and its purchases from the production of useful goods and socially valuable services were presented not only to fellow members of the leisure class but also to the eyes and ears of multitudes who could not afford such luxury. Whether envy will be aroused to anger and resentment or sublimated by such ostentatious acts is one of the greatest problems for any society characterized, as was Veblen's America, by both great disparities in wealth and unqualified public display of it. The wealthy in such societies have abandoned that protection derived from modesty. They may hope for a continued belief in the rightfulness of the rank order that prevails in the society or demand the protective security afforded them by the agencies devoted to law and order. Moreover, they may insist that any serious complaint about their own excesses is motivated not by a sincere wish for social amelioration but rather by an avaricious desire to substitute the complainant for the party complained about.

Thus, Helmut Schoeck argues that luxury will remain politically acceptable despite leveling ideologies that animate resentment over conspicuous displays of wealth. Collective sentiments of opposition to social and economic inequality, he argues, can at best only generate the creation of a new ruling caste that bases its own life-style on that of the caste that it supersedes. Without exception, Schoeck asserts on the basis of his examination of the history of leveling movements, "The new ruling caste has become a bourgeoisie or a plutocracy."[30] Moreover, as the newly established inequities and privileges of rank become recognized as an integral part of the new order they also become acceptable and to that extent fail to arouse malign envy.

ENVY AND ETHNICITY

Envy, emulation, and competition may also arise in the national, cultural, and social spheres. One example is found in the relations that are alleged to obtain between immigrant peoples and the American host society during the formative years of their adjustment to one another. According to one well-known hypothesis, immigrants and host share the same fundamental attitude toward the positive value of becoming full-fledged societal members.[31] The immigrants, so the argument goes, can achieve their goal, and at the same time allay fears and reduce interethnic tensions, by adopting the culture and emulating the social, economic, and political practices of their hosts. Restated in our own terms, social adjustment and the gradual elimination of ethnic prejudices are accomplished because of the subtle operations of a sublimated envy. Immigrants admire their hosts and wish to become just like them; hosts admire only those immigrants who praise the culture and social arrangements of the established classes. An unchallenged elite, the hosts award recognition to those who openly and avowedly identify with and imitate themselves.

In the United States the competition for assimilation and accultura-tion at first took the form of a contest wherein each group sought to gain the approval of the host society by becoming "Americanized" as speedily and completely as possible. Leadership among the various contending groups seems for the most part to have accepted the terms of this contest uncritically. Urged on by spokesmen for the host society, most minority and immigrant leaders encouraged their own compatriots to compete vigorously with other groups for unqualified acceptance as "Americans." Israel Zangwill, perhaps the outstanding example, championed the idea of the "melting pot" as a solution to problems of anti-Semitism. That the competition was keen is suggested by the rewards anticipated for the winners—economic advancement, political rights, and social privileges equal to those of the host group.

Having assumed that only the capacity for rapid, unreserved, and complete assimilation could qualify a group for the rights and privileges of citizenship, ethnic leaders boasted about their own compatriots and accused other groups of being unassimilable. At various times, Nordic immigrants claimed competitive superiority to Slavs and Italians, blacks to Chinese, American Indians to all European immigrants, and white Anglo-Saxons to all others.[32] Some ethnic spokesmen became frustrated by the slowness of their own group's progress and envious of the speed of others. A poignant example is found in the final work of the late Chinese American sociologist, Rose Hum Lee. Chagrined by her discovery that the Chinese remained for the most part confined to a ghetto existence after more than a century of immigration and settlement, while the Japanese in little more than half the time had achieved much greater integration into white society, Lee accused the Chinese of lacking the will and courage to assimilate. She charged that ghetto leaders, rather than encouraging Americanization, had a selfish interest in keeping the Chinese penned up in a closed quarter of the city.[33] Thus, transmuted envy of and admiration for the host society led to emulation, competi-tion, and in some cases to a painful assessment of the moral character of one's own and other ethnic groups.

Not all immigrant leaders or advocates, however, urged their compatriots toward assimilation. Some argued that emulation of the host society required a concomitant but unacceptable abandonment of pride in one's self and one's culture. Moved to establish a cosmopolitan, coopera-tive, and confederated America, some of the more eager advocates of pluralism were led to treat overzealous moves toward the host society as motivated by an unworthy sin, envy; yet they regarded their own advocacy of a multiplicity of ethnic identities as consistent with moral order, social virtue, and societal well-being. It was not chargeable to the sin of pride.

A fine early example of resistance to the blandishments of an unalloyed Americanism is to be found in Randolph Bourne's advocacy of a "trans-national America" and his support for Zionism among America's Jews.[34] Not Jewish himself, Bourne, an adherent of Horace Kallen's thesis favoring a pluralistic democracy, came to appreciate both the group pride and the preservationist ethic that prevailed inside the Jewish community as his own fears about the effects of an uncompromising Americanism grew. Essentially, to restate his thesis in the language of our own study, Bourne's apprehensions about assimilation grew out of his conviction that it would result in an even greater sin than the sublimated envy that motivated it. The melting-pot ideology, he argued, would produce "in the long run ... exactly that terrible unity of pride, chauvinism, and ambition that has furnished the popular fuel in the armed clash of nationalism in Europe ... Who can doubt that, if we ever obtained this homogeneous Americanism that ... the latent imperialism of our ruling class would flame forth and America would follow the other States into their plunge to perdition?"

Support for subnational allegiances and pride, argued Bourne, would root out the frenetic envy that currently moves the assimilating immigrant. At the same time it would reduce that jealous guardianship of its own prerogatives that animates the Anglo-Saxon host. In place of the melting-pot ideology, which forced those seeking a societal ideal to look to the past, when a supposedly fine American culture had already reached its zenith, Bourne favored a progressive, forward-looking ideal whose final outcome was yet to be seen. The Anglo-Saxon who supported the melting-pot ideal, was, in effect, guilty of the sin of pride; he sought to sublimate that sin by encouraging admiration, envy, and emulation of the Anglo-Saxon culture among the immigrants. As Bourne saw it:

> For the Anglo-Saxon now in his bitterness to turn upon the other peoples, talk about their "arrogance," scold them for not being melted in a pot which never existed, is to betray the unconscious purpose which lay at the bottom of his heart. It betrays too the possession of a racial jealousy similar to that of which he is now accusing the so-called "hyphenates."[35]

However, Bourne was not blind to the potentially deleterious effects of the social pluralism that he favored. It might evoke its own competitive struggles, foster excessive zeal in the conservation of outmoded cultural ideals, and encourage the preservation not only of valued Old World cultural forms but, more dangerously, the continuance of abhorrent political identifications. Bourne insisted on the necessary distinction between German American support for "Deutschtum," a cultural form, and "Kaisertum," a patriotic fervor. A "dangerous corollary to trans-nationalism," Bourne wrote, "is that the national groups, if this patriotic and cultural emphasis are [sic] too great, if their Deutschtum and their Kaisertum become too intensified, might tend to become actual political groups of social rivalry within the American nation. This is a consummation even more sinister."[36]

Another possible danger in the development of ethnic subnations, according to Bourne, is the preservation of outworn cultural forms that have since been dropped in the home country but are maintained in a kind of suspended animation abroad. In terms of the argument of our present study, such mummification of cultural elements is at least in part a product of jealous guardianship over elements of a culture that, in the absence of these shielding and sustaining activities, would have drifted into disuse. In brief, then, the desublimation of the immigrants' pride and identification with the host society could also prop up excessive pride in and an envious regard for the society and culture of the world that had been left behind.

In a pluralist society characterized by ambivalence over whether individuals or groups ought to conform to the dictates of the predominant set of values, envy of the successes of fellow ethnics can lead to a limitation on social and economic advancement.[37] Where any kind of cooperation with, accommodation to, or acceptance of the opportunities offered by the larger society might be denounced by ethnic chauvinists as betrayal of the ethnic group and its culture, an individual must evaluate the offers and chances that come his way not only with respect to their intrinsic worth but also in relation to their effect on his standing in the community. Pejorative labels attached to those who move up and out— such as "Uncle Tom," "Tio Taco," and "Banana," for example— manifestly reprove those ethnics who have acquiesced to the demands of or taken advantage of opportunities in the mainstream society. However, they also may mask a malign envy of all those who achieve, or who might achieve, in the larger society. Disguised as ingroup loyalty and solidarity, an unconscious envy of all those who might succeed operates as a social and psychic control device, limiting advancement and change. Envy in such cases retards individual progress and group mobility but is sublimated in the form of a prideful ethnocentrism.

Yet, other problems of disillusion, renewed envy, and bitter *ressentiment* await those who take up the assimilative cause with zealotry, only to discover that no matter how hard they try, and, indeed, how much they succeed, they are still not accepted by the host society as full-fledged members. The situation of the Jews provides an outstanding but no longer unique example. The emancipation of the Jews in the Napoleonic era did not lead to a wholesale cosmopolitan obviation of the special character of Jewishness in the minds of either gentiles or Jews, as, to take two prominent nineteenth-century examples, Rahel Varnhagen and Karl Marx were to discover in quite different ways.[38] American

sociologists who looked to the conversion, intermarriage, or accultura-
tion of the Jews as the final step in an assimilative process that would also
bring an end to anti-Semitism have been disappointed on both counts:
most assimilated Jews did not marry gentiles, abandon all Jewish customs,
or convert to Christianity, and assimilation did not bring about the end of
anti-Semitism.[39]

However, those who assimilated sometimes found themselves at a
loss for personal identity and social esteem. Randolph Bourne described
those descendants of immigrants who had moved away from the cultural
nucleus of their own ethnic group as a rootless mass, "hordes of men and
women without a spiritual country, cultural outlaws, without taste,
without standards but those of the mob."[40] Contrasting such persons with
the proud and secure unassimilated ethnic who is "likely to be a better
citizen of the American community," Bourne argued that the victims of
the melting pot "make for detached fragments of peoples":

> Those who came to find liberty achieve only license. They become
> the flotsam and jetsam of American life, the downward undertow of
> our civilization with its leering cheapness and falseness of taste and
> spiritual outlook, the absence of mind and sincere feeling which we
> see in our slovenly towns, our vapid moving pictures, our popular
> novels, and in the vacuous faces of the crowds on the city street.
> This is the cultural wreckage of our time, and it is from the fringes
> of the Anglo-Saxon as well as other stocks that it falls.

As Bourne saw it, the rejected would-be assimilates make up the
"detritus of cultures." But, disregarding the excesses of Bourne's
rhetoric, what of the attitudes of this rootless, not-quite-cosmopolitan
mass? The problem looms even larger for members of racially visible
minorities in the United States. Having departed from the cultural center
of their originating group and been refused entrance to the seemingly
more attractive center of the host people, they reside in limbo, somewhere between cultures, products of two traditions, members of neither.
The admiration and sublimated envy that led them to an ambitious
emulation of mainstream Americans have been frustrated. One consequence is an anguished, ambivalent, and sometimes bewildered *ressentiment*, as is indicated in this statement from a second-generation Japanese
in America:

> I feel that the Japanese, second generation as well as first genera-
> tion, are viewed with suspicion. Unwritten laws favor the whites
> and keep Orientals down. We are not considered Americans. We
> are regarded as aliens and people believe we will always remain
> Japanese. We of the second generation, on the other hand, are aliens
> to our parents. That makes us a lost generation! Our children will
> feel better—but what good does that do us? Perhaps intermarriage

will solve the problem, but again, what good will that do us of this generation?[41]

Perhaps the most poignant example of this problem is illustrated by the situation of Blacks in America. Uprooted long ago from all but the vestiges of their African cultural origins, these people can neither return to an Old World folk culture nor can they yet obtain unreserved entrance into American society. For some members of the Black middle classes, an anxiety-provoking and imitative ethnic *embourgeoisement* has served as a tentative and precarious resolution of this dilemma.[42] But for other Blacks both resentment and *ressentiment*, in the forms of a hostile opposition to American values, a deprecation of achievement norms, a rejection of middle-class life-styles, a search for African, Oriental, or other more exotic cultural forms, or a sullen refusal to accommodate to generally recognized social practices, indicate how deep a fissure has opened in the psychic and social fabric of the country.[43] Envy, benign and malign, seems to be embedded in ethnicity.

ENVY AND ASCRIPTION

Nature distributes its gifts unevenly, seemingly arbitrarily, and without apparent regard to the worth or worthiness of the recipients. Physical appearance, bodily form, gender, race, and family are acquired at birth without wish, will, or utterance. Yet they are elements not only in the categorization of human kind but also in the evaluation, rating, and grading of individuals and groups. Their distribution is thus not merely a matter of natural fact but more significantly an issue for social understanding and personal concern. The ascriptive elements of existence follow us into the commerce of our lives, with differential and varying effects on occupations, politics, marriage, friendship, and all the other aspects of our humanity and associations. Even when a society is founded on the ideals of universality and achievement, when each person stands formally equal with all others and awaits rewards on the basis of his own efforts and personal achievements, there remains what one writer calls the secret ranking: the evaluation of one's worth according to the standards of beauty, grace, and sexuality.[44]

Body

Of the "property" over which humans have, or seek to have dominion, the body, as Simmel pointed out, is first in place.[45] The body is not merely one's anatomical and physiological inheritance. More significantly it is the primary material extension of the ego, that material which is, or ought to be, obedient to the will of the owner. As the primary object of ego identification the body participates in social life as the most immediate and manifest expression of the ego. The image and the appearance of the human body is a fundamental element in the ego's understanding of itself and in the social estimation of a person. Yet that image and appearance are not entirely under the control of ego, and the perception of the body is subject to divergent interpretation and distorted visualization. Moreover, since both the bodies of ourselves and others are visually or descriptively available to us, these bodies can become the focus of jealous regard and protection and envious resentment and revenge.

Precisely because our bodies are aspects of the biosocial system, our control over their appearance is incomplete.[46] Our bodies are a feature of our *fortuna*, while our *virtù* can only summon up whatever powers, skills, and abilities it has to cope with, manipulate, beautify, and adorn them. Thus, from the beginning of our lives our bodies threaten to betray us. Shaping themselves in accordance with their innate engines of development, they become what it is in their nature to become, regardless of the will of the owner. Yet humans are not without tools, devices, and plans wherein they can modify and limit, and in rare occasions, altogether revoke nature's bodily decrees.

Gender Envy

Nature may decree sex but cultures and personality indicate gender.[47] Thus, while the former is measured by chromosomes, external and internal genitalia, gonads, hormonal states, and secondary sex characteristics, gender is experienced as a facet of identity and expressed in role behavior. Generally sex falls into two categories—male and female—with certain residual categories—hermaphrodite, intersexed, and chromosome mixtures—also recognized as rare but real. Gender, on the other hand, seems more complex. Precisely because it is a socially bound and culturally conditioned phenomenon, it is subject to variation, vagary, and vanity. The correspondence of gender and sex is by no means secure. Among the issues and problems that arise because of this lack of congruency is gender envy. As a powerful sentiment that can arise out of the curious and indeterminate intersections of nature and nurture, gender envy becomes a significant sociocultural force.

Among the middle classes of the Occident, gender envy and other related complications arising out of the long process of nurturance and socialization are prominent features of cultural life. Talcott Parsons has given special emphasis to those gender-role-related issues and noticed their relationship to basic patterns of aggression.[48] Writing at the close of

World War II and addressing himself to the general conditions that had led to that war, Parsons observed that both boys and girls undergo trying maturation periods that tax their capacity for developing gender roles corresponding to their respective sexes.

Parsons' observations can be translated into a study in the etiology and consequences of envy. For middle-class white boys, a long period of maternal guidance, modified by the mother's ambivalent orientation toward boyish masculinity, the working father's absence from home for long periods of the day, the separation of boyish activities from the worlds of men, and the development of male bonding among adolescents makes for varying degrees of anguish, resentment, and resistance to the assumption of adult masculine roles and identities.[49] On the one hand, young men may envy the condition of childishness that they are required to leave behind as the inevitability of age demands an acceptance of serious and competitive activities and the establishment of a career; on the other hand, they might envy the condition of their mothers and sisters, and by extension that of women in general, as they measure the degrees and kinds of difficulty in the duties and obligations assigned to the separate sexes. In either case, however, the envious feelings are experienced with guilt and shame. In turn the envy and resentment are repressed and help in the development of a powerful and more general sense of frustration. Ultimately the original objects of these frustrations are displaced, and other objects are substituted for them. Aggressive antipathy toward Jews and Blacks becomes one form in which this expression of envy is ultimately manifested. In the imagination of the white Anglo-Saxon middle classes, Jews and Blacks live, respectively, beyond or beneath the role expectations that fall to the Gentile Caucasians of the Occident and are freed from the latter's onerous obligations. As the moral equivalent of women, Jews and Blacks become the unfortunate victims of an original envy of gender and sex.

However, boys are not unique in the development of envy and resentment over gender; girls, too, suffer from the dilemmas and contradictions occasioned by the social circumstances and cultural conditions of their own sex. As Parsons has pointed out, middle-class white girls are likely to suffer from the shock of recognition that suddenly occurs when they discover that the movement from their own status as single women to that of wives and mothers requires a successful marketing of sociability and pulchritude. Since they have learned the roles of housewife and mother from watching and participating in the domestic scenes of their own homes, these girls feel cheated because of their lack of knowledge in how to acquire a husband. Wishing to *be* wives and mothers, they wonder how to *become* sweethearts and fiancées. Envious of their mother's secure position, they come to resent them for not teaching them the art of competitive courtship. In addition, they come to envy the freedom and resent the looser morals of boys on whom they are dependent for their futures. These antipathetic sentiments must be suppressed lest they interfere with the girls' ultimate objective—finding a husband.

Even after the courtship game has ended in marriage, frustrations and envious sentiments continue for members of both sexes. Intelligent and talented women are likely to feel cheated by the occupational and marital norms that restrict their chances. In addition, the relegation of marital sex to a scheduled occasion, the reliance for status on the successes of their husbands, the retreat from romance that follows successful courtship, and the restriction of wifely roles to that of good companion or community servant are not infrequently stifling. Unable or unwilling to break out of their marital prisons, such women may fantasize a more exciting sex life than the one that they actually experience—dreaming of being carried off by a lusty Negro, envying Black women who, they suppose, have sexual access to both Black and White men, wishing that they had married a rich Jew who could be dominated, and resenting men in general, and Blacks, Jews, and their husbands in particular. Facing their husbands, who are also suffering from unexalting competition at work, unexpressed longings, and inexpressible frustrations, women may find some small consolation in the common feeling that they share with their mates: they both secretly envy and openly show contempt for Blacks and Jews.

Gender envy most probably arises from a diversity of causes, not all of which are yet known or understood. Whatever its etiology, it finds expression in various epochs in history and across cultures. One mode of existence taken up by those who cannot abide or will not accept the sex nature has given them is "passing," that is, assuming the identity and roles of the opposite sex. History provides numerous examples of men who posed as women and women who posed as men. From the Chevalier d'Eon, who, disguised as a woman, served as a French secret agent in Russia and England, to "Agnes," the transsexual individual who success-fully masked a childhood lived as a boy and obtained a sex-change operation thereby, a few persons have expressed what is, ultimately, at any rate, an envy of the opposite sex by "becoming" what is their ideal.[50] Envy leads to emulation; emulation to assumption—or to *ressentiment*.

Psychoanalysis recognizes one aspect of this form of frustrated desire under the designation "penis envy." For a boy, as Freud contended in 1925, fear of castration adds new dimensions to his recognition that girls have no penis and reinforces his own anxieties; ultimately the boy's relations to women might be permanently distorted by that recognition, in the form of either a repellent horror of mutilated creatures or a triumphant contempt of them.[51] For a girl, on the other hand, penis envy emerges immediately upon perception: "She has seen it and knows that she is without it and wants to have it." Freud depicted the consequences of penis envy as both positive and negative. On the less fortunate side it led to the so-called "masculinity complex," wherein women become fixated on obtaining a penis, deny the fact that they do not have one, or take over the same contempt for their own sex that is felt by men. Furthermore penis envy may persist in displaced form as jealousy of other children, in rejection of the mother as one who has brought into the world a person without a penis, or in a sense of inferiority about the clitoris.

However, Freud also hinted at a possibly positive effect of sublimated penis envy. A girl may equate "penis" with "child," give up her wish for the former and substitute for it a wish to have a child. Even here, however, negative aspects remain. She might develop an Oedipal regard for her father, become jealous of her mother, and, in the event that her attachment to her father comes to grief and must be abandoned, she might in turn replace it by identification with him and a return to a masculinity complex. Sublimated penis envy, thus, like envy of the rich, might encourage emulative actions. In the normal case these move the woman to assume feminine and maternal roles; on the other hand, fixations and failures of sublimation contribute to pathological development and to jealousy.

ANATOMY, DESTINY, AND DEATH: THE DRAMATIZATION OF ENVY

It is now widely recognized that the body is a significant and complex medium of expression.[52] One aspect of that expression is pulchritude. Beauty, however, is neither universal nor is it equally distributed among humans. Beauty partakes of fashion and culture; it tends to locate its traits among those found in the predominant and powerful groups in any society, and to drift in accordance with aesthetic trends. Nevertheless, no matter what shape it assumes, beauty does not embrace all who might benefit from it. As a scarce "commodity," beauty is an object for envy.

The shape of the human body is measurable not only in anatomical but also in aesthetic terms. Its visual design is an object for art and also for identification. In the Occident, body shape ideals have varied over time, rooted essentially in the changing evaluation of proportions and the shifting aesthetic priorities placed on different areas of the human anatomy.[53] As different body types achieved idealization and were widely represented in art and drama, individuals and groups discovered the aesthetic and anatomical distance that separated them from the prized human model. Possessed of what Bernard Rudofsky calls an unfashionable human body, these unfortunates in turn have to live with a visible stigma.[54] Clothing, cosmetics, diet, exercise, surgery, and seclusion become techniques for neutralizing nature's arbitrary gifts. Moreover, those sanctified with classic proportions and socially lauded shapes become objects of envy, targets of resentment, or highly priced commodities in the marketplace of human beauty.

An illustration of this phenomenon—drawn from the work and the life of a Japanese intellectual—can perhaps stand for the much wider range of possibilities that does in fact prevail. The late novelist Yukio Mishima provides in both his stories and his own life remarkable examples of the envy of culturally specific body types. In his novel *Forbidden Colors*, Mishima offers a dramatistic perspective on the Japanese homosexual demi-monde.[55] The scene is set so that entrance to a certain Tokyo bar serves as a parvenu's first move on stage. Unsuspecting young men who pass through the doorway are carefully observed and fully evaluated by the patrons, who form an audience. Youth and anatomical elegance are the only elements that count. The sudden appearance of a remarkably handsome young man will result in an alteration in the relations between the actor and his audience. First there will be an aesthetic reevaluation of all other males present, then a contest for the erotic conquest of the newly discovered beauty, and, during all of this action, a variety of displays of envy and jealousy by all those who lose out in the rating and dating process. Precisely because established masculine beauty is subject to dethronement whenever a better-endowed man appears, each Adonis guards against his own descent from the pinnacle, depreciates the admired form of a newcomer, and envies the loveliness that fate has awarded to another. Only age and wealth can alter the role one plays in this half-world drama of the Tokyo homosexual. Once the years have removed a man from the contest, if he is lucky enough to be rich, he can become a consumer of beauty, purchasing for his own use what once he longed to be. He moves off the stage of the envied and onto the sidelines of the envying audience.

Mishima's own life story reflects the role that envy of human beauty plays. In his own words, he had "a romantic impulse towards death, yet at the same time I required a strictly classical body as its vehicle; a peculiar sense of destiny made me believe that the reason why my romantic impulse towards death remained unfulfilled in reality was the immensely simple fact that I lacked the necessary physical qualifications." Mishima had been to Greece and admired the classical Greek body form. He determined to reshape his rather average body in accordance with the Attic design, and at the age of 30 embarked on a strenuous program of exercise ("sun and steel") in order to prepare for the glorious death vouchsafed to those whose physiques so qualified them. ("A powerful, tragic frame and sculpturesque muscles were indispensable.")[56]

Just as Mishima portrayed the homosexual life in dramatistic perspective in his novels, so also he envisioned his own death in terms related to public display, physical beauty and recognized athleticism. To Mishima the emotions had their dramatic counterpart and visual design in the musculature: "Thus feeble emotions ... correspond to flaccid muscles, sentimentality to a sagging stomach, and overimpressionability to oversensitive white skin." Moreover, to Mishima these outward signs of inner failure were also repulsive: "I had always felt that such signs of physical individuality as a bulging belly (sign of spiritual sloth) or a flat chest (sign of unduly nervous sensibility) were excessively ugly ..."[57] Mishima, in effect a romantic version of Kretschmer, the German theorist who based a theory of personality on body types—or, to choose a different image, a twentieth-century novelist who interpreted anatomy in a fashion similar to those sixteenth-century Englishmen who upon first espying black Africans equated the black skin with a black heart— believed that only a perfected anatomical frame could achieve a perfect death.[58] Envying the ancient Greek athletes whom he imagined had magnificent physiques and died in their twenties, he desired to repeat their glorious existence in his own. Yet, as he wrote, "For me, beauty is always retreating from one's grasp: the only thing I consider important is what existed before, or ought to have existed." And so, by lifting weights and exposing himself to the sun, Mishima "restored the classical balance that the body had begun to lose, reinstating it in its natural form, the form that it should have had all along."[59] He believed that for himself and his followers at least, "Bulging muscles, and a tough skin ... would correspond to an intrepid fighting spirit, the power of dispassionate intellectual judgment, and a robust disposition."

Ultimately, he realized his physical ideal, and, encased in his rippling musculature, he committed suicide in a carefully staged real-life drama that was also a plea for a restoration of traditional Japanese military values. In one of his novels he hints at the suicidal theme that haunted his existence: "Just before the pinnacle when time must be cut short is the pinnacle of beauty." Having attained his aesthetic anatomical ideal he jealously preserved it by killing himself before it could wither and decay.

SIX

Gluttony

The human world, it was said [in the *Puranas*, an ancient Indian collection of stories], formed a series of concentric circles around Mount Meru—a succession of ring-like continents separated from one another by seven oceans. The ocean immediately surrounding Mount Meru was composed of salt; the next of *jaggeri*, a very coarse, sticky, dark brown sugar; the third of wine; the fourth of *ghi* (boiled and clarified butter); the fifth of milk; the sixth of curds; and the seventh of fresh water.

*Reay Tannahill**

APPROACHES TO A DEFINITION

The glutton is one who exhibits almost insatiable desire and enormous capacity for engorgement. Typically gluttony is associated with eating or drinking, but it need not be confined to these two alone. The popular phrase "He's a glutton for work" refers to the person who seems never to tire, who toils on when all others have stopped, who labors on into the wee hours of the morning, and yet is able to arise early, fresh and refreshed, and return to his work. On the other hand, the phrase "He's a glutton for punishment" suggests something more sinister or more pathetic—the masochist who seems to derive some personal pleasure from or has a fatal attraction to instruments of torture, or the unresisting victim who suffers the continued outrages of cruel taskmasters while never raising a finger in his own defense. Gluttony may also indicate uncontrollable addiction—a fascination with drugs, liquor, food, or some activity which for others takes up little or no time or attention. Gluttony, thus, is excessive and greedy absorption in the immediate appetitive pleasures of the self.

That gluttony can focus on such a variety of objects lends to it a sense of moral ambiguity. Not all forms of self-absorption seem equally bad, and some seem to promote social good. The glutton for work, for example, could be recognized as in the Russian example as a Stakhanov, whose prodigious efforts were not only rewarded but institutionalized as the norm of production for all other workers.[1] On the other hand, the "rate-buster," discovered in the Hawthorne Studies, was regarded as an enemy of his fellow laborers, working so rapidly and without fatigue or faltering that he threatened to shame them before their foremen, inspire assembly-line "speedups," and, perhaps, invite a reduction in the labor force.[2] Consider the "bookworm" as a glutton for knowledge. On the one hand he seems overcommitted to his own education and less interested in the immediate pleasures of his social world. Yet his expertise, a product of his long hours of study and his refusal to stray from the intellectual task to which he has committed himself, may prove more worthy and useful than the limited knowledge of the much vaunted well-rounded man. Or, in a perhaps extreme example, examine the social uses of the masochist. As one who has mastered the acceptance and, indeed, taken up the joy of suffering, he is useful in the role of saboteur and spy. If captured by the enemy, he will be far less likely to break under torture than one who abhors pain and avoids punishment.[3] The glutton, repudiated as he indulges his desire, may yet be valuable for his sinfulness.

Where an apparent gluttony arises from uncontrollable addiction, as in the case of the habitual heroin user, the social attitude is a mixture of pity and contempt. To the extent that the addict cannot control his appetite for the drug, he is seen not as acting out of sinful desire but rather out of victimization.[4] On the other hand some regard the craving for opiates as a moral default, a breakdown of personal control, an acquiescence to the less honorable aspects of self. True gluttony is related to acts which arise when choice is free, when one may decide to indulge or abstain, and when an individual or a group under such freedom elects to gorge, to feast, to fill the belly, the veins, or whatever, with the object of insatiable desire.

But precisely because gluttony can only be firmly established under conditions of free choice, it is difficult to establish its existence incontestably. Where the alleged gluttonous acts may depend on biological drives over which the individual has no control, where the political, social, economic or personal constraints on choice are unknown, where, as the law puts it, *mens rea*, or criminal intent, is in doubt, acts that seem overindulgent might be attributable to other sources. Hence there arises not only the possibility of nagging doubt with respect to whether apparent indulgences are moral defaults, but also a potentiality for absolution from the charge of willful sin. The accused might plead lack of control, enslavement to natural or social directives that will cannot overcome. And since ambivalence prevails about these matters among the experts as well as laymen, such exculpations may carry considerable weight.

History of the Sin of Gluttony

Why is gluttony a sin? Gluttony has been regarded as a sin from the earliest recording of the seven deadly sins, the pseudepigraphical *Testament of the Twelve Patriarchs* of 109–106 B.C.[5] When in the sixth century the Gregorian list of these sins began to displace that of Cassian, it retained gluttony along with the other fleshly sins probably because the latter were more especially the problem of cloistered monks, who had taken vows to oppose these temptations. The sculptured pillars of the fourteenth-century ducal palace at Venice depicted gluttony among the vices as a woman holding in one hand a jeweled cup and in the other the limb of a bird at which she is gnawing. From its earliest usages, gluttony is associated not only with overeating but with drunkenness and places to purchase drink. In the fourteenth-century *Piers Plowman*, whose confession scene is one of the most brilliant dramatistic representations of the cardinal sins, Gluttony is personified as one who decides to go to confession but is lured into a tavern on the way, intoxicated, sunk into a two-day hangover, and only absolved when he drags himself to Repentance and confesses to having trespassed with his tongue. The continuous association of gluttony with fleshly overindulgence, and especially its association with the mouth, leads toward recognition of its particular sinful quality.

Gluttony is sinful because it indulges the body at the expense of the mind and the soul. Gluttony partakes of two other sins—greed and lust—and employs these to aggrandize the body. In one sense gluttony is recognizable as a sin because of a prior recognition of the Occidental division into body and soul and, in the post-Cartesian era, body and mind. Once the human was perceived as partaking of spiritual qualities, qualities that raise man above the animal, those actions that indulge the animal nature became inferior, immoral, and chargeable to a sinful reorganization of priorities.

When earlier theologians took up the divisions of the soul into its parts and sources they recognized a distinction among animal and spiritual elements. Thus, during the Carolingian Age Alcuin, in *De animae ratione liber ad Eulaliam virginem*, distinguished concupiscent, irascible, and rational divisions.[6] The first two are shared with animals, he argued, while the latter is purely human. These animal elements evoke sinful acts: from concupiscence arise gluttony, lechery, and avarice; from irascibility there comes anger, sadness, and *accidie*. However, the purely human elements partake of what Alcuin considered the four virtues—prudence, justice, fortitude, and temperance. These human virtues in turn were to do battle with the sinful vices. Man's existence consecrated a dualism and a struggle, a structure and process of conflict in which the virtuous human elements would win out over their vicious animal opponents. However, locked in the soul, the vices and virtues are permanently entangled. Their struggle is engaged from the beginning of life, or of consciousness, and does not end until death extinguishes the struggle by extricating the soul from its fleshly encasement. Concupiscence, when it finds its expression in the ardent longing for food, drink, or drugs, presents itself as gluttony. So long as the individual lives, he must employ prudence in his gustatory choice, justice in the distribution to his appetite, fortitude in his refusal to succumb to ravenousness, and temperance in moderating his diet. The possibility of falling into gluttony is ever present and follows individuals throughout life. It threatens to engulf the individual in a wave of indulgence from which he cannot escape—except if he employs watchful self-restraint or is restrained by others.

When cynics and dissenters sought to reverse the direction of the moral idea behind the great chain of being, the striving of humans to reach up from their base animal nature toward a station just below that of the angels, they did not challenge the fundamental dualism of human existence but rather emphasized the power of the baser elements, acknowledged the potency of the animal nature, or grimly satirized the victory of flesh over spirit. The Elizabethan Age in England, the Italian Renaissance in Florence, focused on the vices of humankind that tended to thrive and indeed even thwart the virtues.[6] Humans did not reach so near to the angels, they argued, but rather rose only slightly above the animals. Gluttony, lust, and avarice would better describe the world's work than pursuit of the virtues. And in subsequent eras, as secular thought replaced theological, there still remained a recognized dualism and a moral hierarchy—mind and body—and the division in humankind separating agency for self-control from appetitive desires.

GLUTTONY AND THE SOCIAL STRUCTURE

Although gluttony is a recognized sin, it is rarely considered a social problem. Gluttony's removal from the societal list of prominent issues stems primarily from its location in the personal and individual aspects of life, its dissociation from group action, and its limited and confined effects. To speak of gluttony in a sociological manner, we must recognize the division in society between public and private realms and between group and mass phenomena. Whereas some of the sins—envy, for example—find direct or sublimated expression in recognized societal values, gluttony, with certain important exceptions, such as drug addiction, alcoholism, and compulsive gambling, remains a private and individual phenomenon or finds its effects in mass rather than group organization.

Although gluttony may not provide a major avenue for social amelioration, it nevertheless is related to cultural ideals and partakes of the social process. Precisely because overindulgence is not possible for those unable to satisfy their appetites we may expect to find it, or the image of it, among the better off and wealthy. Thus it is common to find those who scoff at the rich also including in their criticisms that the rich are gluttons.[8] While ordinary folk eat moderately and the poor go hungry, the rich, it is argued, gorge themselves, consuming meals that are orgiastic feasts rather than merely extraordinary banquets. The rich may may be pictured as a glutton, fat, oleaginous, unceasingly appetitive, and satisfying his desires by preying upon the poor. To the extent that gluttony is an excess characterizing the moral character of the ruling classes, it serves to fuel the fires of resentment, resistance, and revolution that arise in unjustly stratified society.

Gluttony may also arise as a temporary release from impoverishment. As the long-hungry masses in a corrupt society take up arms against the plutocracy, they may storm the granaries, steal large amounts from the great storehouses, and celebrate their temporary liberation from starved conditions by a bacchanalian feast. Satiated for the moment, these masses may fail to take precautions for or prepare a defense against counter-revolution and the resurgence of the old order. The moment of overindulgence may be only a memento of liberation, a memory to the poor of what a more just world might have provided, a reminder to the plutocrats of how precarious are their positions. A gluttonous indulgence might serve as a pseudorevolution, a kind of saturnalian reversal of roles and habits, as the poor gorge themselves for one day, and after satiation return to their lowly stations. Indeed, such moments of rebellious indulgence—rare but wonderful—might dampen the ardor and indeed weaken the support for real revolutionary or reformist groups. The slow, orderly development of wordy ideology and the rational, calculating buildup of an organization leave no room for the playing out of dramatic scenes, the propaganda of the decisive deed, the visible and sensual feel of vital social action and primitive satisfactions. Bread riots in eighteenth-century London and Paris, the ghetto revolts in American cities in the mid-1960s, and the riotous response to the distribution of food demanded by the Symbionese Liberation Army in San Francisco in 1974, though not gluttonous in themselves, provide fascinating examples of gluttonous revolutionary moments.[9]

However, gluttony is linked, negatively, to the sociocultural process in ways other than those described by stratification and its effects. In every culture and civilization there develops an approved ideal body type. This type in turn is related to the social virtues and cultural values celebrated for and urged on every individual. Thus the classic Greek masculine figure, which became an Occidental model after the Renaissance, was in turn associated not only with athleticism but also with heroic stature.[10] According to Orrin E. Klapp, writing in 1962, American culture is characterized by a cult of the physical that finds its expression in admiration for the strong man, champion, he-man, cowboy, stunt man, and prize fighter.[11] In addition to their physical strength and perfection of body, such persons are endowed with leadership skills, social virtues, and the capacity (if not always the sense) to solve social problems. However, Klapp rejects arguments that seek to explain this accent on physique by the attraction to primordialism or the fear of feminity, instead proposing an explanation that links muscular physique to heroism and domination. The physique fulfills a popular demand for simple, universal, visible, and readily available criteria by which people determine their leaders. Surface qualities, easy to recognize and evaluate, have an advantage over those that are hidden from view, inner, spiritual, or complicated. The former have the greatest immediate appeal to the most heterogeneous mass audience; the latter are likely to be overlooked, misperceived, or ambiguous. At any rate, and for whatever reason, the classical physique and its attendant consequences—beach culture, body building, health programs, and an emphasis on physical fitness—are a discouragement to gluttony.

Where a lean, hard muscular body is a male cultural ideal, and a thin, curvaceous, large-breasted figure is favored for women, the social opposition to gluttony becomes patterned and institutionalized. The public educational program will include emphasis on proper diet and physical fitness. Children will be encouraged at home and taught in school to eat balanced meals and engage in regular exercise. Standards of mate choice will emphasize the distinct advantage of the bodily ideal for those of marital age. Adults will wonder and worry about their image and appearance as age and fatigue begin to take their toll. In extreme cases individuals will reinstate themselves in imaginary bodies, fantasize heroic physiques or voluptuous figures for themselves, and develop pathological separations of their identities from their anatomies. Mass media will celebrate the physical ideal with honorific pictures of those who come closest to achieving it, and mass audiences will pin these to walls, lockers, suitcases, albums, and articles of clothing. Criticism, comment, gossip, and humor will aid in keeping individuals and masses within range of the norm. Gluttons will be stigmatized as deviant, and then pitied, condemned, ostracized, or converted into figures of vulgar fun.

Gluttony sometimes is recognized as a problem for an entire society. Anatomical perfection and the Attic physique have not been maintained. Typically this is noticed in times of military danger, or international athletic competition, when physical fitness is discovered to be in short supply and dietary practice to be scandalous.[12] Blame for mass physical failure is placed upon the agencies of cultural transmission: parents, schools, media. Efforts of these institutions are redoubled. Encouragement toward physical fitness, physical beauty, and health is made, and the fat, lazy, and indulgent are excoriated. The sin of gluttony becomes an antisocial act. In such times persons who persist in overindulging their gastronomical habits, who openly display disregard for health and fitness, who celebrate the orgiastic feast and corpulent girth become anathema, subversives to the aristocracy of body that the culture has established.

Societal opposition to gluttony manifests itself in a variety of social control devices and institutional arrangements. Although rarely organized as a group, very fat individuals at times seem to form a much beset minority, objects of calculating discrimination and bitter prejudice. Stigmatized because their addiction to food is so visible in its consequences, the obese find themselves ridiculed, rejected, and repulsed by many of those who do not overindulge. Children revile them on the streets, persons of average size refuse to date, dance, or dine with them, and many businesses, government, and professional associations refuse to employ them. So great is the pressure to conform to the dictates of the slimness culture in America that occasionally an overweight person speaks out, pointing to the similarities of his condition to that of racial and national minorities.[13] Evidence of occupational and educational discrimination against fat people includes cases wherein a civil engineer is told to lose weight or find another job, overweight schoolteachers are fired for refusing to lose weight in accordance with an administratively imposed time table, college entrance requirements give preference to slim applicants, and the president of a major corporation states that he refuses to hire fat people because he believes that excessive weight is indicative of a general lack of discipline. For those who refuse to acquiesce to the chorus of demands, threats, and medical opinions that exhort them to lose weight, a retreat into seclusion sometimes seems to mitigate the oppression. Other oppressed minorities have formed defensive group associations and structured their enforced segregated existence so as to embrace group sentiment, and in a few cases so have the overweight. However, most fat people are rarely in a position to resolve their painful situation in this manner. Lonely and isolated, the fat person, or the fat couple, perhaps finds solace alone, eating to heart's and stomach's content. Ironically, this isolation and loneliness may add considerably to the vexatious situation in which overindulgence occurs, creating a vicious circle.

Other excesses that bear the stigma of gluttony may, ironically, be more resistant to the worst features of prejudice and discrimination. Consider drunkenness and drug addiction. Few would doubt that these cravings are stigmatized, and overindulgence in alcohol has been associated with gluttony since the earliest codification of deadly sins. Fewer still would deny that a great many persons known to be frequently drunk, or individuals who cannot control their desire for drugs, are subject to moral denunciation, social deprecation, and occupational eviction. Yet many distinguish between the obstinately obese person and the addict. The obese person, so some medical and social science argues, indulges because he wants to, the addict because he must. To be sure, it is not so clear to the scientists as the statement here makes it appear. The craving for food is in some cases recognized to be a product of glandular disturbance or some hereditary factor. Nevertheless, the corpulent person is all too often regarded as capable of freely choosing to depart from his habit, while the drug addict and the alcoholic are more often defined as victims of physiological drives that have severed their connections from the will. Hence, while the addict and the alcoholic enjoy even fewer of the occupational, social, and interpersonal privileges of the overweight, they are not regarded as so responsible for their condition as fat people. And even when the ever-hungry fat man is perceived as ill, he is all too often told that he holds the remedy for his disease in his own hands—control over his appetitive desire. Let him but exercise moderation, self-restraint, and girth control, and he will be relieved of the burden of his weight. For the addict and the drunk, however, self-control is seen as insufficient and ineffective. Truly ill beyond self-cure, he is neither responsible for his craving nor required to cure himself alone. To be sure there is a certain praise for the drug addict who goes "cold turkey" to end his habit, and the former alcoholic is on his guard to remain "on the wagon" without others' reminders. Yet special hospitals, clinics, and new methods are established far more often in behalf of addiction and the alcoholic than of corpulence. Spas and resorts established to aid the overweight are all too often places of retreat for the rich and for ridicule by those people who cannot afford them. Our purpose here is not to argue a petition in behalf of the overweight minority but rather to point to the distinctions that prevail among the forms of gluttony.[14] So long as any one form is seen as under the voluntary control of the individual who engages in it, then so long will that practice be regarded as sinful. Redemption and absolution are possible as efforts of will.

The willful aspect of gastronomic gluttony goes far in explaining the resistance to recognizing it as a social problem. Typically, truly social problems are directed toward the institutions that shape or create them. When a problem that might arise from institutional failure is instead redefined as one of human frailty, the social response to it becomes indirect, diffuse, and mediated. Thus when, as has happened in thinking about two other social problems, race prejudice is related to misadventure in the earliest formation of the human psyche, and war is seen as a product of primordial human aggressiveness, solutions to these hitherto perceived social problems evoke pallid proposals for voluntary plans and weak pleas for individual commitment.[15] So it is with food gluttony. Although cultural institutions might be less than successful in encouraging the physical ideal, although commercial institutions might feel free to market foods high in calories and low in nutrients, and although educational institutions might be inadequate in health and physical education, at bottom the problem of body weight is seen as personal. If society suffers from an excess of gluttons and libertines, these sins await the individual's own personal repentance.

The apparently voluntary character of food gluttony serves to point up why it is more likely to seem "criminal" than sick, an act of moral defalcation rather than medical pathology.[16] Although gluttony is not proscribed by the criminal law, it partakes of some of the social sanctions and moral understandings that govern orientations toward those who commit crimes. If, however, gluttony is a "crime," it would appear at first inspection to fall into that category of one without victims.[17] Gluttony supposedly injures only the person who overindulges his appetite, increasing his weight beyond normal proportions, slowing and marring his gait, reducing his motor speed and physical grace, and, if medical science is to be believed, shortening life itself. As a "victimless crime," gluttony is perhaps closer to suicide than any other crime of its type, for it not only facilitates an earlier death for the glutton but also creates a kind of living death for him as well. Deprived all too often of the admiration, companionship, and love of his nongluttonous peers, the overindulgent eater carries on an isolated, asocial existence. He not only consumes too much food; he is consumed by it.

However, it is precisely this overemphasis on consumption that renders gluttony ambiguous with regard to the number of its victims. Gluttony is an excessive *self*-indulgence. Even in its disrespect for the body it overvalues the ego that it slavishly satisfies. Such acts of overindulgence of self and individual constitute a resistance to—indeed a quiet rebellion against—the demands of sociality.[18] The glutton all too frequently eats alone and often; in the extreme case he concentrates his attention on obtaining and consuming more and more food. Dining becomes an obsession, the summum bonum of his existence, and gastronomic interests crowd out other aspects of existence, being, and relationship. Like the taboo against incest—or that against love marriage in clan-based societies, which in part stems from the fact that such intimacy is likely to withdraw too much of the services of the couple from the larger societal unit—gluttony's overindulgence of the self is too egoistic for societal toleration. The glutton has so greatly distorted the appropriate allocation of his duties to his ego and his society that, for the benefit of society and its needs for his services, he must be persuaded or coerced to desist in his indulgence. Gluttony in this sense becomes a sin against society. If the glutton is a "criminal," he can be charged not only with injuring himself and lowering his social esteem but also with insulting society by his withdrawal from it.

THE SOCIAL CONSTRUCTION
OF GLUTTONY

Like all other designated socially identifiable practices, gluttony is recognized through interpretation. Indeed the glutton is recognizable as a dramatic type, noticeable because of his looks, manner, and habits. He exists not only as a type but as a character, performing a role that requires setting, props, scenario, and audience. Typically the glutton's is a supporting role, distinctive in its display of a deviant personality, contrastive in its visible departure from that of heroes and heroines, and all too often minor, removed, present only in a brief scene. The glutton performs only momentarily for our benefit; we need but to see him for a short time to apprehend his character, appreciate his problem, appropriate his humanity, and oppose his habit. As a performer in the drama of social reality, the glutton appears as a sinner—sometimes as sinister, more often as simple.[19]

Understanding the dramatic realization of gluttony requires an analysis of its special impositions on time, place, and manner. Let us begin with time.[20] Social time differs from clock time in the sense that the latter is but one measure of duration. Periods of time are defined by rates, pace, and tracks that connect the emptiness of duration to the continua and breaks of activity. These tracks of time are measures to all social phenomena. They are also elements in their evaluation. What are the temporal dimensions of gluttony? First note that gluttony might be noticed in the violation of regular mealtimes. In most cultures and societies and certainly in the Occident, eating is done according to a schedule and each meal varies in content and style according to its temporal place, for example, breakfast in the morning, lunch at midday, dinner after sundown. One sign of gluttony is a careless inattention to the temporal and food-specific occasions for eating. Foregoing both time and custom the glutton gorges himself on whatever satisfies his palate at whatever time he wishes. True, the glutton may observe the meal divisions that prevail, eating breakfast, lunch, and dinner, but he indicates his indifference to their singularity by overeating at each meal and eating between them. Some concession to his practice is recognized in the "between-meal snack," the variety of foods sold solely for consumption at times other than meals, and the late evening meal before retiring. These, however, pale into insignificance before the voracious appetite of the glutton. He is absorbed in his eating, forgetful of occasion and modesty, a master of the table, a slave of what is on it.

The seriousness of the glutton's nonobservance of mealtime is better understood if we speak of it in terms of the temporal aspects of gratification. It is a commonplace of the Protestant Ethic that its adherents are required to postpone fleshly gratification, awaiting the propriety of time and occasion. To be sure this ethical imperative is usually associated with the delay of marriage, the scheduling of sex, and the careful planning for leisure. But eating is one of the basic gratifications. Man as a feeder is expected to rise above the ever-hungry animal who is imagined to eat whenever food presents itself. The glutton's open disregard of the ethical commandment that he delay his satisfaction suggests his fall into sinfulness, lack of regard for his uniquely human nature, a descent into carnal pleasure.

Temporal dimensions of gluttony include more than timing for meals. They also embrace the pace at which he eats. Ordinary dining proceeds at a routinized rate which might be beyond the measure of all but the most precise clock but is easily observed nevertheless. While the shy and fastidious might eat too slowly, the glutton is characterized by the rapidity with which he devours his food. While others are halfway through their entrée, the glutton has emptied his plate and is ready for more. Indeed, as a social diner, the glutton threatens the occasion in a manner not dissimilar from that of the "rate-buster" on the factory assembly line. As one who eats faster than others, he makes an earlier claim on the portions of food left to be distributed to the gathering. In order to ensure equal apportionment the others will have to speed up, hold the glutton in check, or sullenly acquiesce to his disproportionate aggrandizement. Gluttony is a sin to society in that it voids the tacit guaranty of equal protection that undergirds sociability.

The glutton also is noticeable for his departure from the rules of place and territory that typically mark off meals.[21] Dining is territorial in that it usually proceeds at an appointed place, in the presence of others, and employing designated stations for each item of food and places for each diner. The glutton forgoes or forgets his place and violates the space of others. He may begin eating before the meal is served, going into the refrigerator for snacks before meals, getting at the food while it is still in the kitchen, or in an even more ravenous state, before it is fully cooked, reaching into frying pan or oven to snatch a morsel. At table he may spread beyond his place, taking over part of the space allotted to diners on either side or opposite him. "Imperialism" may characterize his table relations as he takes the bread and butter belonging to his neighbors, reaches to secure second and third helpings before others can offer them, and monopolizes dishes set before him but intended for further distribution. The glutton invades the kitchen backstage, raids the icebox, converts the public place at table to a private preserve, and in general eschews or obliterates the interaction territories that are also a part of social dining.

The glutton is also noticeable as a defiler of his own body space. His appetite threatens to engulf the space of others as he spreads out to take more than one person's ordinary allotment of territory. If he grows too large he may no longer fit into ordinary chairs, threaten by dint of his enormous weight to wreck the furniture, and require special arrangements in advance of his coming.[22] Here again we see another way in which the fat glutton burdens sociability. Precisely because his girth and weight call for precautions, he makes more demands on his friends and associates than others of normal size. Seemingly unmindful of the social consequences of his own size, he forces others to be conscious and careful for him. He is more present and better accounted for than others whose social and personal value may be greater than his own. As a potential threat to company and convenience, he may ultimately lose his place altogether, relegated to the back rooms, kitchens, and isolated eating places that will contain him.

Banishment from company is a territorial marker of the unrepentant glutton. Dropped from the invitational lists of his friends, denied access to those dining places where company and comportment are required, destined to seek ever after his cravings, he eats alone, in furtive places, sometimes without benefit of table, dishes, or utensils. Unable to await the setting of the table, eager to devour the food even before it is ready, he may seize it with his bare hands, tear at the meat with his teeth, devour huge chunks without bothering to chew. And in this disregard of utensil, setting, and mastication, his sin is revealed once more. He has sunk to his animal nature, indistinguishable from a dog or a coyote, gorging with tooth and claw. He has not only been banished from society but also given up his step on the ladder that places him above the beast and below the spirit.

From what we have already said, it becomes clear that the glutton is known by his manner. Dining is a delicate matter in a society that prides itself on moderation in all matters of the flesh. One must eat and yet not appear to be absorbed in the process. Indeed, given the choice of eating and attending to matters of business, politics, or education, the prudent and serious person might leave his food altogether. Often enough, popular films picture the central character deep in conversation over some serious matter while his food remains untouched, or jumping up from a hardly started meal to rush off when a message arrives telling of trouble, or even of some significant commercial, political, or personal matter. Eating takes second place. But not to the glutton. To him eating takes precedence over all other matters. Stereotypes picture the glutton attending with more diligence to his cuisine than to his concerns.

Reversing the social priorities he places his gustatorial welfare before his social obligations.

The appropriate manner for eating is sociable. In the ideal case, the group gathered around the table engage in light conversation, break up what limited concentration they must employ for the act of eating by attending to the talk of their table mates. They observe proprieties, giving attention to the food only insofar as politeness requires, and consuming moderate amounts. The glutton is of a different manner. He lacks sociability. Rather than attend to the persons at the table, he engages the food. His concentration on eating subtracts from the occasion, and by that act of unsociable behavior invites rebuke or, more dangerously, emulation. Should others follow him into his kind of engagement with the cuisine, the glutton bids fair to threaten the social fabric. Usually, however, he lacks either the standing or the charisma to evoke a following. Failing to share himself with others, he fails to find others to share his habit with himself.

The glutton challenges the prevailing rule of fraternization in nearly every status group. As Max Weber has observed, "Fraternization at all times presupposes commensalism; it does not have to be actually practiced in everyday life, but it must be ritually possible."[23] The vicissitudes and breakthroughs of civilization into ever widening fraternizations, a topic central to Weber's sociology, need not detain us here. Suffice it to say that three processes—religious integration, establishment of more or less permanent national, racial, and ethnic sodalities, and the secularization of status, led in the Occident to the formation of large numbers of informal sociable gatherings, bonded together not by an oath of brotherhood but by a common style of life. These informal cliques, groups, and associations, in turn, indicate their exclusiveness by placing various kinds of social barriers around their own commensal occasions. Into such gatherings the glutton, possessing rights to participate on the basis of his status, nevertheless forfeits his dining privilege because of his mannerisms, ugliness, aggression, and personal demands. The net result of this denial of commensal sociability is the occasional formation of specific places and the designation of special occasions where gluttons, otherwise denied an opportunity to socialize and gourmandize unmolested, can join together and enjoy the congregative spirit that prevails when outstanding differences have been muted.

Georg Simmel once pointed out that "Eating and drinking, the oldest and intellectually most negligible functions, can form a tie, often the only one, among very heterogeneous persons and groups."[24] Among gluttons, an outcast population, this sometimes occurs in the form of meetings at hideaway towns and certain restaurants, in which all the congregants, refugees from the diets to which they have been sentenced or from the dining tables of ordinary eaters, find solace and surcease, recognition and response, in joint and common participation at an orgiastic feast. Like criminals in their hideout, the gluttons can here throw caution to the winds. Stigma bearers on holiday, they can depart from the customary etiquette with which they ordinarily approach dining when under the scrutiny of others, denounce the fat-free, calorie-reduced diets that a slim-conscious society flaunts, and ridicule the exercises and health fads that promote the slim Greek body type. Durham, North Carolina, is one such gathering place.[25] Known as "Fat City" to the overweight people who migrate there, it is the location of the Kempner Clinic, a special dietary center for the chronically obese. Many of the enrollees, ostensibly present to undergo weeks or months of a strict, experimental regimen permitting only rice and fruit juice, in fact sneak off to the numerous fast-food stands that dot the area. Just outside Durham is a stretch of road known to the dieters as "Destruction Row" or "Sin Alley." Lined with short-order houses advertising roast beef sandwiches, Kentucky fried chicken, pizza, hamburgers, steaks, doughnuts, and ice cream, these roadside attractions become a classic temptation to patients just released from the clinic. Starved for months, the homeward-bound dieters pull their cars over, discuss the matter among themselves, agree finally that they are all in it together, and enter the fast-food establishments. Rabid, they move from place to place, eating everything, buying bags of food to take away, and eventually giving in completely to the gluttonous license to which their enforced diet entitles them. The roadside restaurants open up the opportunity for a sinful spree.

ABSOLUTION FROM THE SIN OF GLUTTONY: STRATEGIES OF EXCUSE AND JUSTIFICATION

The sin of gluttony is not so great that the sinner is without sources and resources of relief. All activities have value—in accordance with the evaluative label placed upon them. These labels in turn are subject to negotiation, debate, redesignation, and reevaluation. Hence acts that might be called sinful on one occasion can be matters of virtue on another. Even in the same situation an act need not evoke a single uniform evaluation. It might be praised or condemned, excused or justified. The sins are not absolute in their recognition, designation, or specification. For an act to become an example of sinfulness or virtue, it must partake of the vocabulary of motives, the rhetorics of right and wrong.

Precisely because gluttony falls along the line of acts of the will, it requires for its sinful designation an accurate imputation of motives.[26]

Motives can only be inferred from behavior, but the range of behavior from which these inferences can be drawn is great and varied. In fact, gluttony itself requires a labeling of the acts of eating, an inference as to the motives behind these acts, an evaluation of the propriety of these motives, and a final designation of the entire process—act-connected-to-will—as a sin. Between each of these operations gapes a chasm of mystery and opportunity. The overeater, heavy drinker, and drug addict can relieve themselves of the charge of sinful gluttony by an artful employment of the rhetoric of exculpation, a clever exploitation of the vocabulary of motives, or even an accidental invocation of the redeeming words that bring redemption, forgiveness, or salvation.[27]

In general, the putative glutton can relieve himself of the accusation that he is a sinner by invoking an excuse or a justification.[28] If the former, the accused admits to the sinfulness, wrongfulness, badness, or evil of the charge but denies full responsibility; if the latter, the accused admits responsibility but denies the pejorative quality of the act in question. Excuses and justifications articulate a rhetoric of relief, a linguistic strategy for the release from sin.

Let us begin with excuses. Typically there are four model forms of excuse available to the putative glutton—the appeal to accidents, appeal to defeasibility, appeal to biological drives, and scapegoating. Employing any one or a combination of these, as in a sad tale, the accused sinner might carry off the sinful act without having to suffer the full burden of being a sinner.

Excuses that claim *accident* as the source of a charge of gluttony seek mitigation if not absolution from sin by pointing to recognized hazards of dining situations, the undeterrable claims of hunger's demand, and the inattention to controls that might have been operant. Since a gluttonous act might interrupt an otherwise normal eating regimen, the indulgence stands out, invites a searching motivational question, and leaves room for exculpatory maneuver. Since food habits vary among ethnic groups, cliques, and classes, a young man upon returning home from an evening out with friends of a different background than his own can claim that he did not intend to eat so much, did not know what he was getting into, had no idea how much his friends would invite him to eat, did not know that such foods or drinks are so filling and so forth. Or he might claim that because he had not eaten all day his hunger pangs overcame his will, that in responding to the demands of his stomach he overlooked the mistake he had made earlier in not eating properly during the day.

Appeals to *defeasibility* respond to recognized difficulties of personal control. They are central to the rhetoric of absolution of the glutton since they strike a blow at the heart of the charge of sinfulness—its willfulness. The putative glutton, by invoking the lack of freedom of his mind, indicating that he lacked either "knowledge" or control of his "will," relieves himself of the charge that he has entered into sin freely. Precisely because knowledge about nutrition and its effects is inexact and not widely understood, an individual can claim ignorance about the meaning, effect, amount, and kind of foods he ingests. Indeed as experts disagree about the physiological and nutritive effects of cholesterol, carbohydrates, and calories, individuals not only find it hard to follow a proper diet but also are in a position to invoke their understandable ignorance as an excuse for excess.

Impairment of the will is a more likely excuse. The individual claims that he is out of control. Some fat people claim that their corpulence dictates their lives. Sometimes derived from the "invalid" theory of obesity, the excuse claims that the desire to eat has overwhelmed all willful checks on it, and that the individual cannot help imbibing, cannot cope. Another "invalid" excuse refers the accusation from the center of the will to the physiological state. Appealing to recognized notions of glandular disorder, duodenal condition, or genetic heritage, the overeater denies personal responsibility, invites sympathy, and, where a medical problem is presented as still incurable, calls upon his accusers to indulge his excesses until research finds a way to relieve him. Finally, persons who are distraught, out of their mind with worry, beset with emotional and personal problems, can claim these departures from ordinary states of mind as excuses for their gorging.

Where temporary pathology or personal distraction cannot be employed, individuals can direct the cause of their overindulgence to *socialization*. Since modern thought tends to recognize that significant effects on habit, attitudes, and actions can be created in the earliest years of life, when the infant cannot control his situation, and since socialization practices can, in turn, be related to idiosyncrasy and subcultural variation, an individual is in a position to account for his gluttonous behavior by referring to his childhood experiences or national background. Hence, the adult individual who claims he is a food addict because his parents fed him whenever he cried as an infant exculpates his own indulgence while blaming his parents. A more benevolent excuse is that which invokes the dictates of culture and ethnicity, for example, the Jew who cannot help but overeat since his peers, family, and friends all encourage the morality of gastronomic pleasure.

Mention has already been made of the body and its inner workings. Ever with us but mysterious, *the body* invites exploitation as a resource for excuses. We have already noticed how putative gluttons can claim that aspects of their physiology, physique, or heritage force them to eat. These bodily drives can be expanded to include racial characteristics, anatomical developments, and somatic factors. The glutton's unfashionable body may be excused as a fateful gift of unkind nature, which has not only endowed some people with lovely bodies and a will to keep them so, but also cursed others with ugly fat that no effort or intention can make beautiful. Fatness can be its own excuse, a "viscerotonic" condition that demands growth and spread, dictates temperament, and does not give in to any external demands or internal pleas.[29]

Some people cannot excuse their indulgence to others but they can relieve their sinfulness to themselves. *Fantasy* here acts as a device to separate the self from its bodily frame and dictates. The corpulent individual sees himself not as obese and gluttonous but as thin, handsome, normal, and lovable. "Inside the fat man is a skinny one" goes the popular proverb. As a fantasized excuse the inner man substitutes for the real one, and taking priority over the latter, also excuses his defaults. If only the inner man could get out, could be recognized for what he is, the imputed state of sinfulness would be obviated.

When we turn to the realm of justifications we enter the kingdom of virtue regained. Whereas in all of the excuses there is an admission of wrongfulness, with justifications the accused denies that there is anything wrong in what he does. Justifications for gluttony do not deny that there is a sinful quality to voracious overeating. Rather, they distinguish between the generally impermissible and the particularly allowable. And in some instances they show that the apparently gluttonous act is not only acceptable but required.

Consider the claims of *occupations*.[30] Certain occupations are so centrally related to nutritive excess or gastronomic concentration that those who enter them are linked inextricably to a zealous regard for dietary excess. The gourmet whose profession as a journalistic food critic requires him to indulge continually in rich foods may overeat as part of his elected task. A man of enormous girth, he might wear his weight well, a badge of his endeavor and expertise. Questioned about his size and refusal to diet, he need only point to his occupation, its requirements and perquisites to relieve him of the charge of sinful intent. Other occupations may require activities that resemble gluttony but are not chargeable to its evil. The actor who is required to gain weight for a part, or who must never lose weight lest he lose his character type along with it, provides one example. Such well-known movie stars of an earlier era as S. Z. "Cuddles" Sakall, Fatty Arbuckle, and Sidney Greenstreet were primarily known for their girth, their manner of "wearing" their fat, and the characters that their physical appearance expressed. Each of these men would probably have lost much more than weight by dieting, but neither needed to bear a charge of gluttony in the face of his success and popularity. Similarly, such activities as espionage agent might require the cover of fat and the characterological masquerade of gluttony to disguise a perfectly laudable and patriotic service for one's country.

There also arise *situations and occasions* where indulgence seems to be warranted, and the prohibition on gluttony is temporarily set aside. Participation in these moral holidays requires no apology and may even be expected and encouraged. On a national level in the United States the Thanksgiving dinner and celebration constitute an easily recognized example. For others with only slightly less mass acceptability, consider the license given to overeating when "southern hospitality" prevails, the relaxation on the bans against intemperate drinking on New Year's Eve, or the latitude given to eating and drinking among soldiers about to go into battle. There may also be special situations that permit dietary excess. Prisoners sentenced to death are traditionally permitted to indulge their fancies in eating on the last night of their lives, but for those sentenced to hang, apprehensions about the indignity occasioned by loss of sphincter control while in the throes of strangulation sometimes inspire moderation or even abstinence. Finally, there are the modern versions of saturnalian role reversal, of which that carried on by body builders provides an excellent example of justified excess. According to Arnold Schwarzenegger, holder of the Mr. Universe and Mr. Olympia titles, body builders, who shun high-caloric foods for most of the week, enjoy having an occasional "food orgy": "That happens about once a week in California," he said. "We'll all get together and have a food orgy and eat for hours and have a good time. Our favorite dish is a mixture of ice cream, whipped cream, nuts, honey, and sugar. No one feels guilty, because all of us are there."[31]

Gluttony may also be justified because it is a tissue-related excess that allows nature to set its own limits. Overeaters occasionally report that their weight does not continue to increase indefinitely but reaches a plateau and then remains the same. Hence, they do not disregard the problems of weight but let nature take its course. A similar line of argument points out that excessive eating is not a problem or a social "crime" since satiation will set in for every human, and no one need worry about persons indulging beyond the point of satiety. Added to this latter justification is the recognition that the charge of gluttony varies according to situation, status, and society. A Buddhist monk might be unable to justify a request for a second cup of rice, while an American football player might be perfectly justified in eating two beefsteaks for dinner, and an anemic woman might find no shame in an extra glass of wine or a large rare beefsteak at dinner or between meals.

The glutton may, however, be bereft of excuses or justifications for his indulgence. Without any account to offer he may have to engage in information control and tension management to keep his sin a secret or mask his excess in subterfuge.

Anticipation of the difficulties involved in extricating oneself from the charge of overindulgence sometimes results in careful planning and the screening of one's habits. A fine example is presented in the film *Gone with the Wind.* Scarlett O'Hara, who is known to overeat, is to attend a gala ball and banquet at which she will be courted by all of the handsome beaux of the county. Her Negro "mammy," aware of how important it is for a southern belle to appear to be a dainty and delicate eater, prepares a special meal for Scarlett to eat just before she goes to the party so that, already filled, she will eat lightly or not at all while under the scrutiny of the gathered socialites. Gluttons who announce they are on diets may find that their flesh is weaker than their spirit. However, unwilling to admit defeat, they eat secretly and alone, while in the presence of peers and family they observe the proprieties of abstinence or moderation. In one remarkable instance, a woman who had enrolled in the rice-and-fruit juice diet required at the Kempner Clinic, stole a turkey from the kitchen, hid it under her dressing gown, and devoured the whole bird during the late night hours. Her theft and dietary violation went undetected, and the next day, eleven pounds heavier, she baffled the doctors who weighed her and could not guess how such a large spontaneous gain could occur.[32]

Fear of being taken for a glutton can act as a deterrent to eating, but often enough it provokes an opposite reaction. For some people, anxiety is a goad to eating, so that the fear of overindulgence leads to raids on the refrigerator, devouring of snack foods, and mindless excesses at table. Moreover, anxiety often betrays the secret that provokes it. As the secret glutton widens his eyes, licks his lips, plays nervously with his utensils, and finally flinches at his first refusal of food, he gives himself away. Unable to control his expression of fear, he is undone by his eyes, mouth, finger, and voice. Although he has not sinned he has indicated his cravings, and this may be enough to evoke condemnation, or pity, for him.

THE SUBLIMATION
OF GLUTTONY

Gluttony may not only be forgiven or justified, it may also be a diversion of energy from other sources or possible actions. From certain psychoanalytic perspectives as well as a common-sense point of view, overindulgence in food is interpreted as a deflection from sexual appetite. The sublimation may have a variety of etiologies, and its course may meander before eventually finding discharge in food excess. One possible scenario is that gluttony follows rejection by a love object, converting the libidinal energy into an introjective force that redirects the sensual longings, exchanges their content, and indeed may reverse their emotional valence. Unloved by the other, the individual may come to see himself as unlovable by anyone including himself. His body, however, in its normal form remains a potential object of love. When metamorphosed into something corpulent, gross, and grotesque, its outer appearance reveals his inner condition.

Moreover, once the person acquiesces in his fatness, develops a commitment and an attachment to the role that it contains, he may allow its energies and demands to deflect from all other possible activities, from social relations altogether. Fatness becomes a justification for retreating from sociability.

"See, when you're fat you don't have to take responsibility for anything but your fatness [according to a 350-pound man who has attended the Kempner Clinic for twelve years]. You don't have to go out and meet people and you don't have to take the chance of getting hurt that contact always poses. You can just stay in the dark and brood and fester. Nobody is particularly going to take the trouble to try to get to know a fat person. So the fat is a nice protection if you look at it that way. It's literally a nice thick wall insulating you from contact."[33]

But the sublimation of gluttony is not always so sad in its outcome. Consider the much-vaunted jolly fat man. To be sure, much of the argument behind the boasted joyfulness of the obese person is stereotype and misinformation. And many of the more oppressed members of the corpulent population bitterly denouce the situation in which they are expected to enliven every social gathering with their mirth and merriment. Yet much of the release from sin that comes to the glutton arises precisely from the fact that he is regarded as a harmless figure of fun, a cowardly lion of lovable proportions, a sinner who, although fallen from grace himself, nevertheless saves others by his insistence on bacchanalia and feast.

SEVEN

Greed

"Take some more tea," the March Hare said to
Alice, very earnestly.

"I've had nothing yet," Alice replied in an offended tone:
"so I ca'n't take more."

"You mean you ca'n't take *less*," said the Hatter: "it's
very easy to take *more* than nothing."

Lewis Carroll*

DEFINING THE SIN OF GREED

Greed in its most general sense refers to an inordinate desire, an insatiable
longing for the possession of something. As a sin, however, it is associated
not with a diffuse and general cupidity but rather with the excessive
eagerness to accumulate wealth and obtain money. At first inspection
greed might seem close to gluttony, and, indeed, in the voraciousness
associated with both there is a resemblance, but gluttony is limited by the
finite capacity of the body, whereas greed, as Aristotle observed, having
no real aim except acquisition itself, has also no established limit. Greed
is indeed a social phenomenon for it may find expression only in a realm
of objects, values, and human extension. To the psychoanalyst greed
begins with a projection and respecification of bodily acquisitions onto
the world outside the body of the individual. It depends on the valuation
of objects and the transvaluation of money as first an item of exchange
value and ultimately an object in its own right. Furthermore to econo-
mists and sociologists greed is related to inequality, and through the latter
to the sins or sublimations of pride and envy. The condition of inequality
evokes envy of the better off, prideful desire in the self, and propels the
acquisitive action necessary to remove inequities and restore or raise

dignity. However, once undertaken, both as a psychic process and a social action, avariciousness knows no bounds. The inequalities that breed envious competition also engender a permanent restlessness, character- ized on the one hand by the insatiable desire to acquire more and more and on the other by the miserable but nagging apprehension that whatever one has or gets is not and never can be enough.

Greed as a Sin in Society and Culture

The significance and priority of greed among the sins seems to vary in accordance with the place of money and pecuniary values in society. Thus when Gregory the Great placed pride ahead of avarice in his collation of the seven deadly sins he did not have unambiguous biblical authority for his selection; rather, writing largely for monastic orders at the close of the sixth century, Gregory was undoubtedly influenced by the fact that there was little absolute wealth then in society and much of that consisted in land rather than cash. Although Augustine repeatedly warned about the dangers of avarice, the sin of greed seems not to have acquired too much primacy before the rise of a merchant class and a bourgeoisie in the twelfth and thirteenth centuries.[1] Although greed does not require great differences in wealth and station to manifest itself, it seems to come into its own when wants express themselves in the desire for goods, when commodities can be obtained for cash, and when money becomes recognized not only for its utility in exchange but for its own intrinsic worth. Thus, in the thirteenth century Roger Bacon listed avarice at the head of the seven sins and traced all others, except anger, to that one source. Bacon's contemporaries followed suit, even exagger- ating and building upon the importance and danger of greed: Brunetto Latini, that teacher of Dante whom the latter placed in hell among the sodomites, designated two distinct elements of greed, *avaritia* and *cupiditas*, as separate sins, and Antoninus of Florence (d. 1459), while retaining avarice as the first sin, sought to reconcile the growing bourgeois belief in the rectitude of profits with the theological requirement of a just price.

In the period 1000-1400 the Crusades opened Islamic civilization and science to the West, the ancient classics were rediscovered and translated, towns began to grow in importance, inventions flourished, merchant classes formed, and struggles for class, national, and interna- tional wealth erupted. In the thirteenth century, stimulated by the rapid growth and sinful wealth of towns, mendicant orders of friars were established not only to popularize theology, put down heresies, and preach the gospel, but also to proscribe the ever enlarging sin of greed. It is in this period that greed is envisioned specifically in its relation to money: at Amiens Cathedral, Avarice is seated on a bench putting sacks of money into a chest, while a fourteenth-century folio of Friar Laurent's *Somme le Roy* depicts the anthropomorphized sin as a hooded man, perhaps a monk, gathering coins from a chest and putting them in a bag. The latter work speaks of avarice as the root of all evil, having no less than ten branches including simony and wicked games, and the author warns against usury and business as expressions of this sin. That the desire for money would lead ultimately to misery, loneliness, and dis-ease was illustrated in Spenser's *Faerie Queene*, when Avarice, suffering from gout, rides a camel laden with gold. Two iron coffers hang on the sides of the beast of sinful burden, while the old, poorly dressed, and miserly rider counts a heap of coins in his lap.

The especially sinful quality of greed is related to its association with a respecification of the sacred—the shift from the worship of God to the worship of mammon. The early Church's concern over the worldly desire for money is precisely located in its recognition of the terrible potentiality for man to place another god, secular and earthly, before the deity rendered sacred by religious authority. Although the Durkheimian tradition dichotomizes the sacred and secular realms, placing the latter as a superstructure atop a sacred base and locating money in its rationalizing functions for the mundane world, it is in fact the case that money can and does partake of the supernatural. The modern, supposedly secular age is a dialectical inversion of the theological era. Power and awe have passed from the once supreme spiritual authorities to their negation. God's ape, the negation of God, is the devil, and specific to his demonic powers is the money complex. As the devil has overtaken God as the deity of this world, the philosophy of money replaces the theology of grace. The precise condition of this sin is that man finds a deity in things, and in that which can be exchanged for things.

It may at first seem strange to speak of the irrational and preternatural qualities of money.[2] Practically all economic theory insists on its essentially secular character and rational functions. But as we shall see presently, the much-vaunted rationality of money economies is a rationalization, a sublimation, and one of the salvation devices employed to absolve the acquisitive complex from sin. The desublimation of money permits us to see its specifically irrational character, first in the forms and usages it assumed in archaic economies and next in its disguised form as a secular source of wealth, worth, and power in market societies. The "money" of archaic economies included dog's teeth, feather bands, stones and rocks—items that as condensed wealth were useless. Melville Herskovits is among the anthropologists who has noticed that the actual purpose of the objects employed by archaic peoples for money is to bring prestige to those who display them. However, the Veblen-like tone of Herskovits' argument requires a further analysis of what irrational considerations confer prestige value on shells, teeth, and stones. It would appear that the value of these objects is derived from sacred sources. The tokens of archaic money are magical and mystical amulets. The fact that archaic money is "noneconomic" in character, associated with ceremonies and rituals and lacking utility, only serves to emphasize decisively its sacred character.

Having recognized the sacred and irrational character of archaic money, it is but a short step to recognizing the equally irrational character of money in market economies. The minerals employed for basic monetary units in modern market economies—gold and silver—have no practical use. Indeed, they are, as John Locke once observed, valuable solely because mankind has endowed them with an imaginary value.[3] John Maynard Keynes went even further, associating the choice of gold and silver as monetary metals with the magical qualities ascribed to the sun and the moon, and Georg Simmel observed that Greek money, from which modern systems of coinage take their beginnings, has its origin in the temple and not the marketplace. The irrational character of money—modern as well as archaic—is the key to grasping how the insatiable desire for it leads to sin.

Precisely because money is capable of taking on a peculiar and demanding sacred character, it challenges the conventional gods and competes for their congregation. Religion in general tends to excite powerful and vivid passions. When the deity that inspires awe and ascetic action changes from a supramundane spirit to an inner-worldly entity, the passion is not only likely to be as great as before but also to engender severe social conflicts and personal misfortunes. "From avarice," wrote Gregory the Great, "there spring treachery, fraud, deceit, perjury, restlessness, violence, and hardness of heart against compassion."[4] And ten centuries after Gregory's prescient observation, Erich Fromm echoed the point, noting that "Greed is one of the strongest noninstinctive passions in man, and it is clearly a symptom of psychical dysfunctioning, of inner emptiness and a lack of a center within oneself." But Fromm, who sees greed in terms of psychopathology, nevertheless views it at bottom as a fall from virtue. "It is," he concludes, "a pathological manifestation of the failure to develop fully, as well as one of the fundamental sins in Buddhist, Jewish, and Christian ethics."[5]

However, the sacred characterization of money is not confined to pathological mind states. Indeed the spiritual transvaluation of money occurs within the institutional practices and customary codes of supposedly rationalized societies. Consider the establishment of spending as a form of prayer institutionalized in the annual American observance of the birth of Jesus.[6] Commercial exploitation of the Nativity began about 1890 and has increased in scope enormously since the modest campaigns of the

Mauve Era. Essentially the greed of the merchant class has found its fundamental expression and amoral métier in the transubstantiation of money at Christmas. Where once the gift given on that holiday bore the unique mark of the giver, who had shown his personal care and special concern for the recipient by taking time and effort to create a present solely for the occasion, the contemporary store-bought present communicates only its price, bears no intrinsic worth, and can and often is exchanged for something else by the receiver. The Christmas spirit is given substance as cash; the joy of giving is commercialized and depersonalized; the greed of the sellers is barely hidden beneath the tinseled trees; and recorded carols that solemnize the birth of a savior sing out against the cacophony of a thousand cash registers that celebrate the profits of the holiday business.

Even charity is corroded by cash. As Christmas "drives" collect money for widows, orphans, neglected and sick children, aged shut-ins, and the other fallen folk of society, the central fact of altruism is that it caters to the impersonal need or unspoken greed of the less fortunate. In place of the direct and unmediated assistance that a caring human presence might provide, the massification of misfortune has led inevitably to the dehumanization of assistance. Through the medium of money the giver is at one and the same time salvaged through his good work and severed from his connection to the human misery that requires his benevolence.

GREED AND THE SCIENCES: THE SEPARATION OF AVARICE FROM SIN

Above all the sins it is greed that has been most relentlessly investigated for the purposes of absolution. The decline of the sinful qualities once attributed to man has indeed been general, as Karl Menninger recently observed, but while lust, gluttony, and sloth remain recognizable in their pristine form as vices of the body, and pride, anger, and envy are still less than virtuous characterizations of the self, greed has lost much of its vicious quality.[7] In the remarkable transvaluation of greed both religion and science have played important roles. Theological reinterpretations of the relation of worldly practices to ultimate salvation helped pave the way for the elevation of avarice above the vices. Psychological and economic analyses of money and its relation to character and social structure have either relieved men of the responsibility for cupidity or pointed to the public good produced by private vice.

Psychoanalytic Interpretations of Greed

When psychoanalysis considers the drive to amass ever greater piles of money, it sees the phenomenon as biologically determined through the fundamental process of anal eroticism. "We have learnt," wrote Freud, ". . . that after a person's own faeces, his excrement, has lost its value for him, this instinctual interest derived from the anal source passes over on to objects that can be presented as *gifts*." Just as feces are the child's first gift of love to those who nurture him, so also the person comes to value highly just those items that he can possess, display, and give away in order to show and earn love. "After this," Freud continued, "corresponding exactly to analogous changes of meaning that occur in linguistic development, this ancient interest in faeces is transformed into the high valuation of *gold and money* . . ."[8] Moreover, as Freud also observed, the instinctual interest first aroused from the anal source might later find expression in character traits and personality. The anal personality tends to exhibit traits of orderliness, parsimoniousness, and obstinacy. Greed, in the psychoanalytic perspective, is thus removed from the *responsible* arena of sinful conduct. As a consequence of the tortuous path followed by anal eroticism, it cannot be freely elected by men, but only transformed, directed, diluted, or sublimated. In explicating the instinctual basis of anal eroticism, Freud relieved humankind of some of the morbid guilt or shame that might arise if avaricious activities were matters of pure unalloyed sin.

Followers of Freud built upon the original theory, connecting it also to the intake of food and the norm of reciprocity. The excrementa are really the first "savings" held back by the constipated child, who guards his biological economy as a first step toward developing an egoistic economic attitude. Duncan, reviewing the evidence of the Freudians on this subject, points to the story of the banker "who again and again impressed on his children that they should retain the contents of the bowels as long as possible in order to get the benefit of every bit of the expensive food they ate."[9] The anal character traits of collecting, hoarding, and saving that Ferenczi ascribed to early emphasis on excremental savings are related in the first instance to the intake of food, and as Fenichel and Odier added, to anything else that can be introjected pleasurably via the mouth. It "is inherent in the money complex," writes Norman O. Brown, "to attribute to what is not food the virtue that belongs to food."[10] As, in Freud's concise phrase, excrement becomes aliment, it also converts and transvalues what was once a basic need for existence into a craving for substituted objects that are also redefined as essential for existence. Fromm has pointed to the peculiar obfuscation that occurs when greed is identified with self-interest. The latter term, he argues, should refer to a biologically given drive whose aim is to obtain precisely what is necessary for survival. However, the distinction between luxury and necessity is not easy to make.[11] Through the conversion of food to nutrients, nutrients to excrementa, and excrementa either to "savings" or "gifts" in return for food and love, man develops an avaricious orientation. Later, with the transvaluation of the original forms onto worldly objects and especially money, the greedy orientation is extended and shorn of any limitation. Again, however, note how the individual is relieved from chargeable sin in this analysis. Self-interest, anchored in a biologically given striving, is projected onto the passion to accumulate money. The greedy passion is not a product of choice or will. And the individual is released from the accusation that his vice might have been avoided. The sacred is thus once again replaced by the natural.

The attitude toward money discovered by psychoanalysts contains a paradox: the greedy individual feels compelled not only to hoard cash but also to spend it.[12] Indeed, in the studies of such Freudians as Odier, Ferenczi, and Róheim there is a basic recognition of the significance of reciprocity in anal eroticism. On the one hand, the individual "spends," or rather "gives," his feces as a gift to his mother in return for food and love. The seeming contradiction between saving and spending is understandable in light of the egoistic need to ensure continued gratification. It also aids in understanding the onset of avariciousness. In order to receive love and gratification, the individual must be able to give gifts. That ability, in turn, depends on having the cash to purchase them. Money thus finds a further extension of its irrational quality in its designation as the feces substitute that can, if enough of it is available, buy love and gratification from others. Persons must save in order to have something to spend. As an inordinate expression of the need to save, hoarding, parsimony, and noncompassionate orientations multiply into the anal-erotic character recognized as greedy.

At least one psychoanalytic theorist, Norman O. Brown, has extended the anal-erotic thesis to embrace that of the death instinct and to refute Durkheim's and Mauss's idea that a norm of reciprocity arose out of gift giving.[13] The money complex is rooted in a psychology of guilt which in turn arises out of a primal fantasy about the Fall of Adam and the debt owed to ancestors. Gift giving is the expression of this guilt. Money is human guilt refined and drained of anything but the purity of the guilt itself. Since guilt requires expiation, the reciprocity of gift giving mitigates the all-pervading feeling, while the reciprocity entailed adds further to man's relief by allowing the guilt to be shared. However, the necessity of accumulation is again made clear through this analysis, since the practical consequence of having ceaselessly to repay one's ancestors and expiate the original sin is that man must acquire and save for his own self-sacrificial gifts. That the savings are ultimately for self-sacrifice, for presentation to the gods for sins and debts of the past, also ensures that the obligatory greed will be accompanied by an unhappy existence and by hard and joyless work. Brown concludes that the guilt generating this cycle of greed and sacrifice is an illusion necessary for the one animal that has the capacity to remember and to promise—man. Such an animal cannot enjoy life in the present; because of this incapacity, he must organize his nonenjoyment. The establishment of money and the institutionalization of greed are central to that organization.

Ultimately, however, man desires to rise above the death instinct, to depart from his feces and his body, and to attain immortality. The process whereby this is accomplished is sublimation. The place wherein life is assured forever is the city. The connecting link between the sublimation of man's earthly existence and his immortal state is a transvalued greed. The attempt to overcome the limitations of the body (death) first distinguishes and then detaches the soul from the body. Then to give concrete expression to the immortality of the soul, it is reconstituted in its icons and symbols, in what it can leave to endless descendants (who are, of course, through the energy of the penis, the emblems of the immortality of the body). Man constructs culture and civilization, and its most concrete representation, the city, to immortalize his individual and his collective soul. But the city, whose very structures and activities go beyond the necessities of mere existence, requires enormous expenditures of time and money. And so accumulation of money, its transformation into things, its use in construction of the civic existence, at last builds each city as the eternal city, as the embodiment of immortal man. Greed becomes the engine of man's endlessness. Its sinfulness ultimately, then, resides in its use as an instrument for man to assume the unique quality of God, to become eternal, to live forever.

The Economics and Sociology of Greed: Mandeville, Simmel, and Weber

Our concern with the science of economics is neither broad nor deep. Rather, here we wish only to emphasize that a major effort of the science of economic behavior (and we include here several sociological approaches to that science) has been to provide a transvaluation of greed, point to the rational properties of money, and with varying degrees of confidence and qualification, argue for the socially beneficial consequences of accumulation and investment. Whereas psychoanalysis has functioned to *excuse* greed by locating its source in elements outside man's conscious control, economics *justifies* avarice by lifting the stigma of evil from its practice. In the writings of Mandeville, Simmel, and Weber we find a body of commentary that shows how greed and its connection to the acquisition and manipulation of money makes for progress and development in modern society—and yet avarice cannot fully escape from sin.

Mandeville

To Bernard de Mandeville (1670–1733) goes the credit for arguing with stunning cogency the theory of the latent benefits of vice in general and avarice in particular. Subtitling his *Fable of the Bees* "Private Vices, Publick Benefits," Mandeville expatiated on how publicly abhorred sinful practices in fact produce the very conditions and effects that are everywhere recognized as virtuous and appropriate to the welfare of society. Consider alcohol. Mandeville is at great pains to rehearse the unhealthy and dangerous effects of excessive drinking. But after his recital of these evils, he turns to the advantages that arise from the free market in malt. The duties on the sale of gin enrich the public treasury; the varieties of labor employed to husband the grain, distill the spirits, ferment the wines, bottle and box the several types produced, and distribute and sell them to the public produce tillers of ground, keepers of draught animals, renters of land, manufacturers of tools, and above all a multitude of poor people who are maintained in employment. "The short-sighted Vulgar in the Chain of Causes seldom can see further than one Link," Mandeville concluded, "but those who can enlarge their View, and will give themselves the Leisure of gazing on the Prospect of concatenated Events, may, in a hundred Places see *Good* spring up, and pullulate from *Evil*, as naturally as Chickens do from Eggs."[14]

As for avarice itself, Mandeville observed that those who railed against it did so out of self-interest, "for the more the money is hoarded up by some, the scarcer it must grow among the rest." However, the acquisitive impulse springs from the surplus value that individuals place upon their own services: ". . . every Body esteeming his Labour as he does himself, which is generally not under the Value, most People that want Money only to spend it again presently, imagine they do more for it than it is worth." Hostility to covetousness springs from the difficulties of obtaining money. Yet avarice also has its advantages. "Was it not for Avarice," Mandeville pointed out, "Spendthrifts would soon want Materials; and if none would lay up and get faster than they spend, very few could spend faster than they get." Further, greed was the slave to prodigality as the miser hoarded cash for the idle benefit of his profligate legatees who spent the money all too lavishly, even borrowing against their inheritance at usurious rates, and by that act enriching the lender who takes the risk and acts as the catalyst to put the money back into circulation. Beyond miserly greed, Mandeville concluded, there is "a sort of Avarice which consists in a greedy desire of Riches, in order to spend them . . ." A sort of reciprocity evolves from this as the greedy party is avidly in pursuit of the wealth of others while lavish in his own expenditure of it. Completing his argument Mandeville asserted that "I look upon Avarice and Prodigality in the Society as I do upon two contrary Poysons in Physick, of which it is certain that the noxious qualities being by mutual mischief corrected in both, they may assist each other, and often make a good Medicine between them."

Simmel

Of the classical sociologists, it is Georg Simmel who deserves much credit for seeing the effects of the objectification and rationalization of greed in the modern money economy. Emphasizing the role of money in depersonalizing exchange, leveling social differences, and requiring self-sacrifice, he removes the subjective, willful, and therefore greedy, imputations from the impulses to acquire and expend by dissolving them in the flux of economic activity itself. "The fact of economic exchange," wrote Simmel, "confers upon the value of things something super-individual." To Simmel the essence of economic activity is the communicative and substitutive process that it entails. Or as he once put it, "the specific character of economic activity as a special form of commerce exists, if we may venture the paradox, not so much in the fact that it exchanges *values* as that it *exchanges* values."[15] Money is the supreme arbiter of exchange in that, having no value of its own, it becomes the talisman of the exchange value that anything is worth. "Money," as S. P. Altmann put it in expounding Simmel's *Philosophie des Geldes*, "is the objectivation of the relation which as exchangeability plays a part in economics, but beyond that it is the expression for the formula that things are determined by each other, that only the mutuality of relations determines their being, and their being as they are."[16] Money removes the individual from the commerce of his transactions because "money expresses the general element contained in all exchangeable objects, that is, their exchange value," and hence money "is incapable of expressing the individual element" in objects.[17]

Precisely because the money economy is rooted in and exists for object exchange, Simmel argues, it liberates man from an all-encompassing commitment of himself to another and widens the circles of his contacts with equally impersonal others. Greed, herein, is banished from the exchange, as personal motives do not so much give way but become dissolved in the mutuality of reciprocity and the preservation of the self from unnecessary and contaminating involvements. It is true that money is literally "degrading," argues Simmel, but in that very degradation lies the institutionalization of personal liberty.

In economic exchange, as distinct from the erotic exchange of lovers or the emotional exchange of friendship, there is the prospect of parting with only that which one wishes to give up, independent of one's whole or true self, and obtaining only what one wishes to purchase, independent of the entangling elements of its personal connection to the seller.[18] Of course the selling of one's own labor forces one to make an object of oneself, a degrading act because it is so inhumanly reductionist in nature. But here again is contained the paradox of personal liberty, for the individual sells only that portion of himself that is marketable, his labor power, and reserves all other portions to the private nonmarket arenas.[19] Finally, the money economy objectifies sociable relations, reducing them to the question of exchange value pure and simple. Objects acquire their value in this communicative situation itself, not in any intrinsic or permanent sense, but precisely in the sense that the buyer is willing to sacrifice just so much in order to obtain what he wants from the seller. Thus the economy of exchange includes not only ordinary market relations but also the exchange by a starving man of a diamond for a crust of bread. Every exchange has its specific elements, its aura of feelings and sentiments, its pursuits and promotions, but these are in principle indifferent to exchange itself. "There can be no doubt, at any rate," Simmel concludes on this matter, "that in the moment of exchange, that is, of the making of the sacrifice, the value of the exchanged object forms the limit which is the highest point to which the value of the sacrificed object can rise." Thus, in the negotiation of price, the selling of self or of objects, the variability of value drowns the sin of greed in the ocean of exchange.

According to Simmel there is yet another positive function of the establishment of an objectified money economy, namely, the detachment of exchange from the qualities of those party to it.[20] Money frees the servant from his master, and by extension the servant class, ethnic group, or race from its social superiors, by permitting the former to sell what it acquires regardless of the mode of acquisition and to sell itself as a limited and still *essentially* free commodity in the market. Money, as the most impersonal medium of exchange, permits the memory to forget all other values, sentiments, prejudices, and feelings in the concentration on the definite but limited act of exchange itself. Money decreases the geographic and social distances in life by bringing together persons and groups who are interdependent with respect to goods and services, but independent with respect to personality, life-style, and creed. Thus, money aids in liberating the expression of personality from traditional suppressive forces at the very moment that it plunges man into the market and into acquisition of goods, services, and self-esteem. Greed is absolved from sin in the higher liberation of man's ego that money, its instrument and objective, permits.

Lastly money rationalizes and objectifies what was once a powerful religious virtue, self-sacrifice, and connects it inextricably to daily life. An economy built upon money and the exchange values of goods and services requires that individuals and groups so organize their lives that self- and group-sacrifice must precede acquisition. Moreover, the sacrifice aids in establishing the value of the object attained thereby, while the nature and extent of the sacrifice reflects also on the virtue of the sacrificing agent. "If we observe which human achievements obtain the highest honors and appraisals, we find it to be always those which betray a maximum of humility, effort, persistent concentration of the whole being, or at least seem to betray these."[21] Simmel thus introduces the significance of a dramatic display of virtuous self-sacrifice as a feature of the establishment of value itself. Since money must be obtained in some manner to purchase wants, it is the manner of obtaining it and choosing how to spend it that supplies both virtue and value. Neither objects nor desires establish value. Rather it "is only the postponement of the satisfaction through obstacles, the anxiety lest the object may escape, the tension of struggle for it, which brings into existence that aggregate of desire elements which may be designated as intensity or passion of volition." If the drama of self-sacrifice and anxious action in behalf of satisfying wants is the central factor in attaching value to goods and services, it is the persistence of dissatisfaction, the permanence of tension between desire and satiety, that preserves self-sacrifice as a process. "The desire, therefore, which on its part came into existence only through an absence of feelings of satisfaction, a condition of want or limitation, is the psychological expression of the distance between subject and object, in which the latter is represented as a value." The economy promotes self-sacrifice by establishing a permanent condition of nonsatiety; greed sublimated as sacrificial effort is given hostage to virtue.

Weber

In Weber's studies of the sociology of capitalism we find the most significant analysis of how greed has been sublimated by religious practice, and yet how through capitalism greed has become the most fundamental of sins—man's usurpation of the power of God.[22] The details of Weber's argument need not detain us here since they are too well known—and debated—to require recapitulation.[23] Suffice it to note that Weber specifically rejected the connection of greed to capitalism.[24] "The impulse to acquisition, pursuit of gain, of money, of the greatest possible amount of money," he wrote, "has in itself nothing to do with capitalism." Indeed, unlimited "greed for gain is not in the least identical with capitalism, and is still less its spirit. Capitalism *may* even be identical with the restraint, or at least a rational tempering, of this irrational impulse."

But, Weber insists, "capitalism is identical with the pursuit of profit, and forever *renewed* profit, by means of continuous, rational, capitalistic enterprise." And, as Weber presciently observes, the pursuit of profit is inextricably connected to survival. "In a wholly capitalistic order of society, an individual capitalistic enterprise which did not take advantage of its opportunities for profit-making would be doomed to extinction." Thus it is that Occidental capitalism separates the greedy pursuit of gain from the ascetic pursuit of profit. The latter, as Weber is at great pains to show, is endowed with virtue and encumbered with the obligation of a religious calling, while the former is naked, vicious, and alienating from God.

However, the instrumentality for the separation of vice from virtue, for differentiating the pursuit of sinful gain from the acquisition of ascetic profits, for distinguishing the demonic avatar of wealth from the secular saint of industry, is *the firm*.[25] As Weber shows, the religious prohibition against laying up treasures on earth is resolved to the benefit of ascetic pursuers of profits through their creation of an unusual entity— the corporation—that not only relieves them of the temptations to engage in sinful excess, but also flourishes and grows independent of its progenitors and thrives beyond their lifetimes. Money is first the product of successful pursuit in a calling, second the instrumentality that gives life and motion to the firm, and finally the master that enslaves generations of Puritan descendants, long since removed from their religious tradition, but now in yoke to the instrumentality that the religion had first inspired.

Crucial to the character of the firm is its immortality. This miracle of life everlasting is accomplished in the first place by its vampiric origins.[26] The corporation contains none of the blood, sentiments, or feelings of those who in the very act of founding it also drain it of these human characteristics. No longer bound by the limitations of body, blood, emotions, or age, the firm is, in effect, a zombie—a creature of death-in-life, that, having been created, cannot be destroyed unless it ceases to make profits. The sinful aspects of the creation of an immortal creature were imagined nearly a half century before Weber's birth in a fantasy by Mary Shelley.[27] A doctor, fired both by his advanced scientific knowledge and dreams of immortality sacrifices self, career, esteem, wife, and family in the construction of, and subsequent enslavement to, a monster. A modern Prometheus, Dr. Frankenstein has arrogated to himself the power of the gods and must be punished for his sin. So also the creators of and the creatures in service to the corporation. Psychoanalytic theory has hinted at the curious mental operations that connect feces to penis, penis to money, money to power, and power to procreation. The Puritans and their descendants are like both the gothic and the psychoanalytic characters—creators and victims of their creation, Prometheans and prisoners of their immortal monster.[28] As Weber saw so clearly in the final pages of his great study, the retribution for man's seeming escape from sin had come full circle. Seeking immortality and relief from his guilt, he had fathered an immortal "son," who, free from social controls and moral conscience, had, in turn, enslaved his creators and their descendants forever. The sin of greed had led man to the most heinous blasphemy—seeking to become God. Through sublimated greed an impersonal capitalism had at last been repaid for its creation. Man's self-imposed sentence to eke out his existence in an iron cage becomes his judgment for blasphemy.

Going beyond Weber, we can see that it is the overwhelming desires of the devil-vampire that drive the lifeless-yet-living spirit of the corporate firm. Drained of its creators' blood in order that it might be free from sin and guilt, it in turn drains the blood of its owners, converting them into its soulless servants. Just as the mythological vampire must roam the earth in search of new sources of sanguine energy, so also the firm must expand over the face of the earth in search of life-restoring slaves. It was machinations in the international world of the firm that, in Robert Park's memorable phrases, put "a king in business" and extracted "blood money from the Congo."[29] Moreover, the joint-stock company, as Ralf Dahrendorf has shown, permits a more widely shared control and complicity in what we here are calling the sin of institutionalized death-in-life-giving greed.[30] That the vampiric monster of the firm would in turn convert first its founders and more significantly their descendants into blood-seeking, arrogant creatures like itself was in fact foreseen by Weber. The last stage of capitalism's cultural development, he gloomily predicted, would be characterized by the predominance of "'Specialists without spirit, sensualists without heart; this nullity imagines that it has attained a level of civilization never before achieved.'"[31]

GREED AND THE HUMANITIES: SIN RESTORED

If the social and behavioral sciences have provided psychological excuses or economic justifications for greed, the tendencies in literature and drama have been to portray it as punishable sin. Whether it is in the personification of greed in Molière's *Miser*, or the overwhelming terrors and woeful ironies of the unceasing pursuit for gold in von Stroheim's film classic *Greed*, there remains a basic avariciousness at the core of modern man's dilemma and downfall.

The conflicts between the greedy father Harpagon and his wastrel son Cléante in Molière's *L'Avare* provide a portrait of an antagonistic duo archetypically associated with avarice—the miser and the spendthrift.

Simmel would later show these two types to be more similar than Molière's apparent polarization of them would indicate.[32] Money, Simmel observed, is "almost as important to the spendthrift as to the miser, only not in the form of possessing it, but in its expenditure." The spendthrift in a money economy derives his pleasure not from a senseless gift of his money to the world, but rather from a foolish expenditure of it on commodities and services inappropriate to his station in life. "The pleasure of waste depends simply on the instant of the expenditure of money for no-matter-what objects. For the spendthrift, the attraction of the instant overshadows the rational evaluation either of money or of commodities." For the miser, on the other hand, bliss is attained "in the sheer possession of money, without proceeding to the acquisition and enjoyment of particular objects." To the miser money provides a sense of power uncontaminated by the exchange of it for goods, which resist complete incorporation into the self. "Money alone do we own completely and without limitations." Its possessive power arises precisely in its potentiality for use rather than in the employment of it. Money "alone can be completely incorporated into the use which we plan for it." The process that connects the miser to the spendthrift is found precisely in this: "The goal of enjoying the possession of an object is preceded by two steps—first, the possession of money and, second, the expenditure of money for the desired object. For the miser, the first of these grows to be a pleasurable end in itself; for the spendthrift the second."[33] Two of the faces of greed—that of the miser and of the spendthrift—are mirrors of the sin that encourages their anxiety.

However, Molière wishes to make a different point—the close relationship between the miser and misery.[34] For all his money, indeed precisely because of it, Harpagon is miserable, but he cannot escape his misery. Among the unhappy consequences of his greed are fear and, indeed, paranoia. He suspects everyone—even the members of the audience watching Molière's comedy—of harboring designs on his money. Harpagon's daily life is beset with anxieties: rumors of burglary, suspicions about the honesty of his servants, and doubts about the filial devotion of his own children. Even the barking of a stray dog arouses his fears about the security of his precious gold. When at last his money box is stolen he gives way completely, demanding the arrest and execution of everyone in the town and suburbs and in the theater audience, and, in an introjection of his paranoid delusion, he seizes his own arm as that of the thief. When a loyal servant is accused he repeats his pathological self-accusation.

Because of his own fears and delusions, Harpagon acts like the classic paranoid.[35] He secretly lends money at usurious rates, employing go-betweens and detectives, only to discover that he has been led into negotiating with his own wastrel son. He tricks his son into a confession of love for his own fiancée and then uses that confession to deny his son's suit for the marriage. And just as the paranoid's own fears may be partly grounded in fact, as Lemert has shown, so Harpagon's fearful miserly greed leads to plots against him by his servants, his daughter's suitor, and his own son.[36] Truly the miser establishes his own misery. The sin of greed sets in motion the vicious circle of its own hellish torture.

Molière is also willing to see the miser as a figure of fun—a fool as much as a knave, and therefore one who can be redeemed through renouncing his own foolishness or establishing role distance from it. Harpagon, however, is not redeemed. He remains unchanged in character from the beginning of the play to its final line, when, the young lovers having been properly sorted out and reunited, the marriages of his children assured of financial solvency through an agency other than his own, and his stolen gold returned intact, Harpagon rings down the curtain with "and let me go and see my beloved money box" (V:6). There is, it would seem, a deeper and darker aspect of his greed argued by this fact. Greed, as Norman O. Brown has argued, is related to the death instinct and to the desire for immortality as well. Certainly Harpagon's thoughts about and allusions to death haunt the drama. In Harpagon's imagination loss of money is related to loss of life, so that when his money box is stolen he cries out:

> Oh! my poor money, my darling money! They've taken you away. And because you're not here, I've lost my strength, my consolation, my happiness. All is over for me. I can't go on. I'm dying. I'm dead and buried. Is there no one who will bring me back to life, and give me back my beloved money, or tell me who took it? (IV:7)

The connection of money to life leads also to Harpagon's muted wish and ambivalent steps toward immortality. As a miser his immortality is not assured by his adult children, the daughter who will be given over to another family in marriage, the son who is a prodigal and a gambler.[37] Indeed, Harpagon is glad when he is told that his health is so good that he will live to be a hundred and twenty and bury his children and grandchildren. And when his daughter reveals that her secret lover, suspected by Harpagon of stealing his gold, is in fact the man who rescued her from drowning, Harpagon rages in reply, "That's of no consequence. It would have been better for me if he had let you drown rather than do what he has done" (V:4). His money, Harpagon admits, is his heart's blood. Without it he cannot live. With it, and a new young wife—purchased at no cost to himself and with the promise of the glitter that his gold will reflect on her, and perhaps the furtherance of his own immortality by means of the children produced through her—Harpagon can live forever. Caught in the miser's grip, he cannot give up life (money) nor afford to part with it as an inheritance to his offspring. But power (penis, money) is communicated through sexuality. Paralyzed in his desire for live everlasting, the miser is irredeemably miserable.

When we turn to von Stroheim's *Greed* we see the frightful terrors that avarice holds in store for those caught up in its viselike passion. Von Stroheim himself saw the film as a revelation of the riddle of life, a universal theme. Opposed to the then current trends in films to "spiritualize" life with uplifting plots and morally redemptive themes, von Stroheim perceived in the struggles of McTeague, the central character in Frank Norris' novel from which *Greed* was adapted, the actual and illogical nature of life—"monstrous, unfathomable, beautiful, ominous.[38] Scenarios had plots, he observed, but "life, raw, immense, swirling, has no plot. Its riddle can never be solved." McTeague, gripped by his passion for success, becomes a slave to greed's ineluctable dictates. Yet von Stroheim sees him as a character in a drama of the absurd, posing his puny *virtù* against an overwhelming but mysterious *fortuna*. "Our McTeague," he concludes, "struggles futilely against the hard swipes of destiny and goes down to death beneath the beating sun out there in the vast lonely desert."[39]

That avarice might become a feature of man's destiny was powerfully illustrated in the film.[40] McTeague, the son of a drunken father and a worn-out drudge of a mother, is a "human beast," a giant strong man capable of battling other humans but not of opposing fate. His *virtù* is in his powerful hands, at first an instrument for fighting off claim jumpers in the roaring goldfields of California, and later, under the guidance of a benevolent physician, the source of his skill as a dentist in San Francisco. He marries Trina, the former sweetheart of his false friend Marcus. When Trina wins a lottery of $5,000, the die is cast for a fateful struggle for the money that stands between all of its victims and happiness. Marcus, jealous of McTeague's magically acquired fortune, sees to it that the latter is suspended for practicing without a license. Trina, fearful of starvation, becomes a haunted miser, changing her winnings into gold pieces and sleeping with her money spread on the mattress. McTeague, sunken into alcoholism and misery, torments his wife for her money, and in a fit of rage maims her by biting her grasping fingers. Driven to distraction by hunger and drink, McTeague at last murders his wife and makes off with the gold. Pursued into the wastelands of California by Marcus and a posse, McTeague flees into the barren desert of Death Valley. Only Marcus will follow him to that deadly place. They fight, and McTeague kills Marcus, but not before all the life-preserving water has been spilled out onto the sand, and the two men have become unbreakably chained together by the handcuffs that Marcus carries and by the greed that calls them both to their death.

The power of greed to wreck even strong men is presented as a major theme. Man's physical strength is no match for the demonic power of avarice. When McTeague's brute power has been tamed by civilization and a healing profession, his now sublimated strength is symbolized by a giant tooth hanging outside his dental office. When fate denies him his chance to practice his profession, the tooth must be sold for living expenses, and McTeague is reduced to relying on his animal strength again, only now, against the force of greed, it cannot prevail. That money equals financial power and sexual potency is dramatically symbolized by Trina's substitution of gold pieces for her husband's penis in bed. As Norris put it, "Her avarice had grown to be her one dominant passion; her love of money for the money's sake brooded in her heart, driving out by degrees every other natural affection."[41] Trina's fingers, ceaselessly counting her coins, constitute a veritable display of her castration of McTeague, and, in raging revenge at his lost manhood, he bites off her fingers and steals the gold. But the wages of this greedy sin are death, and this ultimate fate overtakes McTeague and Marcus in the desert. Greed, in the form of the thirst for gold (death), overpowers the natural thirst for water (life), and in the end chains the dead Marcus and the living dead man McTeague to the cask of gold, useless in the barren valley of death.

GREED AND SOCIETY: COLLECTIVE BEHAVIOR, WHITE-COLLAR CRIME, AND THE CONFIDENCE GAME

Lewis Coser has coined the term "greedy institutions" to describe those arrangements, administrations, and corporate forms that totally absorb the loyalty of those who serve them and cut them off from entangling contracts and deep commitments to other persons or organizations.[42] Although the nature and scope of Coser's study is outside the terms of our own more literal and direct approach to greed, it is worth noting that greed itself is capable of establishing patterns of undivided commitment, all-encompassing behavior, and total absorption of the personality of the individual and character of the group. The miser and the spendthrift personify two character types of complex personal commitment to greed; the capitalistic firm presents avarice's organizational weapon against virtue; and the all-pervading duties of the mafioso "soldier" in the ranks of organized crime certainly take up the whole of his lifetime in service to his superiors' rapacious pursuit of gain. However, the patterned and collective institutionalization of greed takes on even more dramatic, spontaneous, and colorful forms. Here we shall consider greed's role in manias and outbursts, in the penetration of licit middle-class business operations, and in the clever creation of an underworld profession that preys on the avarice of honest men.

Popular Delusions and the Madness of Crowds: Tulipomania, The South Sea Bubble, and the Gold Rush

The Tulip Craze in Holland

It is an almost established truth, known certainly to philosophers of coinage, that just about anything might become an item of great value, an object for speculation, a focus for greedy grasp. Certainly one of the best illustrations of the fantastic in the motley variety of items that avarice might seize for its own is the tulipomania that swept over the Netherlands in the sixteenth and seventeenth centuries.[43] First introduced into Europe from Constantinople, the tulip became the single most significant symbol of wealth and status to the upper classes of Holland, Germany and, to a more limited extent, England and France. Like the hat, stick, and patent-leather shoe that came to symbolize the leisure class of the late nineteenth century in America, the tulip emerged as the master symbol of leisure and station in Holland by 1634, when "it was deemed a proof of bad taste in any man of fortune to be without a collection of them." However, the tulip did not remain a tasteful possession of the very rich for long. Already costly to import and inflated in value by the status competition among Amsterdam's nouveaux riches, the tulips rose to preposterous value when the passion for owning, cultivating, and displaying them spread to the burgeoning middle and shopkeeping classes, and soared beyond imagination when they became a commodity for speculation in futures.

Attempts to explain why the tulip became such an object for mass speculation are only suggestive. To the Freudian analyst the transubstantiation of feces to tulips might emphasize the inversion of aroma, the delicacy of the petals and stem, and the noticeable eroticism which the flower inspired. Poets of the day waxed rapturously over its capacity to change its hue, sang of it as feminine, and insisted on its aesthetic superiority to manufactured beauty. Perhaps also related is the discovery that varieties of tulips might be produced through careful cultivation and crossbreeding: new types might be created by the employment of man's scientific ("reproductive") powers. The offspring of these cultivations are thus the "children" of a sublimated sexual power, giving new forms to nature's bounty, and challenging God's creative powers. Whatever the motivation, however, the rage for tulips and tulip cultivation, the growth, competition, and sale of new varieties, and speculation on tulip futures swept the whole of Holland. Lands were sold to raise cash for tulip purchases, ordinary businesses were neglected as merchants shifted their pursuit of profits to the tulip market, and laborers, servants, and the criminal classes entered into the mania for tulips.

The height of the mania was reached during the years 1634 to 1636.

Individual investments in tulips rose to hundreds of thousands of florins. A new weight of less than a grain, the "perit," was developed, and the prices of various varieties pegged accordingly, and astronomically: an Admiral Liefken, 400 perits, at 4,400 florins; an Admiral Van der Eyck, 446 perits, 1,260 florins; a Childer, 106 perits, 1,615 florins; a Viceroy, 400 perits, 3,000 florins; and the most precious of all, the Semper Augustus, 200 perits, was sold for 5,500 florins or more. Stories of frustrated owners and conniving dealers abounded, and the accidental destruction of a bulb became a very serious penal offense. When an ignorant sailor inadvertently ate a bulb of the invaluable Semper Augustus, mistaking it for an onion, he was clapped into prison for several months, convicted on a felony charge preferred against him by the bulb's owner. In another instance—illustrating how greed had led, as Gregory the Great had said the sin of avarice would lead, to "restlessness . . . and hardness of heart against compassion"—an English botanist, knowing little of the value of tulips, came upon a tulip root in the conservatory of his Dutch host, picked it up, peeled it, and cut it in two. His enraged host hailed him before a magistrate, charged him with destroying the value of an Admiral Van der Eyck worth 4,000 florins, and despite the hapless botanist's pleas of extenuating circumstances, had him imprisoned until he was able to ransom himself from this most innocently incurred debt.

The tulip craze spurred even greater speculation. In 1636 a special market for trade in tulip futures was established at the stock exchanges of Amsterdam, Rotterdam, Haarlem, Leyden, Alkmar, Hoorn, and other towns. From then on money was to be made not on the plant's value, but in speculation on its stock's worth. The money to be made in tulips encouraged both national and international speculation. Jobbers, sellers, buyers, and speculators found themselves caught up in the scramble for the fragile flower that was worth so much. Those with experience in stock manipulation turned their nefarious skills to profiteering in the tulip market. As in other stock manias, it was widely believed that the passion for tulips was permanent, that money could only be *made* in the purchase of tulip shares, and within a year tulip speculation had overcome class barriers and become a mass phenomenon. Noblemen, burghers, peasants, mechanics, tradesmen, sailors, servants, and chimney sweeps invested in tulips. Inflation set in as tulip investors prospered. New laws and codes, and new staffs of clerks, notaries, and bookkeepers arose to handle the boisterous trade. In small towns the tulip notary replaced the public notary, the tavern became the tulip market, and banquets of the investors were graced by vases containing the almost priceless flowers.

Then, as suddenly as it had begun, the bottom fell out of the tulip market. Those who bought tulips ceased planting them; gardens of tulips were sold off, and new ones not planted. Tulips became a commodity of pure exchange, and then, recognized as of exchange value only, the price began dropping rapidly. Growers found that buyers could not be found for their crop; speculators were caught with paper stocks that were valueless; buyers turned away from the purchase of the flower. Thousands of people were ruined, commercial ventures bankrupted, fortunes lost, savings evaporated, and careers dashed. Special governmental commissions failed to satisfy the demands of the angry and frustrated tulip investors for relief, repayment, and restoration. The economy of the state as well as that of its citizens was damaged severely and did not recover for many years. The wages of the greedy in tulip selling were ruin for most; a few escaped the financial fall intact, however, and went on to search for other sources of endless wealth.

The South Sea Bubble

Eighty years after the tulip mania had ended, two other schemes for untold riches emerged—this time in England and in France. The South Sea Bubble and the Mississippi mania were both stock-manipulation schemes that aroused and absorbed the avaricious character of just about the entire populations of the two European powers.[44] Because they are in so many ways alike, we shall here consider only the British example. Both schemes were indeed products of greedy institutions in the literal sense of that phrase. Premised on the appetite for gold that was said to animate all of mankind, these schemes absorbed the undivided commitment, the vital energies, the total lives, the accumulated fortunes, and the meager savings of untold thousands. The avid desire for money brought about the delusion of multitudes; individuals and groups praised for their usual caution and sober-minded approach to matters of finance plunged into a mania of speculation and gambling. The newly created gamblers risked reputation, wealth, and life itself in their obsession to obtain the riches promised by a seemingly magical formula of modern finance.

The intricate economic details of the South Sea Bubble need not detain us here. Suffice it to say that a group of financiers agreed to assume a portion of the British national debt in return for the right to float stock certificates in behalf of a venture proposing to extract gold and silver from as yet untapped mines in two Spanish colonies, Chile and Peru. Backed by the British Parliament and buoyed by the investment risks taken by the nobility and members of the royal family, the scheming financiers caused all manner of rumors to be spread, raising the value of the stock. Despite the firm opposition of the Spanish king to British economic expansion in South America, the spate of planted rumors caused an inflation in the value of the stock—money invested, in effect, in a nearly nonexistent venture. In addition, spurred by the money to be made in stock manipulations, groups of financiers proposed nearly one hundred other ventures. Some of these were for internal improvements and for inventions; others were for secret purposes, and for a variety of disparate projects, many of them farfetched fantasies of the most preposterous nature. Once the venture was announced, stocks were offered; then after a considerable sale, the scheme was abandoned and the purchasers left with worthless paper. Eventually the flood of fatuous bubbles was brought to a halt by parliamentary legislation and royal proclamation. That the mass of the population was caught up in these unregulated "bubbles," as they came to be called, is vivid testimony to the greed in human character.

The South Sea Bubble prospered for a time. Built almost entirely on rumors, false reports, and promises of new finds in exotic South America, the Bubble eventually bulged out by a thousandfold of its original cost. Then, suddenly, it broke. Attempts to rescue the debentures by quick purchases, hastily called meetings, parliamentary sessions, and further manipulation of stock proved unavailing. The cupidity of disillusioned stockholders gave way to disbelief and then to anger. Public meetings held throughout England demanded that the Parliament take vengeance on the directors of the South Sea Company. "Nobody," as Mackay points out, "blamed the credulity and avarice of the people—the degrading lust of gain, which had swallowed up every nobler quality in the national character, or the infatuation which had made the multitude run their heads with such frantic eagerness into the net held out for them by scheming projectors." Eventually some but not all the directors of the burst Bubble were brought to justice, fined, and imprisoned. A clever scheme by Walpole and others who had opposed the Bubble in the first place helped restore public confidence. And the credulous subscribers to the illusion of a South Sea hoard of gold? These people redefined themselves as "a simple, honest, hard-working people, ruined by a gang of robbers," who, they felt, ought to have been "hanged, drawn, and quartered without mercy." Fools in the beginning, they had become the victims of avarice; in the end they returned, quite uneducated by their experience, to the foolish pride with which they had begun. A century later, their descendants paid a similar price investing in the new, less dramatic "bubbles" that again swept over England. Avarice had not died; it had only gone to sleep for a while.

The Gold Rush: An Excursus on the Sociology of Karl Marx

Karl Marx has made a science out of the social economics of greed and linked that science to an apocalypse that will bring an end to history, class struggle, and avarice. During his lifetime, Marx thought he saw the

coming together of his science of greed with the final stages of history
itself. The place where the doom of the old order would be sealed and the
first elements of a new unfettered life begun was, he thought, California.
In the gold rush of 1848 and after, Marx thought he saw the unfolding of
the final act in the drama of history, a drama wherein greed for gold
translated itself and was itself translated by class, class struggles, and,
ultimately a final Armageddon.

Although a full explosion of Marxian theory is beyond the scope of
the present work, a few words on Marx's ideas on money are in order
before we turn to the California gold rush and his view of its importance.
Relevant to our concerns are Marx's economic and philosophical texts,
written during the five months from April through August, 1844.[45]
"Money," wrote Marx, "since it has the property of being able to buy
anything, and to appropriate all objects to itself, is thus the object par
excellence." Money was omnipotent, and he likened it to a god. More
specifically Marx argued that money is "the pander between need and its
object, between man's life and his means of subsistence." Precisely
because money mediated the existence of man to every other and to
himself, it was the most valuable of objects, the object that made moral
and material existence realizable. Marx credited Shakespeare with the
proper understanding of money, quoting from *Timon of Athens* (IV, iii):

> Gold? Yellow, glittering, precious gold? No, gods,
> I am no idle votarist: roots, you clear heavens!
> Thus much of this will make black, white; foul, fair;
> Wrong, right; base, noble; old, young; coward, valiant.

And, seconding Shakespeare's shrewd prescience, Marx argued that
money was the source of identity, itself:

> What . . . money can buy, that is what I the possessor of the money
> am myself. My power is as great as the power of money. The
> properties of money are my (its owner's) properties and faculties.
> Thus what I am and what I am capable of is by no means determined
> by my individuality. I am ugly, but I can buy myself the most
> beautiful women. Consequently I am not ugly, for the effect of
> ugliness, its power of repulsion, is annulled by money. As an
> individual, I am lame, but money can create twenty-four feet for
> me; so I am not lame; I am a wicked, dishonest man without
> conscience or intellect, but money is honoured and so also is its
> possessor. Money is the highest good and so its possessor is good.
> Money relieves me of the trouble of being dishonest; so I am
> presumed to be honest . . .

Money, being at the same time the source of all identity and
transformations and also all powerful and universal, was in Marx's terms

both the "visible god-head" and "the universal whore." Because money could make demands realizable, Marx regarded it as the resource of true existence. "Money," Marx observed, "is the universal means and power, exterior to man, not issuing from man as man or from society as society, to turn imagination into reality and reality into imagination." But precisely because of its great power to transform, money was evil, turning everything to confusion and exchange into its opposite. "As this perverting power, money then appears as the enemy of man and social bonds that pretend to self-subsistence. It changes fidelity into infidelity, love into hate, hate into love, virtue into vice, vice into virtue, slave into master, master into slave, stupidity into intelligence and intelligence into stupidity." Money, thus, is the philosopher's stone. Capable of transposing everything, transubstantiating base metal into precious, physical defects into beauty, and stigma into honor, it is no wonder that money is the supreme object of man's desires—and of his greed.

Money as the transsubstantial substance of greed was in turn related to the conditions of its own significance in the epochs of historical development. Ultimately it and its vicious meanings would be overcome by the workings of the dialectical process. To Marx history was a great drama unfolding according to its own dialectical scenario across the epochs of civilization.[46] People made their own history, but they did not make it as they chose. Rather they enacted the roles of progenitor and revolting son, founder turned villain, and heir turned epoch-destroyer. Moreover, people enacted these roles not as self-constructed free individuals but rather as collectivities, as classes. Furthermore, these collectivities also stood against humanity, embodying the constrained elements of existence against which the individual struggled for liberation. Only when history itself had come to an end, when the last class struggle had been fought, would humanity emerge unshackled from the chains of illusion—chains that bound them to perform history's ineluctable will. In the final outcome avarice and its substance would disappear.

The signs of the beginning of the last class struggles were all around, thought Marx. History had already passed through the great epochs of Asiatic, Ancient, and Feudal methods of productive relations, and was now in its final evolutionary phase, that of modern bourgeois production.[47] Like all previous epochs, this one would begin with a revolution and a consolidation of a ruling class—the bourgeoisie. But in accordance with the dialectics of its own development, this epoch would engender within itself a conflict between the material forces of production and existing social relations. At a certain moment the great final revolution would break out. That moment was at hand, Marx thought. And the place for its momentous occurrence was California.

Marx's observations about the general properties of money and the imminence of revolution were given a more specific focus by the

discovery of gold in California in 1848.[48] News of the strike spread
around the world causing one of the largest mass migrations in history.[49]
From nearly every continent there came men—but very few women—
into the gold fields of California. Within eight years California was a
polyglot society, where races, nations, tribes, and peoples from all over
the world rubbed shoulders, dug gold, bought and sold goods, and
struggled against one another for the precious metal or for the fortunes to
be made from those who looked for it.[50] The very same greed that would
animate early scenes of California mining life in Norris' *McTeague*
inspired Marx to perceive the California gold fields as the setting for the
final chapter of world history.[51] To the end of his life Marx kept up with
the news of the "golden state," the state given nurturance by man's greed
for gold, and the place where, Marx thought, the forces of capital and
labor were arrayed against one another in a struggle to the death.[52]

California, as Marx saw it, brought together the naked forces of
greed and the nexus of history. "The hunt for gold in all countries leads
to its discovery; to the formation of new states; initially to the spread of
commodities, which produce new needs, and draw distant continents into
the metabolism of circulation, i.e., exchange." Back of this hunt, Marx
continued, a hunt that "precedes the development of modern industrial
society," is the "general greed for money on the part of individuals as
well as of states."[53] And the activation of that general greed in California
would, according to Marx, change history, indeed had already begun to
do so. Marx wrote in January, 1850, that "the most important thing that
has occurred [in America], even more important than the February
Revolution [in Europe], is the discovery of gold in California."[54] This
event would turn out to be more important than the discovery of
America itself, for it would change the entire structure of European
trade, draw the Asian continent and Oceania into the world orbit, and
submerge the native races of those newly engulfed lands in the deadly
struggles between capital and labor. "California's gold mines were
discovered only eighteen months ago," Marx wrote breathlessly in 1850,
"and the Yankees have already started a railroad, a great highway, and a
canal from the Mexican Gulf; steamers from New York to Chagres, from
Panama to San Francisco, are already in regular service; trade with the
Pacific Ocean is already concentrating in Panama, and the trip around
Cape Horn is obsolete."

The drama of history was being enacted as before, Marx perceived,
and "New York, San Francisco, San Juan de Nicaragua [Greytown],
Chagres, and Leon are now becoming what Tyre, Carthage, and
Alexandria were in antiquity, what Genoa and Venice were in the
Middle Ages, and what London and Liverpool have been hitherto—the
emporia of world commerce." However, this time the drama was casting
new and culturally distant peoples into its central parts and being

performed in a place geographically far from but socially near to the old stage of history. "A coast of 30 degrees longitude, one of the most beautiful in the world, hitherto practically uninhabited, is being visibly transformed into a rich and civilized land, thickly populated with people of all races, from Yankees to Chinese, from Negroes to Indians and Malays, from Creoles and mestizos to Europeans." And even where the greed for gold did not send teeming immigrants off to California, its power still was felt, for "California gold is flowing in streams over America and the Asian coast of the Pacific Ocean, drawing recalcitrant barbaric peoples into world commerce, into civilization." Indeed, Marx believed that the "center of gravity of world trade—in Italy in the Middle Ages and in England in Modern times—is now the southern half of the North American hemisphere," and that very soon "the Atlantic Ocean will decline to the level of an inland sea." If Europe wished to avoid its fate—becoming a dependency of the new civilization developing around the Pacific—it would have to embark on social revolution immediately.

However, although Marx believed that Europe had now experienced its sixteenth century for the second time, a repeat performance of an epoch that would "sound its death knell just as the first one thrust it into existence," he was pessimistic about the chances for revolutionary success there. The European bourgeoisie had performed its historic duty, Marx argued, by establishing a world market and by creating a productive system based on that market. "Since the world is round," Marx observed, "this seems to have been completed by the colonization of California and Australia and the opening up of China and Japan." But since bourgeois life was on the ascendancy in the Pacific area, a socialist revolution "in this small corner" of Europe was bound to be crushed.[55]

Nevertheless, there remained a possibility that the forces of history would move forward in Europe more rapidly because of the naked confrontation of greed and misery on the California frontier. However, instead of facilitating the polarization of social classes in Europe, gold fever led to a speculative mania in France. Marx's analysis of this mania furthered his despair for revolution in Europe. Like the earlier "bubbles" that had aroused people from all walks of life in England to covet the wealth to be made from speculations in mines in Peru and Chile, the "growth of capital in France led to a series of speculations, for which the exploitation of the California gold mines on a large scale served as a pretext." And, as Marx lamented, the nature if not the extent of the popular delusion was almost as great as in the earlier stock-market rush. "A swarm of companies have [sic] sprung up"; Marx wrote, "the low denomination of their shares and their socialist-colored prospectuses, appeal directly to the purses of the petty bourgeois and the workers, but all and sundry results in the swindling which is characteristic of the

French and Chinese alone."[56] One of these "bubbles" was particularly nefarious, involving a scheme to make money through a gold bars lottery, the proceeds of which would be used to ship Parisian vagabonds to California. Its secretary was Alexandre Dumas, *fils*, and it was advertised with much fanfare in California as well as France.[57] Marx inveighed against the weak-spirited French working class that succumbed to the appeal to human avarice. "On the one hand, golden dreams were to supplant the socialist dreams of the Paris proletariat, the seductive prospect of the first prize, the doctrinaire right to work. Naturally the Paris workers did not recognize in the glitter of the California gold bars the inconspicuous francs that were enticed out of their pockets." Marx exposed the man behind the lottery, Louis Napoleon Bonaparte, "who precisely because he was a bohemian, a princely lumpen proletarian, had the advantage over a rascally bourgeois in that he could conduct the struggle meanly." Marx showed how the future emperor saw to it that false lottery tickets were manufactured. "The vagabonds who wanted to open California gold mines without troubling to leave Paris," Marx wryly observed, "were Bonaparte himself and his debt-ridden Round Table." In France, Marx argued, this act in the historical drama was being played out not as a profound tragedy but rather as a ludicrous farce.[58]

There remained California in particular and America in general as the site for revolution. Marx waxed warmly on the subject, seeing in the organization of greed and class struggle there the chance for history to advance a giant step. In the great industrial exposition of 1851 Marx exulted over the fact that America carried off the prize, and especially that it "showed a colossal lump of California gold ore, and, alongside, a golden service of pure gold."[59] Speculation in America, occasioned by the discovery of gold in California, seemed to promise a more restive situation, suitable for hostile outbursts and revolutionary development. "I see," Marx wrote to Engels in 1852, ". . . the most frantic speculation in railways, banks, house building, unheard of expansion in the credit system, etc. Is this not approaching a crisis? The revolution may come sooner than we wish. Nothing is worse than for revolutionists to have to worry about bread."[60] That California would be the site for a Socialist resurgence buoyed Marx through the Civil War. When Engels wrote to him praising the virtues of the Confederate general Stonewall Jackson, Marx replied that the South would not win the war, since such a victory would permit California, as well as New England, to be "under the acknowledged supremacy of the slaveholders," a retrogressive class.[61] Seven years later, angered by Liebknecht's preference for bourgeois democracies over revolutionary politics, Marx again pointed to developments in California and to the consequences of bourgeois avarice in that state for impending revolution: "[T]he railway to California was built by the bourgeoisie," Marx thundered, "the latter presenting to itself, through Congress, an enormous mass of 'national land'; that is to say, they expropriated the workers from it by importing a rabble of Chinese to force down wages, and finally formed themselves into a new sprig of 'financial aristocracy.'"[62] As the years dragged on and workers' movements in California showed a decidedly greater interest in racist demagoguery than in socialist politics or revolutionary action, Marx still clung to his dream.[63] The state where greed had been represented by its metallic substance would be the place where epoch-changing events would occur. Less than thirty months before his death, while feverishly attempting to put the final touches on the second and third volumes of *Kapital*, Marx wrote to Friedrich Adolph Sorge, a German Socialist who had moved to America, closing his letter with a postscript that evinced his continued hope for California: "I should be very pleased if you could find me something good (substantial) on economic conditions in California, of course at my expense. California is very important to me, because nowhere else has the upheaval caused so shamelessly by capitalist centralization taken place—with such speed."[64] Marx died in 1883; no revolution had broken out in California.

And what of the gold rush and the fate of California? Like other "bubbles" and manias, this one came to an end in a few years, but not before a few fortunes had been made and a great many more lost. Just as the gold strike in California was petering out, other discoveries in British Columbia, Oregon, Idaho, Montana, and in Australia kept the rushes going. In 1898 the Klondike strike attracted gold seekers from many parts of the world. California's population settled down, and the state remained a stronghold of organized labor for many decades. As the golden state, it continued to attract new migrants: the restless and rejected, the passionate and the desperate, the eager and the enchanted— all hoping to realize a dream.[65] Sometimes avaricious, sometimes just disillusioned, the dreams that drove them on varied over the years, but all too few were ever realized. The migrants might have thought they were marching to utopia, but California's gold fever—like that for the gold of Ophir—had set in motion a process of desecration, perhaps beyond redemption.[66] Yet, California, and the Western frontier continue to beckon: It was in an erstwhile setting of gold strikes that F. Scott Fitzgerald set his absurdist black comedy about a diamond as big as the Ritz Carlton Hotel, and it was in the tinseled dream factory of Hollywood that Nathanael West foresaw the apocalyptic day of the locust.[67] California seems ever destined to be a place of dreams and nightmares.

White-Collar Crime

"There is something in the handling of money for gain that tends to the demoralization of the finer faculties." So wrote Hubert Howe Bancroft in the opening of his chapter on money and monopoly in the American West.[68] Bancroft went on to describe the occupations of bank teller, bank manager, jeweler, and the several institutions of monopoly all with an eye to showing how these positions and organizations are unfavorable for mind and moral development. The lowly teller was merely bored because his job required him to become "a counting machine, the mind being forced to fix itself attentively on the work in order to avoid mistakes, while ground down by dead monotony." But the managers, jewelers, monopolists, and corporate leaders suffered alike from soul-destroying work, for their tasks were occasioned by the institutionalization of greed. As Bancroft saw it in 1890: "During these days of strong competition and well-defined business channels, the largest fortunes are not made by merchants or manufacturers, but by manipulators of mines, railways, or grain." The wealth to be made in manipulation, argued Bancroft, cannot be obtained by honest means. Rather "gambling ventures, trickery, on a mighty magnificent scale, or downright rascality barely shielded by all-accommodating law" were the practical means to the opulent end. The net effect of these modes of moneymaking on the individual was to attenuate his moral moorings, erode his ethics, and undermine the higher purposes that make for human virtue. Indeed, in speaking of the terrible human wreckage that arises from indulgence in the sin of avarice, Bancroft echoes Gregory the Great:

> In the race for wealth loftier aspirations are too often trampled under foot, many devoting themselves heart and soul throughout life to the fascination of gambling and cheating within the pale of law. Barren in all the nobler attributes of intellect, and in heart and feeling as cold as ice and hard as stone, the souls of these *pauvres riches* are shrivelled to slag, their consciences utterly benumbed.

But in addition to the subversion of the soul, there is the crime itself. In later years, sociology would come to distinguish these kinds of crime from more violent ones by the term "white-collar" crime. "White-collar crime," wrote Edwin H. Sutherland, who coined the term, "may be defined approximately as a crime committed by a person of respectability and high social status in the course of his occupation."[69] The white-collar criminal is performing a role familiar to his position and permitted by or winked at by his colleagues and fellow respectables. Although he may benefit personally and financially from his criminal act, it is in principle the case that his crime is beneficial to his firm. White-collar crime is a crime created by the separation of the office from the individual, by the endowment of the office with all the characteristics of a human except a conscience, by the reduction of respectable people to the formal status of agents for an artificial entity—by, in short, the obviation of sin from crime. Sin being absent, the question remains whether there is guilt. Sutherland answers this by showing that the white-collar crimes are indeed violations of the law, and therefore worthy of punishment and that they are costly to the public. Yet, as Sutherland grudgingly admits, white-collar criminals do not feel themselves to be criminals; at best they see themselves as "law violators," a status they hold to be quite different from that of the ordinary felon and quite without guilt as well. More often than not, he also allows, the public does not regard the dishonest businessman as a criminal either. Modern business practice has, in effect, obviated the sinful aspect of greed, when it is indulged by men of high station and respect.

Yet, in the period of "the robber barons," both the moralists of the day and the white-collar criminals more readily assented to their guilt.[70] In the same year that saw the closing of the frontier and the publication of Bancroft's essay on money and morals, 1890, A. B. Stickney, a railroad president, addressed sixteen other railroad executives assembled at the home of J. P. Morgan: "I have the utmost respect for you gentlemen individually, but as railroad presidents, I wouldn't trust you with my watch out of my sight." And another railroad magnate, from one of America's most famous families, Charles Francis Adams, pointed to the central significance of cupidity and its attendant characteristics in managing the railroads: "One difficulty in railroad management . . . lies in the covetousness, want of good faith, low moral tone of railway managers, in the complete absence of any high standard of commercial honesty."[71] Bancroft was more direct and harsh in picturing the greedy characters that arose from the new corporate organizations and monopolies:

> Selfish and unprincipled, they play upon the necessities of others, using the power their wealth gives them to increase its already enormous bulk, by impoverishing poor producers; by lying in wait for opportunities to get something for nothing; by regulating elections so as to put their tools in power; by originating plausible schemes to rob the people; by inflating or breaking the stock-market at pleasure, so as to gather at one fell swoop the small accumulations of those thousands of smaller gamblers who are foolish enough to stake their all on games beside which faro and three card monte are honorable and fair; by bribing assessors so that the burden of taxation shall fall on the laboring classes and honest merchants.[72]

How men can commit crimes without feeling like criminals deserves fuller attention than either Bancroft or Sutherland has given it. In terms of our own thesis, we seek the methods of absolution that white-collar criminals employ to relieve themselves of the guilt from which they might otherwise suffer. Greed, which we hold is the basis of that kind of crime, is perhaps the one sin for which modern Occidental civilization itself has had the greatest success in providing ready-made salvation devices. One sociologist recently put it this way: "In the eighteenth and nineteenth centuries, the Industrial Revolution under (ultimately) Calvinist auspices took hold of European avarice (one of the 'seven deadly sins') and organized it in rational-bureaucratic forms in such a way that avarice was transubstantiated into something else."[73] That "something else" was either a virtue or a neutral passion. Those who assimilated the ethical culture of the rational bureaucratic ethos (or its Calvinist underpinnings) received as well a rhetoric of exculpation and absolution, through which the sin was sublimated.

A salvation device, as Kenneth Burke has pointed out, is any "conscious or unconscious, adequate or inadequate way of saving one's soul, saving one's hide, or saving one's face."[74] In general these devices (which elsewhere we have called "accounts") may be distinguished according to whether one admits commission of a sin or crime but denies full responsibility (an "excuse"), or whether one admits commission of an act but denies that it is tainted (a "justification").[75] The acts of white-collar avarice are subject to accusations of sinful indulgence or of more specific crimes. In most cases, aided by the social developments mentioned earlier, those who commit the allegedly evil deeds justify their actions. The foremost justifications for the "crimes" of capitalism are found in various elements of Protestant thought. John Wesley sensed the difficulties of the position, but he nevertheless argued that "we ought not to prevent people from being diligent and frugal; we must exhort all Christians to gain all they can, and to save all they can; that is, in effect, to grow rich."[76] And, as Burke has noted, salvation devices tend to start out at the top of the social order, in quite sophisticated forms, but soon become democratized and seep through to the general population, gaining more adherents but losing much of their philosophical quality.[77] The casuistic stretch of the Protestant Ethic salvation device is well illustrated by the embarrassing but apparently persuasive rhetoric employed by Bruce Barton in his widely read book of 1924, *The Man Nobody Knows: A Discovery of the Real Jesus*. Insisting that Jesus' famous phrase referring to his "Father's business" was not meant to refer only to preaching, healing, or teaching, Barton asserted that "the business itself is far larger, more inclusive . . . The race must be fed and clothed and housed and transported, as well as preached to, and taught and healed. Thus all business is his Father's business. All work is worship; all useful service, prayer."[78] The corporate and business leaders who operate in restraint of trade, collect secret rebates from clients or workers, engage in unfair labor practices, infringe on patents, trademarks, and copyrights, misrepresent their products in advertising campaigns, and undertake stock and futures manipulations might justify these actions by referring to their religious adherence to God's command that they grow rich. Greediness comes close to godliness.

However, Protestant ethics are not the only justifications for white-collar crimes. Indeed, the well-known techniques of neutralization by which juvenile delinquents relieve themselves of guilt for their misdemeanors are also artfully employed by white-collar criminals.[79] When stock swindlers *deny that they injured* anyone, they usually denigrate their victims, charging that they in fact did not suffer, or if they did it was because of their own greed, stupidity, or incautiousness. When *denying their victim*, these same swindlers shift the burden of guilt as well as the blame onto the people who gambled their savings with them. Arguing that the subscribers are either fools or knaves, the stockjobbers insist that their victims deserved whatever they got. In some cases white-collar criminals justify their violation of the public law by arguing that in fact business is conducted according to the law of the jungle.[80] In effect the white-collar criminal here *condemns his condemners*, in some cases presenting an entire casuistic ideology in his defense. Bancroft gives a nice summary of the creed of this type of criminal:

> Here is their creed. Let your watchword be expediency. Policy is the best honesty. Strict integrity does not pay; a little of it, mixed with policy, will suffice as leaven for a large loaf of appearance, which may be fed to those from whom favors are desired . . . Love yourself; hate your enemies; let neither friends nor sentiment stand in the way of success. Keep within the pale of the law; forgive your creditors. Finally, clothe your misbehavior in sanctimonious garb, and thus be happy and virtuous.[81]

Lastly, a dishonest businessman might *appeal to loyalties*. When employed as a justification, this appeal argues that precisely because knowledge of the act was widely shared, the putative criminal is absolved from guilt. "Everybody does it" serves to permit the accused to do "it" too and with impunity. An *appeal to loyalties* can also be an excuse when an accused party responds that he committed the crime under duress, the threat of loss of his job, or other loss.

Among the excuses for criminal avarice are those denials of responsibility based on having been overwhelmed by some psycho-biological state—a predisposition to kleptomania, for example—or based on cultural dictates, such as the well-known religious injunction to be frugal. A particular excuse for white-collar crime is made available by the separation of the firm from the individuals who own it and by the subsequent shearing off of ownership from control. The crimes are not the actions of conscience-bound individuals, argues this appeal, but rather those of that soulless vampire, the corporation. As Bancroft put it, "The conscience of a corporation is remarkable only for its absence; where such a thing as a corporate conscience exists at all it is extremely callous. The individuality which loses itself in the body corporate does not scruple to receive the cruelly or illicitly extorted gains of the corporation."[82] No longer responsible for the acts from which he obtains his ill-gotten gains, the sinner claims he has been sinned against by all those forces and powers that govern his choices and place him in his position of inadvertent advantage.

In these ways white-collar criminals violate laws and subvert morality and yet escape the charge of crime and sin. Even public benefices support private vices with impunity. Thus, Bancroft observed that, "Railway companies present the most conspicuous form of incorporation in the United States for public benefit, but they have too often proved vampires as well." Justifying their appropriation of public lands at the peoples' expense by pointing to the many general advantages to be obtained by improvement in transporation, the corporate managers felt little guilt or shame over the depredations. However, "not content with such easy acquisition, such munificent rewards, the managers, once in possession, turn alike on immediate associates and on the public, to plunder friends and patrons either by insidious manipulations or brazen trickery and extortion. To this pernicious end is used the very money and power entrusted to them for individual and general benefit." Mandeville's argument on the latent beneficial aspects of avarice is here shown to be father to a monster grown quite out of control and removed from the commands of conscience.

THE CONFIDENCE GAME: AN EXCURSUS ON THE "SOCIOLOGY" OF HERMAN MELVILLE

Greed has a curious and paradoxical relationship to trust: each is related to authority but in quite opposed ways. For greed to find an open field for extensive operations there must be no supreme arbiter over the market for money, or so little authority that a free reign is given to the clever and diligent. For trust to prevail there must be a basic code of authorized custom, a level of predictable reciprocity, an infrequency of nasty surprises, a legitimated authority, ultimately enforced by law, but in fact governed by the tacit understandings of the social contract.[83] Greed negates trust and opposes authority; trust abhors greed and depends on established confidence. Greed and trust, although seeming antagonists, find their joint representation in the confidence man and the confidence game. And perhaps nowhere were greed and trust to be better combined as partners in crime than in America, a land founded in the name of Providence and dedicated to the pursuit of wealth. By the time that Max Weber pronounced his doleful prophecy on the fate of the Protestant Ethic, America had all but shed its cloak of ethical responsibility and turned to the all-out pursuit of money. "In the field of its highest development, in the United States," wrote Weber, "the pursuit of wealth, stripped of its religious and ethical meaning, tends to become associated with purely mundane passions, which often actually give it the character of sport."[84]

If we are to search for the sport par excellence associated with the greedy pursuit of gain we should find it in the games of confidence played by sharpsters on the credulous but avaricious citizens of the United States. That these games were the inevitable consequence of the restless search for wealth that preoccupied nearly all Americans can scarcely be doubted. In 1845 an editorial in the leading Whig review in the United States noticed that a definite and peculiar anxiety had appeared in the American countenance and attributed it to the fact that in the United States, "there are no bounds among us to the restless desire to be better off; and this is the ambition of all classes of society."[85] The writer went on to observe that since "No man in America is contented to be poor, or expects to continue so," there "are here no established limits within which the hopes of any class of society must be confined, as in other countries." Equality had removed limitations on every individual's desires for money. But the excitement produced by this peculiar form of equality—equality of opportunity to pursue the will-o'-the-wisp of financial success—led not only to the entrance of nearly everyone into some kind of commercial venture, but also to a pervasive and general restlessness, worry, and anxious concern. It also led to a diminution of kindliness and grace and a greater distrust of one's fellow men. These developments are, continued the editorialist, "natural to the circumstances, but not natural to the human soul. It is good and hopeful to the interests of the race, but destructive to the happiness, and dangerous to the virtue of the generation exposed to it." Catering to the soul's desire for trust and security and preying upon the body's desire for wealth, the confidence man became a familiar figure in American society.

The persistence of the confidence man and his endless variety of tricks is explicable in great part because he provides not only a chance for his victim to make money but also an illusion of confidence and trust. The sharpster is, in effect, an applied ethnomethodologist, providing the background and invoking the background expectancies that make for the "mark's" fatal confidence in him. The very greed that animates his victim's restlessness and sharpens his distrust also evokes his interest in and ultimate victimization by the con-man. Perhaps no American understood the nature and psychology of this phenomenon better than

Herman Melville. In his novel *The Confidence Man* he unveiled the peculiar American obsession with money. The way of life spawned by the restless pursuit of riches is represented as a black comedy of grotesque absurdity.[86] A ship embarks from St. Louis on what appears to be an ordinary voyage. In fact, however, it is a ship of fools. Its passengers are ultimately fleeced by a masterful and mysterious confidence man who appears in innumerable disguises—as a mute youth, as a cripple, as a slave, as an older man, as an intellectual. The confidence man takes from the motley group of passengers all their wealth in return for restoring their confidence in mankind in general and himself in particular. His is the ultimate con. When, at the last, he has "taken" an old man, telling him "in Providence, as in man, you and I equally put trust," the lights must be dimmed because the lamp is giving off an awful stench. He guides the old man to his stateroom, and the novel concludes with the confidence man thinking about the endless possibilities that beckon such an artful swindler as himself: "Something further may follow of this Masquerade."[87]

As Melville seems to see it, greed in an anarchic society turns every man into a competitive, distrustful enemy of his fellow man. But it also creates a deep, brooding, and restless anxiety, a search for someone to trust, someone in whom to place one's confidence. Cautious and alone, men seek to make their desires the children of their shrewdness, but they are not really so smart as they suppose. Prideful in their belief that they can only take and not be taken, they are vulnerable to an even more shrewd con man.

There is more.[88] The ship is named *Fidele*, but as the strange sharpster disguised as a cripple points out, neither captain nor officers are in evidence. In short the leaderless ship represents the condition of absolute *laissez-faire, laisser-aller*. Devoid of authority, guidance, or custom, every man must watch out for himself, each must look askance on the other, none may repose confidence or have faith in any but himself. When the confidence man reappears as a black slave, moaning "Oh, sar, I am der dog widout massa," he points up the missing element in the lives of the whites who abuse him. They too are "widout massa," without any unifying principle to which they can adhere and with which they can form an authoritative and legitimate communion amongst themselves. Misers and greedy speculators in a strange and uncertain setting, they lack both the psychic self-sufficiency to produce self-confidence and the trust in one another to provide security.

The confidence game takes place in a world of interdependent strangers, who are obliged to interact but cannot know one another.[89] It is the scene of the quintessential social masquerade, as Melville so correctly portrays it, a scene in which each individual is required to ration his trust but not abandon it altogether. The most successful confidence man is he who can extract the greatest amount of faith and reliance from the other while giving the least value in return. The emporia of commerce provide the peculiarly adaptable settings in which the confidence game and its attendant masquerade can go on; indeed, in the argot of the American swindler the "big store" is "the swanky gambling club or fake brokerage establishment in which the modern pay-off or rag is played."[90] These establishments float in a free, unregulated market in the same manner that Melville's ship *Fidele* drifts in its unnavigated waters. And, just as the lonely, leaderless ship becomes the stage on which the confidence man plays his magnificent masquerade, so the "big store is a carefully set up and skillfully managed theater where the victim acts out an unwitting role in the most exciting of all underworld dramas."

The search for trust which accompanies the pursuit of gain in an unregulated economy takes on aspects of an urgent and sometimes realized psycho-biological regression to a more infantile stage of human development. Melville depicts this significant aspect of greed's effects by presenting an old miser, who, after the confidence man has artfully tricked him out of his gold, begins to behave like a child and finally cries out that he does have confidence in his victimizer. The theme is repeated when the confidence man, disguised as a Natural Bone-Setter, speaks of a "destitution, not of cash, but of confidence," and again when, as a herb doctor, he urges the passengers to "gladly seek the breast of that confidence begot in the tender time of your youth, blessed beyond telling if it returns to you in age." However, this return to infancy seems to be a reintrojection and return to the original source of greed, without being relieved of its basic drive. In the final chapter of Melville's enigmatic tale, an old man is approached by a youth who cons him into buying a lock, then a money belt resembling a truss, and, finally, as a gift the old man accepts a book to serve as a "counterfeit detector." Then the confidence man appears. When the old man asks him for a life preserver, he gives him a brown stool with a curved tin compartment underneath. The stool is a chamber pot within which the man can retain his feces, i.e., his life. The confidence man allows that he thinks it a very good life preserver, but that he himself never uses one. Man seems trapped and doomed in Melville's grotesque sociology of greed. He can either continue to sail on the ship of greedy but credulous fools, an unwitting party to a conniving masquerade controlled by cruel sharpsters, or he can return to the pseudo-innocence of childhood where unrequited anality will still haunt his existence.

CONCLUSION

Greed has been the bane and boon of mankind. As a sin it has been condemned by philosophers of both the Orient and the Occident. Lao-

Tzu believed that no greater disaster could overtake man than to sink into his desires, to become a slave to greed. Adam Smith asserted, "The great source of both the misery and disorders of human life seems to arise from overrating the difference between one permanent situation and another. Avarice overrates the difference between poverty and riches: ambition, that between a private and a public station: vainglory, that between obscurity and extensive reputation."[91] Poets and politicians have waxed eloquent on greed. When Kipling urged that every Englishman should "Take up the White Man's burden," the London wags replied "Pile on the Brown Man's burden/To satisfy your greed."[92] And when Abraham Lincoln wished to satirize the supporters of his corpulent opponent, Stephen A. Douglas, he pointed out, "They have seen in his round, jolly, fruitful face, post offices, land offices, marshal-ships, and cabinet appointments, charge-ships and foreign missions, bursting and sprouting out in wonderful exuberance, ready to be laid hold of by their greedy hands."[93] Political leaders have found it a potent theme upon which to enlarge and sermonize. A fine example is found in the speeches of America's only four-term president. Franklin D. Roosevelt opened his first term with the triumphant claim that "the moneychangers have fled from their high seats in the temple of our civilization."[94] Three years later he stated, "I should like to have it said of my first Administration that in it the forces of selfishness and of lust for power met their match. I should like to have it said of my second Administration that in it these forces met their master."[95] Less then three months later, at his second inaugural, Roosevelt added a utilitarian argument to the ethical one: "We have always known that heedless self-interest was bad morals; we know now that it is bad economics."[96] That greed had not been mastered was admitted in 1940: "It is an unfortunate human failing that a full pocketbook often groans more loudly than an empty stomach."[97] And fourteen months before his death President Roosevelt still said he believed he was battling the forces of greed. Vetoing a tax bill, he told the Congress, "It is not a tax bill but a tax relief bill providing relief not for the needy but for the greedy."[98] The evils of greed seemed to be not only a worthy but an insuperable opponent.

But greed is also a source of good. Sublimated as the ethical imperative to follow an earthly calling diligently and to live frugally and piously, it became the basis for modern capitalism and the central cultural impetus in the Occident. Moreover, believing that the Puritan model might be emulated with the same effect, planners, politicians, and political analysts have urged that the native races of Africa, Asia, Oceania, and Latin America be imbued with some functional equivalent of the Protestant Ethic so that they too can participate in the progress of civilization.[99] The anxieties, fears, crimes, and corruption spawned by the sin of greed still persist, perhaps as a price reluctantly paid by the melancholy servants of civilizational advance.

Society and Evil

Because of evil, history is a drama of conflict, not of gradual improvement.

*C. T. McIntire**

It is in the modern era that man seems to be overwhelmed by evil and yet obscured from sin. What is missing in the relation of evil to sin in the contemporary era is a tissue of guilt and responsibility that connects individuals and groups to institutions and corporate structures. At the level of the individual there is the predicament of the self—social but amorphous, surrounded but in a lonely crowd, singular but not secure. "The self," writes William Irwin Thompson, "is not defined in terms of eternity, God, or even, absolutely, in terms of itself." Rather, Thompson goes on, "the self is defined by others. Each man looks over his shoulder at other men to find out what he is himself." But this drama of interpersonal mirror imagery renders man all but immune from responsibility. Not responsible to himself, he is also irresponsible toward others, engaged in a never-ending display of antagonism, cooperation, and antagonistic cooperation. "He is not responsible to himself; therefore he cannot know guilt, expiation, or tragic illumination." The alienation of man from himself has resulted in his loss of a defensible sense of moral worth. In its place there gnaws the existential void, the nothingness that faces evil with neither comprehension nor feeling. We seek to find the guilt in the other, to excuse or justify our own behavior. And most often we are inert. Our moral accounting creates a new theater of absurdity. As Thompson observes, "There is no meaning in all this, of course: we observe a line of men, each pointing the guilty finger at the man next to him. Here there is a disappearance of meaning in which no central term can be found by which the self can be finally known."[1]

However, a self-pitying sense of alienation of the self does not reach to the core of the matter. Instead, as the late Ernest Becker once observed, "Man must confront the underlying alienation that exists in every age, and alienation exists *whenever the individual does not have a commanding view, a unitary critical perspective* by which to take in hand and react to the determinants of his social existence."[2] With Becker we confront the series of obstacles that holds us back from our discovery of evil, sin, and guilt. These include the inevitable inequities in *power* that prevail among men, the multiplicity of *visions* that compete for the position of commanding views, the plurality of *voices* giving explanations for the evils that do exist and remedies for their elimination. The drama of power over the human condition reveals in turn the power of dramas to intimidate, coerce, or confuse men's minds.

Ultimately our own drama of evil reality concludes on a pithy note that returns us to the beginning of the story of sin. The drama is in part a masquerade. Evil is hiding, and sin lurks behind a benign persona. True hell is not in the afterlife; rather, it is here in the darkness of our own uncritical ignorance. "True hell," as Nicola Chiaromonte once remarked, "is in the unnecessary, in all that hides us from ourselves, hiding from us the fact that we are living in a morally dead world." In this masquerade we enjoy or lust after luxury, money, sensuality, and ease, and hope to carry these off while maintaining permanent spiritual blindness. As Chiaromonte continues, this "possessiveness and greed are walled within the most deadly of the passions: inert self-satisfaction."[3] However, inert self-satisfaction can prevail as a habit of mind and conduct only so long as the world retains its capacity to reward our efforts or, at least, not undo them. The masquerade is between man and society—each plays the game of "as if" as long as it can. But things fall apart. The mutual suspension of disbelief cannot hold. Sooner or later, one confronts the other—naked and revealed. At the point of a crisis in the life-world the masks are lifted from men's eyes and—if only for a moment—the fragile structure of reality is revealed. And evil is then made visible.

Our analysis of evil—especially of the sin of greed, but implicit in our other discussions as well—has emphasized the powerful effects of crushing individuation and the transformations of corporate structures into soulless evildoers. As man's control over his own existence has diminished, some men have engineered the *exploitation of things* for evil purposes. Such exploitations date from the first sin. "Satan's single action—the exploitation of the serpent—is a model for what man does every day of his sinful life."[4] The corporate structure of shoddy production and unequal distribution, the coercive domination of man by the authoritarian state, the employment of armaments as an extension of the violence in the human soul are each examples. Man, or rather some men, make *things* and other men and women the vehicles of evil and thereby hope to remove themselves from sin. If the evil is discovered the things or other people are blamed, and the evildoer excuses himself and escapes guilt, penance, and expiation. God punished the serpent for beguiling Eve, but the devil went unscathed. Human devils are often as fortunate in their own exploits. Man emulates God in punishing the agency of evil, and at the same time he exculpates himself from responsibility for the acts of his zombielike creations.

Theologically sin refers to humanity's separation from the powers and protections of the gods. Sin from this point of view is the human condition, the condition of alienation from God. In his separation from the divine he feels uncertain of his being and unknowing of his future. The material and fleshly world obsesses him, but he gains no peace of mind thereby. It is life itself that becomes a problem, and not merely particular acts in that life. Sin thus creates a drama of lifelong anxiety, as lonely, oppressed, and weighted-down individuals act or are acted upon in a theater of increasing absurdity.

As the anxieties of life itself become too much to bear, individuals seek an escape from evil, a release from sin, virtually a departure from the human condition. In their heroic struggle to release themselves from the captivity of sinful life they exchange one *form* of life for another, each new *form* promising both liberation and security, the end of man's separation from himself, from God, from history. Harold Rosenberg is thus quite correct when he interprets Marx's theory of history as a great theatrical drama.[5] It is a play that unfolds in five mammoth, era-long acts—Asiatic, Ancient, Feudal, Bourgeois, and Socialist Production. In terms of Simmel's theory of the dialectics of *form* and *life*, each epoch is an act in the drama of mankind's release from the formal conditions of human enslavement and its ultimate emergence into an existence that is life itself, freed from all forms. But the forms are man's own contribution to life—he gives it structure, meaning, rules, and customs. Encased in his own creations, architectonic man cannot escape. He can only hope for release.

Ernest Becker saw a possibility for escape from evil: Guilt must somehow be sublimated. "The task of social theory is not to explain guilt away or absorb it unthinkingly in still another destructive ideology, but to neutralize it and give it expression in truly creating and life-enhancing ideologies." Becker believed that a new science of society—synthesizing ideas of Marx with those of Freud—might in its critical and tragic dimensions provide a moral equivalent of religion for the expiation of sin. "A science of society," he wrote, "will be a study similar to one envisaged by Old Testament prophets, Augustine, Kierkegaard, Max

Scheler, William Hocking: it will be a critique of idolatry, of the costs of a too narrow focus for the dramatization of man's need for power and expiation."[6]

A dramatistic comprehension of power and moral accountancy might go far to illuminate the social construction of virtuous and sinful realities. A central tenet of dramatism is that the style of something may count as much or more than the substance of it—indeed, may *be* the substance of it. The sins we have studied here are labeled such insofar as the dramatic presentations of actions performed on a life stage are identified as transgressions of moral law. A Florentine ideal of appearances rules our reason, even when we reject it as such. Both sin and virtue must be seen to be such, or else each goes unrecognized. A science of society that dramatizes the multifarious ways in which the social construction of reality is accomplished, performed, and perceived will also uncover the social architecture of evil.

As both a critique of idolatry and a recognition of the tragic dimension of humanity, a new science of society should avoid the pitfalls of excessive conservatism or utopian dogmatism. The former is skeptical about melioristic change and too concerned with the evils that arise from well-intentioned endeavors. The latter is too sure of its own perspective on history and events and too little concerned with measures that hasten an allegedly ineluctable march toward liberation. These concerns are not in fact proper concerns for sociology; rather they are the issues that arouse the interest and action of the social actors. It is in their taking risks with freedom and responsibility that social actors intentionally or inadvertently exhibit heroic, cowardly, insouciant, humble, aroused, or apathetic displays of human character. It is in the customs and mores, institutions and organizations, power and resistance that society fosters conservatism or emancipation. In the relationships of character and social structure are formed the scenarios, the props, the stages, and the backdrops for the dramas of good and evil and indifference that encompass life.

A science of society that takes sin and evil for its *topics* will avoid taking society's definitions of these twin demonic elements as its *resources*. The dramas of social reality are like Shakespeare's plays—they illustrate and are made up of alienation, absurdity, the struggle between Dionysian and Apollonian forces, the occurrence of too many anticlimaxes and events *in medias res*, the absence of beginnings or of teleological promise. The human actors in life's dramas sometimes include Hamlets, Macbeths, and Caesars but are more likely to be like Rosencrantz and Guildenstern, Osric and Falstaff, Horatio and Ophelia. Less than heroic in stature, they sometimes rise to an occasion, become victims of forces beyond their control, or dupes of malevolent powers. Most die less than honorably and can only hope that like Antony or Brutus, or Malcolm reporting on

Cawdor, they will be credited with being worthy. A new dramatistic science of society must be prepared for the vast range of characters that will populate its scenes.

However, the scenes of sin are now much different from those imagined by the early thinkers on the subject. Three moods or leitmotivs dominate the modern dramas of sin and evil—immensity, impersonality, and ambiguity.

The scale of evil committed in the world today seems to defy puny man's attempt to understand, much less to prevent it. The Holocaust of the European Jews from 1933 to 1945 provides the most terrifying example—an organization of planned and executed horror of a scope not hitherto imagined as part of the conscious intent of rational men. Indeed it is precisely the combination of scale and planning, the employment of reasoned unreason for the constructions of engines of death and—far worse—of social engines of death-in-life that make every comprehension, each study, and all literature on the subject inadequate to embrace it. Men escape from this evil by denying its reality altogether, repressing it from consciousness, relegating it to history, or accepting the opiate of forgetfulness as a release from responsibility. Yet that scale of planned human destruction may be surpassed by others now possible. Fission, thermonuclear, and neutron bombs promise to annihilate many millions—more than the six million Jews killed by the Nazis—and to do so in a manner that, if recent reports are to be believed, will protect property while destroying life. Thus do pride and avarice, envy and blood lust, anger and gluttony, and acedic despair join together to plan a conflagration of humanity. This latest conflagration promises to provide concrete ruins—historical mementos left for whatever beings who survive to find and marvel at.

The serpent was Satan's deputed servant. This otherwise silent and often unnoticed animal was made to speak, indeed to entice and cajole hapless Eve. Thus also modern sin. It speaks in monotones, impersonally, technically, without apparent feeling or moral recognition; yet it also activates man's evil orientations. Hannah Arendt captured the harbinger of this form of sinful expression in the idea of the *banality of evil*. In the character and conduct of Adolf Eichmann there is revealed the modern bureaucrat of mass murder. Characteristically he is distinguished by his indistinguishability—he might have been replaced by any number of fellow Germans who would have done the same things, carried out the same directives, engineered the same efficient dispatch of millions to their deaths. "The trouble with Eichmann," as Hannah Arendt points out, "was precisely that so many were like him, and that the many were neither perverted nor sadistic, that they were, and still are, terribly and terrifyingly normal."[7] It is the normalcy of this new type of criminal, his willingness to become part of a bureaucracy of execution, that makes both the crime and the criminal so terrifying, so hard to bear, and in the end so easy to accept. The modern agent of societal evil is able to commit his crimes without knowing or feeling that he is doing wrong. The techniques of neutralization by which a criminal excuses or justifies his acts are, so to speak, preempted in advance by the agencies for which he works, rendered obsolete by the separation of technologies from purposes and purposes from ethics. The older idea of sin and the modern idea of crime make much of the significance of intent, premeditation, and passion. However, intent and premeditation are divisible into their moral and technical parts, and passion is removable altogether. Modern dramas of evil occur on stages where the originating actions are all too routine.

The meaning of action grows increasingly hard to comprehend. Social science has long since banished moral judgments from its pronouncements, preferring to hide its feelings behind pious phrases extolling objectivity, painstaking techniques of measurement, and public disavowals of any but scientific interest. Ordinary folks are not in a similarly privileged situation. They must find or make meaning—moral as well as existential—in the events and happenings of their lives.

The world is God's great achievement, writes Leszek Kolakowski, a leading Marxist humanist. Created, so Kolakowski argues, for the relief of God's loneliness and to satisfy his craving for glory, it is, nevertheless, "chaotic, without a guiding principle and indisputably . . . tawdry, botched, and tasteless . . ." It is "also a fact that the world is improvable in certain respects, which is the most important point in the matter of judging it."[8] For these improvements, then, an interpretive principle, a guiding set of understandings, is required. So also is leadership. For the moment social science has abandoned a once-promising lead in the development and exhortation of such understandings and principles. Like Martin Buber's conception of God's recent orientation toward the world, the social sciences have turned their backs on man's problematic struggle for moral comprehension and societal guidance. Perhaps, like God, or like Grant at Galena, the social sciences are biding their time, waiting for situations to ripen or man to mature sufficiently to be worthy of scientific endeavor. Pride, here, goes before the incomprehensibility of the world, leaving it in a strange kind of enlightened darkness.

But an absurd world waits for no one in its struggle for self-understanding. The abdication of the social sciences—or, more commonly, the prostitutive sale of them to the state or to sundry social movements and sanguinary ideologies of redemption—have left the field of principle and action to social philosophers, moral leaders, and practical politicians. The first named are closest to the social sciences and draw upon them for inspiration. Thus, as an example, we may contrast two such approaches that arise out of the seemingly ever-fertile thought of Karl Marx. To Kolakowski improvements in the world are "tiny changes for the better [that] can be made in it by the utmost endeavors of myriad masses of people." To this somewhat forlorn optimist, "History furnishes particular proofs in support of this view."[9] More aggressive and less optimistic is the view of Jean-Paul Sartre.[10] Sure that there is a "coming revolution," Sartre is equally confident that it will be different from all previous ones and that it "will last much longer and will be much harsher, much more profound." The French philosopher believes "that at least fifty years of struggle will be necessary for the partial victory of the people's power over bourgeois power." After many advances and retreats the revolution "will bring into existence a new society in which all the powers have been done away with because each individual has full possession of himself." For Sartre the nemesis of human liberation is power: "Revolution is not a single moment in which one power overthrows another; it is a long movement in which power is dismantled." With neither a guaranty of success nor a surety of failure, Sartre urges this revolution because "the alternatives really are socialism or barbarism."

However, Sartre's ominous forebodings are quite mistaken. The alternatives are not so simply dichotomized. Much of life proceeds and will continue to proceed along the vast stretches of social space between the Sartrean poles of socialism and barbarism. Dramas of good and evil play themselves out between, before, and beyond revolution. Corrupt men and corrupt institutions will perform against scenes of benign moral neglect, crusading virtuous exposure, and cruel or condign punishments. Rather than a promise of apocalyptic redemption, the world holds out scenarios of infinite existential variety.

To recognize this immense dramaturgical lifescape requires abandonment of social science's preeminent pride and privileged status. All too often both social science and moral philosophy have imagined a bolder prouder vision—one that is described by Kolakowski's devil:

> No devilishness at all—nothing; to be—what a bold idea!—purged of sin in order to sail straight to Heaven, to sit on the right of the Heavenly Father, to enjoy the delight of external rest at the foot of the Lord's throne, to have an invitation to eternal joy . . .[11]

The earthly utopias of contemporary revolutionaries are secular versions of the older sacred visions. A world devoid of power, of roles, of division of labor, of envy and iniquity—a world, in short, where *form* itself has been overthrown and where *life*, free, pulsating, unbounded, and irrepressible flourishes in everlasting triumph. But, as Kolakowski's devil reminds us, "this would be a terrible sin, the greatest sin on earth, the sin of shameless pride . . ." Better to take Satan as one's companion than blaspheme God in such a way. Take up Satan! As Kolakowski tells us, "if with humility you deepen your sinfulness by adding one more sin to another daily, hourly, minute by minute, if you combine evil with greater evil, then . . . you will be rewarded according to the measure of your sins." If we are to avoid the sin of pride and the train of terrible evils that flow from it, we have to settle for less than utopian redemption. Indeed, perhaps for no redemption at all. A world of endless drama—and also of dramas that begin but do not end, that start in the middle, that stop without resolution; that may or may not have scenarios and pre-texts; that have actors with and without talent; that audiences see or do not see, understand or do not understand; that are criticized, attacked, applauded, or ignored—that is, in short, essentially absurd and existentially meaningful. As the devil concludes, "we are brothers here, bound together by a common fate for centuries. World without end. Amen."

Notes

SIN AND SOCIOLOGY

*Reinhold Niebuhr, "The Foolishness of the Cross and the Sense of History," in *God, History, and Historians*, ed. C. T. McIntire (New York: Oxford University Press, 1977), p. 70.

**Kenneth Scott Latourette, "The Christian Understanding of History," in ibid., p. 66.

1 See Lucy S. Dawidowicz, *The War Against the Jews, 1933-1945* (New York: Holt, Rinehart, and Winston, 1975).

2 An important exception is Edward Alsworth Ross, *Sin and Society: An Analysis of Latter Day Iniquity* (New York: Harper Torchbooks, 1973; orig. pub. 1907).

3 See Karl Menninger, *Whatever Became of Sin?* (New York: Hawthorn, 1973).

4 This was one of the main arguments made by Ross in his all too neglected work. See Ross, *Sin and Society*, pp. 1-42, 105-131.

SLOTH

*Jacques Choron, *Death and Western Thought* (New York: Collier, 1963), p. 260.

**The Journal of Andrew Bihaly*, ed. Anthony Tuttle (New York: Thomas Y. Crowell Co., 1973), p. 33.

1 Morton Bloomfield, *The Seven Deadly Sins: An Introduction to the History of a Religious Concept, with Special Reference to Medieval English Literature* (East Lansing: Michigan State University Press, 1967), pp. 57-60.

2 Ibid., pp. 72-74, 356-357.

3 Gregory the Great, *Morals on the Book of Job* (Oxford: J. H. Parker; London: F. and J. Rivington, 1845), III, 490.

4 Bloomfield, *Seven Deadly Sins*, pp. 74, 106, 80-81, 362, 96, 172. See also Siegfried Wenzel, *The Sin of Sloth: Acedia in Medieval Thought and Literature* (Chapel Hill: University of North Carolina Press, 1960).

5 See Aldous Huxley, "Accidie," *On the Margin: Notes and Essays* (New York: Harper and Brothers, 1951; reprinted in *Mass Leisure*, ed. Eric Larrabee and Rolf Meyersohn (Glencoe: Free Press, 1958), pp. 15-18. See also Mark D. Altschule, "Acedia: Its Evolution from Deadly Sin to Psychiatric Syndrome," *British Journal of Psychiatry*, 3 (February 1965), 117-119.

6 For a literary survey see Reinhard Kuhn, *The Demon of Noontide: Ennui in Western Literature* (Princeton: Princeton University Press, 1976).

7 Gregory the Great, *Morals*, p. 490.

[8] Geoffrey Chaucer, "The Parson's Tale," in *Canterbury Tales*, trans. Frank Ernest Hill (New York: McKay, 1964), pp. 549–553. See also Bloomfield, *Seven Deadly Sins*, p. 146 and Huxley, "Accidie," p. 16.

[9] Bloomfield, *Seven Deadly Sins*, pp. 181, 176.

[10] Ibid., pp. 176–177.

[11] Chaucer, "Parson's Tale," p. 551. See also Bloomfield, *Seven Deadly Sins*, p. 199. Although a full analysis of the relation of sleep to sloth will not be attempted here, some observations are in order. Sleep lies somewhere in the mysterious limbo connecting life to death. Its quite unawake form seems close to death, while its dreams are clues to life's secrets. Periodic sleep seems necessary for wide-awake energetic activity, but the amount, rates, and tempo of sleep vary by culture, class, and constitutional state. A sociology of sleep has not yet been written but helpful and sensitive guides will be found in Vilhelm Aubert and Harrison White, "Sleep: a Sociological Interpretation," reprinted in Vilhelm Aubert, *The Hidden Society* (Totowa, N.J.: Bedminster Press, 1965), pp. 168–200; and Barry Schwartz, "Notes on the Sociology of Sleep," in *People in Places: The Sociology of the Familiar*, ed. Arnold Birenbaum and Edward Sagarin (New York: Praeger, 1973), pp. 18–34.

[12] *The Pilgrimage of the Life of Man*, trans. John Lydgate (1426), ed. F. J. Furnivall and K. B. Locock (London, 1899–1904); cited in Bloomfield, *Seven Deadly Sins*, pp. 269 et passim.

[13] Bloomfield, *Seven Deadly Sins*, pp. 229–232, 222–223.

[14] See Franz R. Goetzl, "Root of Discontent and Aggression," in the volume he edited, *Boredom: Root of Discontent and Aggression* (Berkeley: Grizzly Peak Press, 1975), pp. 55–109.

[15] Bloomfield, *Seven Deadly Sins*, pp. 131, 142, 214, 117, 155.

[16] The following is based on two works by Gershom S. Scholem, *Sabbatai Sevi: The Mystical Messiah, 1626–1676*, trans. R. J. Zwi Werblowsky (Princeton: Princeton University Press, 1973), pp. 299–308; and *Kabbalah* (New York: Quadrangle, 1974), pp. 125–127 et passim.

[17] Scholem, *Kabbalah*, p. 126.

[18] Chaucer, "Parson's Tale," p. 553.

[19] See Mircea Eliade, *The Myth of the Eternal Return*, trans. Willard R. Trask (New York: Pantheon, 1965).

[20] Karl Abraham, "Notes on the Psycho-Analytical Investigation and Treatment of Manic-Depressive Insanity and Allied Conditions," in *The Meaning of Despair: Psychoanalytic Contributions to the Understanding of Depression*, ed. Willard Gaylin (New York: Science House, 1968), pp. 26–49.

[21] Sigmund Freud, "Mourning and Melancholia," *Collected Papers*, trans. under the supervision of Joan Riviere (New York: Basic Books, 1959), IV, pp. 152–170.

[22] Sandor Rado, "The Problem of Melancholia," *International Journal of Psycho-Analysis*, 9 (1928), 420–438; reprinted in Gaylin, *Meaning of Despair*, pp. 70–95.

[23] Cf. the comment by Gregory the Great, *Morals*, p. 491; "Melancholy also arises from anger, because the more extravagantly the agitated mind strikes itself, the more it confounds itself by condemnation; and when it has lost the sweetness of tranquillity, nothing supports it but the grief resulting from agitation. Melancholy also runs down into avarice; because when the disturbed heart has lost the satisfaction of joy within, it seeks for sources of consolation without, and is more anxious to possess external goods, the more it has no joy on which to fall back within."

[24] Perhaps the most profound discussion of despair will be found in Sören Kierkegaard,

Fear and Trembling and the Sickness unto Death, trans. Walter Lowrie (Princeton: Princeton University Press, 1968), pp. 141-262.

25 Franz Alexander, "Buddhistic Training as an Artificial Catatonia: The Biological Meaning of Psychic Occurrences," in *The Scope of Psychoanalysis: Selected Papers of Franz Alexander, 1921-1961* (New York: Basic Books, 1961), pp. 74-89. For analyses less harsh than Alexander's, see Karlfried Graf von Durckheim, *The Japanese Cult of Tranquillity* (New York: Samuel Weiser, 1974); and two works by Eugen Herrigel, *Zen in the Art of Archery*, trans. R. F. C. Hull (New York: Vintage, 1971); and *The Method of Zen*, ed. Herman Tausend, trans. R. F. C. Hull (New York: Vintage, 1974).

26 Alexander, "Buddhistic Training," p. 89.

27 Cf. Willard Gaylin, "The Meaning of Despair," in Gaylin, *The Meaning of Despair*, pp. 3-25.

28 See particularly Ernest Jones, *Hamlet and Oedipus* (Garden City: Doubleday Anchor, 1954, orig. pub. 1949, pp. 51-80.

29 Consider the remark of Gregory the Great, *Morals*, p. 491: "Melancholy is also wont to exhort the conquered heart as if with reason, when it says, What ground hast thou to rejoice, when thou endurest so many wrongs from thy neighbors? Consider with what sorrows all must be looked on, who are turned in such gall of bitterness against thee."

30 See Andrew L. Bowman, "Poor, Nasty, Brutish, and Short—But Seldom Boring," in Goetzl, *Boredom*, pp. 11-33.

31 See W. K. C. Guthrie, *The Greeks and Their Gods* (Boston: Beacon Press, 1955); and E. R. Dodds, *The Greeks and the Irrational* (Berkeley: University of California Press, 1951).

32 Albert G. Keller, "The Study of Homeric Religion," *American Journal of Sociology*, 15 (March 1910), 641-656; quotation from p. 652.

33 The following draws on Bowman, "Poor, Nasty, Brutish, and Short. . . ," pp. 13-15.

34 Gregory the Great, *Morals*, p. 490.

35 M. I. Finley, *The World of Odysseus* (New York: Viking, 1965), pp. 53-55.

36 Bowman, "Poor, Nasty, Brutish, and Short. . . ," p. 15.

37 Finley, *World of Odysseus*, pp. 66-70.

38 Homer, *The Odyssey*, trans. E. V. Rieu (Harmondsworth: Penguin, 1971), Book VIII, p. 126.

39 Finley, *World of Odysseus*, p. 70.

40 See W. B. Stanford, "Ulysses in the Early Epic Tradition—From his Birth to the Fall of Troy," in *The Quest for Ulysses*, ed. W. B. Stanford and J. V. Luce (New York: Praeger, 1974), pp. 11-34.

41 See W. B. Stanford, "Ulysses in Later Greek Literature and Art," in ibid., p. 144.

42 Homer, *Odyssey* (Book IX), p. 149.

43 Ibid., p. 153.

44 Bowman, "Poor, Nasty. . . ," p. 16.

45 Georg Simmel, "The Metropolis and Mental Life," in *The Sociology of Georg Simmel*, ed. Kurt Wolff (Glencoe: The Free Press, 1950), pp. 409-424, esp. pp. 414, 415.

46 Ibid., p. 422.

47 Robert E. Park, "Community Organization and the Romantic Temper," in *The City*, ed. Robert E. Park, Ernest W. Burgess, and Roderick D. McKenzie (Chicago: University of Chicago Press, 1925, 1967), pp. 113-122, esp. p. 117.

48 See two essays by Park, "Community Organization and Juvenile Delinquency" and "Magic, Mentality and City Life," *The City*, pp. 99-112 and 123-141.

49 Park, "Community Organization and the Romantic Temper," p. 118.

[50] Goetzl, *Boredom*, pp. 55–109; quotations from pp. 90 and 92.

[51] Kenneth Burke, "On Stress, Its Seeking," in *Why Men Take Chances: Studies in Stress-Seeking*, ed. Samuel Z. Klausner (Garden City: Doubleday Anchor, 1968), pp. 75–103.

[52] Kenneth Burke, "White Oxen," in *The Complete White Oxen: Collected Short Fiction of Kenneth Burke* (Berkeley: University of California Press, 1968), pp. 9, 41.

[53] Adam Smith, *The Theory of Moral Sentiments* (New Rochelle, N.Y.: Arlington House, 1969; orig. pub. 1759), pp. 427–428.

[54] Kenneth Burke, *Permanence and Change: An Anatomy of Purpose* (Indianapolis: Bobbs-Merrill, 1965), pp. 197–198, 198n.

[55] See George Rosen, *Madness in Society: Chapters in the Historical Sociology of Mental Illness* (New York: Harper Torchbooks, 1969), pp. 73–74; and Judith S. Neaman, *Suggestion of the Devil: The Origins of Madness* (Garden City: Doubleday Anchor, 1975), pp. 7–8.

[56] Rosen, *Madness*, pp. 96–97, 237–238.

[57] Robert Burton, *The Anatomy of Melancholy*, ed. Holbrook Jackson (New York: Vintage, 1977; orig. pub. 1621), p. 200.

[58] J. Huizinga, *The Waning of the Middle Ages* (Garden City: Doubleday Anchor, 1954), pp. 31–56.

[59] Goetzl, *Boredom*, p. 60.

[60] Bloomfield, *Seven Deadly Sins*, p. 96.

[61] For the desert fathers see Jean Decarreaux, *Monks and Civilization: From the Barbarian Invasions to the Reign of Charlemagne*, trans. Charlotte Haldane (London: Allen and Unwin, 1964), pp. 70–116. For the role of the *daemon meridianus* see Kuhn, *Demon of Noontide*, pp. 39–100; Goetzl, *Boredom*, pp. 60–61; Bloomfield, *Seven Deadly Sins*, p. 28.

[62] Bloomfield, *Seven Deadly Sins*, pp. 96, 147–148, 440.

[63] Max Weber, *The Protestant Ethic and the Spirit of Capitalism*, trans. Talcott Parsons (London: G. Allen, 1930), pp. 156–164 (quotations from pp. 157, 158, 161).

[64] Ibid., p. 181.

[65] Huxley, "Accidie," p. 17.

[66] John G. Cawelti, *Apostles of the Self-Made Man in America* (Chicago: University of Chicago Press, 1965).

[67] See Max Weber, "The Protestant Sects and the Spirit of Capitalism," in *From Max Weber: Essays in Sociology*, trans. and ed. Hans H. Gerth and C. Wright Mills (New York: Oxford University Press, 1946), pp. 302–322; and David Brion Davis, "Stress-Seeking and the Self-Made Man in American Literature, 1894–1914," in Klausner, *Why Men Take Chances*, pp. 104–131.

[68] See Raymond Williams, *Keywords: A Vocabulary of Culture and Society* (New York: Oxford University Press, 1976), pp. 94–95.

[69] See two works by Raymond Williams, *Drama in a Dramatised Society* (Cambridge: Cambridge University Press, 1975); and *Drama in Performance* (Harmondsworth: Penguin, 1972), pp. 170–188.

[70] A growing sociological literature on life as theater is now available. Among the more important recent works are Sheldon E. Messinger, Harold Sampson, and Robert D. Towne, "Life as Theater: Some Notes on the Dramaturgic Approach to Social Reality," *Sociometry*, 25 (September 1962), 98–110; Richard Schechner, *Public Domain: Essays on the Theatre* (New York: Avon-Discus, 1969); Elizabeth Burns, *Theatricality: A Study of Convention in the Theater and in Social Life* (London: Longmans, 1972); Dennis Brissett and Charles Edgley, eds., *Life as Theater: A Dramaturgical Sourcebook* (Chicago: Aldine, 1975); James E. Combs and Michael W. Mansfield, eds., *Drama in Life: The Uses*

of Communication in Society (New York: Hastings House, 1976); Richard Schechner and Mady Schuman, eds., *Ritual, Play, and Performance: Readings in the Social Sciences/Theatre* (New York: Seabury, 1976). On the performance element in everyday life, see Stanford M. Lyman and Marvin B. Scott, *The Drama of Social Reality* (New York: Oxford University Press, 1975), pp. 101-114.

71 I first developed the idea of the drama in the routine in my essay entitled, "Cherished Values and Civil Rights," *The Crisis: A Record of the Darker Races*, 71 (December 1964), 645-654, 695.

72 Kuhn, *Demon of Noontide*, pp. 43-49; Bloomfield, *Seven Deadly Sins*, p. 28.

73 George Brown Tindall writes: "The lazy South cultivated the art of relaxation long before the greening of America and the fashion of 'overhauls' long before the jeaning of America." *The Ethnic Southerners* (Baton Rouge: Louisiana State University Press, 1976), p. 10. For a complete analysis see David Bertelson, *The Lazy South* (New York: Oxford University Press, 1967).

74 See Paul Ricoeur, "The Model of the Text: Meaningful Action Considered as a Text," *Social Research*, 38 (Autumn 1971), 529-562; and Schechner, *Public Domain*, pp. 84-105, 189-191.

75 For some sensitive observations on the subject see Everett C. Hughes, "The Social Drama of Work," *Mid-American Review of Sociology*, 1 (Spring 1976), 1-7.

76 Weber, *Protestant Ethic*, p. 181.

77 Clark Kerr, "Plant Sociology: The Elite and the Aborigines," in his *Labor and Management in Industrial Society* (Garden City: Doubleday Anchor, 1964), pp. 43-82. See also Elton Mayo, *The Human Problems of an Industrial Civilization* (New York: Viking, 1960; orig. pub. 1933), pp. 30-32; J. A. C. Brown, *The Social Psychology of Industry* (Harmondsworth: Penguin, 1954), pp. 206-209.

78 See Robert Blauner, *Alienation and Freedom: The Factory Worker and His Industry* (Chicago: University of Chicago Press, 1964), pp. 28, 82-83, 116-118, 132-142, 155-158.

79 Free [pseudonym for Abbie Hoffman], *Revolution for the Hell of It* (New York: Dial Press, 1968).

80 Daniel Cohn-Bendit and Gabriel Cohn-Bendit, *Obsolete Communism: The Left-Wing Alternative*, trans. Arnold Pomerans (New York: McGraw-Hill, 1968), pp. 34-40.

81 F. J. Roethlisberger and William J. Dickson, *Management and the Worker* (Cambridge, Mass.: Harvard University Press, 1966), pp. 409-447.

82 Sir Geoffrey Vickers, *Towards a Sociology of Management* (New York: Basic Books, 1967), p. 123.

83 Roethlisberger and Dixon, *Management and Worker*, pp. 420-423.

84 Ibid., pp. 421-422.

85 See Edward George Hartmann, *The Movement to Americanize the Immigrant* (New York: AMS Press, 1967; orig. pub. 1948); Colin Greer, *The Great School Legend: A Revisionist Interpretation of American Public Education* (New York: Basic Books, 1972). For regional studies in eastern and western America see Diane Ravitch, *The Great School Wars, New York City, 1805-1973: A History of the Public Schools as Battlefield of Social Change* (New York: Basic Books, 1974); and William Warren Ferrier, *Ninety Years of Education in California, 1846-1936: A Presentation of Educational Movements and Their Outcome in Education Today* (Berkeley: Sather Gate Book Shop, 1937). For the special situation affecting American Indians see Francis Paul Prucha, ed., *Americanizing the American Indians: Writings by the 'Friends of the Indian,' 1880-1900* (Cambridge, Mass.: Harvard University Press, 1973).

[86] See Willard Waller, *The Sociology of Teaching* (New York: Wiley, 1965; orig. pub. 1932), pp. 441–447.

[87] The following draws on Bowman, "Poor, Nasty," pp. 17–22.

[88] See Richard Dehlinger, "The Yawning Student," in Goetzl, *Boredom*, pp. 44–54.

[89] See John A. Hostetler, *Amish Society*, rev. ed. (Baltimore: Johns Hopkins University Press, 1968), pp. 193–208; John W. Bennett, *Hutterian Brethren: The Agricultural Economy and Social Organization of a Communal People* (Stanford: Stanford University Press, 1967), pp. 101–102, 118, 128, 192, 219, 247, 253, 277; Harry Leonard Sowatzky, *They Sought a Country: Mennonite Colonization in Mexico* (Berkeley: University of California Press, 1971), pp. 305–321; Harry B. Hawthorn, ed., *The Doukhobors of British Columbia* (Vancouver: University of British Columbia, 1955), pp. 19–20, 118–120, 141–144, 184–186, 218; George Woodcock and Ivan Avakumovic, *The Doukhobors* (London: Faber and Faber, 1968), pp. 208–224.

[90] Cf. David Matza, *Delinquency and Drift* (New York: Wiley, 1964), pp. 88–90, 188–191.

[91] Waller, *Sociology of Teaching*, p. 182.

[92] See David McLellan, *The Thought of Karl Marx* (New York: Harper & Row, 1971), pp. 76–79.

[93] Karl Marx and Friedrich Engels, "Manifesto of the Communist Party," in *Marx and Engels: Basic Writings on Politics and Philosophy*, ed. Lewis S. Feuer (Garden City: Doubleday Anchor, 1959), p. 23.

[94] Karl Marx, *Grundrisse: Foundations of the Critique of Political Economy (Rough Draft)*, trans. Martin Nicolaus (Harmondsworth: Penguin, 1973; orig. pub. 1939), p. 611, renders this sentence poorly. I have used the translation in *The Grundrisse*, ed. and trans. David McLellan (New York: Harper & Row, 1971), p. 124.

[95] Karl Marx and Friedrich Engels, "The German Ideology," in *Writings of the Young Marx on Philosophy and Society*, trans. and ed. Loyd D. Easton and Kurt H. Guddat (Garden City: Doubleday, 1967), pp. 424–425.

[96] The following is taken from Nicolaus' trans. of *Grundrisse*, p. 111.

[97] Paul La Fargue, *The Right to Be Lazy, Being a Refutation of the 'Right to Work' of 1848*, trans. Charles H. Kerr (Chicago: Charles H. Kerr, 1883). An excerpt from this work entitled "The Right to be Lazy" may be found in Larrabee and Meyersohn, *Mass Leisure*, pp. 105–118.

[98] See Joffre Dumazedier, *Sociology of Leisure*, trans. Marea A. McKenzie (Amsterdam: Elsevier, 1974), pp. 10, 59, 107.

[99] Sebastian de Grazia, *Of Time, Work, and Leisure* (Garden City: Doubleday Anchor, 1964), pp. 181–206.

[100] The following is based on ibid., pp. 189–195, and on the essays in Frederick A. Hayek, ed., *Capitalism and the Historians* (Chicago: University of Chicago Press, Phoenix Books, 1963).

[101] Hannah Arendt, *The Human Condition* (Garden City: Doubleday Anchor, 1959), p. 47.

[102] Fernando Diaz-Plaja, *The Frenchman and the Seven Deadly Sins*, trans. Ernst Schrader (New York: Scribner, 1972), pp. 147–148.

[103] Arendt, *Human Conditions*, pp. 47–48.

[104] Ibid., p. 115.

[105] Paul Weiss, "A Philosophical Definition of Leisure," in *Leisure in America: Blessing or Curse?* ed. James C. Charlesworth (Philadelphia: American Academy of Political and Social Science, 1964), p. 29.

[106] Marion Clawson, "How Much Leisure, Now and in the Future?" in ibid., pp. 1–2.

107 Robert M. MacIver, "The Great Emptiness," in Larrabee and Meyersohn, *Mass Leisure*, pp. 118–122.

108 Paul La Fargue, "The Right to Be Lazy," in ibid., pp. 109, 113–115. For some sensitive perceptions on the subject see John W. Loy, "The Nature of Sport: A Definitional Effort," in *Sport, Culture and Society*, ed. John W. Loy and Gerald S. Kenyon (New York: Macmillan, 1969), pp. 56–71. See also Benjamin R. Barber, *Superman and Common Man: Freedom, Anarchy and the Revolution* (New York: Praeger, 1971), pp. 37–80.

109 See Jessie Bernard, "The Eudaemonists," in Klausner, *Why Men Take Chances*, pp. 6–47.

110 Bruno Bettelheim, *The Uses of Enchantment: The Meaning and Importance of Fairy Tales* (New York: Knopf, 1976), pp. 41–45; quotations from pp. 44, 45.

111 Park, "Community Organization and Juvenile Delinquency," p. 109.

112 See Charles Loring Brace, *The Dangerous Classes of New York and Twenty Years Work Among Them* (New York: Synkoop and Hallenbeck, 1880; Montclair, N.J.: Patterson Smith, 1967); and Louis Chevalier, *Labouring Classes and Dangerous Classes in Paris During the First Half of the Nineteenth Century*, trans. Frank Jellinek (London: Routledge and Kegan Paul, 1973).

113 David Matza, "The Disreputable Poor," in *Class, Status, and Power: Social Stratification in Comparative Perspective*, 2nd ed., ed. Reinhard Bendix and Seymour Martin Lipset (New York: The Free Press, 1966), p. 289.

114 Diaz-Plaja, "Frenchman," p. 150.

115 Matza, "The Disreputable Poor," pp. 292–296.

116 See Charles Booth, "A Picture of Pauperism," in *Charles Booth on the City*, ed. Harold W. Pfautz (Chicago: University of Chicago Press, 1967), pp. 243–249.

117 See Brian V. Street, *The Savage in Literature* (London: Routledge and Kegan Paul, 1975).

118 See Stanley Elkins, *Slavery: A Problem in American Institutional and Intellectual Life*, 3rd ed., rev. (Chicago: University of Chicago Press, 1976), pp. 81–139, 147–163, 206–302; J. L. Gillin, "Vagrancy and Begging," *American Journal of Sociology*, 25 (November 1929), 424–432; Albert Perry, *Garrets and Pretenders*, rev. ed. (New York: Dover, 1960; orig. pub. 1933), and Cesar Grana, *Bohemian Versus Bourgeois: French Society and the French Man of Letters in the Nineteenth Century* (New York: Basic Books, 1964), pp. 157–212; Jan Yoors, *The Gypsies* (New York: Simon and Schuster, 1967); Donald Kenrick and Grattan Puxon, *The Destiny of Europe's Gypsies* (New York: Basic Books, 1972); Werner Cohn, *The Gypsies* (Reading, Mass.: Addison-Wesley, 1973); E. B. Trigg, *Gypsy Demons and Divinities: The Magical and Supernatural Practices of the Gypsies* (London: Sheldon Press, 1975); Thomas Acton, *Gypsy Politics and Social Change: The Development of Ethnic Ideology and Pressure Politics Among British Gypsies from Victorian Reformism to Romany Nationalism* (London: Routledge and Kegan Paul, 1974); Fred Davis, "Why All of Us May Be Hippies Someday," and Bennett Berger, "Hippie Morality—More Old than New," both in *Trans-Action*, 5 (December 1967), 10–18, 19–27.

119 See Stanford M. Lyman and Marvin B. Scott, *A Sociology of the Absurd* (New York: Appleton-Century-Crofts, 1970; Pacific Palisades: Goodyear, 1970), pp. 205–206.

120 See Noah Webster's well-argued opposition to this stereotype reprinted in Louis Ruchames, *Racial Thought in America* (Amherst: University of Massachusetts Press, 1969), pp. 228–234.

121 Oscar Wilde, certainly one who was sensitive to the issues involved in *acedia*, described the Chinese he saw in San Francisco in 1882 as "strangely melancholy Orientals," insistent on "having nothing about them that is not beautiful." H. Montgomery Hyde, *Oscar Wilde: A Biography* (New York: Farrar, Straus, & Giroux, 1975), p. 67.

[122] For a discussion and refutation of this stereotype see Stanford M. Lyman, *Chinese Americans* (New York: Random House, 1974), pp. 54-118.

[123] For a general picture see D. G. Cochrane, "Racialism in the Pacific: A Descriptive Analysis," *Oceania*, 40 (September 1969), 1-12.

[124] See Douglas Oliver, *The Pacific Islanders*, rev. ed. (Garden City: Doubleday Anchor, 1961), pp. 3-173; Cyril S. Belshaw, *Changing Melanesia: Social Economics of Culture Contact* (Melbourne: Oxford University Press, 1954), pp. 90-97; Andrew W. Lind, *An Island Community: Ecological Succession in Hawaii* (New York: Greenwood Press, 1968; orig. pub. 1938), pp. 90-97.

[125] The definitive work on the subject is W. H. R. Rivers, "The Psychological Factor," in his *Essays on the Depopulation of Melanesia* (Cambridge: Cambridge University Press, 1922), pp. 84-113; reprinted in *Frontiers of Anthropology*, ed. Ashley Montagu (New York: Putnam, 1974), pp. 391-409.

[126] Hawaii provides a strategic research site for studying these phenomena. For the definitive history see Ralph S. Kuykendall, *The Hawaiian Kingdom, 1778-1893*, 3 vols. (Honolulu: University of Hawaii Press, 1953, 1957, 1967).

[127] A. Grenfell Price, *The Western Invasions of the Pacific and its Continents* (Oxford: Clarendon Press, 1963), pp. 143-175.

[128] See Bruno Lasker, *Human Bondage in Southeast Asia* (Chapel Hill: University of North Carolina Press, 1950).

[129] See, e.g., Andrew W. Lind, *Hawaii: The Last of the Magic Isles* (London: Oxford University Press, 1969).

[130] Samuel Taylor Coleridge, "Hamlet, 1813," *Selected Poetry and Prose of Coleridge*, ed. Donald A. Stauffer (New York: Modern Library, 1951), pp. 452-453.

[131] Sigmund Freud, *The Interpretation of Dreams*, ed. and trans. James Strachey (New York: Discus-Avon, 1965), pp. 298-300.

[132] On political forms of affectlessness, see David Riesman and Nathan Glazer, "Criteria for Political Apathy," in *Studies in Leadership: Leadership and Democratic Action*, ed. A. W. Gouldner (New York: Russell and Russell, 1965), pp. 505-559. For sociological studies of affectlessness and alienation, see Georg Simmel, "The Stranger," in *The Sociology of Georg Simmel*, pp. 402-408; Alfred Schutz, "The Stranger: An Essay in Social Psychology," *Collected Papers II: Studies in Social Theory*, ed. Arvid Brodersen (The Hague: Martinus Nijhoff, 1964), pp. 91-105; Margaret Mary Wood, *The Stranger: A Study in Social Relationships* (New York: AMS Press, 1969; orig. pub. 1934); Everett V. Stonequist, *The Marginal Man: A Study in Personality and Culture Conflict* (New York: Russell and Russell, 1961; orig. pub. 1937); Howard M. Bahr, ed., *Disaffiliated Man: Essays and Bibliography on Skid Row, Vagrancy, and Outsiders* (Toronto: University of Toronto Press, 1970); Bahr, *Skid Row: An Introduction to Disaffiliation* (New York: Oxford University Press, 1973). See also Margaret Mary Wood, *Paths of Loneliness: The Individual Isolated in Modern Society* (New York: Columbia University Press, 1960); Clark E. Moustakas, *Loneliness* (Englewood Cliffs, N.J.: Prentice-Hall Spectrum, 1961; Moustakas, *Loneliness and Love* (Englewood Cliffs, N.J.: Prentice-Hall, Spectrum Books, 1972); Robert S. Weiss, *Loneliness: The Experience of Emotional and Social Isolation* (Cambridge, Mass.: MIT Press, 1973); David Riesman, Nathan Glazer, and Reuel Denney, *The Lonely Crowd: A Study of the Changing American Character*, abridged ed. (Garden City: Doubleday Anchor, 1953); and Jose Ortega y Gasset, *The Revolt of the Masses* (London: T. Fisher Unwin, 1961; orig. pub. 1930).

[133] Albert Camus, *The Stranger*, trans. Stuart Gilbert (New York: Vintage, 1946).

[134] See Nathan Leites, "Trends in Affectlessness," in *Personality in Nature, Society, and Culture,* 2nd ed., rev. and enl., ed. Clyde Kluckhohn and Henry A. Murray with the collaboration of David M. Schneider (New York: Knopf, 1961), pp. 618-632.

[135] The life and politics of Sergei Nechayev as well as a translation of the "Catechism of the Revolutionist" will be found in Max Nomad, *Apostles of Revolution,* rev. ed. (New York: Collier, 1961), pp. 214-256. Quotations below are from this work.

[136] Hannah Arendt, *Eichmann in Jerusalem: A Report on the Banality of Evil* (New York: Viking, 1963).

[137] Anton Chekhov, *The Three Sisters,* trans. Tyrone Guthrie and Leonid Kipnis (New York: Avon, 1965). For useful commentary and criticism see Albert Bermel, *Contradictory Characters: An Interpretation of the Modern Theatre* (New York: Dutton, 1973), pp. 75-104; Robert Brustein, *The Theatre of Revolt: An Approach to the Modern Drama* (Boston: Little, Brown, 1962), pp. 135-180; and Ronald Hingley, *A New Life of Anton Chekhov* (New York: Knopf, 1976), pp. 263-287.

[138] Quoted in Brustein, *Theatre of Revolt,* p. 161n.

[139] Anton Chekhov, *My Life,* quoted in ibid.

[140] Albert Camus, "The Myth of Sisyphus," in *The Myth of Sisyphus and Other Essays,* trans. Justin O'Brien (New York: Vintage, 1955; orig. pub. 1942).

[141] The reference is to Dante's description of boredom and sloth in *The Inferno.* See the discussion in John S. Carroll, *Exiles of Eternity: An Exposition of Dante's Inferno* (Port Washington, N.Y.: Kennikat Press, 1971; orig. pub. 1904), pp. 133-135. See also Goetzl, *Boredom,* p. 61.

[142] See Robert A. Nisbet, *The Quest for Community: A Study in the Ethics of Order and Freedom* (New York: Oxford University Press, 1953). For the ambiguous and anguished attempts to found new forms of community see Lawrence Veysey, *The Communal Experience: Anarchist and Mystical Counter-Cultures in America* (New York: Harper & Row, 1973); Rosabeth Moss Kanter, *Commitment and Community: Communes and Utopias in Sociological Perspective* (Cambridge, Mass.: Harvard University Press, 1972); Keith Melville, *Communes in the Counter-Culture: Origins, Theories, Styles of Life* (New York: Morrow, 1972); Elia Katz, *Armed Love* (New York: Bantam, 1972); Sallie Teselle, ed., *The Family, Communes, and Utopian Societies* (New York: Harper Torchbooks, 1972).

[143] Edward Gibbon, *The History of the Decline and Fall of the Roman Empire,* abr. D. M. Low (New York: Washington Square Press, 1972), II, 640-658. A much deserved revival of interest in Gibbon is expressed in "Edward Gibbon and the Decline and Fall of the Roman Empire," ed. John Clive and Edward Bowersock, *Daedalus,* 105:3 (Summer 1976). I am also the beneficiary of lectures on Gibbon and Macaulay given by H. R. Trevor-Roper at Oxford University in the Michaelmas term, 1975.

[144] Gibbon, *Decline and Fall,* p. 647.

LUST

*Denis de Rougemont, *Love in the Western World,* trans. by Montgomery Belgion, rev. and augmented ed. (New York: Harper Colophon, 1974), p. 238.

[1] Morton W. Bloomfield, *The Seven Deadly Sins: An Introduction to the History of a Religious Concept, with Special Reference to Medieval English Literature* (East Lansing: Michigan State University Press, 1967), pp. 46-56; quotation from p. 51.

[2] Augustine, *Concerning the City of God Against the Pagans,* trans. Henry Bettenson, ed. David Knowles (Harmondsworth: Penguin, 1972), Book XIV, ch. 16, p. 577.

[3] Ibid.

[4]Ibid., (Book XIV, Ch. 17), pp. 578-579.

[5]Ibid.

[6]Ibid., p. 579.

[7]Ibid.

[8]Ibid., (Book XIV, Chs. 18-19), pp. 581, 579, 580.

[9]Ibid., (Book XIV, Ch. 20), p. 582.

[10]Ibid., (Book XIV, Ch. 21), p. 583.

[11]Ibid.

[12]See Stanford M. Lyman and Marvin B. Scott, "Accounts," *American Sociological Review*, 33 (February 1968), 46-62.

[13]See Panos D. Bardis, "Family Forms and Variations Historically Considered," in Harold T. Christensen, ed., *Handbook of Marriage and the Family* (Chicago: Rand-McNally, 1964), pp. 440-451.

[14]Tertullian, *Adversus Marcionem* I, 29; quoted in Bardis, "Family Forms," p. 449.

[15]Jerome, *Letters*, XXII; quoted in Bardis, "Family Forms," p. 449.

[16]John Chrysostom, *De Virginitate*, IX; quoted in Bardis, "Family Forms," p. 449.

[17]Emory S. Bogardus, *The Development of Social Thought*, 4th ed. (New York: McKay, 1960), p. 157.

[18]Jay Haley, *The Power Tactics of Jesus Christ and Other Essays* (New York: Avon-Discus, 1971), pp. 39-44.

[19]Augustine, *City of God*, p. 591.

[20]John of Damascus, *De Fide Orthodoxa*, IV, 24; quoted in Bardis, "Family Forms," p. 449.

[21]The following depends heavily on Bardis, "Family Forms," pp. 450-451.

[22]*Monogamia*, III; quoted in Bardis, "Family Forms," p. 450.

[23]Jerome, *Epistola*, XXII; cited in Bardis, "Family Forms," p. 441.

[24]Jerome, *Epistola*, LIV; cited in Bardis, "Family Forms," p. 446.

[25]Summarized in Bardis, "Family Forms," p. 442.

[26]Athenagoras, *Legatio pro Christianis*, 33; quoted in Bardis, "Family Forms," p. 442.

[27]Jerome, *Epistola* LIV; quoted in Bardis, "Family Forms," p. 442.

[28]The following is from Thomas Aquinas, *On the Truth of the Catholic Faith*, bk. III, pts. I and II, trans. Vernon J. Bourke (Garden City: Doubleday, 1956); reprinted in D. P. Verene, ed., *Sexual Love and Western Morality: A Philosophical Anthology* (New York: Harper Torchbooks, 1972), pp. 119-133. All quotations are from this edition unless cited otherwise.

[29]Aquinas pointed out that "Man's desire to enjoy God belongs to that love of God falling under love of concupiscence. But because the divine good is in itself greater than our share of good in enjoying Him, we love God with the love of friendship rather than with that of concupiscence." *Summa of Theology* II, q. 26, a. 3, ad. 3; reprinted in *An Aquinas Reader: Selections from the Writings of Thomas Aquinas*, ed. Mary T. Clark (Garden City: Doubleday Image, 1972), pp. 276-277.

[30]See Georg Simmel, "The Conflict in Modern Culture" in *The Conflict in Modern Culture and Other Essays*, trans. K. Peter Etzkorn (New York: Teachers College Press, 1968), pp. 11-26.

[31]The following depends on Bardis, "Family Forms," pp. 447-448.

[32]For cross-cultural and historical studies of incest, see Russell Middleton, "A Deviant Case: Brother-Sister and Father-Daughter Marriage in Ancient Egypt," *American Sociological Review*, 27 (October, 1962), 603-611; and Reo F. Fortune, "Incest," in Rose

Laub Coser, ed., *The Family: Its Structure and Function* (New York: St. Martin's, 1964), pp. 70-74.

33 Martin Luther, "Preface to the Epistle of St. Paul to the Romans," in John Dillenberger, ed., *Martin Luther: Selections from His Writings* (Garden City: Doubleday Anchor, 1961), p. 22-34; quotations from pp. 22 and 25.

34 The following draws upon the section on marriage in Martin Luther, "The Pagan Servitude of the Church," in ibid., pp. 326-340; quotations from pp. 331, 337-338, and 339.

35 The preceding discussion, including the references to Clement of Alexandria (*Stromata* VII: 12), Tertullian (*De Cultu Feminarum* I:1), and John of Chrysostom, depends on Bardis, "Family Forms," p. 445.

36 The following is from Augustine, *City of God*, p. 1057.

37 See, e.g., Ludovico Maria Sinistrari, *Demoniality*, trans. Rev. Montague Summers (New York: Benjamin Blom, 1972). Written in 1701, *Demoniality* was published in French in 1875, and in English translation in 1927 in London.

38 See Ruth Nanda Anshen, *The Reality of the Devil: Evil in Man* (New York: Dell-Delta, 1972), pp. 114-115. Anshen (p. 115) goes on to suggest, however, that Eve might be superior to Adam: "If we agree that to be lead [sic] astray by the Devil is more justifiable and in some ways more honorable than to be led astray by one's wife, then Adam is left in a rather dubious position. Eve had been misguided, but she herself misguided Adam."

39 The following is based on Martin Luther, "The Natural Place of Women," in Verene, *Sexual Love*, pp. 134-143; quotations from pp. 135, 136, 140, 137, 139, 138, 141, 142.

40 See Martin Luther, "A Commentary on St. Paul's Epistle to the Galatians," in Dillenberger, *Martin Luther*, pp. 99-165.

41 *The Diary of Michael Wigglesworth, 1653-1657: The Conscience of a Puritan*, ed. Edmund S. Morgan (New York: Harper Torchbooks, 1965), pp. 47, 80-81, 106-107.

42 See Edmund S. Morgan, *The Puritan Family: Religion and Domestic Relations in Seventeenth-Century New England* (New York: Harper Torchbooks, 1966), pp. 166-167.

43 See Robert Middlekauf, *The Mathers: Three Generations of Puritan Intellectuals, 1596-1728* (London: Oxford University Press, 1971), pp. 201-208; quotation from p. 204.

44 See, e.g., Morgan, *Puritan Family*, pp. 63-64; John Demos, *A Little Commonwealth: Family Life in Plymouth Colony* (New York: Oxford University Press, 1970), pp. 82-99, 152-155; Bernard Farber, *Guardians of Virtue: Salem Families in 1800* (New York: Basic Books, 1972), pp. 30-33.

45 See Richard Slotkin, *Regeneration Through Violence: The Mythology of the American Frontier* (Middletown, Conn.: Wesleyan University Press, 1973), pp. 46-47 et passim. See also Alden T. Vaughan, *New England Frontier: Puritans and Indians, 1620-1675* (Boston: Little, Brown, 1965), and the interesting discussion in D. H. Lawrence, *Studies in Classic American Literature* (New York: Viking, 1961; orig. pub. 1923), pp. 9-64.

46 William J. Goode, "The Theoretical Importance of Love," *American Sociological Review*, 24 (February, 1959), 41.

47 R. F. Fortune, "Incest," in Rose Laub Coser, ed., *The Family: Its Structure and Function* (New York: St. Martin's, 1964), p. 71.

48 Augustine, *City of God*, pp. 623, 624.

49 Fortune, "Incest," pp. 71-72.

50 Augustine, *City of God*, p. 625.

[51] Talcott Parsons, "The Incest Taboo in Relation to Social Structure," in Rose Laub Coser, The Family, pp. 48-70; quotations from pp. 65, 56.

[52] See Philip Slater, "Social Limitations on Libidinal Withdrawal," American Journal of Sociology, 67 (November 1961), 296-311.

[53] Dante Alighieri, The Divine Comedy, trans. Lawrence Binyon, in The Portable Dante, Paolo Milano, ed. (New York: Viking, 1947); all excerpts from The Inferno are from this edition.

[54] Useful commentaries will be found in W. H. V. Reade, The Moral System of Dante's Inferno (Port Washington, N.Y.: Kennikat Press, 1969; orig. pub. 1909). John S. Carroll, Exiles of Eternity: An Exposition of Dante's Inferno (Port Washington, N.Y.: Kennikat Press, 1971; orig. pub. 1904). Erich Auerbach, Dante: Poet of the Secular World, trans. Ralph Manheim (Chicago: University of Chicago Press, 1961; orig. 1929). Francis Fergusson, Dante's Drama of the Mind: A Modern Reading of the Purgatorio (Princeton: Princeton University Press, 1953). Francis Fergusson, Dante (New York: Collier, 1966).

[55] See, e.g., Philippe Ariès, Centuries of Childhood: A Social History of Family Life, trans. Robert Baldick (New York: Vintage, 1965), pp. 164-175 et passim.

[56] Carroll, Exiles of Eternity, pp. 243-244.

[57] See Ariès, pp. 321-326; Oscar Handlin and Mary F. Handlin, Facing Life: Youth and the Family in American History (Boston: Atlantic-Little, Brown, 1971), pp. 76-91.

[58] Carroll, Exiles of Eternity, pp. 242-243.

[59] The actual facts of the story, known to Dante at the time he wrote his poem, are less favorable to the doomed lovers. Paolo was already married when he took Francesca as his mistress. At the time they were killed, Francesca and Gianciotto had been married for ten years and had a daughter, aged nine; Paolo, married for sixteen years, was father to two sons. See Carroll, Exiles of Eternity, p. 94.

[60] Fergusson, Dante, pp. 11-12, 105.

[61] Inferno V:119-120.

[62] Slater, "Social Limitations," p. 242.

[63] Goode, "Theoretical Importance," pp. 39-42.

[64] Ralph Linton, The Study of Man: An Introduction (New York: Appleton-Century, 1936), p. 175.

[65] Margaret Mead, Coming of Age in Samoa: A Study of Adolescence and Sex in Primitive Society (New York: New American Library, 1949; orig. pub. 1928), pp. 95-96.

[66] The following is from Geoffrey Gorer, "Adolescence in Different Cultures," in The Danger of Equality and Other Essays (London: Cresset Press, 1966), pp. 91-104.

[67] Ernest R. Mowrer, The Family: Its Organization and Disorganization (Chicago: University of Chicago Press, 1932), pp. 102-118.

[68] Floyd Mansfield Martinson, Family in Society (New York: Dodd, Mead, 1970), pp. 256-257.

[69] Willard Waller, The Family: A Dynamic Interpretation (New York: Dryden Press, 1938), pp. 189-192.

[70] William M. Kephart, The Family, Society, and the Individual, 2nd ed. (Boston: Houghton Mifflin, 1966), pp. 310-311.

[71] Bernard Farber, Family: Organization and Interaction (San Francisco: Chandler, 1964), pp. 346-351.

[72] See Ernest W. Burgess, "The Prediction of Adjustment in Marriage," and "Adjustment in Marriage," both in Ernest W. Burgess on Community, Family, and Delinquence, eds. Leonard S. Cottrell, Jr., Albert Hunter, and James F. Short (Chicago: University of Chicago Press, 1973), pp. 107-123, 124-137.

[73] Ernest W. Burgess, Harvey J. Locke, and Mary Margaret Thomes, *The Family: From Tradition to Companionship*, 4th ed. (New York: Van Nostrand Reinhold, 1971), pp. 271–277.

[74] Sigmund Freud, "The Most Prevalent Form of Degradation in Erotic Life," *Collected Papers*, trans. Joan Riviere (New York: Basic Books, 1959), IV, 203–216.

[75] See Larry L. Constantine and Mary M. Constantine, *Group Marriage: A Study of Contemporary Multilateral Marriage* (New York: Collier, 1973); William A. Rossi, *The Sex Life of the Foot and Shoe* (New York: Saturday Review Press, Dutton, 1976); for the Chinese variant of this phenomenon, see Howard S. Levy, *Chinese Footbinding: The History of a Curious Erotic Custom* (New York: Walter Rawls, 1966).

[76] For a general discussion of this process and one that goes beyond the confines of homosexuality see Richard Sennett, *The Fall of Public Man* (New York: Knopf, 1977), pp. 6–12.

[77] See the many instances reported in Gordon Westwood, *A Minority: A Report on the Life of the Male Homosexual in Great Britain* (London: Longmans, 1960); D. J. West, *Homosexuality* (Chicago: Aldine, 1967); Lionel Oversey, *Homosexuality and Pseudohomosexuality* (New York: Science House, 1969).

[78] See A. L. Rowse, *Homosexuals in History: Ambivalence in Society, Literature and the Arts* (New York: Macmillan, 1977); Martin Hoffman, *The Gay World: Male Homosexuality and the Social Creation of Evil* (New York: Bantam, 1969); Evelyn Hooker, "The Homosexual Community," in *Observations of Deviance*, ed. Jack D. Douglas (New York: Random House, 1970), pp. 115–128; Carol A. B. Warren, *Identity and Community in the Gay World* (New York: Wiley, 1974). See also the many illuminating insights in Robert Brain, *Friends and Lovers* (New York: Basic Books, 1976).

[79] Laud Humphreys, *Tearoom Trade: Impersonal Sex in Public Places* (Chicago: Aldine, 1970); John Gerassi, *The Boys of Boise: Furor, Vice and Folly in an American Society* (New York: Collier, 1966); Albert J. Reiss, Jr., "The Social Integration of Queers and Peers," in *The Other Side: Perspectives on Deviance*, ed. Howard S. Becker (London: Free Press, Collier-Macmillan, 1964), pp. 181–210.

[80] Cf. Harold Garfinkel, "Conditions of Successful Degradation Ceremonies," *American Journal of Sociology*, 61 (March, 1956), 420–424; and Troy Duster, "Conditions for Guilt Free Massacre," in *Sanctions for Evil: Sources of Social Destructiveness*, ed. Nevitt Sanford and Craig Comstock (Boston: Beacon Press, 1971), pp. 25–36.

[81] See George Williamson, Jr., "Homosexuality and Sin," *New York Times* (August 9, 1977), p. 33.

[82] See Erving Goffman, *Stigma: Notes on the Management of Spoiled Identity* (Englewood Cliffs, N.J.: Prentice-Hall, 1963).

[83] See Robin Lloyd, *For Money or Love: Boy Prostitution in America* (New York: Vanguard, 1976).

[84] Mirra Komarovsky, *Dilemmas of Masculinity: A Study of College Youth* (New York: Norton, 1976), pp. 120–121, 133–134, 144–145, 167–169.

[85] See Laud Humphreys, *Out of the Closets: The Sociology of Homosexual Liberation* (Englewood Cliffs, N.J.: Prentice-Hall, 1972).

[86] See John Lauritsen and David Thorstad, *The Early Homosexual Rights Movement (1864–1935)* (New York: Times Change Press, 1974).

[87] I have borrowed the phrase from Herbert Marcuse, *An Essay on Liberation* (Boston: Beacon Press, 1969), pp. 34–35.

[88] Max Weber, "The Chinese Literati," in *From Max Weber: Essays in Sociology*, ed. and

trans. Hans Gerth and C. Wright Mills (New York: Oxford University Press, 1946), pp. 442–444.

89 See Lewis A. Coser, "The Political Functions of Eunuchism," *American Sociological Review*, 29 (December 1964), 880–885.

90 See Taisuke Mitamura, *Chinese Eunuchs: The Structure of Intimate Politics*, trans. Charles A. Pomeroy (Rutland, Vt.: Charles E. Tuttle, 1970).

91 See Roland Mousnier, *Social Hierarchies: 1450 to the Present*, trans. Peter Evans (New York: Schocken Books, 1973), pp. 91–102, and the discussion in Mitamura, *Chinese Eunuchs*, pp. 65–73.

92 See Eric Chou, *The Dragon and the Phoenix: Love, Sex and the Chinese* (London: Michael Joseph, 1971); Jolan Chang, *The Tao of Love and Sex: The Ancient Chinese Way to Ecstasy* (New York: Dutton, 1977), pp. 36, 81–83, 111.

93 Mitamura, *Chinese Eunuchs*, pp. 37, 123–126.

94 Magnus Hirschfeld, *Curious Sex Customs of the Far East: The World Journey of a Sexologist* (New York: Capricorn, 1965), pp. 201–202.

95 Mitamura, *Chinese Eunuchs*, pp. 123–125.

96 R. H. van Gulick, *Sexual Life in Ancient China: A Preliminary Survey of Chinese Sex and Society from ca. 1500 B.C. till 1644 A.D.* (Leiden: Brill, 1961), pp. 255–256.

97 For cases of self-mutilation in the Occident see George M. Gould and Walter L. Pyle, *Anomalies and Curiosities of Medicine: Being an Encyclopedic Collection of Rare and Extraordinary Cases, and of the Most Striking Instances of Abnormality in All Branches of Medicine and Surgery . . .* (New York: Bell, 1956; orig. pub. 1896), pp. 732–734.

98 Peter Abelard, *The Story of Abelard's Adversities*, trans. with notes of the *Historia Calamitatum* by J. T. Muckle (Toronto: Pontifical Institute of Mediaeval Studies, 1964), pp. 26–41; quotations from pp. 26, 27, 36, 39.

99 Heloise, on the other hand, became the object of sympathetic novels imitating her sacrifice and extolling the transformation of *eros* into *agape*. See Denis de Rougemont, *Love in the Western World*, trans. Montgomery Belgion (New York: Harper Colphon, 1974), pp. 213–216.

100 See Angus Heriot, *The Castrati in Opera* (New York: Da Capo, 1975), pp. 54–55.

101 See James Elbert Cutler, *Lynch-Law: An Investigation into the History of Lynching in the United States* (Montclair, N.J.: Patterson Smith, 1969; orig. pub. 1905); Arthur F. Raper, *The Tragedy of Lynching* (Montclair, N.J.: Patterson Smith, 1969; orig. pub. 1933); Frank Shay, *Judge Lynch: His First Hundred Years* (Montclair, N.J.: Patterson Smith, 1969; orig. pub. 1938); Ralph Ginzburg, ed., *100 Years of Lynchings* (New York: Lancer Books, 1962).

102 See Walter White, "Sex and Lynching," *Rope and Faggot* (New York: Arno Press, 1969; orig. pub. 1929), pp. 54–81.

103 Howard W. Odum, "Lynchings, Fears, and Folkways," *The Nation*, 133 (December 30, 1931), 719–720.

104 Buck v. Bell 274 U.S. 200 (1927).

105 See Arthur E. Fink, "Human Sterilization," *Causes of Crime: Biological Theories in the United States, 1800–1915* (New York: Barnes, 1962; orig. pub. 1938), pp. 188–210.

106 John S. Haller and Robin M. Haller, *The Physician and Sexuality in Victorian America* (New York: Norton, 1977), pp. 91–113.

107 The novel was translated by Pearl S. Buck as *All Men are Brothers* (New York: Grove Press, 1937), 2 vols.

108 The code is realized among traditional Chinese martial artsmen. For a complete

analysis I am indebted to my student Ying-jen Chang, "The Rise of the Martial Arts in China and America," Ph.D. diss., New School for Social Research, 1977.

109 See C. J. Hsia, *The Classic Chinese Novel: A Critical Introduction* (New York: Columbia University Press, 1968), pp. 88–92.

110 See Melville J. Herskovits, *The American Negro: A Study in Racial Crossing* (Bloomington: Indiana University Press, 1956; orig. pub. 1928); Edward Byron Reuter, *The Mulatto in the United States—Including a Study of the Role of Mixed-Blood Races Throughout the World* (New York: Negro Universities Press; orig. pub. 1918).

111 The following is based on Stanford M. Lyman, *Chinese Americans* (New York: Random House, 1974), pp. 86–118.

112 Max Weber, *The Protestant Ethic and the Spirit of Capitalism*, trans. Talcott Parsons (New York: Scribner, 1930), pp. 180–183.

113 See Jessie Bernard, "The Eudaemonists," in *Why Men Take Chances: Studies in Stress-Seeking*, ed. Samuel Z. Klausner (Garden City: Doubleday Anchor, 1968), pp. 6–47.

114 The following draws on Georg Simmel, "The Conflict in Modern Culture" and "On the Concept and Tragedy of Culture," in Simmel, pp. 11–26, 27–46.

115 Gregory the Great, *Morals on the Book of Job* (Oxford: J. H. Parker; London: F. and J. Rivington, 1845), III, 490.

116 Among Artaud's writings available in English translations are the following: *The Theater and Its Double*, trans. Mary Caroline Richards (New York: Grove Press, 1958); *The Peyote Dance*, trans. Helen Weaver (New York: Farrar, Straus & Giroux, 1976); *Anthology*, 2nd ed., rev., ed. Jack Hirschman (San Francisco: City Lights Books, 1965); *Selected Writings*, ed. Susan Sontag (New York: Farrar, Straus & Giroux, 1976).

117 For assessments of Artaud's work see Naomi Greene, *Antonin Artaud: Poet Without Words* (New York: Simon and Schuster, 1970; Bettina L. Knapp, *Antonin Artaud: Man of Vision* (New York: Discus-Avon, 1969); Eric Sellin, *The Dramatic Concepts of Antonin Artaud* (Chicago: University of Chicago Press, 1968). For purposes of my discussion the most useful work is Martin Esslin, *Antonin Artaud* (Harmondsworth: Penguin, 1977).

118 Artaud achieved something of this in his own performances. Of his screen portrayal of the monk who stands beside Joan of Arc at her burning Herman G. Weinberg observed: "[T]he actor takes the personality of the being he undertakes to portray, he incarnates it, he no longer belongs to the mechanical world, he is what the director wanted him to be. From now on . . . Artaud with his fixed eyes will have in life hallucinations of the corpse of a saint burned at Clamait [the name of the studio where *Jeanne D'Arc* was filmed]—pardon, at Rouen." Herman G. Weinberg, "The Actors in Dreyer's *Jeanne D'Arc*," (November, 1929) reprinted in Weinberg's anthology, *Saint Cinema: Writings on the Film, 1929-1970*, 2nd rev. ed. (New York: Dover, 1973), pp. 12–13.

119 The following is from Artaud, "The Theater and Culture," in *The Theater and Its Double*, pp. 7–13.

120 I have borrowed the term from Nietzsche and from Fredric Jameson, *The Prison-House of Language: A Critical Account of Structuralism and Russian Formalism* (Princeton: Princeton University Press, 1972).

121 See Maurice Natanson, "Alienation and Social Role," *Social Research*, 33 (Autumn 1966), 375–388.

122 Artaud, "Eighteen Seconds, A Screenplay (1925-26)," in *Selected Writings*, p. 115.

123 Freud, *Collected Papers*, IV, 215.

124 Esslin, *Artaud*, p. 30.

125 Artaud, "General Security: The Liquidation of Opium," *Selected Writings*, p. 99.

[126] Artaud, *Oeuvres Complètes* (Paris: Gallimard, 1956) X, 16; trans. and quoted in Esslin, *Artaud*, p. 56.

[127] See Naomi Greene, *Artaud*, pp. 165-166.

[128] Translated as "Shit to the Spirit," in Artaud, *Anthology*, pp. 106-112.

[129] Artaud, "The Alfred Jarry Theater," *Selected Writings*, pp. 155-157.

[130] Artaud, "Alfred Jarry Theater: First Season: 1926-27," *Selected Writings*, pp. 157-158.

[131] Artaud, "The Theater and Cruelty," in *The Theater and Its Double*, p. 85.

[132] Ibid., p. 86; emphasis added.

[133] Artaud, "The Theater of Cruelty (First Manifesto)," in *The Theater and Its Double*, pp. 90, 91.

[134] Artaud, "The Theater and the Plague," in *The Theater and Its Double*, pp. 15-32; quotations from pp. 25, 28, 30-31, 31.

[135] Rudolf Bultmann, *Primitive Christianity in Its Contemporary Setting*, trans. R. H. Fuller (New York: New American Library, 1956), p. 196.

[136] Artaud, "The Theater and the Plague," in *The Theater and Its Double*, pp. 30-31.

ANGER

The Iliad of Homer, trans. Richmond Lattimore (Chicago: University of Chicago Press, 1961), Book I, lines 1-8, p. 59.

[1] Gregory the Great, *Morals on the Book of Job* (Oxford: J. H. Parker; London: F. and J. Rivington, 1845), III, 490.

[2] Arnobius, *Adversus Gentes* II: 16; cited in Morton W. Bloomfield, *The Seven Deadly Sins: An Introduction to the History of a Religious Concept, with Special Reference to Medieval English Literature* (East Lansing: Michigan State University Press, 1967), p. 54.

[3] Bloomfield, *Seven Deadly Sins*, pp. 76, 47, 213, 199, 142, 166-435.

[4] Georg Simmel, "A Contribution to the Sociology of Religion," *American Journal of Sociology*, 11 (November 1905), 363.

[5] Cf. Gregory Rochlin, *Man's Aggression: The Defense of the Self* (New York: Dell-Delta, 1973), pp. 191-194.

[6] Harry Stack Sullivan, *The Fusion of Psychiatry and Social Science* (New York: Norton, 1971), pp. 250, 251.

[7] The following is adapted from Harry Stack Sullivan, *The Interpersonal Theory of Psychiatry* (New York: Norton, 1953), pp. 211-216.

[8] Ibid., p. 214.

[9] The following is adapted from several studies by Stanford M. Lyman: "The Structure of Chinese Society in Nineteenth Century America," Ph.D. diss. University of California, Berkeley, 1961; *The Asian in the West*, Social Science and Humanities Publication No. 4, Western Studies Center (Reno: Desert Research Institute, 1970), pp. 33-56; *Chinese Americans* (New York: Random House, 1974), pp. 22-27, 37-53, 86-111; "Conflict and the Web of Group Affiliation in San Francisco's Chinatown, 1850-1910," *Pacific Historical Review*, 43 (November 1974), 473-499; *The Asian in North America* (Santa Barbara: American Bibliographic Center-Clio Press, 1977), pp. 11-150, 177-200.

[10] See Hans H. Gerth, "The Nazi Party," *American Journal of Sociology*, 45 (January 1940), 524-529. For the thesis that support for the Nazis is better explained by the influx of nonvoters and nonpolitical persons into the ranks of the electorate see Reinhard Bendix, "Social Stratification and Political Power," in R. Bendix and S. M. Lipset,

eds., *Class, Status, and Power: A Reader in Social Stratification* (Glencoe: The Free Press, 1953), pp. 596–609.

11 Reinhard Bendix and Seymour Martin Lipset, *Social Mobility in Industrial Society* (Berkeley: University of California Press, 1959), p. 36.

12 Harold D. Lasswell, "The Psychology of Hitlerism," *Political Quarterly*, 4 (1933), p. 374.

13 Frederick L. Schuman, *The Nazi Dictatorship* (New York: Knopf, 1950), pp. 288–290.

14 Lucy S. Dawidowicz, *The War Against the Jews, 1933–1945* (New York: Holt, Rinehart and Winston, 1975).

15 Marie Jahoda, Paul F. Lazarsfeld, and Hans Zeisel, *Marienthal: The Sociography of an Unemployed Community* (Chicago: Aldine–Atherton, 1971), esp. pp. 36–44, 78–98.

16 Horace R. Cayton, "The Psychology of the Negro Under Discrimination," in Arnold Rose, ed., *Race Prejudice and Discrimination: Readings in Intergroup Relations in the United States* (New York: Knopf, 1953), pp. 276–290.

17 See Horace R. Cayton, *Long Old Road: An Autobiography* (New York: Trident Press, 1965), pp. 255–291; quotation from p. 265.

18 William H. Grier and Price M. Cobb, *Black Rage* (New York: Basic Books, 1968). See also Ronald T. Takaki, *Violence in the Black Imagination: Essays and Documents* (New York: G. P. Putnam, 1972), pp. 79–102.

19 See Richard Wright, *White Man, Listen!* (Garden City: Doubleday Anchor, 1964), pp. 1–43; and Richard Wright, *Native Son* (New York: Signet, 1961; orig. pub. 1940).

20 Frantz Fanon, *The Wretched of the Earth*, trans. Constance Farrington (New York: Grove Press, 1963).

21 Kingsley Davis, "Jealousy and Sexual Property: An Illustration," *Human Society* (New York: Macmillan, 1948), pp. 175–194; quotation from p. 176.

22 There is a rich and diversified literature on the problems and processes attending marriage across forbidden lines. For some representative works see Milton L. Barron, ed., *The Blending American: Patterns of Intermarriage* (Chicago: Quadrangle, 1972); Noel P. Gist and Anthony Gary Dworkin, eds., *The Blending of Races: Marginality and Identity in World Perspective* (New York: Wiley, 1972); Albert J. Gordon, *Intermarriage: Interfaith, Interracial, Interethnic* (Boston: Beacon Press, 1964); Fernando Henriques, *Children of Conflict: A Study of Interracial Sex and Marriage* (New York: Dutton, 1975); Irving R. Stuart and Lawrence E. Abt, eds., *Interracial Marriage: Expectations and Realities* (New York: Grossman Publishers, 1973).

23 The terms are from Robert K. Merton, "Intermarriage and the Social Structure: Fact and Theory," *Psychiatry*, 4 (August 1941), 361–374.

24 See Kingsley Davis, "Intermarriage in Caste Societies," *American Anthropologist*, 43 (July–September 1941), 388–395.

25 Herbert Blumer, "Race Prejudice as a Sense of Group Position," *Pacific Sociological Review*, 1 (Spring 1958), 3–7.

26 See James Elbert Cutler, *Lynch-Law An Investigation into the History of Lynching in the United States* (Montclair, N.J.: Patterson Smith 1969; orig. pub. 1905); Ralph Ginzburg, ed., *100 Years of Lynchings: A Shocking Documentary of Race Violence in America* (New York: Lancer Books, 1962); Arthur F. Raper, *The Tragedy of Lynching* (Montclair, N.J.: Patterson Smith, 1969; orig. pub. 1933); Frank Shay, *Judge Lynch: His First Hundred Years* (Montclair, N.J.: Patterson Smith, 1969; orig. pub. 1938); Walter White, *Rope and Faggot* (New York: Knopf, 1929). Perhaps the most famous modern court trial on the subject took place in Alabama in 1931. See Haywood Patterson and Earl Conrad, *Scottsboro Boy* (New York: Bantam, 1951); Dan T. Carter, *Scottsboro: A Tragedy of the American South*

(Baton Rouge: Louisiana State University Press, 1969). During the same period, racial tensions between the white naval social elites and the several Asian and Oceanic minorities living in Hawaii exploded over an accusation of rape and led to the notorious Massie-Fortescue case. See Theon Wright, *Rape in Paradise* (New York: Hawthorn, 1966); Peter van Slingerland, *Something Terrible Has Happened* (New York: Harper & Row, 1966).

[27] See Allison Davis, Burleigh B. Gardner, and Mary R. Gardner, *Deep South: A Social Anthropological Study of Caste and Class* (Chicago: University of Chicago Press, Phoenix Books, 1965), pp. 25–27.

[28] See Karl Menninger, *Whatever Became of Sin?* (New York: Hawthorn, 1973), pp. 38–132.

[29] See David Matza, *Delinquency and Drift* (New York: Wiley, 1964), pp. 1–32. See also Fred Montanino and Edward Sagarin, "Deviants: Voluntarism and Responsibility," in Sagarin and Montanino, eds., *Deviants: Voluntary Actors in a Hostile World*, (Morristown, N.J.: General Learning Press, 1977), pp. 1–17.

[30] See Reinhard Bendix, *Social Science and the Distrust of Reason*, University of California Publications in Sociology and Social Institutions, Vol. I (Berkeley: University of California Press, 1951); Philip Rieff, *The Triumph of the Therapeutic: Uses of Faith After Freud* (New York: Harper & Row, 1966).

[31] Sigmund Freud, *Civilization and Its Discontents*, trans. and ed. James Strachey (New York: Norton, 1962), p. 67.

[32] See Freud, *Three Essays on the Theory of Sexuality*, standard ed. (London: Hogarth Press, 1949), VII, 158, 193n.

[33] Freud, "Analysis of a Phobia in a Five-Year-Old Boy," *Collected Essays*, authorized trans. Alix and James Strachey (New York: Basic Books, 1959), III, 281.

[34] Freud, "Instincts and Their Vicissitudes," *Collected Essays*, authorized trans. under the supervision of Joan Riviere, IV, 81–82.

[35] Freud, *Beyond the Pleasure Principle*, trans. and ed. James Strachey (New York: Norton, 1961).

[36] Freud, *The Ego and the Id*, trans. Joan Riviere, ed. James Strachey (New York: Norton, 1960), p. 31.

[37] Freud, *New Introductory Lectures on Psychoanalysis*, trans. James Strachey (New York: Norton, 1964), pp. 104–105.

[38] For a good discussion see Erich Fromm, *The Anatomy of Human Destructiveness* (New York: Holt, Rinehart, and Winston, 1973), pp. 439–478.

[39] Freud, *New Introductory Lectures*, p. 105.

[40] John Dollard et al., *Frustration and Aggression* (New Haven: Yale University Press, 1939).

[41] John Dollard, *Caste and Class in a Southern Town*, 3d ed. (Garden City: Doubleday Anchor, 1957). For a discussion of the place of this work in the sociology of race relations in the United States see Stanford M. Lyman, *The Black American in Sociological Thought: A Failure of Perspective* (New York: G. P. Putnam, 1972), pp. 71–98.

[42] Dollard, *Caste and Class*, pp. 250–314.

[43] See Richard Hofstadter, *Social Darwinism in American Thought, 1860–1915* (Boston: Beacon Press, 1955) and Stow Persons, ed., *Evolutionary Thought in America* (New York: George Braziller, 1956).

[44] See Kenneth E. Bock, "Darwin and Social Theory," *Philosophy of Science*, 22 (April 1955), pp. 123–134; Stanford M. Lyman, *The Black American*, pp. 15–26.

[45] See Daniel Gasman, *The Scientific Origins of National Socialism: Social Darwinism in Ernst Haeckel and the German Monist League* (New York: Elsevier, 1971); Alfred Rosenberg, *Race and Race History and Other Essays*, ed. Robert Pois (New York: Harper & Row,

1970); Robert Cecil, *The Myth of the Master Race: Alfred Rosenberg and Nazi Ideology* (New York: Dodd, Mead, 1972).

46 Ashley Montagu, *The Nature of Human Aggression* (New York: Oxford University Press, 1976), pp. 23–39.

47 Niko Tinbergen, "On War and Peace in Animals and Man," *Science*, 160 (1968), pp. 1411-1418; Raymond Dart, *Adventures with the Missing Link* (New York: Harper & Row, 1959); Konrad Lorenz, *On Aggression* (New York: Harcourt, Brace, and World, 1966); Desmond Morris, *The Naked Ape* (New York: McGraw-Hill, 1967; *The Human Zoo* (New York: McGraw-Hill, 1969); Ramona and Desmond Morris, *Men and Apes* (New York: Bantam, 1968); Marston Bates, *Gluttons and Libertines: Human Problems of Being Natural* (New York: Random House, 1958). For a critical disagreement with the thrust of this literature see Duncan Williams, *Trousered Apes: Sick Literature in a Sick Society* (New York: Dell-Delta, 1973). See also Albert Szent-Györgyi, *The Crazy Ape* (New York: Philosophical Library, 1970).

48 See Hilary Callan, *Ethology and Society: Towards An Anthropological View* (Oxford: Clarendon Press, 1970), pp. 72-103.

49 See also Desmond Morris, *Intimate Behaviour* (New York: Random House, 1971).

50 See L. Harrison Matthews, "Overt Fighting in Mammals," in J. D. Carthy and F. J. Ebling, eds., *The Natural History of Aggression* (London: Academic Press, 1964), pp. 23-32.

51 Konrad Lorenz, "Ritualized Fighting," in Carthy and Ebling, *The Natural History of Aggression*, pp. 39-50.

52 Nicolas Evreinoff, *The Theatre in Life*, trans. and ed. Alexander I. Nazaroff (New York: Benjamin Blom, 1970; orig. pub. 1927), pp. 7-21. For a discussion of the value of Evreinoff's work for a dramatistic sociology see Stanford M. Lyman and Marvin B. Scott, *The Drama of Social Reality* (New York: Oxford University Press, 1975), pp. 110-112.

53 See Don H. Zimmerman and Melvin Pollner, "The Everyday World as Phenomenon," in Jack D. Douglas, ed., *Understanding Everyday Life: Toward the Reconstruction of Sociological Knowledge* (Chicago: Aldine, 1970), pp. 80-103.

54 Harold Garfinkel, *Studies in Ethnomethodology* (Englewood Cliffs, N.J.: Prentice-Hall, 1967); Lyman and Scott, *Sociology of the Absurd*.

55 Cf. Hans Jonas, "The Abyss of the Will: Philosophical Meditation on the Seventh Chapter of Paul's Epistle to the Romans," *Philosophical Essays: From Ancient Creed to Technological Man* (Englewood Cliffs, N.J.: Prentice-Hall, 1974), pp. 335-348.

56 Matza, *Delinquency and Drift*, pp. 1-32.

57 See Harold Garfinkel, "Conditions of a Successful Degradation Ceremony," *American Journal of Sociology*, 61 (March 1956), 420-424, and Troy Duster, "Conditions for Guilt-Free Massacre," in Nevitt Sanford and Craig Comstock, eds., *Sanctions for Evil: Sources of Social Destructiveness* (Boston: Beacon Press, 1971), pp. 25-36.

58 See Erving Goffman, "On Cooling the Mark Out: Some Aspects of Adaptation to Failure," *Psychiatry*, 15 (November 1952), 451-463.

59 See, however, Robert Ardrey, *The Territorial Imperative: A Personal Inquiry into the Animal Origins of Property and Nations* (New York: Atheneum, 1966); and Lyman and Scott, "Territoriality: A Neglected Sociological Dimension," *Sociology of the Absurd*, pp. 89-110.

60 For an excellent discussion see Raymond Aron, *Peace and War: A Theory of International Relations*, trans. Richard Howard and Annette Baker Fox (Garden City: Doubleday, 1966), pp. 181-209.

61 Sir Halford J. MacKinder, *Democratic Ideals and Reality: A Study in the Politics of*

Reconstruction (New York: Henry Holt, 1919). See also Frederick J. Teggart, "Geography as an Aid to Statecraft: An Appreciation of MacKinder's *Democratic Ideals and Reality*," *Geographical Review*, 8 (October–November 1919), pp. 227–242; and Teggart, "Human Geography, An Opportunity for the University," *Journal of Geography*, 18 (April 1919), pp. 142–148. For a study inspired by MacKinder's perspective see Stuart Legg, *The Heartland* (London: Secker & Warburg, 1970).

[62] Frederick J. Teggart, "The Geographical Factor in History," *Theory and Processes of History* (Berkeley: University of California Press, 1941), pp. 247–267.

[63] Ibid., pp. 253–267. See also Howard Becker, "Forms of Population Movement: Prolegomena to a Study of Mental Mobility," *Social Forces*, 9 (December 1930), 147–160; (March 1931), 351–361.

[64] Karl von Clausewitz, *On War*, ed. Anatol Rapoport (Harmondsworth: Penguin, 1968), p. 208.

[65] Ibid., p. 368.

[66] An impressive historical and sociological literature has grown up on this subject. Among the works are Leonard Bloom and Ruth Riemer, *Removal and Return: The Socio-Economic Effects of the War on Japanese Americans* (Berkeley: University of California Press, 1949); Leonard Broom and John Kitsuse, *The Managed Casualty: The Japanese-American Family in World War II* (Berkeley: University of California Press, 1956); Alan R. Bosworth, *America's Concentration Camps* (New York: Norton, 1967); Roger Daniels, *Concentration Camps U.S.A.: Japanese Americans and World War II* (New York: Holt, Rinehart, and Winston, 1972); Roger Daniels, *The Decision to Relocate the Japanese Americans* (Philadelphia: Lippincott, 1975); Anne Reeploeg Fisher, *Exile of a Race* (Seattle: F & T Publishers, 1965); Audrie Girdner and Anne Loftis, *The Great Betrayal: The Evacuation of the Japanese Americans During World War II* (New York: Macmillan, 1969); Morton Grodzins, *Americans Betrayed: Politics and the Japanese Evacuation* (Chicago: University of Chicago Press, 1949); Dillon S. Myer, *Uprooted Americans: The Japanese Americans and the War Relocation Authority During World War II* (Tucson: University of Arizona Press, 1971); Charles Kikuchi, *The Kikuchi Diary: Chronicle from an American Concentration Camp*, ed. John Modell (Urbana: University of Illinois Press, 1973); Edward H. Spicer et al., *Impounded People: Japanese Americans in the Relocation Centers* (Tucson: University of Arizona Press, 1969); Dorothy Swaine Thomas et al., *The Salvage* (Berkeley: University of California Press, 1952; Dorothy Swaine Thomas and Richard Nishimoto, *The Spoilage* (Berkeley: University of California Press, 1946); Jacobus ten Broek, E. N. Barnhart, and F. Matson, *Prejudice, War, and the Constitution* (Berkeley: University of California Press, 1954); Michi Weglyn, *Years of Infamy: The Untold Story of America's Concentration Camps* (New York: Morrow, 1976).

[67] See *Final Report: Japanese Evacuation from the West Coast, 1942* (Washington: Government Printing Office, 1943), pp. 151–236.

[68] Allen H. Eaton, *Beauty Behind Barbed Wire: The Arts of the Japanese in Our War Relocation Camps* (New York: Harper & Brothers, 1952).

[69] See, e.g., Anthony L. Lehman, *Birthright of Barbed Wire: The Santa Anita Assembly Center for the Japanese* (Los Angeles: Westernlore Press, 1970), pp. 19–70.

[70] See Paul Bailey, *City in the Sun: The Japanese Concentration Camp at Poston, Arizona* (Los Angeles: Westernlore Press, 1971), esp. pp. 103–161; and Alexander H. Leighton, *The Governing of Men: General Principles and Recommendations Based on Experience at a Japanese Relocation Camp* (Princeton: Princeton University Press, 1945), pp. 90–210.

[71] See Jeanne Wakatsuki Houston and James D. Houston, *Farewell to Manzanar* (Boston: Houghton Mifflin, 1973), pp. 108–122.

⁷²Langdon Gilkey, *Shantung Compound: The Story of Men and Women Under Pressure* (New York: Harper & Row, 1975), pp. 80, 81.

⁷³Georg Simmel, "The Aesthetic Significance of the Face," trans. Lore Ferguson, in *Georg Simmel, 1858-1918*, ed. Kurt H. Wolff (Columbus: Ohio State University Press, 1959), pp. 276-281.

⁷⁴See Charles Darwin, *The Expression of the Emotions in Man and Animals* (Chicago: The University of Chicago Press, 1965. Orig. pub. 1872). The following owes much to R. Dale Guthrie, *Body Hot Spots: The Anatomy of Human Social Organs and Behavior* (New York: Van Nostrand Reinhold, 1976), pp. 25-72.

⁷⁵Judy Klemesrud, "What Bodybuilding King Finds Uplifting," *New York Times*, May 8, 1976, p. 12.

⁷⁶See Lyman and Scott, "Game Frameworks," in *Sociology of the Absurd*, pp. 29-70.

⁷⁷See the chapter on "Hamlet" in Lyman and Scott, *Drama of Social Reality*, pp. 21-42; Jacob Black-Michaud, *Cohesive Force: Feud in the Mediterranean and the Middle East* (Oxford: Blackwell, 1975); Roland Mousnier, *Peasant Uprisings in Seventeenth-Century France, Russia, and China*, trans. Brian Pearce (New York: Harper Torchbooks, 1970); Ernest J. Hiller, *The Strike: A Study in Collective Action* (Chicago: University of Chicago Press, 1928), pp. 5-11, 25-78, 125-155, 192-206.

PRIDE

*Richard L. Rubenstein, *The Religious Imagination: A Study in Psychoanalysis and Jewish Theology* (Boston: Beacon Press, 1971), pp. 114-116.

¹Morton W. Bloomfield, *The Seven Deadly Sins: An Introduction to the History of a Religious Concept, with Special Reference to Medieval English Literature* (East Lansing: Michigan State University Press, 1967), pp. 44, 45, 53-54.

²Translated in *Nicene and Post-Nicene Fathers*, 2nd ser., XI, 281; quoted in ibid., p. 69.

³Bloomfield, *Seven Deadly Sins*, pp. 69-81.

⁴Gregory the Great, *Morals on the Book of Job* (Oxford: J. H. Parker; London: F. and J. Rivington, 1845), III, 489-490.

⁵Gregory the Great, *Moralia*, XXIV:48; quoted in Robert Payne, *Hubris: A Study of Pride* (New York: Harper Torchbooks, 1960), p. 73.

⁶Ibid., pp. 72-73.

⁷Ibid., p. 32.

⁸The following is taken from Aristotle, *Nichomachean Ethics*, IV, 3, 1124a, 1124b, 1125a, 1125b in *The Basic Works of Aristotle*, ed. Richard McKeon (New York: Random House, 1941), pp. 992-997.

⁹Adam Smith, *The Theory of Moral Sentiments* (New Rochelle, N.Y.: Arlington House, 1969; orig. pub. 1759), pp. 362-388.

¹⁰Ibid., p. 383.

¹¹Alanus de Insulis, *De Planctu Naturae*, VII, 5-66; quoted in Payne, *Hubris*, pp. 77-78.

¹²Georg Simmel, "Exkurs über den Schmuck," trans. as "Adornment," in *The Sociology of Georg Simmel*, trans. and ed. Kurt H. Wolff (Glencoe: The Free Press, 1950), pp. 338-344.

¹³The following is based on Geoffrey Chaucer, *The Canterbury Tales*, trans. Frank Ernest Hill (New York: McKay, 1964), pp. 526-533.

¹⁴See Erving Goffman, *Relations in Public: Microstudies of the Public Order* (New York: Basic Books, 1971), pp. 62-237.

[15] See Rene Konig, *A La Mode: On the Social Psychology of Fashion*, trans. F. Bradley (New York: Seabury, 1973), pp. 154-164.

[16] Ibid., pp. 133-138, 154-165. For a general discussion emphasizing the interplay of erotic sensibilities and cultural meanings see Ernst Harms, "The Psychology of Clothes," *American Journal of Sociology*, 44 (September 1938), 239-250.

[17] The following interprets J. C. Flugel, *The Psychology of Clothes* (New York: International Universities Press, 1969), pp. 108-121.

[18] For a modern prescription of this thesis in contemporary America see John T. Molloy, *Dress for Success* (New York: Warner Books, 1976).

[19] Flugel, *Psychology of Clothes*, pp. 211-215.

[20] Quentin Bell writes: "Certainly one reason for this development is that student ideology favours an intransigent attitude towards age and authority and what is believed to be non-conformity. As with the art student so with all modern students the desire to *épater les bourgeois* is important. Thus we have seen long hair, gaily blatant effeminacy, sheer dirtiness, the rejection both of fashion and sumptuosity, the defiant display of battered jeans and ragged T-shirts, the tendency to abolish distinctions, not only of sex but of class. Although such manifestations may involve an element of pretense and even of affectation, still they exemplify the passions and the ideology of a genuine revolt." *On Human Finery*, 2nd ed. (New York: Schocken, 1976), p. 172.

[21] Tom Wolfe, "Introduction," in König, *A La Mode*, pp. 15-28. Quentin Bell disagrees, believing that fashion is being replaced by anarchy. See his discussion, *On Human Finery*, pp. 173-178.

[22] The following is drawn from a book and three essays by Louis Dumont. See *Homo Hierarchicus: The Caste System and Its Implications*, trans. Mark Sainsbury (Chicago: University of Chicago Press, 1970), pp. 1-20, 201-216; "Caste: A Phenomenon of Social Structure or an Aspect of Indian Culture?" *CIBA Foundation Symposium on Caste and Race: Comparative Approaches*, ed. A. V. S. de Reuck and Julie Knight (London: J. and A. Churchill, 1967), pp. 28-38; "The Modern Conception of the Individual," *Contributions to Indian Sociology*, 8 (1965), 13-61; "The Individual as an Impediment to Sociological Comparison and Indian History," *Religion, Politics and History in India* (The Hague: Mouton, 1970), pp. 133-150.

[23] Max Weber, *The Protestant Ethic and the Spirit of Capitalism*, trans. Talcott Parsons (London: G. Allen and Unwin, 1930), p. 222, n. 22.

[24] See the latest work available in English by Dumont, *From Mandeville to Marx: The Genesis and Triumph of Economic Ideology* (Chicago: University of Chicago Press, 1977).

[25] Dumont, "The Individual as an Impediment," p. 144.

[26] For a critical rejection of these views, and one that bids fair to restore a proper respect for the histories of mankind, see Kenneth E. Bock, *The Acceptance of Histories: Toward a Perspective for Social Science*, University of California Publications in Sociology and Social Institutions, Vol. 3, No. 1 (Berkeley: University of California Press, 1956). For a discussion of the implications of the varieties of history for social science see Stanford M. Lyman, "The Acceptance, Rejection, and Reconstruction of Histories: An Examination of Certain Controversies in the Study of Social and Cultural Change," in *Structure, Consciousness, and History*, ed. Richard Harvey Brown and Stanford M. Lyman (Cambridge: Cambridge University Press, 1978).

[27] Bruce Mazlish, *The Revolutionary Ascetic: Evolution of a Political Type* (New York: Basic Books, 1976), p. 22.

[28] Payne, *Hubris*, pp. 13-14.

[29] See Robert Jewett and John Shelton Lawrence, *The American Monomyth* (Garden City: Doubleday Anchor, 1977).

[30] See Jenni Calder, *There Must Be a Lone Ranger: The American West in Film and in Reality* (New York: Taplinger, 1975).

[31] See Edward Alsworth Ross, "Individuation," *American Journal of Sociology*, 25 (January 1920), 469-479.

[32] Sigmund Freud, "On Narcissism: An Introduction" (1914), *Collected Papers*, trans. under the supervision of Joan Riviere (New York: Basic Books, 1959), IV, 30.

[33] The summary is adapted from Ovid, *Metamorphoses*, 3:342-510, reprinted in Mark P. O. Morford and Robert J. Lenardon, *Classical Mythology* (New York: David McKay, 1971), pp. 194-198.

[34] Freud, "Narcissism," pp. 31, 30.

[35] Ibid., p. 48.

[36] Ibid., p. 48.

[37] Ibid., pp. 48-49, 49.

[38] Ibid., pp. 45, 47.

[39] Ibid., p. 59.

[40] See Kingsley Davis, *Human Society* (New York: Macmillan, 1948), pp. 96-117.

[41] Max Weber, *The Sociology of Religion*, trans. Ephraim Fischoff (Boston: Beacon Press, 1963; orig. pub. 1922), pp. 114-115.

[42] Cf. Max Weber, *Ancient Judaism*, trans. Hans H. Gerth and Don Martindale (Glencoe: The Free Press, 1952), pp. 149-404, with Arturo Castiglioni, "The Contribution of the Jews to Medicine," and Charles Singer, "Science and Judaism," in *The Jews: Their History, Culture and Religion*, 3rd ed., ed. Louis Finkelstein (New York: Harper & Row, 1960), II, 1349, 1376, 1429.

[43] Werner Keller, *Diaspora: The Post-Biblical History of the Jews*, trans. Richard and Clara Winston (New York: Harcourt, Brace and World, Inc., 1969), p. 61.

[44] See Julius B. Maller, "The Role of Education in Jewish History," in Finkelstein, ed., *The Jews*, II, 1234.

[45] The definitive work is that of Gershom S. Scholem, *Sabbatai Sevi: The Mystical Messiah, 1626-1676*, trans. R. J. Zwi Werblowsky (Princeton: Princeton University Press, 1973).

[46] The following is drawn from Keller, *Diaspora*, pp. 317-324.

[47] The following is from Augustine, *Concerning the City of God Against the Pagans*, trans. Henry Bettenson (Harmondsworth: Penguin, 1972), Bk. XIV, Chap. 13, pp. 571-573.

[48] For a recent discussion of unbelief see *The Culture of Unbelief: Studies and Proceedings from the First International Symposium on Belief Held at Rome, March 22-27, 1969*, ed. Rocco Caporale and Antonio Grumelli (Berkeley: University of California Press, 1971).

[49] The following is from Thomas Aquinas, *Summa Theologiae*, ii-2, q. clxii, a. 3, 4, 6.

[50] Quoted in John S. Carroll, *Exiles of Eternity: An Exposition of Dante's Inferno* (Port Washington, N.Y.: Kennikat Press, 1971; orig. pub. 1904), p. 158n.

[51] Dante Alighieri, *The Divine Comedy*, trans. Lawrence Binyon, in *The Portable Dante*, rev. ed., Paolo Milano, ed. (New York: Viking, 1969), pp. 3-544.

[52] Payne, *Hubris*, p. 87.

[53] Ibid., pp. 85, 91.

[54] The following leans heavily on Carroll, *Exiles of Eternity*, pp. 153-168.

[55] Robert K. Merton, *Science, Technology and Society in Seventeenth-Century England* (New York: Harper Torchbooks, 1970; orig. pub. 1938), pp. 55-79.

[56] *The Diary of Michael Wigglesworth, 1653-1657: The Conscience of a Puritan*, ed. Edmund S.

Morgan (New York: Harper Torchbooks, 1965), pp. 102-105; quotations from pp. 104-105.

[57] Sören Kierkegaard, *The Present Age and Of the Difference Between a Genius and an Apostle*, trans. Alexander Dru (New York: Harper Torchbooks, 1962), pp. 87-108; quotations from pp. 102, 103.

[58] Contrast Kierkegaard's defense of apostleship against the transitory nature of genius with Eissler's defense of Freud's genius against the talented but less original and overdependent discipleship of Tausk, who committed suicide. In a profound sense the contrast that emerges upon coincidental reading of the two texts points to the distinctive difference between Jewish and Christian attitudes toward intellect. See K. R. Eissler, *Talent and Genius: The Fictitious Case of Tausk Contra Freud* (New York: Grove Press, 1971).

[59] See Peter Berger, Brigitte Berger, and Hansfried Kellner, *The Homeless Mind: Modernization and Consciousness* (New York: Random House, 1973).

[60] See J. Glenn Gray, *The Warriors: Reflections on Men in Battle* (New York: Harper Perennial, 1973; orig. pub. 1959); the following is from J. Glenn Gray, *The Promise of Wisdom: A Philosophical Theory of Education* (New York: Harper Torchbooks, 1972; orig. pub. 1968), pp. 134-140.

[61] See Joseph Tussman, *Obligation and the Body Politic* (New York: Oxford University Press, 1960).

[62] Berger, Berger, and Kellner, *Homeless Mind*, pp. 83-96.

[63] See Max Weber, "Science as a Vocation," in *From Max Weber: Essays in Sociology*, trans. and ed. Hans H. Gerth and C. Wright Mills (New York: Oxford University Press, 1946), pp. 129-158.

[64] See the essays by Norman O. Brown, Kay Johnson, Paul Goodman, Michael McClure, Charlotte Selver, Pablo Neruda, and Dennis Saleh gathered together under the heading "Body" in *Sources: An Anthology of Contemporary Materials Useful for Preserving Personal Sanity While Braving the Technological Wilderness*, ed. Theodore Roszak (New York: Harper Colophon, 1972), pp. 109-189.

[65] Berger, Berger, and Kellner, *Homeless Mind*, p. 90.

[66] See Marshall Berman, *The Politics of Authenticity: Radical Individualism and the Emergence of Modern Society* (New York: Atheneum, 1972), pp. 163-230.

[67] See Richard Sennett, *The Fall of Public Man* (New York: Knopf, 1977).

[68] For a representative discussion see *On the Margin of the Visible: Sociology, the Esoteric and the Occult*, ed. Edward A. Tiryakian (New York: Wiley, 1974); Jean-Paul Sartre, "Bad Faith," *Being and Nothingness: An Essay on Phenomenological Ontology*, trans. Hazel E. Barnes (New York: Philosophical Library, 1956), pp. 47-70; also see the analysis in Ian Craib, *Existentialism in Sociology: A Study of Jean-Paul Sartre* (Cambridge: Cambridge University Press, 1976), esp. pp. 14-36.

[69] Nathan Adler, *The Underground Stream: New Life Styles and the Antinomian Personality* (New York: Harper Torchbooks, 1972), p. 35.

[70] Carl Jung, *Psychology and Alchemy* (London: Pantheon, 1954), p. 461; quoted in ibid.

[71] See Benjamin R. Barber, *Superman and Common Man: Freedom, Anarchy, and the Revolution* (New York: Praeger, 1971).

[72] See David C. Gordon, *Self-Determination and History in the Third World* (Princeton: Princeton University Press, 1971); Georges Balandier, *The Sociology of Black Africa*, trans. Douglas Garman (New York: Praeger, 1970), pp. 13-81, 473-504; Samuel de Calo, *Coups and Army Rule in Africa: Studies in Military Style* (New Haven: Yale University

Press, 1976); A. James Gregor, *The Fascist Persuasion in Radical Politics* (Princeton: Princeton University Press, 1974).

73 See two works by Pierre L. van den Berghe, *Race and Racism: A Comparative Perspective* (New York: Wiley, 1967); and *Race and Ethnicity: Essays in Comparative Society* (New York: Basic Books, 1970); Robert Blauner, *Racial Oppression in America* (New York: Harper & Row, 1972). On the feminist movement see among many others, Edith Hoshino Altbach, ed., *From Feminism to Liberation* (Cambridge, Mass.: Schenkman Publishers, 1971).

74 See Theodore Roszak, *Where the Wasteland Ends: Politics and Transcendence in Postindustrial Society* (Garden City: Doubleday, 1972), pp. 3–73, 142–219, 225–236.

75 Among many works see Michael Albert, *What is to Be Undone: A Modern Revolutionary Discussion of Classical Left Ideologies* (Boston: Porter Sargent, 1974); George Fischer, ed., *The Revival of American Socialism: Selected Papers of the Socialist Scholars Conference* (New York: Oxford University Press, 1971); Andre Gorz, *Socialism and Revolution*, trans. Norman Denny (Garden City: Doubleday Anchor, 1973). For two representative works in sociology see Norman Birnbaum, *The Crisis of Industrial Society* (London: Oxford University Press, 1969); and T. B. Bottomore, *Sociology as Social Criticism* (New York: Pantheon, 1974).

76 For some sensitive discussions of the rise of ethnic group consciousness see Donald L. Horowitz, "Ethnic Identity"; Martin Kilson, "Blacks and Neo-Ethnicity in American Political Life"; Orlando Patterson, "Context and Choice in Ethnic Allegiance: A Theoretical Framework and Caribbean Case Study"; William Petersen, "On the Subnations of Western Europe"—all in *Ethnicity: Theory and Experience*, ed. Nathan Glazer and Daniel P. Moynihan with the assistance of Corinne Saposs Schelling (Cambridge, Mass.: Harvard University Press, 1975). See also Harold Isaacs, *Idols of the Tribe: Group Identity and Political Change* (New York: Harper & Row, 1975); John Higham, *Send These to Me: Jews and Other Immigrants in Urban America* (New York: Atheneum, 1975), pp. 196–246.

For a process analysis of ethnicity as an element in the repertory of individual performances and group presentations see two essays by Stanford M. Lyman and William A. Douglass, "Ethnicity: Strategies of Collective and Individual Impression Management," *Social Research*, 40 (Summer 1973), 344–365; and "L'Ethnie: Structure, Processus et Saillance," trans. Alain Kihm, *Cahiers Internationaux de Sociologie*, 61 (July–December, 1976), 197–220.

77 For aspects of this clash among two Asian American minorities see Stanford M. Lyman, *The Asian in the West*, Social Science and Humanities Publication No. 4, Western Studies Center, Desert Research Institute (Reno: University of Nevada System, 1970), pp. 81–118; and Stanford M. Lyman, *Chinese Americans* (New York: Random House, 1974), pp. 158–185. See also Lemuel F. Ignacio, *Asian Americans and Pacific Islanders: Is There Such an Ethnic Group?* (San Jose, Calif.: Filipino Development Associates, 1976).

78 See Erich Fromm, *Escape from Freedom* (New York: Rinehart, 1941); and Albert Salomon, *The Tyranny of Progress: Reflections on the Origins of Sociology* (New York: Noonday, 1955).

79 The following draws on and interprets Albert Salomon, *In Praise of Enlightenment: Essays in the History of Ideas* (Cleveland: Meridian Books, 1963), pp. 387–398; both quotations from p. 391.

80 On the idea of faith in religion, in men, and in ideas see Georg Simmel, *Sociology of Religion*, trans. Curt Rosenthal (New York: Philosophical Library, 1959), pp. 29–37.

81 See Herbert Blumer, *Symbolic Interactionism: Perspective and Method* (Englewood Cliffs,

N.J.: Prentice-Hall, 1969), pp. 1-116, 140-152; Reinhard Bendix, *Social Science and the Distrust of Reason*, University of California Publications in Sociology and Social Institutions, Vol. I (Berkeley: University of California Press, 1951).

[82] See Stanford M. Lyman and Marvin B. Scott, *A Sociology of the Absurd* (Pacific Palisades, Calif.: Goodyear, 1970).

[83] See Pico della Mirandola, *On the Dignity of Man and Other Works*, trans. Charles Glenn Wallis (Indianapolis: Bobbs-Merrill, 1965), pp. 1-34.

[84] See Gilbert Highet, *Man's Unconquerable Mind* (New York: Columbia University Press, 1954), pp. 63-102.

[85] Lyman and Scott, *Sociology of the Absurd*, pp. 1-28, 213-221; Alfred McClung Lee, *Multi-Valent Man* (New York: George Braziller, 1966), esp. pp. 77-94.

[86] Augustine, *City of God*, Bk. XIII, sec. 2, p. 510.

[87] See Maurice Friedman, "Death and the Dialogue with the Absurd," in *The Phenomenon of Death: Faces of Mortality*, ed. Edith Wyschogrod (New York: Harper Colophon, 1973), pp. 149-165.

[88] Miguel de Unamuno, *The Tragic Sense of Life*, trans. J. E. Crawford Flitch (New York: Dover, 1954), p. 45-51; quotations from pp. 45, 46-47, 47, 45, 47-51.

[89] Miguel de Unamuno, *Our Lord Don Quixote: The Life of Don Quixote and Sancho, with Related Essays*, trans. Anthony Kerrigan (Princeton: Princeton University Press, 1967), p. 283.

[90] See Jack D. Douglas, *The Social Meanings of Suicide* (Princeton: Princeton University Press, 1967), pp. 310-319.

[91] See Otto Rank, *The Don Juan Legend*, trans. David G. Winter (Princeton: Princeton University Press, 1975), pp. 61-77.

[92] Cf. the discussion in Julian Marias, *Miguel de Unamuno*, trans. Frances M. Lopez-Morillas (Cambridge, Mass.: Harvard University Press, 1966), pp. 197-199.

[93] For the following see Alan Harrington, *The Immortalist* (Millbrae, Calif.: Celestial Arts Publishers, 1969), pp. 233-250.

[94] See Robert S. Morison, "Death: Process or Event?" and Leon R. Kass, "Death as an Event," both in *Death Inside Out: The Hastings Center Report*, ed. Peter Steinfels and Robert M. Veatch (New York: Harper & Row, 1974), pp. 63-80.

[95] J. Glenn Gray, *The Warriors*, pp. 119-120.

[96] See Philippe Ariès, *Western Attitudes Toward Death from the Middle Ages to the Present*, trans. Patricia M. Ranum (Baltimore: Johns Hopkins University Press, 1974), pp. 27-52.

[97] Ibid., pp. 85-107; John Langone, *Vital Signs: The Way We Die in America* (Boston: Little, Brown, 1974); David Dempsey, *The Way We Die: An Investigation of Death and Dying in America Today* (New York: McGraw-Hill, 1975). See also the sensitive discussion in Edwin S. Schneidman, *Deaths of Man* (New York: Quadrangle, 1973).

[98] For a frank revelation of what death in hospitals is like in America, see the two volumes by Barney Glaser and Anselm Strauss, *Awareness of Dying* (Chicago: Aldine, 1965) and *Time for Dying* (Chicago: Aldine, 1968). See also the following studies for amplification of this subject: Orville G. Brim, Jr., et al., eds., *The Dying Patient* (New York: Russell Sage Foundation, 1970); Robert Fulton, ed., *Death and Identity* (New York: Wiley, 1965); David Sudnow, *Passing On: The Social Organization of Dying* (Englewood Cliffs, N.J.: Prentice-Hall, 1967). For an interesting cross-cultural account see William A. Douglass, *Death in Murelaga: Funerary Ritual in a Spanish Basque Village* (Seattle: University of Washington Press, 1969).

[99] See Nancy Lee Beaty, *The Craft of Dying: The Literary Tradition of the Ars Moriendi in England* (New Haven: Yale University Press, 1970), pp. 1-53.

100 The following is based on *ibid*., pp. 10–18 et passim.

101 J. McManners, *Reflections at the Death Bed of Voltaire: The Art of Dying in Eighteenth-Century France* (Oxford: Clarendon Press, 1974), pp. 4–5.

102 Ariès, *Western Attitudes*, pp. 11–12.

103 The following is based on McManners, *Reflections*.

104 See John Lofland, "The Dramaturgy of State Executions," in *State Executions Viewed Historically and Sociologically* (Montclair, N.J.: Patterson Smith, 1977), pp. 275–325.

ENVY

*Shakespeare, *The Tempest*, III, 2.

1 Here we can present only a sketch. For a comprehensive approach upon which we have drawn liberally, see Helmut Schoeck, *Envy—A Theory of Social Behavior*, trans. Michael Glenny and Betty Ross (New York: Harcourt, Brace, and World, 1970).

2 Max Scheler, *Ressentiment*, trans. William W. Holdheim, ed. Lewis A. Coser (New York: The Free Press, 1961; orig. pub. 1912), p. 52.

3 Robert Owen, "Report to the County of Lanark," *A New View of Society and Other Writings* (London: J. M. Dent, 1966; orig. pub. 1821), p. 297.

4 *The Utopian Vision of Charles Fourier: Selected Texts on Work, Love, and Passionate Attraction*, trans. and ed. Jonathan Beecher and Richard Bienvenu (Boston: Beacon Press, 1971), p. 87.

5 R. F. Fortune, *Sorcerers of Dobu: The Social Anthropology of the Dobu Islanders of the Western Pacific* (New York: Dutton, 1932), p. 135.

6 Melville J. Herskovits, *Life in a Haitian Valley* (Garden City: Doubleday Anchor, 1971), pp. 135–136.

7 Colin M. Turnbull, *The Mountain People* (New York: Simon and Schuster, 1972), p. 289.

8 Pitirim A. Sorokin, *Hunger as a Factor in Human Affairs*, trans. Elena P. Sorokin, ed. T. Lynn Smith (Gainesville: University Presses of Florida, 1975), p. 275.

9 W. G. Runciman, *Relative Deprivation and Social Justice: A Study of Attitudes to Social Inequality in Twentieth-Century England* (Berkeley: University of California Press, 1966), p. 252.

10 Adam Ferguson, *An Essay on the History of Civil Society*, ed. Duncan Forbes (Edinburgh: Edinburgh University Press, 1966; orig. pub. 1767), p. 39.

11 Ibid., p. 40.

12 For an enlivening discussion of the many complex issues glossed in our own formulation see Jacobus ten Broek and the editors of the *California Law Review*, eds., *The Law of the Poor* (San Francisco: Chandler, 1966).

13 Cf. Nathan Glazer, *Affirmative Discrimination: Ethnic Inequality and Public Policy* (New York: Basic Books, 1975) and Herbert Hill, "The New Judicial Perception of Employment Discrimination: Litigation under Title VII of the Civil Rights Act of 1964," *University of Colorado Law Review*, 43 (March 1972), 243–268; see Runciman, *Relative Deprivation*, pp. 249–257; also John Rawls, *A Theory of Justice* (Cambridge, Mass.: Harvard University Press), pp. 530–541; Kingsley Davis, *Human Society* (New York: Macmillan, 1948), pp. 96–117.

14 Rawls, *Theory of Justice*, pp. 532–533.

15 William Graham Sumner, *Folkways: A Study of the Sociological Importance of Usages, Manners, Customs, Mores, and Morals* (Boston: Ginn, 1940), pp. 515–519.

16 Schoeck, *Envy*, pp. 32–45.

17 Sumner, *Folkways*, p. 515.

[18] Anne Parsons, "Expressive Symbolism in Witchcraft and Delusion: A Comparative Study," *Belief, Magic, and Anomie: Essays in Psychosocial Anthropology*, ed. Rose Laub Coser et al. (New York: The Free Press, 1969), pp. 177-203; quotations from p. 201.

[19] Adam Smith, *The Theory of Moral Sentiments, or, An Essay Towards an Analysis of the Principles by Which Men Naturally Judge Concerning the Conduct and Character First of Their Neighbours, and Afterwards of Themselves* (London: Bohn, 1853; orig. pub. 1759), pp. 55-56.

[20] Runciman, *Relative Deprivation*, pp. 253-255; Rawls, *Theory of Justice*, pp. 111-114.

[21] George Cornewall Lewis, *A Treatise on the Methods of Observation and Reasoning in Politics* (New York: Arno Press, 1974; orig. pub. 1852), I, 453-479.

[22] Jacobus ten Broek and Joseph Tussman, "The Equal Protections of the Law," *California Law Review*, 37 (September 1949), 341-381.

[23] Rawls, *Theory of Justice*, p. 533.

[24] Smith, *Theory of Moral Sentiments*, pp. 166-167, 167, 86.

[25] Ping-ti Ho, *The Ladder of Success in Imperial China: Aspects of Social Mobility, 1368-1911* (New York: Columbia University Press, 1962).

[26] Mao-tse Tung, "Oppose the Party 'Eight-Legged Essay,'" *Selected Works of Mao-Tse Tung* (London: Lawrence and Wishart, 1956), IV, 46-62; see also Thomas Taylor Meadows, *The Chinese and Their Rebellions, Viewed in Connection with Their National Philosophy, Ethics, Legislation, and Administration: To Which Is Added an Essay on Civilization and Its Present State in the East and West* (London: Smith and Elder, 1856; Stanford University Academic Reprints, 1953).

[27] Thorstein Veblen, *The Theory of the Leisure Class* (Boston: Houghton Mifflin, 1973), p. 39.

[28] The following is from Georg Simmel, "Exkurs über den Schmuck," trans. as "Adornment" in *The Sociology of Georg Simmel*, ed. and trans. Kurt H. Wolff (Glencoe: The Free Press, 1950), pp. 338-339.

[29] Veblen, *Theory of the Leisure Class*, pp. 120-121.

[30] Schoeck, *Envy*, p. 222.

[31] The reference is to Robert E. Park's "race relations cycle." See Robert E. Park, *Race and Culture* (The Collected Papers of Robert Ezra Park), ed. Everett Cherrington Hughes, et al. (Glencoe: The Free Press, 1950), I, 81-255. For a related theoretical perspective that focuses on the status competition among ethnic groups, see W. Lloyd Warner and Leo Srole, *The Social Systems of American Ethnic Groups*, Yankee City Series, Vol. III (New Haven: Yale University Press, 1945). For a critical discussion see Stanford M. Lyman, *The Black American in Sociological Thought: A Failure of Perspective* (New York: G. P. Putnam, 1972), pp. 27-70.

[32] John Higham, *Strangers in the Land: Patterns of American Nativism, 1860-1925* (New York: Atheneum, 1963), pp. 87-105; Leon Litwack, *North of Slavery: The Negro in the Free States, 1790-1860* (Chicago: University of Chicago Press, 1961), pp. 167-168; Arthur C. Parker, "Problems of Race Assimilation in America, with Special Reference to the American Indian," *American Indian Magazine*, 4 (October-December 1916), 285-304; Barbara Miller Solomon, *Ancestors and Immigrants: A Changing New England Tradition* (New York: Wiley, 1965).

[33] Rose Hum Lee, *The Chinese in the United States of America* (Hong Kong: Hong Kong University Press, 1960). For a critical assessment see Stanford M. Lyman, "Overseas Chinese in America and Indonesia" *Pacific Affairs*, 34 (Winter 1961-1962), 380-389.

[34] See Randolph Bourne, "The Jew and Trans-National America," *War and the Intellectuals: Collected Essays, 1915-1919*, ed. Carl Resek (New York: Harper Torchbooks, 1964), pp. 124-133.

35 Ibid., p. 112.

36 Ibid., pp. 130–131.

37 Cf. Schoeck, *Envy*, pp. 57–61.

38 Rahel Varnhagen (1771–1833) lived at the time of the "Jewish emancipation" in Europe, founded the Goethe cult, and sought for many years to escape her Jewish identity. On her deathbed she is reported to have said, "The thing which all my life seemed to me the greatest shame, which was the misery and misfortune of my life—having been born a Jewess—this I should on no account now wish to have missed." For the definitive treatment see Hannah Arendt, *Rahel Varnhagen: The Life of a Jewish Woman*, rev. ed. (New York, Harcourt Brace Jovanovich, 1974). Karl Marx (1818–1883), son of a Jewish lawyer (who had been baptized) and a descendant on both his mother's and father's sides of generations of rabbis, wrestled with "the Jewish question" in one of his early writings. At one point he asked: "Has the standpoint of political emancipation the right to demand from the Jews the abolition of Judaism and from men the abolition of religion?" At another place he answered his question, "The social emancipation of the Jew is the emancipation of society from Judaism." See Karl Marx, "On the Jewish Question," in *Writings of the Young Marx on Philosophy and Society*, trans. and ed. Loyd D. Easton and Kurt H. Guddat (Garden City: Doubleday, 1967), pp. 217, 248.

39 See Louis Wirth, *The Ghetto* (Chicago: University of Chicago Press, Phoenix Books, 1956), pp. 260–261; Ellsworth Faris, "If I Were a Jew," *The Nature of Human Nature and Other Essays in Social Psychology* (New York: McGraw-Hill, 1937), pp. 350–353.

40 Bourne, "Trans-National America," p. 114.

41 Quoted in Everett V. Stonequist, *The Marginal Man: A Study in Personality and Culture Conflict* (New York: Russell and Russell, 1961), pp. 103–104.

42 E. Franklin Frazier, *Black Bourgeoisie: The Rise of a New Middle Class in the United States* (Glencoe: The Free Press, 1957).

43 See Rhoda L. Goldstein, ed., *Black Life and Culture in the United States* (New York: Thomas Y. Crowell, 1971).

44 Hans Zetterberg, "The Secret Ranking," *The Journal of Marriage and the Family*, 28 (1966), 134–142.

45 Georg Simmel, "Types of Social Relationships by Degrees of Reciprocal Knowledge of their Participants," in *The Sociology of Georg Simmel*, p. 322.

46 Davis, *Human Society*, pp. 31–50.

47 Here we follow Robert J. Stoller, *Sex and Gender: On the Development of Masculinity and Femininity* (New York: Science House, 1968), pp. 8–16.

48 See Talcott Parsons, "Certain Primary Sources and Patterns of Aggression in the Social Structure of the Western World," *Essays in Sociological Theory*, rev. ed. (New York: The Free Press, 1954), pp. 298–322.

49 See Lionel Tiger, *Men in Groups* (New York: Random House, 1969).

50 See Cynthia Cox, "The Chevalier d'Eon: Man or Woman?" in *The Real Figaro: The Extraordinary Career of Caron de Beaumarchais* (London: Longmans, 1962), pp. 90–102; Harold Garfinkel, *Studies in Ethnomethodology* (Englewood Cliffs, N.J.: Prentice-Hall, 1967), pp. 116–185, 285–288; for representative case studies see C. J. S. Thompson, *The Mysteries of Sex: Women Who Passed as Men and Men Who Impersonated Women* (New York: Causeway Books, 1974).

51 Sigmund Freud, "Some Psychological Consequences of the Anatomical Distinction Between the Sexes," *Collected Papers*, ed. James Strachey (New York: Basic Books, 1959), V, 186–197.

[52] See Jonathan Benthall and Ted Polhemus, eds., *The Body as a Medium of Expression* (London: Allen Lane, 1975).

[53] Erwin Panofsky, *Meaning in the Visual Arts* (Garden City: Doubleday Anchor, 1955), pp. 55-107.

[54] Bernard Rudofsky, *The Unfashionable Human Body* (Garden City: Doubleday, 1971); Erving Goffman, *Stigma: Notes on the Management of Spoiled Identity* (Englewood Cliffs, N.J.: Prentice-Hall, 1963).

[55] Yukio Mishima, *Forbidden Colors*, trans. Alfred H. Marks (New York: Avon, 1970), esp. pp. 89-106.

[56] Yukio Mishima, *Sun and Steel*, trans. John Bester (Tokyo: Kodansha International, 1970), pp. 27-28.

[57] Ibid., pp. 26, 17.

[58] See Winthrop Jordan, *White over Black: American Attitudes Toward Negroes, 1550-1812* (Chapel Hill: University of North Carolina Press, 1968), pp. 4-11.

[59] Henry Scott-Stokes, *The Life and Death of Yukio Mishima* (New York: Farrar, Straus & Giroux), pp. 172-173, 216-227, 26.

GLUTTONY

[*] Reay Tannahill, *Food in History* (New York: Stein and Day, 1973), p. 158.

[1] The name gave rise to a Soviet system of individual incentive, *Stakhanovism*, from the efforts of A. G. Stakhanov, an efficiency expert.

[2] See F. J. Roethlisberger and William J. Dickson, *Management and the Worker: An Account of a Research Program Conducted by the Western Electric Company, Hawthorne Works, Chicago.* (Cambridge, Mass.: Harvard University Press, 1966), p. 522.

[3] Cf. Philip P. Hallis, *The Paradox of Cruelty* (Middletown, Conn.: Wesleyan University Press, 1969).

[4] There is a rich and extensive literature on the history and sociology of drug use, addiction, and narcotics control. Some representative works include George Andrews and Simon Vinkenoog, eds., *The Book of Grass: An Anthology of Indian Hemp* (New York: Grove Press, 1967); Richard Ashley, *Cocaine: Its History, Uses and Effects* (New York: St. Martin's, 1975); Bingham Dai, *Opiam Addiction in Chicago* (Montclair, N.J.: Patterson Smith, 1970); Richard C. DeBold and Russell C. Leaf, eds., *LSD, Man and Society* (Middletown, Conn.: Wesleyan University Press, 1967); Troy Duster, *The Legislation of Morality: Law, Drugs, and Moral Judgment* (New York: The Free Press, 1970); Sigmund Freud, *Cocaine Papers*, ed. Robert Byck (New York: Stonehill Publishing, 1974); Michael J. Harner, ed., *Hallucinogens and Shamanism* (New York: Oxford University Press, 1973); Alfred R. Lindesmith, *The Addict and the Law* (New York: Vintage, 1967); and *Addiction and Opiates* (Chicago: Aldine, 1968); Tod H. Mikuriya, ed., *Marijuana: Medical Papers, 1839-1972* (Oakland, Calif.: Medi-Comp Press, 1973); David F. Musto, *An American Disease: Origins of Narcotic Control* (New Haven: Yale University Press, 1973); John A. O'Donnell and John C. Ball, eds., *Narcotic Addiction* (New York: Harper & Row, 1966); J. L. Simmons, ed., *Marihuana Myths and Realities* (North Hollywood, Calif.: Brandon House, 1967); David Solomon, ed., *The Marihuana Papers* (New York: Signet, 1966); Norman Taylor, *Narcotics: Man's Most Dangerous Gift* (New York: Delta, 1963). Two classic autobiographical accounts are Thomas de Quincy, *Confessions of an English Opium Eater and Other Writings*, ed. Aileen Ward (New York: Signet, 1966) and Jean Cocteau,

Opium: The Diary of a Cure, trans. Margaret Crosland and Sinclair Rood (London: NEL, 1972).

5 Morton W. Bloomfield, *The Seven Deadly Sins: An Introduction to the History of a Religious Concept, with Special Reference to Medieval English Literature* (East Lansing: Michigan State University Press, 1952, 1967), pp. 44, 74, 104, 198.

6 Ibid., pp. 80–82.

7 See E. M. W. Tillyard, *The Elizabethan World Picture* (New York: Vintage, n.d.), pp. 18–82, 94–99; Theodore Spencer, *Shakespeare and the Nature of Man*, 2nd ed. (New York: Collier, 1966), pp. 1–50; J. H. Plumb, *The Italian Renaissance* (New York: Harper Torchbooks, 1965), pp. 47–62, 111–126.

8 See Fernand Braudel, *Capitalism and Material Life, 1400–1800*, trans. Miriam Kochan (New York: Harper & Row, 1973), pp. 121–191.

9 See George Rudé, *Paris and London in the Eighteenth Century: Studies in Popular Protest* (New York: Viking, 1973); the excellent discussion in Joe R. Feagin and Harlan Hahn, *Ghetto Revolts: The Politics of Violence in American Cities* (New York: Macmillan, 1973); Steven Weed with Scott Swanton, *My Search for Patty Hearst* (New York: Warner Books, 1976), pp. 179–259 et passim.

10 See Erwin Panofsky, *Meaning in the Visual Arts* (Garden City: Doubleday Anchor, 1955), pp. 88–107. The Occidental celebration of the classic Greek frame is usually associated with the publication of Joachim Winckelmann's *Erinnerung über die Betrachtung der Alten Kunst* in the latter half of the eighteenth century. See Paul Schilder, *The Image and Appearance of the Human Body* (New York: Wiley, 1964), pp. 270–273. According to Yukio Mishima (*Forbidden Colors*, trans. Alfred H. Marks, New York: Avon, 1970, p. 91): "The establishment of the system of male beauty in Greek sculpture in the field of esthetics had to wait for the advent of Winckelmann, who was a homosexual." For a biography of Winckelmann see Wolfgang Leppmann, *Winckelmann* (New York: Knopf, 1970).

11 Orrin E. Klapp, *Heroes, Villains and Fools: The Changing American Character* (Englewood Cliffs, N.J.: Prentice-Hall Spectrum, 1962), pp. 98–101.

12 See, e.g., the irreverent article by Grace Lichtenstein, "A Nation of Fat Heads," *Esquire*, 80 (August 1973), 94–95, 138.

13 Lew Louderback, "More People Should Be Fat," *Saturday Evening Post* (November 4, 1967), pp. 10, 12.

14 The sociological literature on alcoholism, its causes, conditions, and control is voluminous. Some representative works include Joseph R. Gusfield, *Symbolic Crusade: Status Politics and the American Temperance Movement* (Urbana: University of Illinois Press, 1966); Craig MacAndrew and Robert B. Edgerton, *Drunken Comportment: A Social Explanation* (Chicago: Aldine, 1969); James P. Spradley, *You Owe Yourself a Drunk: An Ethnography of Urban Nomads* (Boston: Little, Brown, 1970); Harrison Trice, *Alcoholism in America* (New York: McGraw-Hill, 1966); Samuel E. Wallace, *Skid Row as a Way of Life* (Totowa, N.J.: Bedminster Press, 1965); Jacqueline P. Wiseman, *Stations of the Lost: The Treatment of Skid Row Alcoholics* (Englewood Cliffs, N.J.: Prentice Hall, 1970). F. Scott Fitzgerald chronicled his own nervous breakdown, attended by alcoholism and social failure, in "The Crack-Up," in *The Crack-Up*, ed. Edmund Wilson (New York: New Directions, 1959), pp. 69–84. A novel exaggerating but thinly disguising Fitzgerald's alcoholism and its effects is Budd Schulberg, *The Disenchanted* (New York: Viking, 1975). For a discussion of the obese and their attempts to organize protective organizations, see Edward Sagarin, *Odd Man In: Societies of Deviants in America* (Chicago: Quadrangle, 1972), pp. 71–75.

[15] See, e.g., T. W. Adorno et al., *The Authoritarian Personality* (New York: Harper & Row, 1950), and Gordon W. Allport, *The Nature of Prejudice*, abridged ed. (Garden City: Doubleday Anchor, 1958). See Sigmund Freud, "Thoughts for the Times on War and Death," in *Collected Papers*, trans. supervised by Joan Riviere (New York: Basic Books, 1959), IV, 288-317. For a sociological criticism of research on war and conflict see Kenneth E. Bock, "The Study of War in American Sociology," *Sociologus*, 5 (November 1955), 104-113.

[16] See Vilhelm Aubert and Sheldon S. Messinger, "The Criminal and the Sick," *Inquiry*, 1 (1958), 137-160; reprinted as chapter 1 of *The Hidden Society* by Vilhelm Aubert (Totowa, N.J.: Bedminster Press, 1965), pp. 25-54.

[17] See Edwin M. Schur, *Crimes Without Victims: Deviant Behavior and Public Policy* (Englewood Cliffs, N.J.: Prentice-Hall Spectrum, 1965).

[18] See Georg Simmel, "The Sociology of Sociability," trans. Everett C. Hughes, *American Journal of Sociology*, 55 (November 1949), 254-261.

[19] For this term see Stanford M. Lyman and Marvin B. Scott, *The Drama of Social Reality* (New York: Oxford University Press, 1975).

[20] See Stanford M. Lyman and Marvin B. Scott, "On the Time Track," *A Sociology of the Absurd* (New York: Appleton-Century Crofts, 1970; reissued Pacific Palisades, Calif.: Goodyear Publishing, 1970), pp. 189-212.

[21] See Lyman and Scott, "Territoriality: A Neglected Sociological Dimension," *A Sociology of the Absurd*, pp. 89-110.

[22] In the extreme he becomes a "freak," no longer suitable for ordinary social occasions but an object of curiosity, fear, or pity. See Frederick Drimmer, *Very Special People* (New York: Bantam, 1976), pp. 265-281.

[23] Max Weber, "India: The Brahman and the Castes," *From Max Weber: Essays in Sociology*, ed. and trans. Hans Gerth and C. Wright Mills (New York: Oxford University Press, 1946), p. 402.

[24] Georg Simmel, "Fundamental Problems of Sociology: Individual and Society," *The Sociology of Georg Simmel*, trans. and ed. Kurt H. Wolff (Glencoe: The Free Press, 1950), p. 33.

[25] Burr Snider, "Fat City: Durham, North Carolina. Where the Obese Meet to Cheat," *Esquire*, 79 (March 1973), 112-114, 174-182.

[26] See Robert M. MacIver, "The Imputation of Motives," *American Journal of Sociology*, 46 (July 1940), 1-12.

[27] C. Wright Mills, "Situated Actions and Vocabularies of Motives," *American Sociological Review*, 5 (December 1940), 904-913.

[28] See Stanford M. Lyman and Marvin B. Scott, "Accounts," *American Sociological Review*, 33 (February 1968), 46-62; reprinted in Lyman and Scott, *Sociology of the Absurd*, pp. 111-144.

[29] See William H. Sheldon, *The Varieties of Temperament* (New York: Harper and Brothers, 1942) and the discussion of temperament and body type in Tamotsu Shibutani, *Society and Personality: An Interactionist Approach to Social Psychology* (Englewood Cliffs, N.J.: Prentice-Hall, 1961), pp. 544-548.

[30] Notice that these claims might be an *excuse* if the individual employs them as countervailing his own intentions, ethics, desires, etc.

[31] Judy Klemesrud, "What Body-Building King Finds Uplifting," *The New York Times*, May 8, 1976, p. 12.

[32] Burr Snider, "Fat City," p. 182.

[33] Ibid., p. 174.

GREED

*Lewis Carroll, "Alice's Adventures in Wonderland," *Complete Works* (New York: Vintage, 1976), p. 81.

1 See Morton W. Bloomfield, *The Seven Deadly Sins: An Introduction to the History of a Religious Concept, with Special Reference to Medieval English Literature* (East Lansing: Michigan State University Press, 1967), pp. 74-75, 90-91, 199, 182-183, 241-242.

2 The following owes much to the discussion by Norman O. Brown, *Life Against Death: The Psychoanalytical Meaning of History* (Middletown, Conn.: Wesleyan University Press, 1970), pp. 234-306.

3 John Locke, *Some Considerations of the Consequences of the Lowering of Interest and Raising the Value of Money*, in *Works*, V, 22; cited in ibid., p. 247.

4 Gregory the Great, *Morals on the Book of Job* (Oxford: John Henry Parker; London: F. and J. Rivington, 1845), III, 490.

5 Erich Fromm, *The Anatomy of Human Destructiveness* (New York: Holt, Rinehart and Winston, 1973), p. 208.

6 The following is adapted from Hugh Dalziel Duncan, *Communication and Social Order* (London: Oxford University Press, 1968), pp. 358-360. See also Stuart Ewen, *Captains of Consciousness: Advertising and the Social Roots of Consumer Culture* (New York: McGraw-Hill, 1976), pp. 156-157.

7 Karl Menninger, *Whatever Became of Sin?* (New York: Hawthorn, 1973).

8 Sigmund Freud, *New Introductory Lectures on Psychoanalysis*, trans. James Strachey (New York: Norton, 1965), p. 100.

9 Duncan, *Communication and Social Order*, pp. 351-353.

10 Brown, *Life Against Death*, p. 257.

11 Fromm, *Anatomy of Human Destructiveness*, p. 209. However, Sombart defined luxury as "any expenditure in excess of the necessary" and points to two sources for the determination of the necessary—one is subjective and referable to some ethical or aesthetic value; the other is objective and referable to physiological needs or cultural wants. Of the subjective sources he distinguishes the quantitative luxury that is synonymous with prodigality and the qualitative that leads to the designation of "luxury goods" and "refinement." To Sombart, luxury was a key factor in the development of capitalism. See Werner Sombart, *Luxury and Capitalism*, trans. W. R. Dittmar, (Ann Arbor: University of Michigan Press, 1967; orig. pub. 1913), pp. 59-63.

Even earlier, in 1723, Bernard de Mandeville argued with much wit and verve that "once we depart from calling every thing luxury that is not absolutely necessary to keep a man alive, ... then there is no luxury at all; for if the wants of Men are innumerable, then what ought to supply them has no bounds; what is call'd superfluous to some degree of People, will be thought requisite to those of higher Quality; and neither the World nor the Skill of Man can produce any thing so curious or extravagant, but some most Glorious Sovereign or other, if it either eases or diverts him, will reckon it among the Necessaries of Life; not meaning every Body's Life, but that of his Sacred Person." *The Fable of the Bees, or Private Vices, Publick Benefits*, ed. F. B. Kaye (London: Oxford University Press, 1966), I, 108.

12 Duncan, *Communication and Social Order*, pp. 352-353.

13 Brown, *Life Against Death*, pp. 252-304. See also Ernest Becker, *Escape from Evil* (New York: The Free Press, 1975), pp. 73-90.

14 De Mandeville, *Fable of the Bees*, I, 91, 101, 102, 106.

[15] Georg Simmel, "A Chapter in the Philosophy of Value," *American Journal of Sociology*, 5 (March 1900), 577, 578.

[16] S. P. Altmann, "Simmel's Philosophy of Money," *American Journal of Sociology*, 9 (July 1903), 52. For a related point of view see Charles Horton Cooley, "The Sphere of Pecuniary Valuation," *American Journal of Sociology*, 19 (September 1913), 188-203.

[17] Georg Simmel, "Faithfulness and Gratitude," in *The Sociology of Georg Simmel*, trans. and ed. Kurt H. Wolff (Glencoe: The Free Press, 1950), pp. 390-391.

[18] Ibid., pp. 391-392.

[19] Simmel, "A Chapter in the Philosophy of Value," pp. 582-584. It was his position on the sale of labor power that aroused the criticism of socialist sociologists. For a representative point of view of the latter see Albion W. Small, trans., "Schmoller on Class Conflicts in General," *American Journal of Sociology*, 20 (January 1915), 504-531.

[20] Simmel, "A Chapter," p. 585.

[21] Ibid., pp. 586, 589, 590.

[22] In addition to his famous study of the Protestant Ethic, Weber devoted much of his writings on religion and economic action to the comparative historical and differential study of capitalism. See especially Max Weber, *Economy and Society: An Outline of Interpretive Sociology*, 3 vols., ed. Guenther Roth and Claus Wittich (New York: Bedminster Press, 1968); *General Economic History*, trans. Frank H. Knight (Glencoe: Free Press, 1950); *The City*, trans. and ed. Don Martindale and Gertrud Neuwirth (Glencoe: The Free Press, 1958); *The Theory of Social and Economic Organization*, trans. A. M. Henderson, ed. Talcott Parsons (Glencoe: The Free Press, 1947); *From Max Weber: Essays in Sociology*, ed. Hans Gerth and C. Wright Mills (New York: Oxford University Press, 1946); *On Law in Economy and Society*, trans. Edward Shils and Max Rheinstein (Cambridge, Mass.: Harvard University Press, 1954); *The Rational and Social Foundations of Music*, trans. and ed. D. Martindale, J. Riedel, and G. Neuwirth (Carbondale: Southern Illinois University Press, 1958); *The Agrarian Sociology of Ancient Civilizations*, trans. R. I. Frank (London: New Left Books, 1976); *The Sociology of Religion*, trans. E. Fischoff (Boston: Beacon Press, 1963); *The Religion of China: Confucianism and Taoism*, trans. and ed. Hans Gerth (Glencoe: The Free Press, 1951); *The Religion of India: The Sociology of Hinduism and Buddhism*, trans. and ed. Hans Gerth and Don Martindale (Glencoe: The Free Press, 1958); *Ancient Judaism*, trans. Hans Gerth and Don Martindale (Glencoe: The Free Press, 1952).

[23] For some representative comments over the years see Kemper Fullerton, "Calvinism and Capitalism," *Harvard Theological Review*, 21 (July 1928), 163-195; T. Parsons, "Capitalism in Recent German Literature: Sombart and Weber," *Journal of Political Economy*, 36 (December 1928), 641-661; 38 (February 1929), 31-51; and T. Parsons, "H. M. Robertson on Max Weber and His School," *Journal of Political Economy*, 43 (October 1935), 688-696; Albert Salomon, "Max Weber's Sociology," *Social Research*, 2 (February 1935), 60-73; Werner Falk, "Democracy and Capitalism in Max Weber's Sociology," *Sociological Review*, 27 (October 1935), 373-393; Ephraim Fischoff, "The Protestant Ethic and the Spirit of Capitalism: The History of a Controversy," *Social Research*, 11 (February 1944), 53-77; Winthrop S. Hudson, "Puritanism and the Spirit of Capitalism," *Church History*, 18 (March 1949), 3-17; Benjamin Nelson, "Weber's Protestant Ethic: Its Origins, Wanderings, and Foreseeable Future," in C. Y. Glock and P. Hammond, eds., *Beyond the Classics? Essays in the Scientific Study of Religion* (New York: Harper & Row, 1973), pp. 71-130. I am indebted to Guenther Roth for pointing out the importance of Werner Stark, "Max Weber and the Heterogony of Purposes," *Social Research*, 34 (Spring 1967), 249-264.

24 The following quotations are taken from the "Author's Introduction" to Max Weber, *The Protestant Ethic and the Spirit of Capitalism*, trans. Talcott Parsons (London: Allen and Unwin, 1930), p. 17.

25 A related process was the adoption by Christians of the right to lend money at interest. For the definitive study of how the Deuteronomic double standard prohibiting usury among brothers was extended by first universalizing brotherhood, then transforming that into a universal otherhood, permitting interest-bearing loans, see Benjamin Nelson, *The Idea of Usury: From Tribal Brotherhood to Universal Otherhood*, 2d enl. ed. (Chicago: University of Chicago Press, 1969).

26 The psychoanalytic and symbolic connections of vampirism to sexuality, anti-Semitism, and capitalism deserve much more investigation. As Norman O. Brown *Life Against Death*, (p. 297) has pointed out, "The connection between sublimation, the death instinct, and excrement is not static but subject to the dynamics of the neurosis which is human history." In the mythological vampire, Dracula, is embodied the restoration of immortality in the form of a sentient zombie, who must forever live in the night, revitalizing his life-in-death with human blood sucked from the throats of victims who become his slaves, exchanging their own mortal freedom for everlasting slavery. Furthermore, the vampiric myth evokes the image of blood and its relation to life, menstruation, sexuality, sadism, and murder. (See Freud, "The Taboo of Virginity," *Collected Papers*, IV, 221–227.) Moreover, the anal-feces cathexis, associated with greed, is, as Freud argued, translatable into other objects having to do with other orifices (the mouth, sucking) and to sexuality (penis, power). Note also that vampirism is in some cases a secularized form of anti-Semitism's medieval blood charge against the Jews [See Joshua Trachtenberg, *The Devil and the Jews: The Medieval Conception of the Jew and its Relation to Modern Anti-Semitism* (New Haven: Yale University Press, 1943), pp. 140–158]. Finally, it is clear that the vampire belongs to that realm of the uncanny discussed by Freud, who observed that the term not only referred to that which "arouses dread and creeping horror" but also "that which is concealed and kept out of sight." [Freud, "The Uncanny," *Collected Papers*, IV, 368–407.] Here it is not possible to work out the connections among feces-money-immortality-concealment. Suffice it to suggest that just as Freud disenchanted sublimated anal-eroticism, so Weber and Marx disenchanted capitalism, removing it from its uncanny dark concealment and exposing it to the destructive rays of sunlit, daytime illumination.

27 See Mary Wollstonecraft Shelley, *Frankenstein; or, the Modern Prometheus* (1818 text), ed. James Rieger (Indianapolis: Bobbs-Merrill, 1974). For discussions of the symbolism in this work see Christopher Small, *Ariel like a Harpy: Mary Shelley and Frankenstein*, (London: Gollancz, 1972; and Martin Tropp, *Mary Shelley's Monster: The Story of Frankenstein* (Boston: Houghton Mifflin, 1976). For an attempt to reconstruct the historical background see Radu Florescu, *In Search of Frankenstein* (New York: New York Graphic Society, 1975).

28 The literature on vampires and witchcraft has grown enormously in the last century and received serious attention recently from a variety of perspectives. An excellent general account is to be found in Jeffrey Burton Russell, *Witchcraft in the Middle Ages* (Ithaca, N.Y.: Cornell University Press, 1972); See also Norman Cohn, *Europe's Inner Demons: An Enquiry Inspired by the Great Witch-Hunt* (New York: Basic Books, 1975). The beginnings of sociological interest are presented in Edward A. Tiryakian, ed., *On the Margin of the Visible: Sociology, the Esoteric and the Occult* (New York: Wiley, 1974). The classic gothic fiction includes James Malcolm Rymer (or Thomas Pecket Prest), *Varney the Vampyre, or the Feast of Blood* (New York: Dover, 1972; orig. pub. 1847) 2 vols.; Joseph

Sheridan LeFanu, "Carmilla," in *Best Ghost Stories of J. S. LeFanu*, ed. B. F. Bleiler (New York: Dover, 1964; orig. pub. 1867), pp. 274–339. A good collection is to be found in E. F. Bleiler, ed., *Three Gothic Novels: The Castle of Otranto, by Horace Walpole: Vathek, by William Beckford; The Vampyre, by John Polidori, and a Fragment of a Novel, by Lord Byron* (New York: Dover, 1966). Of course, *the classic* is Bram Stoker, *Dracula* (New York: Modern Library, n.d.; orig. pub. 1897); and Bram Stoker, "Dracula's Guest," in *Dracula's Guest and Other Stories* (London: Arrow Books, 1974; orig. pub. 1914). Interest in Dracula has recently been repaid with Raymond T. McNally and Radu Florescu, *In Search of Dracula: A True History of Dracula and Vampire Legends* (Greenwich, Conn.: New York Graphic Society, 1972); Radu Florescu and Raymond T. McNally, *Dracula: A Biography of Vlad the Impaler, 1431-1476* (New York: Hawthorn, 1973); Gabriel Ronay, *The Truth About Dracula* (New York: Stein and Day, 1972); Leonard Wolf, *A Dream of Dracula: In Search of the Living Dead* (Boston: Little, Brown, 1972), and *The Annotated Dracula* (New York: Clarkson N. Potter, 1975); Siegfried Kracauer, *From Caligari to Hitler: A Psychological History of the German Film* (Princeton: Princeton University Press, 1971), pp. 61–87; Lotte H. Eisner, *The Haunted Screen: Expressionism in the German Cinema and the Influence of Max Reinhardt* (Berkeley: University of California Press, 1969), pp. 17–38; 95–114, and *Murnau* (Berkeley: University of California Press, 1973), pp. 27–58, 108–119, 227–272; Raymond Rudorff, *The Dracula Archives* (New York: Arbor House, 1971). Serious historical literature includes three works by Montague Summers, *The Vampire: His Kith and Kin* (New Hyde Park, N.Y.: University Books, 1960; orig. pub. 1929); *The Vampire in Europe* (New Hyde Park, N.Y.: University Books, 1968; orig. pub. 1929); *The Werewolf* (New York: Bell, 1966; orig. pub. 1933); and Dudley Wright, *The Book of Vampires*, (New York: Causeway Books, 1973); Anthony Masters, *The Natural History of the Vampire* (New York: G. P. Putnam, 1972). For a thoughtful analysis of the genre, see H. P. Lovecraft, *Supernatural Horror in Literature* (New York: Dover, 1973). A recent biography, Daniel Farson, *The Man Who Wrote Dracula: A Biography of Bram Stoker* (New York: St. Martin's, 1975), is useful. For the most famous "Dracula" on stage and screen see Arthur Lennig, *The Count: The Life and Films of Bela "Dracula" Lugosi* (New York: Putnam, 1974); and Robert Cremer, *Lugosi: The Man Behind the Cape* (Chicago: Regnery, 1976).

[29] See three essays by Robert E. Park, "A King in Business: Leopold II of Belgium, Autocrat of the Congo and International Broker," *Everybody's Magazine*, 15 (November 1906), 624–623; "The Terrible Story of the Congo," *Everybody's Magazine*, 15 (December 1906), 763–772; "The Blood-Money of the Congo," *Everybody's Magazine*, 16 (January 1907), 60–70.

[30] Ralf Dahrendorf, *Class and Class Conflict in Industrial Society* (Stanford: Stanford University Press, 1959), pp. 41–48.

[31] Max Weber, *Protestant Ethic*, p. 182.

[32] Georg Simmel, "The Miser and the Spendthrift," trans. Roberta Ash from *Philosophie des Geldes*, 2nd enl. ed. (Leipzig: Duncker and Humblot, 1907), pp. 351–354, 254–257, in G. Simmel, *On Individuality and Social Forms*, ed. Donald N. Levine (Chicago: University of Chicago Press, 1971), pp. 179–186.

[33] Ibid., pp. 183, 182, 179, 183.

[34] Molière, *The Miser* (*L'Avare*), trans. Wallace Fowlie (Woodbury, N.Y.: Barron's, 1964), the play was first produced in 1668.

[35] See Lyman and Scott, "Paranoia, Homosexuality, and Game Theory," *Sociology of the Absurd*, pp. 71–88.

[36] See Edwin Lemert, "Paranoia and the Dynamics of Exclusion," in *Human Deviance,*

Social Problems, and Social Control (Englewood Cliffs, N.J.: Prentice-Hall, 1967), pp. 197-211.

[37] Robert E. Park discovered a real and much more ominous miser in Leopold II, King of Belgium. About this avaricious and cynical king it was said that he had but two dreams: "'To die a milliardaire' (the possessor of one thousand million francs), 'and to disinherit his daughters.'" And Park goes on to point out in terms complementary to our own argument, "But at seventy-one, even the most worldly man must needs think of something other than money and the satisfaction of his personal malice" (Park, "A King in Business," p. 626).

[38] Frank Norris, *McTeague: A Story of San Francisco* (New York: Signet, 1964). Originally published in 1899, the novel was inspired by Emile Zola and became the first American novel in the naturalistic tradition. It is perhaps worth noting that naturalism entered the dramatic literature via Zola's interpretations of Claude Bernard's book on experimental medicine and reflected the profound influence of Auguste Comte. See Emile Zola, *The Experimental Novel and Other Essays*, trans. Belle M. Sherman (New York: Haskell House, 1964), pp. 1-56, 109-160, and Martin Esslin, "Naturalism in Perspective," *Reflections: Essays on Modern Theatre*, (Garden City: Doubleday Anchor, 1971), pp. 11-26.

[39] Quoted from Thomas Quinn Curtis, *Von Stroheim* (New York: Farrar, Straus & Giroux, 1971), p. 175.

[40] Von Stroheim's own summary of Norris' novel is found in ibid., pp. 159-161. The original screenplay is found in *The Complete "Greed" of Erich Von Stroheim*, compiled and annotated with a foreword by Herman G. Weinberg (New York: Dutton, 1973). See also Joel W. Finler, ed., *Greed: A Film by Erich von Stroheim* (New York: Simon and Schuster, 1972).

[41] Norris, *McTeague*, p. 273.

[42] Lewis Coser, *Greedy Institutions: Patterns of Undivided Commitment* (New York: The Free Press, 1974).

[43] The following is adapated from Charles Mackay, *Extraordinary Popular Delusions and the Madness of Crowds* (London: Richard Bentley, 1841; New York: Farrar, Straus, & Giroux, 1932, 1970), pp. 89-97; quotation from p. 89.

[44] The following is adapted from ibid., pp. 1-88; quotations from p. 72.

[45] The following is taken from Karl Marx, *Early Texts*, trans. and ed. David McLellan (Oxford: Basil Blackwell, 1972), pp. 178-183.

[46] For a dramatistic interpretation of Marx's thought, see Harold Rosenberg, *Act and the Actor: Making the Self* (New York: World, 1970), pp. 14-57.

[47] Karl Marx, "Preface to a Contribution to the Critique of Political Economy," trans. N. I. Stone, in *Marx and Engels: Basic Writings on Politics and Philosophy*, ed. Lewis S. Feuer (Garden City: Doubleday Anchor, 1959), pp. 42-46.

[48] John A. Sutter, "The Discovery of Gold in California," *Hutchings' California Magazine*, 2 (November 1857), 194-198.

[49] See Ralph J. Roske, "The World Impact of the California Gold Rush, 1849-1857," *Arizona and the West*, 5 (Autumn 1963), 187-198.

[50] See Frank Soule, John H. Gihon, and James Nisbet, *The Annals of San Francisco, Together with the Continuation Through 1855*, comp. Dorothy H. Huggins (Palo Alto: Lewis Osborne, 1966; orig. pub. 1855), pp. 248-263, 300-310, 357-369, 378-390, 411-426, 484-496. See also Jay Monaghan, *Australians and the Gold Rush: California and Down Under, 1849-1854* (Berkeley: University of California Press, 1966).

[51] For sensitive discussions of California's character in this period see Josiah Royce,

California: From the Conquest in 1846 to the Second Vigilance Committee in San Francisco (New York: Knopf, 1948); David Lavender, *California: Land of New Beginnings* (New York: Harper & Row, 1972), pp. 149–378; Kevin Starr, *America and the California Dream, 1850–1915* (New York: Oxford University Press, 1973); Walton Bean, *California: An Interpretive History* (New York: McGraw-Hill, 1968), pp. 108–124; Roger W. Lotchin, *San Francisco, 1846–1856: From Hamlet to City* (New York: Oxford University Press, 1974), pp. 3–135.

[52] Karl Marx, "The Global Consequences of the Discovery of Gold in California," in Marx, *On America and the Civil War*, trans. and ed. Saul K. Padover (New York: McGraw-Hill, 1972), pp. 14–15.

[53] Kal Marx, *Grundrisse: Foundations of the Critique of Political Economy*, trans. Martin Nicolaus (Harmondsworth: Penguin and New Left Review, 1973), p. 225.

[54] Marx, "The Global Consequences," pp. 14, 15.

[55] Marx to Engels, London, October 8, 1858, in Karl Marx, *On Revolution*, ed. and trans. Saul K. Padover (New York: McGraw-Hill, 1971), p. 139.

[56] Kal Marx, *The Class Struggles in France, 1848–1850*, trans. prepared by the Institute of Marxism-Leninism based on the Engels ed. of 1895 (Moscow: Progress Publishers, 1969); reprinted in Marx, *On Revolution*, p. 231.

[57] See Abraham P. Nasatir, "Alexandre Dumas, Fils, and the Lottery of the Golden Ingots," *California Historical Society Quarterly*, 33 (June 1954), 126–130 et passim.

[58] Karl Marx, *The Eighteenth Brumaire of Louis Bonaparte* (New York: International Publishers, 1963), pp. 84–86, 15.

[59] Marx to Engels, London, November 13, 1851, in Karl Marx, *On America and the Civil War*, p. 37.

[60] Marx to Engels, London, August 19, 1852, in ibid., p. 38.

[61] Marx to Engels, London, August 7, 1862, in ibid., p. 261.

[62] Marx to Engels, London, August 10, 1869, in Karl Marx, *On Revolution*, p. 525. Incidentally it is worth pointing out that Marx was quite wrong about the expropriative function of, or the cheap wages allegedly paid to, Chinese workers. See Alexander Saxton, *The Indispensable Enemy: Labor and the Anti-Chinese Movement in California*, (Berkeley: University of California Press, 1971); and Stanford M. Lyman, *Chinese Americans* (New York: Random House, 1974), pp. 58–85.

[63] See Stanford M. Lyman, *The Asian in the West*, Social Science and Humanities Publication No. 4, Western Studies Center (Reno: Desert Research Institute, University of Nevada System, 1970), pp. 9–26; Herbert Hill, "Anti-Oriental Agitation and the Rise of Working-Class Racism," *Society*, 10 (January–February 1973), 43–54. See also James Bryce, "Kearneyism in California," *The American Commonwealth* (New York: Macmillan, 1901), II, 425–448.

[64] Marx to Sorge, London, November 5, 1880, in Marx, *On Revolution*, p. 536.

[65] See Carey McWilliams, *California: The Great Exception* (New York: Current Books, 1949), and Dennis Hale and Jonathan Eisen, eds., *The California Dream* (New York: Collier, 1968).

[66] See Joan Didion, *Slouching Toward Bethlehem* (New York: Delta-Dell, 1968). Sydney Greenbie and Marjorie Greenbie, *Gold of Ophir: Or the Lure That Made America* (Garden City: Doubleday, 1925).

[67] From F. Scott Fitzgerald, "The Diamond as Big as the Ritz" [in *Babylon Revisited and Other Stories* (New York: Scribner, 1960), pp. 75–113], an allegory that mirrors the greed that had become second nature in America and the illusion of riches that fascinated his contemporaries and would end in a great crash returning everyone to the hell-on-earth

of everyday life. In the novella by Nathanael West, "The Day of the Locust" [in the *Complete Works of Nathanael West* (New York: Farrar, Straus & Giroux, 1971, pp. 257-421], the dreams of fame and fortune in Hollywood are not only shown to be disillusioning and false, but also destroyed in a great holocaust.

68 Hubert Howe Bancroft, "Money and Monopoly," *Essays and Miscellany*, The Works of Hubert Howe Bancroft, vol. 38 (San Fransisco: The History Co., 1890; New York: Arno Press and McGraw-Hill, n.d.), pp. 419-454; quotations from pp. 420 and 421.

69 Edwin H. Sutherland, *White Collar Crime* (New York: Holt, Rinehart, and Winston, 1949), pp. 9-13, 29-55, 222-233; quotation from p. 9.

70 Matthew Josephson, *The Robber Barons: The Great American Capitalists, 1861-1901* (New York: Harcourt, Brace and World, 1962).

71 Sutherland, *White Collar Crime*, p. 10.

72 Bancroft, "Money and Monopoly," pp. 421-422.

73 John Murray Cuddihy, *The Ordeal of Civility: Freud, Marx, Levi-Strauss, and the Jewish Struggle for Modernity* (New York: Basic Books, 1974), pp. 69-70.

74 Kenneth Burke, *Attitudes Toward History* (Boston: Beacon Press, 1961), p. 319.

75 Lyman and Scott, "Accounts," in *A Sociology of the Absurd*, pp. 111-144.

76 Robert Southey, *The Life of Wesley*, 2nd ed. (London: Longman, Hurst, Rees, Orme, and Brown, 1820); quoted in Duncan, *Communication and Social Order*, p. 349.

77 Burke, *Attitudes*, p. 320.

78 Bruce Barton, *The Man Nobody Knows: A Discovery of the Real Jesus* (Indianapolis: Bobbs-Merrill, 1924), pp. 179-180.

79 Gresham M. Sykes and David Matza, "Techniques of Neutralization," *American Sociological Review*, 22 (December 1957), 667-669.

80 Cf. Sutherland, *White Collar Crime*, pp. 235-241.

81 Bancroft, "Money and Monopoly," p. 433.

82 Ibid., pp. 432-433, 435-436.

83 See Harold Garfinkel, "A Conception of, and Experiments with, 'Trust' as a Condition of Stable Concerted Actions," in *Motivation and Social Interaction*, ed. O. J. Harvey (New York: Ronald, 1963), pp. 187-238. The relation of trust to sublimated greed and modest upward mobility was communicated in the stories of Horatio Alger. Young men were advised that if they worked hard in the most menial of jobs, remained chaste, and abstained from liquor and tobacco, they would be in an excellent position to reap the rewards that would come from a lucky accident, e.g., rescuing the boss's daughter from a runaway horse and being rewarded with a promotion on the job, rights to court the girl, and the hope of marrying her and inheriting the business. See R. Richard Wohl, "The 'Rags to Riches Story': An Episode of Secular Idealism," in *Class, Status and Power: A Reader in Social Stratification*, ed. Reinhard Bendix and Seymour Martin Lipset (Glencoe: The Free Press, 1953), pp. 388-395.

84 Max Weber, *Protestant Ethic*, p. 182.

85 Anonymous, "The Influence of the Trading Spirit on the Social and Moral Life in America," *The American Review: A Whig Journal of Politics, Literature, Art and Science*, 1 (January 1845), 95-98. All quotations in this paragraph are from this essay.

86 Herman Melville, *The Confidence Man: His Masquerade* (New York: New American Library, 1964; orig. pub. 1857). I should like to express my appreciation to Herbert Hill, who suggested the significance of this novel and urged its importance.

87 Ibid., p. 260.

88 Cf. Edwin Haviland Miller, *Melville* (New York: George Braziller, 1975), pp. 269-283.

89 Cf. Georg Simmel, "The Stranger," in *The Sociology of Georg Simmel*, pp. 402-408.

⁹⁰David W. Maurer, *The American Confidence Man* (Springfield, Ill.: Charles C. Thomas, 1974), p. 10.

⁹¹Adam Smith, *The Theory of Moral Sentiments* (New Rochelle, N.Y.: Arlington House, 1969; ⁓rig. pub. 1759), p. 210.

⁹²*London Truth*, reprinted in the *Middlebury* (Vt.) *Register*, March 17, 1899.

⁹³Abraham Lincoln, "Second Campaign Speech Against Stephen A. Douglas" (Springfield, Ill., July 17, 1858).

⁹⁴Franklin D. Roosevelt, "First Inaugural Address" (Washington, March 4, 1933).

⁹⁵Roosevelt, "Speech at Madison Square Garden" (New York, October 31, 1936).

⁹⁶Roosevelt, "Second Inaugural Address" (New York, January 20, 1937).

⁹⁷Roosevelt, "Speech" (Brooklyn, November 1, 1940).

⁹⁸Roosevelt, "Tax Bill Veto Message" (Washington, February 22, 1944).

⁹⁹See Niles M. Hansen, "The Protestant Ethic as a General Precondition for Economic Development," *Canadian Journal of Economics and Political Science*, 29 (November 1963), 462-474. See also Niles M. Hansen, "Weber and Veblen on Economic Development," *Kyklos*, 17 (1964), 447-469 and Thelma McCormack, "The Protestant Ethic and the Spirit of Socialism," *British Journal of Sociology*, 20 (1969), 266-276.

SOCIETY AND EVIL

*C. T. McIntire, "The Renewal of Christian Views of History in an Age of Catastrophe," *God, History, and Historians: An Anthology of Modern Christian Views of History* (New York: Oxford University Press, 1977), p. 13.

¹William Irwin Thompson, *Evil and World Order* (New York: Harper & Row, 1976), pp. 57-58.

²Ernest Becker, *The Structure of Evil: An Essay on the Unification of the Science of Man* (New York: George Braziller, 1968), p. 141; emphasis in original.

³Nicola Chiaromonte, "The Worm of Consciousness," in *The Worm of Consciousness and Other Essays*, ed. Miriam Chiaromonte, trans. Barbara Loeb Kennedy (New York: Harcourt Brace Jovanovich, 1976), pp. 158-159.

⁴Stanley E. Fish, *Surprised by Sin: The Reader in Paradise Lost* (Berkeley: University of California Press, 1971), p. 156.

⁵See Harold Rosenberg, *Act and the Actor: Making the Self* (New York: World, 1970), pp. 14-57.

⁶Ernest Becker, *Escape from Evil* (New York: The Free Press, 1975), p. 162.

⁷Hannah Arendt, *Eichmann in Jerusalem: A Report on the Banality of Evil* (New York: Viking, 1963), p. 253.

⁸Leszek Kolakowski, "The Key to Heaven: Edifying Tales from Holy Scripture to Serve as Teaching and Warning," trans. Salvator Attanasio, in *The Key to Heaven and Conversations with the Devil* (New York: Grove Press, 1972), p. 4.

⁹Ibid.

¹⁰The following is from Michel Contat's interview with Sartre that originally appeared in *Le Nouvel Observateur*, June 23, June 30, and July 7, 1975, and is translated and printed as "Self-Portrait at Seventy" in Jean-Paul Sartre, *Life/Situations: Essays Written and Spoken*, trans. Paul Auster and Lydia Davis (New York: Pantheon, 1977), p. 84.

¹¹The following is from "Conversations with the Devil," trans. Celina Wieniewska, in Kolakowski, *Key to Heaven*, pp. 94-95.

INDEX

Abba Isaias, 136
Abelard, Peter, 95–96
Abraham, Karl, 11
Abstinence, 54, 59–61
Absurdity of life, death evoking, 175
Accident, as excuse for gluttony, 226
Acedia. See Sloth
Addiction, as gluttony, 212, 213
Adornment. *See* Clothing
Adultery
    Aquinas' view of, 64–65
    See also Lust
Affectlessness, as trend, 40–42, 119
Africa, 2
Agathogamic marital norms, 118
Aggression
    Freudian view of, as instinct, 121
    gender-roles and patterns of, 206–207
    in school, 28, 30
    sloth and, 14
    work and, 26, 27
    See also Anger
Alanus de Insulis, 141–142, 144
Alcoholism, 240
Alcuin, 6, 214
Alexander, Franz, 11–12
Ambition, envy as goad to, 194–195
American Monomyth, 153
Amiens Cathedral, 233
Amish (community), 29
Amsterdam Jewish Community, 162–163
Anal eroticism
    greed as, 237–239
    See also Greed

Anatomy
    envy of, 209–211
    See also Body
Anatomy of Melancholy (Burton), 22
Anger, 110–134, 139
    Dante's view of, 165
    drama of, 131–134
    in defense of self, 113–119
    display of, and violence, 131
    ethology and, 122–124
    and group defense, 114–117
    nature of, 110–112
    in phenomenological sociology, 124–125
    in psychoanalysis, 120–121
    and sexual property, 117–119
    sloth and, 12
    in social psychology, 121–122
    and territoriality, 125–131
Anger of Achilles, The (Graves and Richards), 112
Animal studies, 122–124
Anshen, Ruth Nanda, 72
Anthropology, denigration of love in, 87–90
Anti-Semitism, 201, 204
Antoninus of Florence, 233
Apathy, 40–42
Apostolic Constitutions, 61
Aquinas, Thomas, 23
    lust as viewed by, 59–68
    pride as viewed by, 164
Arbuckle, Fatty, 228
Arendt, Hannah, 32–33, 41–42, 273

Ariès, Philippe, 179-180
Aristotle, 63
    greed as viewed by, 232
    on pride, 137-139
Arnobius, 110
Arranged marriages, 100-101
Arrogance. *See* Pride
Artaud, Antonin, 102-108
Asceticism
    Christian, 101
    redeeming and revolutionary, 151-154
Ascription, envy and, 205-209
Assimilation (to U.S. society), 200-205
Assortative mating, 99-100
Athenagoras, 61
Augustine, 60, 103, 271
    avarice as viewed by, 233
    on death, 175
    divorce as viewed by, 65
    incest as viewed by, 77-79
    lust as viewed by, 54-58, 69, 71
    male sex organ and, 54, 58, 143
    pride as viewed by, 163-164
    on women, 72
Authenticity, quest for, 170-173
Autoeroticism, 64, 65, 98
Avariciousness. *See* Greed

Bacon, Roger, 82, 233
Bakunin, Mikhail, 41
Bancroft, Hubert Howe, 259, 263-264
Barton, Bruce, 262
Bates, Marston, 123
Baxter, Richard, 23
Beauty, 209-211
Becker, Ernest, 154, 270-272
Behavioral sciences, anger and, 119-125
Bestiality, Aquinas' view of, 64, 65
Bettelheim, Bruno, 35
Bible, 59
Bigamy, Luther's view of, 70, 71
Blacks
    anger of, 116-117
    assimilation of, 205
    and basis of racism, 119
    gender role and, 207, 208
    lust and, 97-98, 100

    reciprocal aggression of whites and,
        122
    sloth of, 37
Blumer, Herbert, 118-119
Boastfulness, 139
Body
    and beauty, 209-211
    classical figure of, 216-218
    envy and, 205-206
    as excuse for gluttony, 227-228
    gluttony defiling, 223
    gluttony as sin of, 214
    nakedness of, 55-57
    as object of love, gluttony and, 230-231
Body language, 131-133
Bogardus, Emory S., 59, 61
Boredom
    modern, 18
    in schools, 28-30
    sloth activated by, 14-18
    and work, 26-27
Bosch, Hieronymus, 105
Bourgeoisie
    civility of, 146
    envy, display and, 198-200
    greed of, 233, 235-236
    and white-collar crime, 259-264
    See also Revolution
Bourne, Randolph, 202-205
Bowman, Andrew L., 17-18
Brown, Norman O., 237-239, 247
Buber, Martin, 274
Buck, Carrie, 98
Buddha, 11-12
Buddhism, melancholy in, 11-12
Bultman, Rudolf, 107
Burgess, Anthony, 123
Burgess, Ernest W., 90
Burke, Kenneth, 20-21, 262
Burton, Robert, 22

Cacogamic marital norms, 118
California Gold Rush, 253-259
Calvinism
    and avarice, 262
    and men's dress, 146
    pride and, 152

withdrawal and lassitude proscribed in, 10
See also Protestant Ethic
Camus, Albert, 40, 47
Canterbury Tales, The (Chaucer), 143
Capitalism, 101, 119, 151, 262
and giving-up syndrome among Oceanic peoples, 38-39
greed and, 119, 243-245, 268
unemployed and disreputable poor under, 35-37
Cartesian duality, 170-172, 214
Carthage, Council of (407), 65
Casanova, 97
Cassian, John, 6, 136, 214
Castrati, 94-98
Castrations, 119
boyhood fear of, 208
castrati, 94-98
early Christian, 61
Catechism of the Revolutionist, The (Bakunin), 41
Catholic thought. See Christian thought
Cayton, Horace, 116-117
Celibates, 94-98
Chaperonage, 98-99
Chaucer, Geoffrey
pride as viewed by, 143-147
sloth as viewed by, 6-7, 10
Chekhov, Anton, sloth as viewed by, 42-50
Chiaromonte, Nicola, 270
Chiavasso, Angelus de Clavassio, 69
Children
anger in, 132
child marriages, 100-101
and divorce, 66
and early Christians, 59-62
and narcissism, 156
and polygamy, 67
and repressed anger, 114
China, 2
civil service in, 197-198
control of lust in, 94, 95
Japanese detention camps in (World War II), 129, 130
lust and, 100

martial arts in, 132
sloth and, 37
Chinese immigrants, 100, 259
anger among, 115
assimilation of, 201
Chiote à l'esprit (Artaud), 104
Christian asceticism, 101
Christian thought
crimes of capitalism in Protestant, 262
early, on pride, 136-137
lust in, 54-76
See also Protestant Ethic; and specific Christian sects and thinkers
Chrysostom, John, 59, 65, 71, 95
Civilization
and impotence, 91
See also Social order
Clausewitz, Karl von, 127-128
Clochard (type), 36
Clothing (dress; adornment)
envy and display in, 198-200
lust-shame origin of, 56-57
pride and, 141-149
Coleridge, Samuel Taylor, 39
Colonialism, 117, 172
Comte, Auguste, 1
Communism, 30-31, 101
Community, 173
Competition, envy and, 194-200
Concentration camps, Japanese Americans in, 129-130
Confidence game, 264-267
Confidence Man, The (Melville), 266
Constantine the Great, 62, 65
Corinthians (Paul), 59, 64, 71
Corporate firms, 3-4, 244, 245, 249, 270
and white-collar crime, 259-264
Corpus Hermeticum, 53
Coser, Lewis, 249
Costa, Uriel da, 162-163
Covetousness. See Envy
Crescas, Hasdai, 163
Crime
aggressive delinquency of youth, 124-125
and anger, 110
white-collar, 259-264

Cromwell, Oliver, 151
Cruelty, theater of, 102–108
Cryonics, 177
Culture
  greed as sin of, 233–236
  See also Social order
Cynics (philosophers), 57–58
Cyprian of Carthage, 60

Dahrendorf, Ralf, 245
Dante Alighieri, 233
  lust as viewed by, 81–86, 88, 165
  pride of, 164–165
  pride as viewed by, 165–168
  sloth as viewed by, 49
Dart, Raymond, 123
Darwinism, 123
Davis, Kingsley, 117
Death
  envy and, 209–211
  of Mishima, 210–211
  pride and dignity in, 175–183
Death instinct, 121
  anal eroticism as expression of, 238, 239
  greed related to, 247
Defeasibility, as excuse for gluttony, 226–227
Degradation
  ceremonies of, to control lust, 92–94
  greed and, 241–242
Deguileville, Guillaume de, 7
Democracy, 168, 169, 172, 174
"Demodernism," 172
Demonology. See Witchcraft
Denigration of love, 87–101
De Planctu Naturae (On the Complaint of Nature; Alanus de Insulis), 141, 144
Descartes, René, 163
Destiny, envy and, 209–211
Determinism, 119, 120
Deuteronomy, 64
Deviance
  evil as, 3
  See also specific forms of deviance
Devil, as deity, 234
Diaz-Plaja, Fernando, 33, 36
Dignity

in death, 175–183
  pride linked to, 169
Dining
  gluttonous, 222–224
  See also Gluttony
Display
  envy and, 198–200
  See also Clothing
Divine Comedy (Dante), 81–86, 164–165
Divorce
  Aquinas' view of, 65, 66
  Luther's view of, 68, 70–71
Dobu, envy among, 187
Dollard, John, 122
Douglas, Stephen A., 268
Doukhobors, 29
Downward mobility, anger and, 115, 116
Dress. See Clothing
Drinking. See Gluttony
DuBois, W. E. B., 159
Dumas, Alexandre, fils, 258
Dumont, Louis, 149–150
Duncan, Hugh D., 237
Durham (N.C.), as "Fat City," 225
Durkheim, Emile, 149, 154, 234, 238
Dyadic withdrawal, 79–81
  in Divine Comedy, 81–86

Eating. See Gluttony
Ecologism, 172
Economics
  of greed, 239–245
  See also Capitalism
Edicts of Constantine (331), 65
Edmond of Pontigny, St., 111
Education
  in Jewish tradition, 161, 162
  sloth and, 28–30
Egocentricism. See Egoism
Ego and the Id, The (Freud), 121
Egoism
  in asceticism, 151–154
  body as extension of, 205–206
  and immortality, 176
  as pride, 149–151
  and temporality, 171–172
  See also Narcissism
Eichmann, Adolf, 41, 48, 273

Eliade, Mircea, 10
Ellis, Havelock, 155
Elvira, Council of (306), 65
Emulation, envy and, 194–200
Engels, Friedrich, 258
England
    death in, 178
    South Sea Bubble in, 252–253
Ennui, 10–14
    See also Sloth
Envy, 184–211
    ascription and, 205–209
    body, 205–206
    Dante's view of, 165
    definition of, 184–185
    display and, 198–200
    dramatization of, 209–211
    emulation, competition and, 194–198
    ethnicity and, 200–205
    gender, 206–209
    greed and, 232
    relative deprivation, resentment and,
        189–194
    as ressentiment, 119
    sloth and, 12
    survival and, 186–189
    as weapon of devil, 111
Eroticism. See Anal eroticism; Sexuality
Essenes, 60
Ethics (Spinoza), 163
Ethnicity, envy and, 200–205
Ethnomethodology, 124
Ethology, and anger, 122–124
Eunuchs, 61, 94–98
Eusebius, 61
Evagrius of Pontus, 136
Evil eye, belief in, 191–192
Evolutionism, 149–151
Evreinoff, Nicolas, 124
Excommunication from Jewish commu-
        nity, 162–163
Exemplar humanae vitae (da Costa), 163

Fable of the Bees (Mandeville), 240
Faerie Queen (Spenser), 7, 234
Faith, 165, 166, 168
Family
    lust and nuclear, 88

    sociology of, 76–77
    See also Incest
Fanon, Frantz, 117
Fatalism, 9, 10, 124
Feminism, 172
Fenichel, Otto, 237
Ferenczi, Sandor, 237, 238
Ferguson, Adam, 190–191
Fitzgerald, F. Scott, 259
Flugel, J. C., 146–148
Food. See Gluttony
Forbidden Colors (Mishima), 210
Fornication. See Lust
Fortuna, 185, 206
Fortune, R. F., 187
Fourier, Charles, 187
Fourteenth Amendment (1868), 194
Fourth Lateran Council (1215), 69
France
    death in 18th-century, 178–182
    leisure in, 32–33
    South Sea Bubble in, 252–253
French Revolution, men's dress and, 146
French uprising (May 1968), 27
Freud, Sigmund, 11, 271
    anger as viewed by, 120–121
    Artaud and, 104
    greed as viewed by, 237
    love as viewed by, 91, 92
    narcissism as viewed by, 155–158
    penis envy as viewed by, 208, 209
    sloth as viewed by, 39
Fromm, Erich, on greed, 235, 237–238
Frustration
    leading to aggression, 122
    See also Anger

Galen, 22
Gaultier, Abbé, 181–182
Gender envy, 206–209
Genesis, 56, 57
Germany under Nazis, 41, 115–116, 123
Gibbon, Edward, 51
Gilkey, Langdon, 130
Giving-up syndrome, 38–39
Gluttony, 111, 136, 212–231
    as addiction, 119
    Dante's view of, 165

definition of, 212–215
excuses and justifications for, 225–230
leisure and, 32
sloth and, 12
social construction of, 221–225
and social structure, 215–221
sublimation of, 230–231
God
  and definition of self, 269
  devil as, 234
  good and evil in, 8
  greed and shift from worship of, to mammon, 234
  greed and usurpation of power of, 243–245
  lust, original sin and, 57, 58, 60
  lust, Puritans and, 75, 76
  lust, women and, 72–74
  and permissible sexual union, 63, 65
  pride alienates from, 136–137
  punishing agent of evil, 271
  sloth and abandonment of, 5, 7–11, 13, 22, 23
  world as creation of, 274
  See also Christian thought; Immortality
Gods, Greek, 14–17, 31
Goetzl, Franz, 19–20
Goffman, Erving, 144
Gold Rush, 253–259
Golding, William, 223
Gone with the Wind (film), 229–230
Goode, William J., 76, 87
Gorer, Geoffrey, 88
Grant, Ulysses S., 274
Graves, Robert, 112
Gray, J. Glenn, 168–169, 177
Greed, 232–268
  in collective behavior, 249–259
  in confidence game, 264–267
  definition of, 232–236
  economics and sociology of, 239–245
  gluttony and, 214
  in hierarchy of sins, 136
  and the humanities, 245–249
  leisure of, 33
  Mandeville's view of, 240–241
  psychoanalytic interpretation of, 237–239

  restored as sin, 245–249
  Simmel's view of, 241–243
  as sin of society and culture, 233–236
  sloth and, 12
  as spirit of capitalism, 119, 243–245, 268
  Weber's view of, 243–245
  in white-collar crime, 259–264
Greed (film), 245, 248–249
Greek gods, 14–17, 31
Greek money, 235
Greenstreet, Sidney, 228
Gregory, John, 111
Gregory the Great (pope)
  on anger, 110
  greed as viewed by, 233, 235, 251, 260
  on lust, 101–102
  pride as viewed by, 56, 136, 137, 140, 144
  sloth as viewed by, 6, 10–11, 15
Grief, 11
Group defense, anger and, 114–117
Grundrisse (Marx), 30
Grunewald, Mathias, 105
Guilt, sublimation of, 271

Hadrian (Roman emperor), 162
Haitians, envy among, 187–188
Haley, Jay, 59
Hamlet (Shakespeare), 12–14, 39, 133
Hate, Freud on, 121
Hawthorne Studies, 213
Heloise, 95–96
Henry of Ostia, 136
Herakleitos, 17, 20
Heresy, knowledge and, 163–168
Hermas, 65
Herskovits, Melville, 187, 234–235
Hippocrates, 22
Hitler, Adolf, 115
Hoffman, Abbie, 26–27
Holland tulip craze, 250–252
Holmes, Oliver Wendell, Jr., 98
Homer, 14–16, 125
  and anger, 110, 112–113
Home territory, 128–131
Homosexuality, 65
  Aquinas' view of, 64
  and dyadic withdrawal, 79–81

among Japanese, 210-211
Luther's view of, 68, 73-74
and men's dress, 148
narcissism in, 156, 158
social control of, 93-94
society and, 79
of teachers, 82
Honor, pride and, 169
Humiliation
anger and. *See* Anger
of dying, 178
Humility, 135, 139
Augustine on, 164
and intellectual pride, 167, 169
Hung Hsiu-Chuan, 198
Hutterians, 29
Huxley, Aldous, 24

Ik (people), 188, 189
Iliad (Homer), 112-113
Immortality
and greed, 239, 244-245, 247
and pride, 175-177
Impairment, as excuse for gluttony, 227
Imperialism
colonialism, 117, 172
and giving-up syndrome among Oceanic peoples, 38-39
Impotence
envy emerging from, 184-186
Freud's view of, 91
Luther's view of, 70
Incest, 88
Aquinas' view of, 65, 67-68
as asocial consequence of lust, 77-80
impotence and, 91
Luther's view of, 69
Individual, the (the self)
anger and defense of, 113-119
defined, 269-270
knowledge and, 159
pride and, 149-159
radical, and quest for authenticity,
170-173
Individuation, 270
process of, 154
pride linked to, 169-170
Intellect

Christian assault on unlimited, 165-168
pride and, in secular age, 168-173
and quest for authenticity, 170-173
Isolation to control lust, 99-100
Israel, 126

Jacob's Hell (anonymous), 7
Jahoda, Marie, 116
James (apostle), 61
Japanese Americans, 129-130
Jealousy, 117
Jerome, 59, 61, 65
Jesus Christ, 59, 104, 165, 167
and children, 61
commercial exploitation of birth of,
235-236
and family, 59-60
Luther and, 68
Voltaire and, 181, 182
Jettatura, 191-192
Jews, 116
anti-Semitism, 201, 204
ban on marriage between Christians
and, 62
emancipation and assimilation of,
203-204
gender role and, 207, 208
gluttony and, 227
Holocaust of, 273
pride, knowledge, and sin in thought
of, 160-163
Zionism among U.S., 202
Johanan ben Zakkai, Rabbi, 161, 162
John (apostle), 61
John of Damascus, 60
Jones, LeRoi, 154
Jose ben Halafta, 162
Judah ben Ilai, 161-162
Jung, Carl, 171-172
Justification of greed, 239-240

Kafka, Franz, 40
Kallen, Horace, 202
Kant, Immanuel, 191
Kapital, Das (Marx), 259
Keller, Albert G., 15
Keller, Werner, 161
Kempner Clinic, 225, 230, 231

Kerr, Clark, 26
Keynes, John Maynard, 235
Kierkegaard, Soren, 167, 168, 271
Kipling, Rudyard, 268
Klapp, Orrin E., 217
Knowledge
   pride and, 159-168
   See also Intellect
Kolakowski, Leszek, 274-276
Komarovsky, Mirra, 93
Kubrick, Stanley, 123

La Fargue, Paul, 31, 34
Lao Ts'ai, 95
Lao-Tzu, 267-268
Lasswell, Harold, 115
Latini, Brunetto de, 81-83, 233
Laurent, Friar, 234
L'Avare (Molière), 245-248
Lazarsfeld, Paul F., 116
Lechery, 111
   See also Lust
Lee, Rose Hum, 201
Leisure, sloth and, 30-34, 50
Lemert, Edwin, 247
Lenin, Vladimir I., 16, 151
Leontius of Neapolis, 136
Leviticus, 64
Lewis, George Cornewall, 193-194
Liberty, and greed, 241-242
Life
   revolt in behalf of, 101, 171, 172, 275
   and theater of cruelty, 102-108
   See also Pleasure
Lincoln, Abraham, 268
Linton, Ralph, 87
Literature, greed in, 245-249
Locke, John, 235
Lorenz, Konrad, 123
Louis Napoleon Bonaparte (Emperor of
   the French), 258
Love
   denigration of, 87-101
   desublimation of, 86
   jealousy and, 117-118
   limiting aggression, 123
Love complex, 87
Love patterns, 87

Lust, 53-109, 137
   Aquinas' view of, 59-68
   asocial consequences of, 77-81
   Augustine's view of, 54-58, 69, 71
   in Christian thought, 54-76
   Dante's view of, 81-86, 88, 165
   dress and, 143, 146
   and dyadic withdrawal, 78-81
   gluttony and, 214
   incest and, 77-79
   leisure and, 32
   and love, 86
   Luther's view of, 68-74
   moral equivalent of, 101-108
   not subject to the will, 55-60
   Puritan view of, 74-76
   as sexual deviance, 119
   sloth and, 12
   social controls over, 92-101
Luther, Martin, and psychology of lust,
   68-74

Macbeth (Shakespeare), 177-178
McDowell, Malcolm, 123
Machiavelli, Nicolo, 185
MacIver, Robert, 34
MacKinder, Sir Halford J., 126
McManners, J., 179
McTeague (Norris), 248, 256
Maimonides, 163
Malatesta, Gianciotto, 83, 84, 86
Malatesta, Paolo, 81, 83-86
Male sex organ
   Augustine and, 54, 58, 143
   in "Parson's Tale," 143
Mandeville, Bernard de, 264
   greed as viewed by, 239-241
Man Nobody Knows: A Discovery of the Real
   Jesus, The (Barton), 262
Mao Tse-tung, 151, 198
Marranos, 162
Marriage
   child and arranged, 100-101
   coitus as locus for, 54, 55
   legitimation of carnal union in, 63
   Luther's view of, 68-70, 73, 74
   role of, in Christian thought, 59-63
   sociology and, 76

Marienthal citizenry, 116
Martinson, Floyd M., 89
Marx, Karl, 33, 52, 154, 203, 271, 274
  and emancipation of individual, 150
  and the Gold Rush, 253-259
  and work, 30-31
Mary (mother of Jesus), 59
Masculinity complex, 209
Masochism, 212, 213
Masturbation (autoeroticism), 64, 65, 98
Mather, Cotton, 76
Matthew, 71
Matza, David, 36
Mauss, 238
Mazlish, Bruce, 151, 152
Mead, George Herbert, 131
Mead, Margaret, 87-88
Medicine, death and, 178
Megalopsychos, 137-139
Meir, Rabbi, 161
Melancholy, 10-14
  See also Sloth
Melville, Herman, 264-267
Menninger, Karl, 236
Mennonites, 29
Merchant class
  greed of, 235-236
  See also Bourgeoisie
Meritocracy, 159-160
Merton, Robert K., 166
Methodius, 60
Micah (prophet), 162
Mishima, Yukio, 210-211
Modesty, 135
  origin of, 56-57
Molière (Jean-Baptiste Poquelin),
  245-248
Monadic withdrawal
  narcissism as quintessential form of,
  155
  as vice of pride, 137, 141
Money
  archaic, 234-235
  and greed, 233-234
  See also Greed
Monotony, work and, 26, 27
Montagu, Ashley, 123
Montesquieu, Baron de (Charles de

Segondat), 126-127
Morgan, J. P., 261
Morris, Desmond, 123
Mowrer, Ernest R., 88-89
Myrdal, Gunnar, 2

Nakedness, 55-57
Narcissism, 113, 154-159
  of ascetics, 151-154
  Jung on, of ego, 172
  and men's dress, 148
Nathan of Gaza, 8
Nationalism, 172
Nations (public territories), 126-128
Native Son (Wright), 117
Nazi regime, 41, 115-116, 123
Nechayev, Sergei, 41, 48
Neo-Ludditism, 172
Nietzsche, Friedrich, 21
Nouvelle Héloise, La (Rousseau), 180
Norris, Frank, 248, 256

Occupations, as justification for gluttony,
  228
Oceanic peoples, giving-up syndrome
  among, 38-39
Odier, 237, 238
Oedipal complex, 88
Organic origin of sloth, 22
Origen, 53, 61, 65
Owen, Robert, 186-187

Parents, and narcissism of children, 156,
  157
Park, Robert, 19, 35, 36, 245
Parsons, Anne, 191-192
Parsons, Talcott, 79-80
  gender-role-related issue as viewed by,
  206-207
"Parson's Tale" (Chaucer), 143-147
Passivity, 8-10
Paul
  and castrati, 96
  incest and, 67
  lust and, 23, 59, 62, 71
  Luther and, 68
Payne, Robert, 137, 165
Peckinpah, Sam, 123

Pèlerinage de la vie humaine (de Deguile-
    ville), 7
Perella, Mrs., 192
Personal territories, 128-130
Phenomenological sociology, anger and,
    124-125
Philip le Bel (King of France), 82
Philosophie des Geldes (Simmel), 241
Pico della Mirandola, 174-175
Piers Plowman (Langland), 214
Ping-ti Ho, 197
Plato, 137
Playfulness
    in school, 28-30
    and work, 26-27
Pleasure
    as evil, in early Christian thought, 60
    modern view of, 51
    See also Life
Polygamy, Aquinas' view of, 65-67
Polynesian sensuality, 34
Poor, the, 35-37
Positivism, 1, 2
Poverty
    the poor, 35-37
    as a root of envy, 186-187
Pricke of Conscience, The (Rolle), 7
Pride, 135-183
    Alanus de Insulis on, 141-142
    Aristotle's view of, 137-139
    and dignity in death, 175-183
    dress and, 146-149
    early Christian view of, 136-137
    greed and, 232
    and the individual, 149-159
    and intellect in secular age, 168-173
    knowledge and, 159-168
    as mental illness, 119
    "Parson's Tale" on, 143-146
    and religion of sociology, 173-175
    Simmel on, 142-143
    sloth and, 12
    A. Smith on, 139-140
    as weapon of devil, 111
Primary narcissism, 156-157
Prostitution, 68, 73
Protestant Ethic, 147
    and fleshly gratification, 222
    and growing rich, 262-263

as model, 268
and Oceanic peoples, 38
sloth and, 21, 23
Weber on, 265
Protestant thought
    crimes of capitalism in, 262
    See also Protestant Ethic
Psychoanalysis
    anger as viewed in, 116, 120-121
    boredom and, 19-20
    denigration of love in, 91-92
    greed as viewed in, 232, 237-239
    narcissism as viewed in, 155-156
    penis envy as viewed in, 208-209
    sloth and, 11-12
Public executions, pride and, 182-183
Public territories, anger and, 126-128
Punishment
    and anger, 114
    glutton for, 212
Puritanism, 268
    lust and, 74-76
    and pride, 166-167

Quixotic madness, 176

Racism, 2, 100, 117
    antiracist, 172
    basis of, 118-119, 219
Rado, Sandor, 11
Rawls, 193, 194
Rebellion
    anger and, 110
    in behalf of life, 101, 171, 172, 275
    See also Revolution
Redemption, asceticism and, 151-154
Reformation, 151, 166
Relative deprivation, envy and, 189-194
Religious movements, extension of lei-
    sure opposed by, 32
Resentment
    envy and, 189-194
    and pride of intellect, 169
Ressentiment
    assimilation and, 205
    envy and, 186
    gender role and, 208
    in Judaism, 160
Revenge, envy and, 186

Revolt
  asceticism and, 151–154
  in behalf of life, 101, 171, 172, 275
Revolution, 1, 275
  and affectlessness, 41
  anger and, 110
  democratized envy as a basis for, 185
  gluttonous revolutionary movements,
    216
  Gold Rush and, 253–259
  presage of, in Russia, 47
Richards, I. A., 112
Right to Be Lazy, The (La Fargue), 31
Rimini, Francesca da, 81, 83–86
Róheim, Géza, 238
Rolle, Richard, 7
Roosevelt, Franklin D., 268
Rosenberg, Harold, 271
Rousseau, Jean-Jacques, 180
Rudofsky, Bernard, 210
Runciman, W. G., 189, 193
Russia, 2, 47

Sabbateans, 8
Sadism, 120–121
Sakall, S. Z. "Cuddles," 228
Salomon, Albert, 173–174
Salpingectomy, 97, 98
Sartre, Jean-Paul, 171, 275
Scarcity
  envy and, 186–187
  See also Envy
Scheler, Max, 184, 271–272
Schoeck, Helmut, 200
Scholem, Gershom, 8
Schools, sloth in, 28–30
Schuman, Frederick L., 115–116
Schwarzenegger, Arnold, 132, 229
Segregation to control lust, 99–100
Self, the. *See* Individual, the
Self-esteem, golden mean of, 135
Self-sacrifice, greed and, 240, 243
Sensuality
  Polynesian, 34
  sloth and, 52
  See also Sexuality
Servius, 53
Sevi, Sabbatai, 162
Sex consciousness, 172, 173

Sexual deviation, 59–68
  See also specific types of deviation
Sexuality
  of the disreputable poor, 37
  and dress, 144–148
  and modern sociology, 76–77
  and narcissism, 157–158
  sadism and, 120–121
  See also Lust
Sexual property, anger and preservation
    of, 117–119
Shakespeare, William, 177–178, 254,
    272–273
Shame, 139
Shelley, Mary, 244
Stylites, St. Simeon, 53–54
Simmel, Georg, 18–19, 35, 101, 102, 271
  on anger, 111
  and body as property, 205
  dress and display as viewed by, 198–200
  greed as viewed by, 239–243, 246
  and human emotions, 131
  money as viewed by, 235
  on pride, 142–143
  on social function of eating and drink-
    ing, 224
Simon bar Kochba, 161
Simon ben Yohai, 162
Sin
  Luther's view of, 68
  modern rejection of, 119–120
  and rise of sciences, 119
  sociology and, 1–4
  See also specific sins
Slater, Philip, 86
Sloth, 5–52, 111
  as affectlessness, 40–42, 119
  in apathy, 40–42
  boredom and, 14–18
  Chekhov's dramatization of, 42–50
  defined, 5–7
  and dramatism, 24–25
  and giving-up syndrome among Oce-
    anic peoples, 38–39
  and leisure, 30–34
  modern versions of, 18–21
  passive aspect of, 8–10
  as roots of melancholy and ennui,
    10–14

in schools, 28-30
as sin or disease, 21-24
as source of all sins, 136
of unemployed and disreputable poor,
    35-37
work and, 25-27
Slums, 36
Smith, Adam, 21
    on emulation, 195-196
    envy as viewed by, 192-193
    on greed, 268
    on pride, 239-140
Social change
    intellect in, 170
    See also Rebellion; Revolt; Revolution
Social controls
    over lust, 92-101
    See also Social order
Social Darwinism, 1-2, 123
Socialization, as excuse for gluttony, 227
Social justice, 189-194
Social order (societal structure; society)
    anger and, 110-13
    confidence game in, 264-267
    construction of gluttony in, 221-225
    envy as organizing principle of,
        186-189
    evil and, 269-276
    gluttony in, 215-221
    greed in progress and development of,
        239-245
    greed as sin of, 233-236
    greedy collective behavior in, 249-259
    new science of, 271-273
    white-collar crime and, 259-264
Social problems, sociology and, 173-174
Social psychology, and anger, 121-122
Social sciences
    abdication of, 274
    anger and, 119-125
Society. See Social order
Sociology
    of the absurd, 124, 174, 175
    denigration of love in, 87-91
    of greed, 239-245
    and the individual, 149, 150
    pride and religion of, 173-175
    sin and, 1-4
Sodomy, 81-83

Somme le Roy (Laurent), 234
Sorge, Friedrich Adolph, 259
Sorokin, Pitirim, 188-189
Soul, departure of the, 53-54
South Sea Bubble, 252-253
Speculum ecclesiae (St. Edmond of
    Pontigny), 111
Spenser, Edmund, 7, 234
Spinoza, Baruch, 163
Sports, ritual expression of anger in, 132
Stakhanovite, 213
Statism, 188-189
Sterilization, 95, 98
Stickney, A. B., 261
Stigmatization to control lust, 92-94
Stranger, The (Camus), 40-41
Stroheim, Erich von, 245, 248-249
Sublimation
    of gluttony, 230-231
    of greed, 239
    of guilt, 271
Sullivan, Harry Stack, 113-114
Summa Angelica (Chiavasso), 69
Sumner, William Graham, 191
Superbia. See Pride
Supreme Deity
    devil as, 234
    good and evil in, 8
    See also God
Surplus humanity, 35
Survival, envy and, 186-189
Sutherland, Edwin H., 260-261
Symbionese Liberation Army, 216
Synod of Elvira (306), 62

Taiping Revolution, 198
Tastelessness, 139
Teggart, Frederick J., 127
Ten Broek, Jacobus, 194
Territoriality
    anger and, 125-131
    gluttony and personal, 223
Terrorism, 41, 115-116
Tertullian, 59, 61, 62, 71
"Testament of Reuben," 136
Testament of the Twelve Patriarchs, 136, 214
Thompson, William Irwin, 269
Three Sisters, The (Chekhov), 42-50
Timon of Athens (Shakespeare), 254

Tinbergen, Niko, 123
Tönnies, Ferdinand de, **154**
Totalitarianism, 2, 189
Toynbee, Arnold, 177
Trans-nationalism, 202–203
Transvestism, 64
Treatise on Religion and Philosophy
    (Spinoza), 163
Trent, Council of (1545–1563), 65, 66
Tristitia. See Sloth
Trust, greed and, 264
Tulip craze, 250–252
Turnbull, Colin M., 188
Tussman, Joseph, 194

Unamuno, Miguel de, 175–177
Unemployed, the, 35–37
Unemployment, envy and, 186–187
Utopias, 2, 3, 186–187, 275

Vagrius, 6
Vainglory. *See* Pride
Vanity, 135
Varnhagen, Rahel, 203, 204
Vasectomy, 97, 98
Veblen, Thorstein, 198–200
Vergil, 84, 165–167
Vickers, Sir Geoffrey, 27
Violence
    and display of anger, 131
    See also Anger
Virtú, 185, 206
Vita sancti Joannis eleemosynaarii (Leontius
    of Neapolis), 53, 136
Vitrac, Roger, 104
Voltaire (François Arouet), death of,
    178–182

Waller, Willard, 29–30, 89
War, 2–3, 126–128
    basis for, 219–220
    soldiers' deaths in, 177
Waste, pride and, 144–145
Water Margin, The (Chinese classic), 99
Weber, Max, 102, 149, 154
    and asceticism, 151, 152
    on Christian asceticism, 101

on fraternization, 224
greed as viewed by, 239–240, 243–245
on Jews, 160, 161
on Protestant Ethic, 265
sloth and, 23
on work, 26
Wei Chung Hsien, 95
Wesley, John, 262
West, Nathanael, 259
Westermarck, Edward, 77, 79
Western Electric Company, 27
White-collar crime, 259–264
Widowhood, early Christian view of, 61,
    62
Wigglesworth, Michael, 74–75, 166–167
Will, the
    gluttony and, 225–227
    lust not subject to, 55–60
Witchcraft
    envy and, 191, 192
    women and, 72
Wolfe, Tom, 148
Women
    anger in, 132–133
    demonology and, 72
    dress of, and pride, 146, 147
    gender role and, 207–208
    penis envy among, 208–209
    primary narcissism and, as sexual ob-
        jects, 157, 158
    See also Lust
Work
    Communists and, 30–31
    glutton for, 212–213
    pride and, 147
    and Protestant Ethic, 23
    sloth and, 25–27, 50
Wright, Richard, 117
Wyklif's Bible, 82

Yawning, 28–29
Youth, aggressive delinquency of,
    124–125

Zangwill, Israel, 201
Zeisel, Hans, 116
Zionism, 126, 202